T0148793

WAR,
REVOLUTION,
AND PEACE
IN RUSSIA

Frank A. Golder
(1877–1929)

WAR, REVOLUTION, AND PEACE IN RUSSIA

*The Passages of
Frank Golder, 1914–1927*

Compiled, edited,
and introduced by
TERENCE EMMONS
and
BERTRAND M. PATENAUDE

HOOVER INSTITUTION PRESS
Stanford University
Stanford, California

Hoover Institution Press Publication No. 411

Hoover Institution at Leland Stanford Junior University,
Stanford, California, 94305-6003

Image on cover is adapted from photograph of military parade before the Winter Palace in Petrograd in March/April 1917. In the right foreground stands Frank Golder.

First printing 1992
Simultaneous first paperback printing 1992
29 28 27 26 25 24 23   9 8 7 6 5 4 3

Library of Congress Cataloging-in-Publication Data
Golder, Frank Alfred, 1877–1929.
  War, revolution, and peace in Russia: the passages of Frank
Golder, 1914–1927 / compiled, edited, and with an introduction by
Terence Emmons and Bertrand M. Patenaude.
        p.   cm. — (Hoover archival documentaries)
(Hoover Institution Press publication ; 411)
  Includes bibliographical references and index.
  ISBN 0-8179-9191-3 (cloth : acid-free paper). —
  ISBN 0-8179-9192-1 (paper: acid-free paper)
   1. Golder, Frank Alfred, 1877–1929—Journeys—Soviet Union.
2. Soviet Union—Description and travel—1917–1944.   3. Golder,
Frank Alfred, 1877–1929—Diaries.   4. Historians—United States—Diaries.
5. Soviet Union-Politics and govemment-1917-1936.
I. Emmons, Terence.   II. Patenaude, Bertrand M., 1956–   .
III. Hoover Institution on War, Revolution, and Peace.   IV.   Title.
V. Series.   VI. Series: Hoover Institution Press publication ; 411.
DK27.G62   1992
914.704´841—dc20   91-45706
                                              CIP

ISBN 978-0-8179-9192-0 (pbk)
ISBN 978-0-8179-9193-7 (epub)
ISBN 978-0-8179-9195-1 (PDF)

CONTENTS

ACKNOWLEDGMENTS

The principal research source for this book was the archives and library of the Hoover Institution, which supported the project with a grant from its publications committee and through its National Fellows Program. Special thanks for this support go to Deputy Director Charles Palm, who also granted the editors access to the Hoover Institution's internal records, and to Senior Research Fellow Robert Hessen.

The Kennan Institute for Advanced Russian Studies in Washington, D.C., provided financial assistance in the form of research grants; our thanks to its director, Blair Ruble, for all his help and to intern Gregory P. Lannon, Jr., for his hard work. The Stanford University history department contributed funds for the making of the index.

We are indebted to the staffs of the following libraries and archives for their assistance: the Hoover Institution Library; the Herbert Hoover Library, West Branch, Iowa; the Manuscripts Division of the Library of Congress; the National Archives; the Harvard University Archives; and the library at Washington State University in Pullman. A special note of thanks to the staff of the Hoover Institution Archives for rendering us patient and helpful service beyond the call of duty. Above all, we owe a debt of gratitude to Associate Archivist Elena Danielson for her early encouragement of the project, her unflagging enthusiasm, and her expert assistance and advice over the past four years.

Finally, to the late Harold H. Fisher, former director of the Hoover Institution and professor of Russian history at Stanford, who succeeded Frank Golder at the Hoover library and who in 1929 began to collect material for a Golder memorial volume, we acknowledge a debt of inspiration.

INTRODUCTION

Frank Golder is remembered today as the man responsible for amassing the extraordinary Slavic collections now housed at the Hoover Institution at Stanford University. These unsurpassed holdings on modern Russia and early Soviet history are a monument to Golder's achievements as a collector.

Scholars also know Golder as the author of pioneering studies on the history of Russian-American relations. Although not abundant, these high-quality works are still valued today. That the total number of Golder's publications was by some standards modest is in large part due to the fact that, during the prime of his career as a historian of Russia, he was repeatedly swept up by historic events inside Russia. This remarkable aspect of Frank Golder's life, largely unknown even to scholars, is brought to light in the present volume.

Golder witnessed some of the most important and dramatic developments in modern Russian history. He was in St. Petersburg in 1914 when Russia entered the Great War; he was in Petrograd in 1917 when the February Revolution ended the three-hundred-year reign of the Romanov dynasty; he was in Soviet Russia in 1921–1923 as a famine relief worker, book and manuscript collector, and political observer of Lenin's government; and he was in the USSR for extended visits in 1925 and 1927, recording the changes in Soviet society after Lenin.

During his Russian travels Golder kept a detailed diary and was a prolific correspondent and so left behind extensive documentation of his

Russian sojourns, most of which has never before been published.[1] His account, bridging the 1917 revolution, provides an overview of the tumultuous period from the last years of imperial rule to the beginnings of Stalinism. The result is a sustained narrative of Russia's agony in war, revolution, civil war, famine, and their aftermath.

Golder was a modest, self-effacing man who recorded the extraordinary events around him as a fascinated and conscientious observer, sensitive to the historical and human impact of Russia's time of troubles. He was not a major actor on the stage of history but had little difficulty establishing professional and personal contacts among tsarist officials and the intelligentsia during his initial visit in 1914. In the subsequent thirteen years (three of which were spent inside Russia), he maintained many relationships with members of the vanquished classes of the old regime and initiated many new ones among the Bolshevik and Soviet establishment. By the early 1920s the range and depth of his contacts in Moscow and Petrograd were unmatched among U.S. observers of Russia. Golder's personality seems to have played a considerable role in this. He was by all accounts soft-spoken and gentle in manner, able to get along with a wide variety of people. Someone he worked closely with characterized him as "a kind, considerate, sympathetic person, who enters into the minds of all sorts of people and to whom they talk with freedom. He is a very likeable person and made many friends in Russia."[2] He was, as well, essentially apolitical in nature. At a time when everyone in Russia seemed intent on converting the next person to his own point of view, Golder was a good listener. This attribute, which helped make him a good observer, makes difficult the task of his biographer, for Golder was especially reticent about his own back-

---

[1]The main source for the present volume is the Frank A. Golder collection at the Hoover Institution Archives, Stanford University, 43 boxes. Golder's diaries are located in boxes 6, 15, and 19; his correspondence is in boxes 14, 32, 33, 35, and 42. This collection is supplemented chiefly by materials from the following sources: the records of the American Relief Administration, Russian Unit, at the Hoover Institution Archives; the Manuscripts Division of the Library of Congress; the National Archives; the Herbert Hoover Presidential Library, West Branch, Iowa; the Harvard University Archives; and the archives of Washington State University at Pullman.

Alain Dubie's *Frank A. Golder: An Adventure of a Historian in Quest of Russian History* (New York, 1989) is a sympathetic and generally accurate biography, though its value is limited by the author's lack of familiarity with the Russian context of the Golder story.

[2]J. Franklin Jameson to Hugh Gibson, October 8, 1917, J. Franklin Jameson papers, box 86, file 626, Manuscripts Division, Library of Congress.

ground. "I do not like to talk much, particularly about myself," he wrote toward the end of his life in a rare "autobiographical sketch."³ As a result there is a lack of detail about his early life.

Frank Alfred Golder was born on August 11, 1877, near Odessa. Biographical sources on Golder offer conflicting information as to when his family emigrated from Russia to the United States, but he stated on two occasions that it was when he was eight years old, after the death of his German-born grandfather.⁴ He also claimed that neither he nor his father had ever been Russian subjects and that he became a U.S. citizen when his father forswore allegiance to Germany in 1890 or 1891. As will be made clear below, there is reason to doubt the veracity of these details. Golder was not a native speaker of Russian or Ukrainian, and his first language was probably Yiddish, possibly German.

As to the reasons for the emigration, we can surmise that this Jewish family of three was, along with many thousands of Russian Jews in the wake of the 1881 pogroms, seeking to escape anti-Semitic persecution. The family eventually settled in Bridgeton, New Jersey, where they endured severe financial hardship. Golder was rescued from this life of poverty by a Baptist minister who found him on the streets, "a little Jew peddler," and who "persuaded him to let me help and share his struggles for a livelihood and an early education."⁵

For Golder this marked a break with his family and his past. His subsequent conversion to Unitarianism put even more distance between

---

³Frank Golder, "Autobiographical Sketch," *Harvard College Class of 1903*, Report VI (Norwood, Mass., 1928), pp. 388–92. Typescript copy in the Golder collection, box 13-C, p. 5.

⁴Golder to A.C. McLaughlin, May 9, 1905, Jameson papers, box 110, file 1079; Golder to Jameson, May 11, 13, 19, 1913, Jameson papers, box 86, file 626.

⁵R.D. Minch to Stanford University, February 12, 1929; on Golder's early life see the handwritten draft biographical article by Harold H. Fisher; both in Hoover Institution Internal Records, box 94, file "Golder"; also Dubie, *Frank A. Golder*, pp. 1–2. For an interesting (and at least in part inaccurate) anecdotal glimpse of Golder's early life, see Bluma Bayuk Rappoport Purmell and Felice Lewis Rovner, *A Farmer's Daughter: Bluma* (Los Angeles, 1981), pp. 56–60. Biographical articles written at the time of Golder's death reveal his closest colleagues' lack of knowledge about his background. For example, Harold H. Fisher, "Frank Alfred Golder, 1877–1929," *Journal of Modern History* 1, no. 2 (June 1929): 253–55; Lincoln Hutchinson, "Frank A. Golder," *A.R.A. Association Review* 4, no. 1 (February 1929): 49; *Washington Historical Quarterly* 20, no. 2 (April 1929): 157–58; Ralph Haswell Lutz, "Professor Frank Alfred Golder," *Stanford Illustrated Review*, February 1929, pp. 249–50.

him and his family, although he maintained warm ties to a brother, Benjamin, who became a successful trial lawyer and U.S. congressman from Philadelphia. Golder seems never to have discussed the hardship of his early life or his Jewish background with even his closest colleagues and friends.[6] He never married, and there is no evidence of a significant romance; his biographer thus has none of the attendant intimate correspondence to illuminate the private side of his life.

Golder enrolled in a preparatory school in Kentucky and then attended Bucknell, where in 1898 he received a bachelor of philosophy degree. From 1900 to 1902 he worked for the U.S. government in Alaska, teaching English to Aleut public school children on a remote island settlement. He became interested in the Aleutian people and their history and later published several articles about them. He came away from this experience intent on writing the history of Alaska.

Golder then attended Harvard University, where he received his bachelor of arts degree in 1903 and then began his doctoral studies in history. At Harvard he was the student of Archibald Cary Coolidge, a pioneer in Russian studies in the United States and one of the great teachers of history, who probably had much to do with the course of Golder's studies and career.[7] During his doctoral program, Golder journeyed to Paris and Berlin (1903–1904), and he later claimed that his research there put him onto the Russian history track. "The discovery of Alaska, which I had regarded as a beginning chapter of American history," he wrote, "I found to be the closing chapter of a period of Russian expansion."[8] And so he turned his attention to the study of Siberia in the seventeenth and eighteenth centuries, the history of Russian settlements in America, and the history of diplomatic relations between the United States and Russia. He received his Ph.D. in 1909 with a dissertation about Russian expansion on the Pacific, which was published in 1914.

While a doctoral student, Golder taught history and economics at Arizona State Teachers' College in Tempe and at the University of Missouri; after receiving his Ph.D. he taught history as an instructor at Boston University in 1909 and at the University of Chicago in 1910. He then became assistant professor in the Department of Economic Science and History at Washington State College in Pullman, where he was later

---

[6]Henrietta to Thomas Eliot, March ? 1958, Golder collection, box 12, file 8.

[7]See Robert F. Byrnes, *Awakening American Education to the World: The Role of Archibald Cary Coolidge, 1866–1928* (Notre Dame and London, 1982).

[8]Frank A. Golder, *Russian Expansion on the Pacific, 1641–1850* (Cleveland, 1914), p. 13. See Golder to Jameson, January 22, 1913, Jameson papers, box 86, file 626.

promoted to professor and where he remained, with long periods away on other projects, until 1920.

From early on in his academic career Golder attempted to get into Russia to investigate the libraries and archives. From Paris in December 1903 he wrote to Herbert Putnam, librarian of Congress, with a proposal "to spend two or three months at St. Petersburg making a bibliography of all the books, maps and manuscripts on Alaska" and requesting the financial assistance of the library. Putnam replied that the library had no funds for such a purpose and he discouraged Golder from undertaking the expedition, saying he doubted that it would prove worthwhile.[9]

In 1912, Golder again began sounding people out about a research trip to Russia, which he seems to have been intent on undertaking at his own expense. From Pullman he wrote to historian J. Franklin Jameson (1859–1937), head of the Department of Historical Research of the Carnegie Institution in Washington, D.C., expressing a desire to spend several months in St. Petersburg and Moscow in the imperial archives and asking Jameson's help in securing the necessary permissions. Either Golder had been tipped off or was lucky, for it so happened that Jameson was contemplating making a guide to materials on American history in the Russian archives. He signed Golder on as his agent, asking him to wait until 1914 to make his trip.[10]

---

[9]Golder to Putnam, December 7, 1903, January 27, 1904; Putnam to Golder, January 6, 1904, Herbert Putnam papers, file "Golder, F.A. (Dr.), 1912–27," Manuscripts Division, Library of Congress.

[10]At this time Golder again requested Putnam's assistance in securing permission to enter Russia and the imperial archives. Putnam still felt that the benefits of such a trip were "problematic" but agreed to help because Golder had evidently made up his mind to go anyway. Putnam to Golder, October 23, 1912, Putnam papers, file "Golder, F.A. (Dr.), 1912–27." Two years earlier, Golder had written to Jameson with a request for Carnegie funds to support such a trip, which Jameson was at that time unable to sponsor. Golder to Jameson, April 4, 1910, Jameson to Golder, April 12, 1910; Jameson papers, box 86, file 627. While at Harvard in 1905, Golder had written to Jameson's predecessor at the Carnegie Institution, A.C. McLaughlin, requesting that if McLaughlin planned to send someone to Russia to collect materials on American history that he be given consideration. Golder to McLaughlin, May 9, 1905, Jameson papers, box 110, file 1079.

Jameson's 1913 correspondence investigating Golder's personal background in order to judge his suitability for work in Russia makes plain that Golder had good reason to be reticent at this time, perhaps even somewhat misleading, about his personal background. In December 1912 the U.S. government abrogated the U.S.-Russian commercial treaty of 1832 to protest the tsarist government's treatment of Russian Jews and its discrimination against American Jews' seeking to enter Russia.

Jameson maintained a broad range of contacts among scholars in the United States and throughout Europe, was well-connected in government circles in Washington, and was the managing editor of the *American Historical Review*. In all these capacities he now began to exert a significant influence over Golder's career. He provided him with letters of introduction to key people in St. Petersburg (renamed Petrograd in 1914), notably the historian Aleksandr Lappo-Danilevskii and Sergei Goriainov (1849–1918), the director of the archives of the Ministry of Foreign Affairs, both of whom Jameson had met in Europe at international conferences of historians.[11]

Golder arrived in Russia in February 1914 and stayed on until November.[12] The result of this research trip was the publication of a unique and still valuable *Guide to Materials for American History in Russian Archives* (Washington, D.C., 1917), most of which deals with the history of diplomatic relations between Russia and the United States. He also published several articles in the *American Historical Review* and other journals based on his archival research on eighteenth- and nineteenth-century Russian diplomatic history, specifically Russia's role in the American Revolution and

---

This left the visa process in limbo for prospective U.S. visitors to Russia, and the official atmosphere was severely strained. See Benson Lee Grayson, *Russian-American Relations in World War I* (New York, 1979), pp. 8–18. Jameson, concerned lest Golder's background become an obstacle to obtaining a visa, wrote to colleagues to inquire whether Golder was of Jewish origin. The only available statements from Golder as to his previous citizenship and family background come from his communications with Jameson during this brief period, which must have been uncomfortable for him. These circumstances must be taken into account when considering Golder's testimony. See Jameson papers, box 86, file 626; box 89, file 679; box 92, file 720; box 110, file 1080.

[11]Aleksandr Sergeevich Lappo-Danilevskii (1863–1919), a lecturer in Russian history at St. Petersburg University and member of the St. Petersburg Academy of Sciences, was regarded throughout Europe as the representative of Russian historical science. Foreign historians visiting St. Petersburg sought out Lappo-Danilevskii for introductions to other important Russian historians and to the directors of the archives and libraries, as well as for invitations to attend the weekly evening seminar at his home. See the memoir of G. Vernadsky in *Novyi zhurnal* (*New journal*), no. 100 (New York, 1970): 214–15.

[12]It is difficult to assess Golder's facility with the Russian language as he set out on his first trip to Russia. His quick success in building up a network of contacts tells us little, as his German and French (which appear to have been quite good), as well as his English, would have enabled him to get by with most of his new Russian acquaintances.

Civil War.[13] During this visit Golder also collected material, supplemented during a later trip, that he used to write *John Paul Jones in Russia* (Garden City, 1927).

Golder found the short hours and the many holidays at the Russian archives a handicap. The situation was made much worse in July when Russia went to war, which not only caused more frequent interruptions in the archives but distracted Golder with all the excitement, a sense of which he conveys in his diary.[14] The diary for 1914 reveals the cracks in the structure of imperial Russian society, an internally stratified society united only in cynicism about the tsarist government.

Beyond the element of distraction brought on by the coming war, Golder soon found that the hostilities had cut off his supply of finances to support his research and pay his living expenses, and he was forced to cut short his work and return home through Siberia and across the Pacific, reaching America at year's end. He later recalled that "when I landed at Seattle, I had fifty cents of borrowed money and a doctor's bill."[15]

Much the same thing occurred when Golder returned to Russia in 1917 to continue his investigations in the Petrograd archives. This time he went as the agent for the American Geographical Society, by whom he had been commissioned to translate, edit, and prepare for publication the journals of the explorer Vitus Bering. He arrived in Petrograd on March 4, eleven days before the fall of Nicholas II. His diary thus records the drama of the initial months of the Russian Revolution.[16] Not only does he take us onto Nevsky Prospekt for the encounters of the Cossacks and the demonstrators, but he introduces us to some of the major actors on the political scene, including

---

[13]See Thomas A. Bailey, *America Faces Russia: Russian-American Relations from Early Times to Our Day* (Ithaca, 1950), pp. 86–88, and Norman E. Saul, *Distant Friends: The United States and Russia, 1763–1867* (Lawrence, Kansas, 1991), pp. 340–43.

[14]With this as with all the documents presented in this volume the editors have made minor editorial modifications, mostly for the sake of clarity or to correct grammar or syntax or the transliteration of Russian words. Extraneous or repetitious parts of the text have been excised and marked with ellipses. Those places where Golder's handwriting is illegible or his meaning unclear are indicated in the text or the notes.

[15]"Autobiographical Sketch," typescript copy, p. 1.

[16]Two versions of the 1917 diary are in the Golder collection: the original handwritten copy and a typescript copy, edited, apparently several years afterward, by Golder. The editors have chosen to reproduce the original handwritten version (located in box 19), which retains much more of the immediacy to the events and the confusion of the diarist than does the typescript copy. (The handwritten version of Golder's 1914 diary has been lost.) The observations of the 1917 diary are amplified by Golder's personal letters to friends.

principal figures in the Provisional Government such as Alexander Kerensky and Paul Miliukov. An overriding motif in Golder's account is how the optimism and hope of the early period of the revolution gave way to dark pessimism, especially as the end of autocracy failed to reverse Russia's military defeats at the front and the country began to slide toward anarchy. On May 17 he wrote:

> If I am not much older in years I see the world differently since the Revolution here. Our joy has turned to sorrow. I should not have imagined that a country could go to pieces in such a short time and the end is not yet.[17]

Golder became a minor player in the events of 1917, escorting, at the request of the U.S. ambassador, an American presidential commission of railroad engineers from Siberia to Petrograd and around European Russia. He departed Petrograd in late summer, before the Bolshevik seizure of power, about which he read in the newspapers in Pullman. Golder came away troubled by the course of events in Russia. Shortly after his return he wrote to Jameson:

> It has been a great year; from now on I shall read history differently. How stupidly I have, until now, interpreted the French Revolution. They are ugly, these revolutions; but since so much in government is artificial and abnormal, revolutions must come. If I had an opportunity I should like so much to talk to you. My theories and ideas are jarred and bruised and I do not know where I am going any more. Although I have no sympathy with the gang of anarchists and disturbers who are now at work in Russia, yet I occasionally catch a glimpse of their ideals and they are not at all bad. What I can not forgive them is their impatience, their unwillingness to wait until the war is over.[18]

Golder related some of his eyewitness testimony on the revolutionary events in Russia in a paper presented to the annual meeting of the American Historical Association in December 1917, which appeared in print the following year.[19] He published another account called "The Russian Revolution" in the Washington State *University Magazine* for April 1918.

---

[17]From the office of the president; Ernest O. Holland records, 1890–1950, Washington State University Libraries at Pullman.

[18]Golder to Jameson, Jameson papers, box 86, file 626.

[19]Alexander Petrunkevich, Samuel Northrup Harper, and Frank Alfred Golder, *The Russian Revolution* (Cambridge, Mass., 1918).

During his stay in Russia, Golder managed to accomplish his scholarly mission as well, the results of which appeared several years later as *Bering's Voyage: An Account of the Efforts of the Russians to Determine the Relation of Asia and America,* 2 vols. (New York, 1922–25).[20] In addition, he published further archive-based articles on Russian-American relations.

Golder's research experience in Russia, especially his recent exposure to the Russian scene, helped win him a place on a committee of men called together by President Woodrow Wilson at the end of 1917 to gather information for the coming peace conference. The committee, under the direction of Colonel Edward M. House, was known as The Inquiry, and it sat for two years. Golder was attached to its East European Division, which was headed by Professor Coolidge and did its work at Harvard. Golder wrote reports on the Ukraine, Lithuania, Siberia, Poland, and the Don province.[21] In a major personal and professional setback, when Inquiry members were selected to attend the Paris Peace Conference in 1919, Golder was not among them. Instead he returned to his teaching position at Washington State University.

In 1920 Golder was teaching summer classes at Stanford University when he was offered a position there at the recently founded Hoover War History Collection (later the Hoover Library), established by Herbert Hoover to collect documents on the causes and course of the Great War. Thus began his association with Stanford, which would last until his death. In 1921 he was made associate professor and in 1924 professor of Russian history, at which time he was also made a director of the Hoover Library.

On being hired as a curator for the Hoover Collection, Golder departed in August 1920 on his first collecting trip, a journey of three years that would have an enduring effect on the field of Slavic studies in America. He traveled during the next year throughout central, eastern, and southeastern Europe and the Near East, collecting books, manuscripts, periodicals, government documents, personal papers, and posters and arranging for their shipment to Stanford.

In his collecting work Golder was aided by his association with the American Relief Administration (ARA), formerly a U.S. government agency and at the time a private relief organization under the direction of Secretary of Commerce Herbert Hoover. The ARA, which had been

---

[20]The original plan was for Golder to publish Bering's journals in 1917, the fiftieth anniversary of the purchase of Alaska; when this target was missed, the publication date was set to coincide with the bicentennial of Bering's first voyage.

[21]See the Golder collection, boxes 2 and 12; Dubie, *Frank A. Golder,* pp. 66–73; Lawrence E. Gelfand, *The Inquiry: American Preparations for Peace, 1917–1919* (New Haven and London, 1963), pp. 55–56, 68–69, 163.

bringing food and medical relief across Europe in the postwar period, enjoyed enormous political clout. Golder found that in most places he visited, the Hoover name had spread goodwill and opened doors for him to officials, librarians, collectors, and others. At the same time, the depressed economic conditions enabled him to purchase literally tons of material at cheap prices.[22]

All the while, Golder was impatient to get into Russia. He knew that books would be extremely cheap there and that he could acquire abundant material for the Hoover Library. His opportunity came in August 1921, when the ARA signed an agreement with the Soviet government to bring food relief into Soviet Russia, at the time threatened with a major famine. The organization established headquarters in Moscow and set up district posts in and beyond the Volga region to the edge of Siberia, throughout the Ukraine and White Russia, and south to the Caucasus. At the height of operations in the summer of 1922, the ARA had a staff of 250 Americans and more than 120,000 local citizens feeding nearly 11 million people a day. The ARA stayed for almost two years, saving millions from starvation and disease and helping to rebuild the Soviet economy.

Golder entered Soviet Russia with one of the first ARA parties at the end of August and remained there for most of the next twenty-one months. He went in principally as an agent for the Hoover Collection; he ended up, however, because of his familiarity with the terrain and the language, as an investigator for the ARA, traveling throughout the famine region and writing reports on famine conditions. During the second year of the ARA mission Herbert Hoover asked him to serve as a political observer and submit weekly reports on developments inside Russia. These activities competed for Golder's time, and he often found himself torn between his obligations to Stanford, Hoover, and the ARA.

As a collector Golder built on past contacts with archivists, scholars, and librarians to acquire an enormous amount of material. He made new connections with the Bolshevik establishment, most important with the Marxist historian and Deputy People's Commissar of Enlightenment Mikhail Pokrovsky, who assisted him in collecting, free of charge, most official publications since 1917, including complete runs of many newspapers and

---

[22]In the subsequent three years estimates are that Golder acquired for the Hoover and Stanford libraries some twenty-five thousand volumes and more than sixty thousand pamphlets, government documents, periodicals, and newspapers. See Byrnes, *Awakening American Education*, p. 144; W.S. Sworakowski, *A Short History of the Collection on Russia in the Hoover Institution* (Stanford, 1969), p. 3. On Golder's collecting feats, see Wojciech Zalewski, *Collectors and Collections of Slavica at Stanford University* (Stanford, 1985), pp. 22–39.

journals. During the first months, Golder found the prices of books on the private market very low and he purchased aggressively. In addition, he also acquired some personal papers of individuals, including the diaries of a Petrograd archivist and a Moscow historian during the Russian Revolution.[23]

His collecting achievement during this period was Golder's most important professional accomplishment. He not only collected for Stanford but acquired duplicates for the Harvard Library and the Library of Congress as well. The importance of Golder's work was recognized at the time by Coolidge, his former teacher. After receiving a letter from Golder in Moscow recounting his most recent collecting successes, Coolidge wrote to the director of the Hoover War Library, Ephraim D. Adams, on April 21, 1922: "I must admit that the thought of it sometimes makes my mouth water." On the same day, he replied to Golder: "I think your acquisitions of Russian works for Stanford and Harvard at this particular juncture will go down to posterity in the annals of book buying."[24]

Much of the correspondence having to do with Golder's collecting efforts has been excluded from this volume, as have selected passages from individual letters bearing on the same subject. The specialist reader can consult these in the Golder collection. Enough of this material has been included here, however, in Golder's letters to Adams and to Ralph H. Lutz, another Hoover library colleague, to give a sense of the scope of Golder's collecting and his methods. The letters to Adams and Lutz form the bulk of chapter 3, which covers the first year of Golder's extended stay in Russia.

Golder's second major activity in Russia—his role as a special investigator for the ARA—took up more of his time than he had originally planned, and during the first year of the mission, when the market for books was exceptionally good, he worried that he was not devoting enough time to collecting. Golder, who accompanied one of the first ARA parties to the Volga in September 1921, was the most traveled of all the ARA Americans, journeying up and down the Volga and to the Ukraine, the Caucasus, and Dagestan. While on the road he was constantly on the lookout for materials for the library, and his collecting habits were a curiosity to his fellow Americans in Russia, who knew him as "Doc" Golder. In the ARA newsletter someone wrote that during a trip to the Caucasus in the company of the economist Lincoln Hutchinson, his fellow

---

[23]The diary of the Petrograd archivist Georgii Alekseevich Kniazev is in the Golder collection, box 16; the Moscow diary has been published as *Time of Troubles: The Diary of Iurii Vladimirovich Got'e, Moscow, July 8, 1917, to July 23, 1922*, trans., ed., introd. by Terence Emmons (Princeton, 1988).

[24]Harvard University Archives, A.C. Coolidge papers, "Correspondence, A-Z 1922/23—A-Winship 1923/4."

ARA investigator, the two men had failed to climb Mount Ararat because Golder had "spent all his time running around trying to find Noah's log book."[25]

Golder's travels are chronicled in his diaries, which, along with material provided by Hutchinson, were published as *On the Trail of the Russian Famine* (Stanford, 1927). That book deals almost exclusively with the experiences of these two men in the famine zone and supplements, but does not duplicate, the present volume's section on this period.

When he was in the capital cities, Moscow and Petrograd, Golder found that he had little time to keep a diary. Instead, he maintained an extensive correspondence, most of which is published here, nearly all for the first time. Sections dealing with internal ARA affairs and other special-interest material have been excised from individual letters, and several such letters have been excluded altogether. Several previously unpublished diary entries, recorded mostly in Moscow and Petrograd, have been included here.

The material in the chapters on the 1921–1923 period that deals with Golder's contribution as a famine relief worker illuminates his central role in helping the ARA to identify the appropriate beneficiaries of its food package program from among the city intelligentsia. These passages, which provide anecdotal evidence of the extent of Golder's role as benefactor, serve as well to document the fate of the old regime intelligentsia.

During the second year of the mission, Golder took on a new assignment in Soviet Russia, that of political observer for Secretary of Commerce Hoover, writing weekly reports in the form of letters to Hoover's assistant, the future secretary of state Christian A. Herter. Golder wrote of the evolving situation in the country generally, especially the development of the New Economic Policy (NEP), the retreat to a mixed-market economic system introduced by the Bolsheviks in the spring of 1921. Together with the letters to Adams and Lutz over the entire two-year period, these documents deepen our understanding of the contradictions and confusion of the early NEP period.

Beyond this, in his reports for Hoover, Golder also documented his meetings with some of the leading Bolshevik and Soviet officials. Acting as a kind of unofficial diplomat during these months, at a time when the United States had no official relations with Soviet Russia, he accompanied in Moscow the former governor of Indiana, James P. Goodrich, another ARA special investigator who was a personal friend of President Warren

---

[25]American Relief Administration, Russian Unit, box 92; *Russian Unit Record,* March 19, 1922.

Harding and who for several weeks in 1922 was an unofficial emissary between the White House and the Kremlin.

The Soviet government eagerly sought to convert ARA food relief into some form of official U.S. recognition and trade. Secretary of State Charles Evans Hughes and Secretary Hoover remained staunchly against the idea in their public statements. Hoover's ARA was feeding starving Russians, but it was not intended to bolster the Soviet government; on the contrary, the quiet hope in Washington at the time was that if the people were fed they would gain the strength to throw off their Bolshevik oppressors (a rationale, incidentally, supported by most of Russia's key political émigrés). As the ARA mission unfolded and the stability of the Bolshevik government became clear to official Washington, however, the idea of establishing official or quasi-official contact with the Soviet government became, for much of the year 1922, a major point of discussion among officials of both governments. The backdoor negotiations between Washington and Moscow on the issues of trade and political recognition, here revealed for the first time, were more considerable than previously known, and Golder played a role in them.

Either alone or with Goodrich, Golder regularly met with influential men in the Kremlin, most often Karl Radek, the Bolshevik journalist and official of the Communist International, and Leonid Krassin, the Soviet diplomat and trade official, both of whom were directly involved in discussions concerning a U.S. government proposal to send a "commission of inquiry" to Soviet Russia to assess trade and business possibilities.

Nothing came of these contacts, and the United States did not grant official recognition to the Soviet government until after President Herbert Hoover left office in 1933. In 1922, Golder, after much agonizing over the question of U.S. recognition, came to support hooking up with the Bolsheviks. This, he reasoned, would make them respectable, "and respectability will kill them."

Golder's reports for Hoover (published here virtually in their entirety) were read by Hughes and circulated at the State Department, where the chief of the Russian desk called them "one of the most valuable sources of information which we have concerning current events and especially the currents of Bolshevik opinion at Moscow." Herter wrote to Golder that Hoover read his reports avidly and felt them to be, in Herter's words, "much the best things that are coming in to this Government at the present time on Russia."[26]

---

[26]D.C. Poole to Herter, December 16, 1922; Herter to Golder, September 20, 1922, Golder collection, box 33.

In his writings from the 1921–1923 period we see Golder the student of history struggling to understand the meaning of the events he witnesses. As a man with many friends among the old intelligentsia, his feelings were bitter as he saw that many in their ranks had died during the Civil War or survived to live through further Bolshevik oppression. Yet as a historian he tried to understand the forces of history that had brought forth such a situation and to be an objective observer of the Bolsheviks, or "Bolos" as he called them, using the term in vogue among foreign relief workers in Eastern Europe.

Golder returned to Stanford in the autumn of 1923 to resume teaching and to begin to sort through the material he had sent to the Hoover Library. He was intent on organizing a series of studies on the Russian Revolution. "The time has come," he wrote, "for the historian to study it objectively as a social movement and not as the psychology of men thirsting for blood."[27]

> The Russian Revolution is the greatest social event in modern history, as great as the French Revolution and as influential. It is worth our careful study, to learn what it attempted to do, what it accomplished, what it failed to do and why.[28]

Golder proposed to establish an institute for the study of the Russian Revolution at Stanford. His original concept was to bring together Russian and American scholars to write the history, based mostly on the material that he had brought out of Russia. In his mind, the role of the American historian was critical. The Russian scholar, he felt, was "broken in body and in spirit and his vision is blurred by his tears"; he could not be objective, whereas the American scholar had the advantage of some distance from the events to be studied.[29]

In 1925 the Laura Spelman Rockefeller Memorial Fund awarded Stanford a grant to establish a Russian institute, the first award by an American foundation for Russian studies.[30] The first fruit of the institute was the publication of *Documents of Russian History, 1914–1917* (New York, 1927), a selection of official decrees, speeches, newspaper articles, and extracts from memoirs, edited by Golder.

---

[27]Golder, "The Tragic Failure of Soviet Policies," *Current History*, February 1924, p. 781.

[28]*The Lessons of the Great War and the Russian Revolution*, a pamphlet of Golder's address at Washington State College, January 7, 1924.

[29]Golder, "The Tragic Failure of Soviet Policies," p. 783.

[30]Byrnes, *Awakening American Education*, p. 144.

To enlist the support and resources of Soviet scholars and institutions, in 1925 Golder returned to Soviet Russia for two months, accepting an invitation to attend the two hundredth anniversary celebrations of the Russian Academy of Sciences in Leningrad (as Petrograd was renamed after Lenin's death in 1924) and Moscow. His diary and a report he made to Hoover about his trip are included here, as well as an article he wrote for an ARA alumni newsletter. These documents provide a small but direct window on Soviet Russia at midpoint in the 1920s. Also included here are excerpts from Golder's diary in Europe after his departure from Soviet Russia, describing his encounters with prominent Russian émigrés.

During his 1925 trip, Golder arranged a preliminary agreement between Stanford and the USSR Society for Cultural Relations with Foreign Countries (a department of the People's Commissariat of Foreign Affairs) to establish a Russian Revolution institute. The parties agreed to sponsor the research and publication of works by American and Soviet scholars on the Russian Revolution.

As a result of the agreement, a Soviet economist named Lev Nikolaevich Litoshenko spent the 1926–1927 academic year at Stanford, where, together with Lincoln Hutchinson, he completed a major study of Bolshevik agricultural policies since 1917.[31] Although drafts of this manuscript reveal an effort to keep the work as free from opinion, as "objective" as possible (that is, as unobjectionable to the Bolsheviks as possible), it nonetheless documented the folly of Bolshevik peasant policy during the Civil War years and prescribed a further privatization of Soviet agriculture.

The problem for Golder (and, much more seriously, for Litoshenko) was that this point of view was becoming politically untenable inside Soviet Russia. The illusion behind Golder's scheme was that somehow by focusing on the study of Russian economics and society, by avoiding politics, his institute could avoid controversy. But in the Soviet Union of the late 1920s everything had become politicized and peasant policy especially so.

When signs of trouble appeared and publication of the Litoshenko manuscript became stalled, Golder returned to Soviet Russia in the autumn of 1927 to try to loosen the logjam; the ostensible occasion for his visit was an official invitation to the celebrations of the tenth anniversary of the October Revolution.

Golder, carrying a proposal to have the Russian Revolution Institute prepare further studies, intended to invite several Soviet economists and

---

[31]See the L.N. Litoshenko collection at the Hoover Archives. Golder made Litoshenko's acquaintance during his 1921–1923 Russian sojourn, at which time he acquired a copy of the economist's unpublished study of Bolshevik agrarian policy from 1917 to 1921 for the Hoover Library. See the Golder collection, box 20.

sociologists to Stanford. In Moscow Golder found his path blocked at every turn. He had numerous and lengthy meetings with officials from the Foreign Affairs Commissariat about his institute and the publication of the Litoshenko manuscript, but wherever he went he found officials afraid to take initiative and assume responsibility and scholars fearful of even applying to go abroad. The xenophobia that was to become a hallmark of the Stalin era had begun to show its face. He left the country empty-handed and depressed.

Golder's diary from this visit, not reproduced here, sketchily outlines his Moscow meetings in a telegraphic style reflecting his state of exhaustion at this time. The article he submitted to the ARA alumni newsletter captures his pessimistic mood.

Most of the scholars Golder intended to enlist in his study of the revolution were arrested and imprisoned just a few years later. A few years beyond that, of course, would come the mass purge. Golder was spared all this by his death from lung cancer, after a brief illness, on January 7, 1929.

Throughout his professional career Golder envisioned a community of American and Russian scholars, and much of his professional activity was directed toward this end. He had seen his *Guide* to the Russian archives as a first step in this direction, concluding its preface with the words: "I join Russian scholars in wishing that this Guide may help to draw the learned men of the two countries together."[32] During his initial visit to Russia, he made arrangements for the publication in Petrograd of a Russian edition of his *Russian Expansion on the Pacific,* but the war intervened.[33]

During his first trip Golder found the Russian scholars and archivists he met "eager to be drawn a little nearer to American scholars."[34] He became especially close to his first Russian contact, Professor Lappo-Danilevskii, and together they planned to edit a four-volume history of Russia by Russian historians, to be published by the Macmillan Company. But most of the scholars who were to be involved in the project died as a result of the deprivations of the Civil War. Golder was not present in those years but followed the course of events from halfway around the world. On March 4, 1919, on reading of the death of Lappo-Danilevskii in the *New York Times,* he wrote to an American friend:

---

[32]Golder, *Guide to Materials for American History in Russian Archives,* p. v. A Russian historian reviewing the book in an issue of a short-lived "bourgeois" publication in 1920 quoted this line and let out a sigh for the memory of the good old days. *Dela i dni (Works and days),* no. 1 (1920): 212.

[33]Golder to Jameson, February 8, 1916, Jameson papers, box 86, file 626.

[34]Golder to Jameson, November 15, 1914, Jameson papers, box 86, file 626.

I have some sad news and my heart is aching and my eyes are full of tears. While in Petrograd I made a friend of one of the greatest of Russian scholars, a man of unusual ability and a beautiful character. He was highly cultured and refined and the visits to his home and family are the bright spots of my Petrograd days. In the summer of 1914 I visited him at his Finland home and spent two happy days in conversation with him. He and I are editors of a four volume work on the history of Russia. Last night I read in the New York Times that the man has starved to death in Petrograd. It is horrible! It haunted me all day. His great crime was being educated and a bourgeois. He did not meddle in politics. All he asked was to be let alone. Think of these fine men and women being sacrificed on the altar of bolshevism. If ever I return to Petrograd I shall probably find all my friends, all those who were with me, dead and buried like dogs. I close my eyes and see their starved bodies and their pitiful faces.[35]

Not all of them starved, as Golder discovered when he returned in 1921. But few had been able to think about scholarship, their time being taken up by the search for daily bread. Of those who survived the physical hardship, many had lost their academic positions and become demoralized by the turn in their personal and professional lives.

Golder could see that the tradition of Russian historical writing, indeed Russian high culture generally, was under threat. "To live in Russia now and to see [the] bearers of Russian culture and tradition dying one after another and to realize that no others are coming to take their place is like living in a community struck by the plague."[36] His idea of enlisting Soviet scholars in the work of a Russian Revolution institute flew in the face of what he knew was transpiring in Soviet Russia. When he journeyed there in 1925 and 1927 intent on engaging Soviet scholars to help write the history of the revolution, he could see that the best men were being elbowed out by new Bolshevik-trained specialists and were increasingly fearful of associating with his institute. Yet Golder fought on, hoping against hope.

Golder's pioneering attempt to establish a community of Russian and Western scholars was aborted, but in the 1990s it may at last be a real possibility. His efforts deserve attention as a historical precedent and a cautionary tale about the unavoidable political context of scholarly enterprises.

---

[35]Golder to Henrietta Eliot, undated (March 4), Golder collection, box 12. Also, Golder to Jameson, March 4, 1919, Jameson papers, box 86, file 626.

[36]Golder, *Lessons of the Great War and the Russian Revolution*, p. 11. In 1925 Golder edited a translation of a major work by one of those "bearers of Russian culture and tradition," the historian Sergei Platonov's *History of Russia* (New York, 1925).

In a Golder obituary, Lev Litoshenko provided a fitting summation of his legacy:

> In losing Professor Golder one of the most remarkable and valuable forms of cultural ties between two countries has been lost—that of equal comprehension by one man of two absolutely different worlds. It is for the Americans to appreciate what he did for their culture. Russian scholars are not likely to forget their debt to this noble man.[37]

One can only wonder whether Litoshenko (who was executed in 1938) later reflected on the tragic irony of this last sentence. As for his charge to Americans, we hope that the present volume goes some way toward meeting it.

---

[37]Published (1929?) in an unidentified Soviet English-language periodical (*Our path?*). See Hoover Institution Internal Records, box 94, file "Golder."

WAR,
REVOLUTION,
AND PEACE
IN RUSSIA

Frank Golder (right) with Donald Renshaw of the
American Relief Administration in front of St. Isaac's
Cathedral, Petrograd, January 1923. (Photo courtesy
of the Hoover Institution Archives.)

JOURNEY I
1914

CHAPTER ONE
RUSSIA GOES TO WAR

St. Petersburg, Russia
March 9/22, 1914[1]

Dear President Bryan:[2]

I have been here not quite three weeks and I have been busily at work almost the whole of that time. It gives me pleasure to tell you that the Russian officials here are doing all that they can to aid me.

Just now I am at work on the diplomatic correspondence of the time of Alexander I.[3] I am learning to admire the man. His motives seem to have been pure and he had the good of all in mind. He was a friend of the United States, although he did not always understand us and we did irritate him occasionally. Unfortunately his representatives in Washington were at times far from able men and they misled him, but he was glad when he could be set right again. Working on such correspondence makes me realize how

---

[1]Golder dated most of his 1914 and 1917 Russian letters and diaries according to both the Julian and the Gregorian calendars. The Julian calendar, thirteen days behind the Gregorian, was used in Russia until the Bolsheviks abandoned it on February 1 (14), 1918.

[2]Enoch A. Bryan (1855–1941), president of Washington State College, 1893–1916. This letter is from the office of the president (Enoch A. Bryan records, 1888–1952, Washington State University Libraries, Pullman, Wash.).

[3]Alexander I was tsar from 1801 to 1825.

very human are kings, emperors, diplomats, and others to whom we unconsciously look up.

It is such a temptation to turn from my task and peep into the correspondence of Alexander with Napoleon, Metternich, et al. It seems to be the only way to study history. I am learning much by absorption and by getting the atmosphere.

In looking over some letters today I was interested to read one from the Russian Minister at Washington (dated 1823) telling Nesselrode that three Americans started overland from Vincennes, Indiana, for Alaska and he was afraid that they were kind of spies.

I have had the good fortune to become acquainted with members of the university faculty. Last week I was invited to attend an historical conference. We met in the evening and the first thing was the drinking of tea. At this gathering were present the members of the historical faculty and a few of the more advanced students. Three of the younger members of the faculty read papers and at the end of each paper the others discussed and criticized. It is very helpful for young writers to have such training. Fortunately for me one of the readers gave a paper on a phase of Eastern Siberian history with which I was familiar. I listened carefully to catch his point of view, his method and in general to be able to measure myself along side of him, who had better advantages. I shall go again and see more before I will express an opinion.

As you know there is as yet no large middle class as in England. Society is divided into (1) official and (2) non-official. Among the non-official there are quite a number of wealthy families who although they may not mingle with those above them try to keep up the same style of life. In general we might say that there is a wealthy class and a poor class. Among the poor class are a great many educated people to whom many doors are closed and their life is not a happy holiday. They are very pessimistic. . . .

On the other extreme one finds the official and wealthy class. I may be mistaken, but I do not think so, that in no large capital or city of the world does the pursuit of pleasure have such a hold on the people (of this class) as here. Society is more or less rigid and when one gets into a certain position he remains there and his purpose in life is to enjoy himself. The fact that a man is a great scholar does not open society doors for him.

Since coming here I have been fortunate enough to become acquainted with a rich family of merchants. They are of course not permitted to mingle with the official class, but in their own way they try to live in the same style and at the same pace. Their house is decorated with precious works of art, their table covered with the best foods and wines, their women covered with jewels, they have their automobiles, and their box in the theatre adjoins to one of the nobility—and yet with all that I can not find that they possess a real appreciation of art, music or literature. There are many such families.

It is theatres, balls, dinners, suppers, cards, races, etc.

It is the proper thing to go to certain theatres and every one who wishes to consider himself of the best families makes an effort to go. As a result the prices are very high and tickets are at a premium. Through the kindness of my friends I went with them once and I assure you it was an eye-opener to me. I had been at the opera in Paris, Berlin, etc., but nowhere have I seen such gorgeous settings, such rich colors, nor such an atmosphere of the orient as here. It was like a page out of the Arabian Nights. In addition to the stage effects the audience was worthy of study—there were many beautiful women bedecked with precious jewels and dressed in most elegant gowns.

I am telling you all this in order to give you the other side of the picture and as a good historian you will be able to draw your own conclusions.

The cost of living is very high, more so than anywhere else in the world. It is not necessary for me to give reasons. One of the results is poverty and there are many beggars. I go to the Greek Church[4] very often and just now being Lent the churches are full of the faithful. The music one hears is very sweet and good.

I have come across here a man who would be an ideal person for our department. I have reference to the American Consul.[5] He studied at Yale and Chicago and from one of these institutions he received the Ph.D. degree. He taught at the University of Pennsylvania. He is especially well prepared in applied economics. He has been for about ten years in the consular service, most of the time in the Far East, and understands commercial conditions. He has a good personality and is a capable man and accustomed to meet business men and just the person to work with Chambers of Commerce and other such organizations. I think that he would like to go back to teaching. He now receives $3500 per year. He would probably take a little less but not a great deal. I suppose he is too high priced a man for us, but he is worth it. He could do the college and state a great deal of good.

I have so much work ahead of me that I can not make plans, so please, disregard me for a time altogether.

I should appreciate very much if you would remember me to Mrs. Bryan and your children.

Sincerely yours,

P.S.   Please address me care of the American Consulate.

---

[4]The services of the Russian Orthodox church.

[5]Jacob Elon Connor (1862–?) was U.S. consul at St. Petersburg from 1909 to 1914. He received his Ph.D. in economics from the University of Iowa in 1903.

Diary

St. Petersburg, May 2/15

Archbishop Nikolai, formerly bishop of Alaska, gave me a card to the meeting of the Imperial Council which I attended today.[6] The hall in which the meeting took place is semicircular and quite artistic. On the platform was the speaker, the secretary, and other officials. Many of the members were in military uniforms, others in clerical gowns, and the rest were dressed in Prince Alberts. Each member had an arm chair. It was difficult to hear, but as most of those present paid little attention themselves, it didn't matter much. In order to collect votes, the ushers passed boxes among the members. There was no applause.

May 4/17

Went with Vernadskii[7] to Narva, passing through a green and flower-bedecked country. Narva is a small frontier town, and has been fought over by Germans, Danes, Swedes, and Russians. There are a number of old fortresses left, some built by the Russians and others by the Swedes, one on one bank and one on the other bank of the Narova. It is said that the Russian fortress was built in the time of Ivan III, Grand Duke of Moscow, and that he put out the eyes of the Polish engineer who built it so that he couldn't give the plans to the Swedes. Within sight of the town is the famous battle field where Charles XII and Peter the Great hacked at each other.

Reval

We arrived here May 5, at 8 A.M. It is a beautiful old city with walls and towers. It has a good museum with a very fine Alaska collection made by Krusenstern, Kotzebue, Wrangel and other Balts who navigated the North Pacific. We visited the old Rathouse, and the old Saint Nikolai church, and other survivals of medieval days, as well as the house where Peter the Great lived.

---

[6]The Imperial Council, or State Council, had been, since the enactment of the Fundamental Laws of 1906, in effect the upper house of the Russian parliamentary system, the lower house being the State Duma. One half the council's members were appointed by the tsar.

[7]Georgii Vladimirovich Vernadskii (George Vernadsky) (1887–1973), historian of Russia, later professor of Russian history at Yale University.

May 8/21

Rodichev[8] gave me an admission card to the Duma. The session took place in the large semicircular hall, not quite as artistic as the one in which the Council of the Empire meets. The Duma is a noisy body, with people running here and there, and with little attention to the speaker. The galleries were well filled.

With several others, I spent the evening with Andrei Tishchenko.[9] We sat around the samovar and talked about history and literature. I doubt whether five American graduate students or instructors could talk on as many subjects as intelligently as the Russians did. After tea, we promenaded in the garden until past midnight.

Sunday, May 11/24

About six o'clock, I went with Mrs. Rogozina[10] to call on Archbishop Nikolai. Mrs. Rogozina drew him out and he talked very brilliantly. He said that in the time of Stolypin,[11] the Emperor [Nicholas II] sent a letter to the right wing of the Council of the Empire indicating how he would like to have the members vote on a certain question. When the letter was received, those to whom it was addressed had a meeting at which the Archbishop and others declared that they were not servants to be told how to vote. It was decided to write a letter to the Emperor intimating why they could not do as he suggested. This was done. But the man who brought the letter from the Emperor would not take back the reply. Trepov,[12] however, volunteered to deliver it. When the Emperor read it, he raised no objections, and since then he has not interfered. He generally makes known how he stands on a question, but does not give any direct instructions.

The question of Rasputin was raised. The Archbishop was loath to commit himself or make any definite statement. He finally came out by

---

[8]Fedor Izmailovich Rodichev (1854–1933), Zemstvo activist, leader of the Union of Liberation, member of the liberal Constitutional Democratic (Kadet) party, and deputy to all four Dumas. He fled Soviet Russia in 1919.

[9]Identity unknown. In an edited version of his diary, Golder noted only that Tishchenko was "killed in East Prussia at the beginning of the war."

[10]Identity unknown.

[11]Petr Arkad'evich Stolypin (1862–1911), president of the Council of Ministers from July 8, 1906, to September 1, 1911, when he was assassinated by a young revolutionary at the Kiev Opera House.

[12]Dmitrii Fedorovich Trepov (1855–1906), governor-general of St. Petersburg and, from October 1905, commandant of the palace.

saying that Rasputin won the good will of the Emperor by disclosing a plot against the Imperial family. The Emperor was so grateful that he told him that the palace would always be open to him. Mrs. Rogozina stated that some time ago Rasputin desired to enter the bedroom of the Grand Duchesses to bless them, but the governess blocked the way. This angered the Empress and she dismissed the governess. When Mrs. Rogozina exclaimed that Rasputin was an immoral man, the Archbishop didn't comment, but he finally admitted that he had refused to meet him or to receive him. Mrs. Rogozina added that Rasputin had made himself priest in order to become the family confessor, and that he is planning to put away his wife in order to have himself made bishop. It is said that the Emperor hates Rasputin, but keeps him near because of his influence over the Empress, and because he quiets her. At the request of Rasputin, the Emperor ordered the Holy Synod to make a bishop out of an ignorant priest, who in turn made Rasputin priest.

At nine o'clock, I went to the home of Harold Williams[13] where I had an enjoyable evening.

Russian society is built in layers, one on the top of the other. At the bottom lie the peasants and workers, on the top of them the small bourgeoisie, and over them the aristocracy. It is difficult but honorable for a peasant to become a bourgeois; it is easy but humiliating for a bourgeois to become a worker. A man's occupation determines his social status and certain kinds of labor are beneath the dignity of a gentleman. At times this medieval point of view brings about amusing situations.

Whenever I rise to leave, the host rings for the servant and follows me into the hallway where the maid is supposed to wait to help me on with my things. If she delays, as she often does, and I try to help myself the host becomes confused. It is poor hospitality not to help me and it is humiliating for him to help me. I usually avoid embarrassing him by throwing the coat over my arm and saying, "I do not believe I will wear it," and walk out to put it on when out of his sight.

This artificiality in social life may be seen on the street and in public places. I asked a lady once why there was so little laughter, so little joy on the streets; "Because," she said, "it is not good form." I have often sat in cafés with Russians and was interested how much one group criticized the other on "good form." The influence of the eighteenth century and French literature is still very marked.

When I reached St. Petersburg in February I went to live in a pension kept by a Scotch lady married to a Russian. They had a son who was about

---

[13]Harold Williams (1876–1928) was a British journalist and an old Russia hand.

thirty-five years of age and who was pretty much broken in health. He was wholly Russian in his point of view. He had been at the university, had belonged to a secret political society, had participated in a plot and had been exiled to Siberia. He used to come to see me quite often to enlighten me. He told about his university career.

When twenty years of age he entered the university with the object of definitely settling to his own satisfaction three profound questions: Is there a God, a soul, a hereafter? For two years he studied biology and at the end of that time he proved to himself that there is no God, no soul, and no hereafter and then quit the university. It is hard to think of any American student of the same age being interested in such problems or presuming that he could prove them. Russian students are not gifted with a sense of humor. They take themselves seriously and talk down to their auditors with a cock-sureness that is irritating. It is true with them as with others that "a little knowledge is a dangerous thing."

One day this man came to me and expounded Rousseau's theory of the Social Contract, though he gave the impression that he was saying something new and original. After going on for a time he turned to me with this question: "How many suits of clothes have you?" I said, "Three." "Are you a Christian?" he asked again. "Yes," I replied. "If you are," he went on, "why don't you follow the teachings of Christ and give the two extra suits to the poor?" It was a hard question to answer and I did what most people do under the circumstances, that is to say, I put some questions to him. "How many suits have you?" I asked. "Three," he said. "Why don't you give two of them to the poor?" I followed up. "Because I live in a state of nature and keep what I have," he replied. He seems to get a great deal of delight in criticizing others for not doing things that he himself is unwilling to do.

As I was eager to get into a Russian family to learn the language and ways of the people, I asked some of my professor friends to keep me in mind in case they heard of a private family that would take me in. One day I received a note from Professor Lappo-Danilevskii informing me that he had heard that on such-and-such a street lived a Russian army officer with his wife, who knew no other language than Russian, and who would be glad to take in a foreigner. I went to the place and found a policeman at the door. Assuming that all Russian officers have guards, I paid no attention and inquired for Captain Troianovskii. I was shown into a waiting room and pretty soon a youngish looking man in uniform came in. After I explained my mission he excused himself for a few minutes and then returned with his wife, a big peroxide blonde with thick lips and large grey eyes. They looked me over, showed me the room and offered to take me in. It seemed just the place I was looking for and so I moved in. A few days later Professor Lappo-Danilevskii came to see me and almost went down on his knees in apologizing to me. He told me what I did not know: that I was living in a police station, that the officer was the Captain of the police of the district, that he did not know what he was doing when he recommended the place to me. He offered to find me another place. During the next few days nearly every Russian friend I had in the capital came to see me to express sorrow and to offer to get me out of the humiliating position I was in.

After thinking over the matter, I decided to stay where I was. In a country so full of police and spies as Russia is, it would do me no harm to live under the roof of the guardian of the law. During my stay in the place, I was surrounded and waited on by policemen. They brushed my clothes, polished my boots, opened the doors for me, ran my errands and watched over my comings and goings.

I never saw the Troianovskiis in the morning for they slept late and I was about early. I had my breakfast alone and it was usually a poor affair. The servants were negligent of their duties and the dining room was full of flies. It was at dinner, late in the afternoon, that the three of us gathered around the table. During the first few days, all went well and then all went wrong. The husband and wife began quarreling and they never let up. It seemed as if they could not agree on anything. Whenever one stepped out the other insisted on telling me in confidence his side of the story. Here is her story.

She is a native of the Caucasus and there she met a Russian officer and married him. Soon afterwards they were transferred to Siberia where she met Troianovskii, fell in love with him, became his mistress, secured a divorce and married him when he was detailed for the police job at the Capital. She is now tired of him and ready to make a third try; she is ready "to go anywhere, the farther the better, even to America." The thrust did not penetrate and I argued with her on the beauties of wifely virtues, on patience.

After I had been in this home about three weeks her father and mother came to visit. The old colonel was a nice old soldier, but the mother was a large, coarse-grained half-breed Tartar. We three became friends and I learned from them a great deal about that far-off country. The old lady assured me that as far back as she knew not a single male member of her family had died a natural death. One and all had lost their lives in battle with the natives. It made cold shivers run down my back to hear her describe the fights. As she talked her face became animated, her large mouth opened wide and disclosed huge white teeth, her eyes shone, her voice grew loud and passionate, her hands reached out for any object near by which she held as a dagger and then with one quick stab she plunged it into the body of the invisible opponent.

When the old folks came, I hoped that the young folks would cease their quarrels. Little did I realize the new tortures that awaited me. No Russian meal is complete without soup and eating soup in Russia is a noisy affair. It got on my nerves after a time. I usually sat next to the old lady, the noisiest of all. To hear her was a torture. I used to close my eyes and wait with bated breath every time she moved the spoon to her lips. When the storm was over I would say to myself, "There," and open my eyes only to close them again a second later.

After two months of Russian family life I was ready to forgo all the knowledge to be gained in that circle. I got out of my awkward position very gracefully when Troianovskii was promoted and transferred to another part of the city too far for my archive work. I then found me a room in a pension where I had less family life and more peace of mind.

Now and then Troianovskii and I went for a walk and I learned much from him on these wanderings. He complained of the dishonesty and inefficiency of the police. It was dishonest he said because it was underpaid; inefficient because it lived on "pull." Sometime ago, he related, he was in a certain part of the city and saw people committing illegal acts. As a police officer he arrested them and led them to the chief of police of the district. The latter turned on him and told him to mind his own business and in his own district. The explanation was that the lawbreakers had an understanding with the police. "Now," says Troianovskii, "when I see lawless and illegal acts outside of my ward, I look the other way and pass by. So long as we keep down political criminals we are in good standing with our chief."

In this land of uniforms and tips it is easy to get into trouble. Before beginning my work in the archives, I asked one of the scholars to tell me whom one may and may not tip. He said that as a rule one tips the man who brings the documents to the table, but there are exceptions. After I had worked in the Ministry of Foreign Affairs for a time I decided to tip the man who brought me manuscripts and one day I handed him a three-ruble bill. He gave me a look of scorn and disappeared. About five minutes later the old director, so angry that he could hardly talk, walked up towards me and began to abuse me: "You think this is America. In Russia we do not bribe or tip gentlemen." Right behind him was the offended man and one or two others to give moral support. I tried to explain but they did not give me a chance and they made me feel that I had committed the unpardonable sin. As soon as I could I left the building not knowing whether I would be sent to Siberia for bribing or merely be prohibited from the use of the archives.

With my troubles I went to Professor Lappo-Danilevskii. He called up the director, who had by that time cooled off, and explained that it was all a mistake and a misunderstanding, and it was agreed to forget the unhappy incident. Before leaving, the good professor gave me this advice. "In the archives never tip the man in civilian clothes. He is an official. Tip the man in uniform. He is a servant."

A few weeks later, when I was almost through in the archives of the Ministry of Foreign Affairs, the director of it offered to secure for me permission to investigate the archives of the Ministry of the Marine. One day as I was working at my desk a man in uniform came up and inquired whether I was the American who desired to work in the Naval archives. I replied in the affirmative. "You have been granted the desired permission," he informed me. I supposed that he had been sent to tell me the news. Instead of going away he engaged me in conversation as to the character and the object of my investigation. It then occurred to me that he was waiting for a tip so I offered him one. He turned pale and then pink and burst out, "I am the director of the Naval archives."[14] It was then my turn to change color and to wish that I were thousands of miles from St. Petersburg. I tried to explain and fortunately for me he accepted the explanation. When I related my adventure to a Russian friend, he said: "Could not you tell an officer's uniform from a servant's?" No, I could not and can not yet.

In the archives of the former Ministry of Industry and Commerce are two curators, both middle-aged men. Their office hours are from one to three, but as they never come on time and always leave before time they are seldom more than an hour and a half at their desk. While in the office they smoke cigarettes, drink tea and paste postage stamps in their albums. One day I gave them a lot of stamps and after that we became very good friends. The archives were in poor condition and they apologized by saying that for the last twenty-five years they have been appealing for funds to put the papers in order but without success. They talked as if they had a real grievance. So far as I could see they had done practically nothing during those twenty-five years but work themselves up into a fit of anger against the government for not giving them the money. They were kind to me and I should not complain. I intimated once that it would be well if I could have a little longer time to work in the archives. "Of course, you may," they said. They led me to a place outside of a door and pointed to a nail. "This is where we hang the key. Should you come earlier than we you will find it there, should you leave after we are gone you will hang it there." After that

---

[14]If Golder is correct, this would be Mikhail Nikiferovich Varfolomeev.

I came at nine and left at five. I was master of all the papers in sight. I could have done with them whatever I pleased. Is there another country in the world where such a state of affairs exists?[15]

Saturday, June 28/July 11

I left St. Petersburg today for Valaam Monastery by way of Finland. My reasons for going this round about way were to spend the week end with Professor Lappo-Danilevskii and to see a bit of Finland. I took a train as far as Trusovo and from there I went by cart, some twenty miles. The "dacha," or summer home, is a roomy building situated on high ground in the midst of a forest and overlooking the Gulf of Finland. It is an ideal place for rest, study and health. Professor Lappo-Danilevskii is one of the rare scholars of the world. He is unusually well equipped linguistically for his historical studies; and he not only speaks a number of modern languages, but also writes them. He has read widely in the literature of the world, he knows of music and appreciates art. To be in his company is an education and delight.

On Sunday morning we strolled along the sea shore and I listened to my learned colleague on men and books. In the afternoon, we took a drive to some of the inland lakes. Finland is as barren, as rocky and as unproductive agriculturally as certain parts of New England. The Finn compares well with the Yankee in industry, honesty and cleanliness; but physically the former is much more robust, much better built than the latter. In Finland the women do much more out-of-door work than in America. They are not afraid to roll up their sleeves and to tuck up their skirts; they are not ashamed to take off all their clothes and go in bathing. If the men do not like it, they can look the other way. Finnish children are well behaved and clean. On our way back to the "dacha" we passed women and children with their shoes in their hands on the way to church. Very few spoke Russian and nearly all resent Russian rule.

Monday, June 30/July 13

This morning I took leave of my kind host and hostess and drove about twenty-five miles through the forest to Uusikirkko, the nearest railway

---

[15]Golder's letters to J. Franklin Jameson during his 1914 trip, none of which are reproduced here, describe his work in the archives in some detail, recording his frustration (and occasional amusement) in dealing with uninspired archive officials and their unpredictable working hours. (Jameson papers, box 86, files 626, 627. See also *Guide to Materials for American History in Russian Archives*, pp. 1–2.)

station. I did not have to wait long before a train came along and carried me to Vyborg, a clean and old fashioned town. In the afternoon I took the train for Imatra which took us through a forest and across the Vuoksen river. It was late in the day when we reached Vuoksenniska and I went on board a small steamer bound for Nyslott. The little ship was crowded with tourists and the good old captain proffered me a chair in front of the pilot house and a rug to put over me and from that vantage point I watched the beauties of Lake Saima. The scenery, the wonderful midsummer night, almost midnight sun, the fishing villages and the primitive life called to mind the inland waters of southeastern Alaska. It seemed like dream-land.

Tuesday, July 1/14

Towards eight in the morning we came along side the wharf of Nyslott and made fast. Nyslott looks spotlessly clean. From the deck as one views the Castle, the stone bridge, the small boats in the harbor, the women with their carts, he tries to recall where he had seen that before and concludes that must have been in a picture book. Within a few feet from the boat are a number of whitewashed booths and kindly old ladies with white aprons inviting the passengers to partake of breakfast. I went into one and had delicious coffee, hot rolls with butter and honey. It was a much better breakfast than one can have in Russia. I offered the good woman a Finnish mark, the equivalent of twenty cents in American money. She returned the money and said something which I did not understand. I added another mark and she gave them back but talked much louder to make me understand. I replied in such languages as I knew but made no impression. By this time a crowd gathered and one of the number acted as interpreter. It seems that I over paid; my bill amounted to five cents and the woman would not take a cent more.

About nine o'clock we steamed away for Punkaharju. The scenery was similar to that we had had all night. I spent the night at the Hotel Punkaharju, situated on a high ridge and shaded by stately pine trees. Numerous shady walks run from the hotel into the deep forest and I used the beautiful sunshiny morning in following some of the trails. After luncheon, I walked to the station, following the shady paths and getting glimpses of rugged scenes. The train ride from here to Sortavala (Serdobol in Russian) in a clean car and through a green country was both restful and enjoyable. Sortavala on Lake Ladoga is not as clean as other Finnish towns. It has a considerable Russian population and Russian is heard everywhere. As my steamer was to leave in the course of the night I went on board late in the afternoon. It was not a large boat but was crowded with pilgrims, about as clean as pilgrims usually are, on their way to the monastery. The captain took pity on me and fixed me a bed on the lounge in his cabin.

Wednesday, July 2/15

When I came on deck this morning I caught a glimpse of Valaam Monastery in the far distance. A little later the sun began to shine on the golden domes of the churches and made them look like one of Bilibin's illustrations of Russian fairy tales. We came along side about ten o'clock and found a large number of people on the dock. Valaam is such an attractive place that many people come here to spend a week or two. It is open to all, rich and poor. No pay is taken for food and lodging, but there are numerous opportunities for contributing towards the support of the church work. Wherever one turns he faces a contribution plate. The monks eye each visitor to determine his capacity either to pay or to work. People who can not afford to contribute are expected to offer their services; if they fail to volunteer, they are asked to do so. Each person is put to such work as he or she can do best. There is work for everybody because the monastery produces its own food, makes its own clothing, shoes, tools and even has its own boats for carrying produce and passengers. No one is overworked. I met here a number of city workmen who are having a very good vacation in return for a little labor.

The Archbishop of Finland gave me a letter to the Abbot and when I presented it at his office, I was well received. At first I was placed in a room with two others, and later I was given a cell by myself. One of my room-mates was in charge of the section of religious art in the Alexander III Museum at the capital and the other was an old peasant who could neither read nor write. As he was alone in the world he decided to become a lay brother and spend the remainder of his years in these walls. He made over whatever property he had to the brotherhood and has been taken in.

While we were talking there came a call to eat. The refectory was a rectangular shaped room with two long rows of tables. At one were the black-robed monks and at the other the male visitors, for the women ate elsewhere. Each person is provided with a wooden spoon, an agate plate and a piece of black bread. When all had gathered the Abbot came in and we stood up to receive his blessing. One of the brothers chanted the service after which all sang. Then we went at it. A big dish of food was placed within reach of four to six people and each dipped into it. For drink we passed the cup of "kwas" (a nonfermented liquid made out of grain) from mouth to mouth. Among the dishes we had to eat in the course of my stay were potato salad with onions and oil, pickled cucumbers and other pickled vegetables, cabbage soup, porridge (kasha), fish, usually boiled whole, head, tail and all. Though I have eaten with all kinds of people yet I could not quite stomach the food because of the table manners. I used to buy bread and make my tea. Sometimes when there was milk to spare I got that. My health did not suffer because of this simple diet.

The main purpose of my visit to the monastery was to examine its archives. Towards the end of the eighteenth century a number of monks went from this monastery as missionaries to Alaska. The poor men had a rather hard time of it; some lost their lives at the hands of the natives, others their vows, and one of them is supposed to have become a saint.[16] The fact that I came to look into the history of these missionaries aroused the interest of the Valaam monks. They placed all their papers before me, the same papers which were used years ago by one of their number in writing the saintly story of the missionaries. In this account many documents were given in the original but the writer forgot to mention that he edited certain portions of them and left out others. It is of such material and by such writers that lives of saints are written. One can trace the growth of this particular legend from one document to another.

My work on the archives left me plenty of leisure to wander over the green and beautiful island, and to watch from the bank the monks as they fished or paddled parties of pilgrims from one shrine to another. Take it all in all, Valaam is one of the most peaceful and picturesque places in the world. What I like best of all was the church service and the wonderful singing. It was especially impressive very early in the morning as it floated through the still air. There is no religious music to compare with that of the Russian Church. On Sundays the church was filled with worshipers who gathered around the tomb of one of the saints to put up candles and lay petitions on it.

After the service the priest took off these prayers one by one and read them aloud. The people stood around to make sure that their humble cry was not left out. The great majority of the monks are peasants or of peasant origin. I dare say that most of them can neither read nor write. Some of their comments on the world outside were, to say the least, naive. They informed me that missionaries from their monasteries had gone to America six hundred years ago. When I raised some doubt as to the date and stated that America had not then been discovered they thought I was joking. They wished to know what I meant by "discovered" and though I tried to explain I am not at all certain that I succeeded.

One day, as I was standing near the church doors watching the brothers enter, one old man came close to me and slipped something into my hands.

---

[16]See F. A. Golder, *Father Herman: Alaska's Saint* (Pullman, Wash., n.d.).

It was a long poem in honor of the Alaska Saint. As I was about to leave several of the brothers were kind enough to honor me by an invitation to join them and remain with them always. I thanked them and promised to consider. On the day the boat was to depart for St. Petersburg I went with the other visitors to receive the blessing of the Abbot. We were a long time in line for those ahead of me asked the old father for advice on many things. At last my turn came and he blessed me too. The steamer that carried us to the capital is owned by the monastery and does a thriving business while navigation is open, which is only a few months each year.

St. Petersburg, July 10/23, 15/28

The city is full of excitement owing to the strike. It is said that the revolutionaries have called out the strike in order to show President Poincaré, who is now here, how much France can depend on Russia. It is whispered about that hundreds of workmen are in prison and that the factory districts are under martial law. Whether these reports are true or not, it is a fact that the center of the city is in the hands of the police.

If that were not enough, there are now rumors of war. The Nevsky Prospekt is full of animated people and they are kept moving by the police with the aid of soldiers.

July 17/30

The war crowded out the strike from the public stage.[17] During the last few days there have been peaceful demonstrations in favor of Serbia. A large part of the paraders is made up of boys, who carry flags and try to sing the national hymn but without much success. They do much better when it comes to shouting "Hurrah!" The police does not interfere and that leads some people to think that these demonstrations are organized by the government.

July 18/31

A mobilization order is out and reserves are called in. Nearly every family is contributing one or more members. The porter of our house has been taken and he leaves behind him a wife and three small children. The crowd on the Nevsky is excited but not gay. These people have lived

---

[17]War broke out between Serbia and Austria-Hungary on July 13 (26), and the Russian army was mobilized on July 18 (31).

through the bitterness of war too many times to take it lightly the way we do in America.

July 19/August 1

At six this morning the reserves had to report at certain barracks for registration and duty. Later in the morning they were taken in charge by officers and led to other places. I saw a number of them lined up in front of the building of the archives of the Ministry of the Marine. Each man was given a number, a copper kettle, and a wooden spoon. Near by were big boilers of cabbage soup and piles of black bread and the men had all the food they wanted. It was pitiful to see the wives and children of these men who clung to them.

The fortification of the city has begun. I witnessed an interesting and amusing scene today. There was a big demonstration with flags and cheering. Some one started the hymn "God Save the Tsar" and the rest took it up. A moment later somebody else started the revolutionary "International," which is strictly forbidden. For a second the police seemed undecided what to do, then they made a move to break up the procession, but before they got under way the crowd began to sing a church hymn and the police retired.

Late in the afternoon I passed in front of two buildings where hundreds of women and children were gathered and were talking to their husbands and fathers who, as reservists, were locked up for the night. Those of the men who could find a place near the windows carried on conversation with those below.

Midnight. War with Germany has been announced by the papers and the Nevsky is boiling with excitement.

Sunday, July 20/August 2

This morning I went to the Kazan Cathedral where a beautiful and impressive service was held. The singing was wonderful. There are all kinds of processions and towards one o'clock many of these formed in front of the Kazan Cathedral and stopped. The clergy in their priestly robes and carrying the Kazan Madonna came out and held a religious service and blessed the people.

I went to the American Consulate and learned that our government has been asked to look after the interests of the Germans and Austrians. Hundreds of these nationals were standing in line waiting to learn what their status is and what they should do. Among them were many men of military age. In addition to the Germans there were many excited Americans who wished to know how to leave the country. There are no steamers and no trains out of Russia.

About the middle of the afternoon the crowd moved towards the square in front of the Winter Palace to hear the Emperor declare war. Along the way we were passed by diplomats with their staffs in their full regalia on their way to the Palace. At 3:30 the square was crowded with thousands of people. The Emperor and his staff appeared at one of the windows and read his declaration of war. After which the guns of the fortress fired thirty shots. I am told that the Emperor read the same declaration of war that was made by Alexander I against Napoleon. After this ceremony the crowd cheered the Imperial family and all those who showed themselves at the window. The people seem to be with the Emperor in this war. All during the night there were processions. At each street corner on the Nevsky there are little groups of men and women, discussing the coming campaign and dividing up the Central Empires.

Monday, July 21/August 3

I spent the day at the American embassy helping with the crowds of Germans and Austrians who flocked there for protection. Many are afraid of a "pogrom" and would like to leave the country but have neither the money nor the means of transportation. Some are afraid that they will lose their savings and their property. In the evening I took President and Mrs. Murlin[18] of Boston University to see the excitement on the Nevsky. Demonstrations still continue. One of the results of the war is the increase in the cost of living. The trains are too much occupied in carrying soldiers and war material to bring in food. Milk is not to be had at all.

Tuesday, July 22/August 4

Our embassy and consulate are still crowded with weeping Germans. In the city all is hustle and bustle in the day time and processions at night. Today the crowd was larger and rougher than usual. German signs on stores are being pulled down and Germans are roughly handled. I passed orators in front of the newspaper office Vechernee vremia[19] who were arousing the crowd against the Germans, the dirty race that ought to be kicked out. Occasionally one sees a Frenchman engaged in this kind of propaganda of hate.

---

[18]Lemuel Herbert Murlin (1861–1935), president of Boston University from 1911 to 1925.

[19]*Evening times,* a conservative daily newspaper.

About eleven o'clock at night as I was on my way home I caught up with a large and seemingly well organized demonstration made up of men, women and many small children. It stopped in front of the Kazan Cathedral and all kneeled while two men and one woman led the singing. It was a rather touching scene and many of the bystanders wept. This war is hitting home and there are many sad faces.

Wednesday, July 23/August 5

Last night the German Embassy was attacked. This building is on St. Isaac's Square and is rather pretentious. Some of the Russians have regarded it as an eye sore.[20] Other German buildings have also been raided. Today German stores are having the windows boarded up and are closing down. Owing to these lawless acts the police have forbidden processions and demonstrations. Tonight there is a large force of police on the street and it has the situation well in hand.

August 6, 7, 8, 9,

All is quiet. People are getting down to work and are becoming somewhat hardened to their sorrows. More women are seen working in the street than before.

August 10

I went to the Finland station to see off some Americans who were going to Sweden. While there a young German reservist, whom I had met at the embassy, came up to bid me goodbye and to tell me that he was going to Germany to fight. I asked him how he had managed it and he gave me a wink and said that his passport was in good order.

Sunday, August 17/30

As the war continues more and more people pray, especially the poor women. Today there was a long religious procession with images and clergy in clerical vestments. It started to rain but the ardor of the pilgrims was not

---

[20]This building, constructed in 1912 by the German architect Peter Behrens, is on the west side of St. Isaac's Square at the corner of Herzen Street. It is the present-day headquarters of Intourist.

dampened. The singing and praying seem to come from hearts full of sorrow and woe.

Monday, September 1/14[21]

The news of the Russian disaster in East Prussia has cast a black gloom over the city.[22]

September, October

I have spent the last two months at Moscow working in the archives. While there I was ill most of the time and had little opportunity to meet people or to learn what is going on. At the archives the officials were helpful and kind.

Petrograd, November 15

Since my return from Moscow I have been trying to find a way to leave Russia. Because of poor mail service my remittances have ceased and I now have a little more than one hundred dollars. In peace times there were four possible ways of going: through Germany, Sweden, Archangel and Vladivostok. The first is in the war zone and the second is closed owing to the thousands of German refugees who are crowding the Swedish ports and can not get passage. I have been assured that a boat will sail from Archangel for New York and on this assurance I sent ahead several boxes of books. Yesterday, however, I was informed that the sailing has been cancelled. The only other route is by way of the Far East. At the city ticket office I was told that the regular Siberian passenger trains have been taken off, that no through tickets or place cards are sold, and that it is not wise to start for one might get stranded somewhere in Siberia. I am going to try it anyway.

November 16

I rose early and started for the station. There were few there and no one ahead of me at the ticket window. After two hours of waiting the window went up and I secured one of the two second class tickets for

---

[21]Hereafter Golder provides only new-style dates.

[22]On August 27 (September 9), General Iakov Zhilinskii's Northwest Army was forced out of East Prussia at heavy human loss, despite having vastly outnumbered the German armies.

Vladivostok. It made a big hole in my finances; for I have only 180 rubles and the ticket cost ninety-nine. The porter put my bag in a coupé occupied by two ladies. I apologized for my intrusion and promised to find another place so as not to embarrass them on this long ride. They laughed and said they would not be embarrassed.

After our train pulled out I looked through the car and found a coupé occupied by only one man and brought my coat there. My coupé mate is a student of Moscow and an intelligent fellow. Our locomotive burns both coal and wood. On the tender was a large wooden frame built up, resembling a hay rack, and at different stations it was filled with wood by gangs of men who throw it up from the ground piece by piece. We saw many women working on the railroad, loading and unloading cars. In the morning, when we left Petrograd we had sunshine, some distance out it became cloudy and towards evening we ran into a snow storm. As I had no blankets and could not get any from the porter, my student friend offered me his heavy sheepskin coat; but it was a bit too warm for comfort and sleep.

                                                          November 17
This morning the ground was white and the snow bedecked trees made a beautiful picture. Yesterday we passed a level country, today the landscape is more hilly. Yesterday peasants asked for papers and news at nearly every station, today there is less eagerness for information. Train loads of cattle are moving westward. In one car I saw cattle with long hair almost like wool.

Everywhere we turn we see old and young women doing hard manual labor. Many of them loading cars with wheelbarrows and by carrying aprons filled with wood and bricks.

Our large passenger car which has accommodations for twenty-eight people has only eight in it. The train is falling behind the schedule owing to the military trains. At each siding were passed cars filled with good natured, musical soldiers. My present coupé mate got into an argument with the two ladies who were my coupé mates over the question as to what the Tsar said to the Commander-in-Chief when they met.[23] The debate became so heated that it ended up in a quarrel. I tried to make peace in the family by suggesting that perhaps the two men talked about the same

---

[23]Grand Duke Nikolai Nikolaevich (1856–1929), supreme commander of the Russian army in 1914–1915 until removed by Rasputin and the Empress Aleksandra Fedorovna and later commander on the Caucasus front. The issue in question is explained below in the entry for November 22.

subject that the Governor of South Carolina discussed with the Governor of North Carolina, but I did not succeed.[24] I left them and went to the other end of the car to talk with a Volga steamboat captain who has come on board. Navigation on the river is closed and he is now on his way home to Viatka to spend the winter. He was an interesting old man and we sat up until two in the morning talking Russia and the war. He did not resent Germany attacking Russia, a country of its size, but jumping on a little nation like Belgium was, he thought, low and cowardly.

Wednesday, November 18

It is a beautiful, clear morning. The foothills in the distance, the nip in the air, the patches of snow on the ground, the wonderful autumn foliage bring to mind Thanksgiving. The soil in these parts seems to be well cultivated. Peasants are threshing grain with old fashioned machines and are hauling their grain to the warehouses.

Late in the afternoon a wounded officer came on board and everybody in the car gathered about him and he entertained us until midnight with stories of war. The conversation turned on the question of prohibition which has been in force since the outbreak of hostilities and it seemed to have been the general opinion that with the decrease of the consumption of vodka there has been an increase in gambling, especially among the peasants and soldiers. My student friend left me. I caught a bad cold and I can barely make myself heard.

Thursday, November 19

This is a glorious morning with the sun shining on the white frosty ground. We are now in the Urals and they remind me of the forested mountains between California and Oregon. At the summit, there was only about six inches of snow on the ground but in the valley there was neither snow nor timber. Our train arrived at Cheliabinsk towards four in the afternoon where we had to get off to change cars. The station is dirty and crowded with stupid-looking soldiers, swash-buckling officers, tired mothers and squalling babies.

---

[24]According to a story antedating the U.S. Civil War, when the governors of the Carolinas became engaged in a heated verbal dispute, the governor of North Carolina relieved the tension by saying, "It's a long time between drinks." Golder was trying to lighten the mood of his traveling companions. (Thanks to F. P. Naber of Menlo Park, Calif.)

The train which is to take me farther was made up about eleven o'clock and when the gate was opened the mob made a rush for it. I tipped two of the porters to find a place and when I located them they had an upper berth for me. In a rush like this it is always best to have an upper, which only one person can occupy, while a lower offers seating space for five or six people.

Friday, November 20

The car was too warm and the snoring too loud for comfort or sleep. Siberia is flat and monotonous, but less so than our Dakotas because of the scrub timber and gulches. This car has no coupés so that we dress and undress, eat, sleep in the sight of all. The person who occupied the bunk below me is an old lady, 72 years of age. She is on her way to join her son at Chita who went there years ago and has built up a good business. Siberia is the land of opportunity. This old peasant woman and I have become good friends. She offered me a green apple, which I declined on the plea that it did not agree with me. She gave me a look of pity and said: "We have come to a sad state of affairs when a young man is afraid to eat a bit extra." My sickly condition has appealed to her motherly instincts and she is suggesting remedies. She assures me that she knows all about it, that she has brought into the world fifteen children, ten girls and five boys, and that fourteen of them have died. This statement convinced me completely of her skill as a dietitian and physician.

Train loads of soldiers on the way to the front are either passing us or we are passing them.

By evening the passengers in the car were like one big family engaged in a general conversation. Everybody had something unkind to say about the government, and many were pessimistic about the outcome of the war and the future of Russia. Whenever the train makes a stop of any length, which is often enough, the passengers rush outside to fill their tea pots with hot water from the "kipiatok" (the boiler) provided by the station. The peasant women from the village come rushing out offering good wholesome food for very reasonable prices.

Saturday, November 21

We are enjoying a beautiful wintry day and are crossing the same kind of country we did yesterday, except that it has more snow on it. At the different stations one sees military trains filled with large, wild looking men with long beards, who fear neither God nor the devil.

Sunday, November 22

We seem to have passed out of the flat lands and are now in a rolling country, something like the woodland meadows of Missouri. Our little family talks nothing but the wickedness of the government and the cruelties of the war. One officer on leave told of a German soldier who was found in a French forest in a demented state singing Wagner and another related the case of a Russian orderly who lost his mind on seeing his officer running without a head. Before our party broke up for the night it got into a friendly quarrel as to what the Tsar and the Grand Duke Nicholas said when they learned that the Kaiser had boasted that he would breakfast at Warsaw, lunch at Petrograd and take dinner at Moscow. After the discussion had been going on for some time one of the officers said he knew what comment the Grand Duke had made. He said that he would take his meals in Russia but would go to Germany to get rid of them.

Monday, November 23

Our train reached Krasnoiarsk about four in the morning. The car in which I was was so stuffy, so full of foul air, tobacco smoke, and snoring that I crawled down from my bunk and went out into the cold air. I walked up and down the platform and once I approached the baggage car where a number of men were laboring hard to get something out. When I came quite close two of the soldiers jumped out, pointed their bayonets at me and ordered me back. I did not argue with them.

We pulled out about seven o'clock and wandered along through a hilly country. The farther we go the emptier the car becomes and of the merry party that left Cheliabinsk the old lady (babushka) and I are the only people left. We get along beautifully. I buy the food and she makes the tea. Today I spent the equivalent of about twenty cents for our dinner. It consisted of a roast chicken, a bottle of milk, bread and butter. This food was bought from the women at one of the stations.

Babushka's ticket has expired and though she knew it she kept the fact concealed and got away with it until today. This evening the new conductor discovered the true situation and told the old lady that she had to get a new ticket. At first she did not have any money at all, then she pulled out five rubles, and a little later seven. One of the women passengers who lives in the same town with the son of the old lady advanced the money for the ticket.

Tuesday, November 24

The country is hilly, wooded and covered with about two feet of snow. We arrived at Irkutsk about midnight and changed into another train and into an up to date car, partly occupied. I took possession of an empty coupé, undressed for the first time in a week and had a good sleep.

Wednesday, November 25

This morning we are following the rocky shores of Lake Baikal, an impressive body of clear and unusually transparent water. It looks particularly picturesque just now with the sun shining on the white cliffs and the light fog as it rises from the water. The ruggedness of the country, the snow covered peaks, the wooded hills and the cold snap in the air is very restful and enjoyable.

I had a long talk today with an engineer who had been sent out here fourteen years ago as an exile. He has built up a practice and has no desire to return to Russia. He is free to travel about within a certain area. The night is cold and clear, with the moon and stars on full duty.

Thursday, November 26

Our train is running through a broad valley on which herds and flocks wander and graze. In the distance one catches glimpses of primitive villages and horsemen dashing over the plains. It would be good to get out of this stuffy train and join them. . . .

Wednesday, December 2

This morning, at six, I arrived at Vladivostok after having been sixteen days on the road. The cost of the journey, including railway ticket, food, and such accommodations as I had, is 130 rubles. This leaves me 50 for returning to America. I wonder how far it will take me. Qui vivra verra. . . .

JOURNEY II
1917

CHAPTER TWO

THE REVOLUTION BEGINS

In the midst of a series of disastrous Russian defeats at the German front, the government of Tsar Nicholas II collapsed in the February (March) Revolution of 1917. Power devolved into the hands of a Provisional Government established by leaders of the former state Duma and consisting initially of "progressive" members of the conservative and liberal political parties with a few moderate socialists. From the start the Soviet of Workers' (later Workers' and Soldiers') Deputies, dominated by socialists and radicals, challenged the new government's authority. The soviet refused to take power, instead issuing orders and instructions intended to keep the "bourgeois" government ministers from backsliding. Throughout its eight-month existence the Provisional Government underwent a series of crises and changes in ministries (whose makeup became increasingly socialist), chiefly because it failed to prosecute the war and to win its test of nerves with the soviet, which grew increasingly radical. This state of dual power persisted until the October Revolution, when the Bolsheviks, having gained ascendancy in the Petrograd and other soviets, took power in their name.

Golder, who left Seattle, Washington, on January 30 and began his diary on that day, would witness the first acts of this revolutionary drama. In Seattle, Russian consul general Nikolai Bogoiavlenskii and his wife entrusted Golder with their two sons for a safe passage to Petrograd. Bogoiavlenskii made out two money drafts for his boys, one on a Petrograd and the other on a Vladivostok account. When Golder arrived in Vladivostok, however, he discovered that both drafts were for Petrograd

*accounts, and thus he was short of money. We pick up the diary on his arrival in
Russia. Entries are dated in new style until March 1 (14).*

★ ★ ★

February 22

Arrived Vladivostok 2:30. Spent hour with different customs officers.
Hurried to bank, got in through the back door and got money. Bogoiavlenskii made a mistake and there was no money here—changed $60 for 210
rubles in order to take the boys along. Had free tickets as far as Manchuria
but must pay for places, etc. In Vladivostok, drunks on the street—many
soldiers, slovenliness. Station agent said that he had 30 million puds[1] of
freight to send and [only] 40 empty cars. Thirteen thousand cars came from
America and all sent to Europe and only a few have come back.

Left 10 o'clock P.M. We have four places for the three of us, two in each
coupé. The "provodnik"[2] provided each of us with two sheets, a blanket, a
pillow case and a towel. This to last until Petrograd—he is not to make up
the beds any more. Cold during the night—windows came open and water
froze.

Friday, February 23

In Manchuria. About two inches of snow on the ground. Sunny, but
chilly. No empty cars on the track. Cup of tea and bread & butter 60
kopeks + 10 kopeks tip. Everything very dear.

Saturday, February 24

8 A.M. Passing through beautiful Manchurian valleys—good for agriculture—but here are wasted. Sun out.

Cost of rail transportation from Vladivostok to Manchuria including
1/10 normal cost of ticket,[3] place cards, and extra fare for speed is 30 rubles.

Nearly everyone is smuggling something in to Russia from Harbin. At

---

[1] One *pud* equals thirty-six pounds.

[2] Russian for "conductor."

[3] In an edited version of this diary, Golder notes that this cut in price was "graft we
got through the efforts of Consul Bogoiavlenskii."

Manchuria, Panov[4] is going to advance me 350 rubles to see us through. Panov said that he was held up at Vladivostok by quarantine because he came from Kobe—but 200 rubles got him out. He has, however, to go to Omsk—there is a quarantine there and it will take more money and detention for 2 or 3 days before he will be allowed to go on his way.

At Mt. Kingan. 11 A.M. Accident happened—coupler on two cars gave away. No one seems to know what to do except talk. Baggage car is being turned upside down for a new coupler. Got under way 1 o'clock.

10 P.M. Manchuria. Ticket from here to Petrograd including place card and extra speed fare is 110 rubles. Panov did give me 350 rubles, but as it turned out we did not need them—we could just have scraped through with the little cash I had. But we kept his money and will give it to his wife in Petrograd.

In the car ahead of us a number of people had a great deal of goods smuggled in and they gave the "provodnik" 50 rubles to hide it and it went through.

A number of army officers caught with smuggled goods.

Sunday, February 25

7:30 A.M. Passing through a country similar to our plains, except hilly and beautiful valleys. Settlers along the way—grazing is the industry. Hardly any snow; sun is shining. During the day the country very much like that about Spokane.

Monday, February 26

Region about Irkutsk—Lake Baikal—very cold, much snow, already 8 hours late. Hot box.

Tuesday, February 27

Same sunny weather—more snow, less cold. Nearly all with whom I speak say that after the war there is going to be a better government for there can

---

[4]Not more fully identified. In the edited version of the diary, Golder writes that he was short of funds to purchase food for the three of them to last the entire trip to Petrograd. The Bogoiavlenskii boys told some of the passengers what had happened, and "a Russian named Panov" forced on Golder a loan of 350 rubles. Golder writes that Panov was sent to Japan "to make some purchases" and that on his way back was held in quarantine at Vladivostok because he had passed through Kobe, where "some kind of disease was raging."

be no worse. One officer, in speaking of the war, said "Germany has made many mistakes, but Russia has put little thought into the war."

In one of the coupés there are three young officers—today a young woman took up the 4th berth. The four seem to get along together pretty well. When I came back from dinner she was lying in her berth in her night gown and night cap and held conversation with the young officers.

At stations people gathered to bid goodbye to soldiers.

Wednesday, February 28

Snow, cold, sunny, Novo-Nikolaevsk. New recruits, stupid-looking, being rounded up and loaded in freight and cattle cars. At stations people bought butter to take to Petrograd for about 1.30 rubles per pound. In Petrograd the rate is 3.50. Silver in coin is almost out of circulation. Postage stamps take its place. Reports of starvation and hardship in Petrograd and Moscow.

Thursday, March 1

Cold. Reached Omsk about 8 A.M. Soldiers trained with a dummy—run at it and spear it. One officer blames Russia for failure to back up Rumania in time. He also said that if the Allies win, it will be chiefly due to England and France, not Russia. No order in Russia.

Friday, March 2

Reached Ekaterinburg in the morning. Snow, sunshine and cold. Engine has gone back on us and can not pull the train. Women shovel snow on tracks and load wood and water on the trains.

Saturday, March 3

Viatka about 8 A.M. Cold, snow, sky overcast.

Sunday, March 4

Snow, cold, cars stuffy, unsanitary, consumption, coughing, spitting, etc. Have a cold. Paid provodnik 2 rubles for bed clothes and 2 rubles tip.

Cost of trip Vladivostok-Petrograd less than 170 rubles.

Reached Petrograd 1:45—about 16 hours late. Was met by Vernadskii and taken to 60 Basseinaia, apt. 22, where I am to live with an intelligentsia family. Hollinger[5] called. I went to Panov's and paid my bills.

---

[5]Ralph W. Hollinger of the Young Men's Christian Association (YMCA).

Monday, March 5

Went to American Consul and registered. No coin in Petrograd—only postage stamps and paper money. Street cars jammed. Izvozchiks[6] very expensive. Scarcity of all foods, especially bread. Petrograd does not feel the war—more luxury, pleasure, expensive clothes than ever. Having a good time is the object. Many are becoming richer. Reports everywhere of corruption of government. People do not trust it. Government condemned openly in all circles. One man high up proposes to take all monarchs of Europe and put them on an island.

Tuesday, March 6

Worked in archives. Evening spent with Prof. Priselkov.[7]

Women conductors, street cleaners, lamp lighters. Lines of people waiting for bread, sometimes they receive only a small piece of black bread. Embarrassing to go for dinner—one is afraid he eats too much.

Wednesday, March 7

Worked in archives. Dined and spent a part of a pleasant evening with Professor A.S. Lappo-Danilevskii. Talked over the history of Russia. He and I are to edit the work.[8]

Thursday, March 8

Archive. Dined with Vernadskiis—pleasant time. Disorder in city and cars interrupted. People hungry and smashing windows—complain no bread or

---

[6]Russian for "cab driver" of a horse and carriage; by Golder's time the word had come to denote the whole conveyance.

[7]Mikhail Dmitrievich Priselkov (1881–1941): historian of early Russia, privatdocent at St. Petersburg University, and later professor of history at Leningrad University.

[8]Here Golder is referring to a planned four-volume history of Russia that he and Lappo-Danilevskii were to edit. A collaborative work of Russian historians, it was to be published by the Macmillan Company. Among the other prospective participants were two Petrograd scholars: the historian and philologist Aleksei Aleksandrovich Shakhmatov (1864–1920) and the academician and historian Mikhail Aleksandrovich D'iakonov (1855–1920). Lappo-Danilevskii died in Petrograd in 1919 of what Golder called "an abscess of the lungs" (probably tuberculosis) brought on by malnutrition. The deaths in 1920 of Shakhmatov and D'iakonov were reportedly also brought on by the deprivations of the Civil War. Golder wrote a detailed letter on the proposed volume (as he envisioned it before the revolution) to Jameson and to R.R. Smith of Macmillan, December 21, 1915. (Jameson papers, box 86, file 626; see also Golder, "The Tragic Failure of Soviet Policies," p. 777.)

poor bread. The refugees who came to the city from the front have been housed and fed, and now that there is work the refugee committee insists that they should take care of themselves for a change. The refugees, however, are displeased and think that they should be cared for and not made to work. Both sides are disgruntled.

Friday, March 9

Disorder on the streets. Crowds on the Nevsky marching and singing revolutionary songs. Cossacks ride up and down and then turn their horses into the crowd and keep turning until mob is scattered to reorganize. Lines stand in front of bakeries and many people have no bread. Since government has issued the order not to use white flour for cake, etc., white flour has disappeared—speculators and well to do people have laid in stores. Black bread available, but the black bread bakeries are unable to bake enough. In addition the bakers find it more profitable to sell the flour for high prices to those who are willing to buy than to bake it and sell it for fixed price. Bread given out at inconvenient times. In the morning the workman can not get it and when he returns after work it is already distributed.

Clothing and shoes are high, yet the question is what has become of the hides of the thousands of cattle killed for the army. Everyone blames the government for the mismanagement, corruption and speculation.

Streetcars crowded to overflowing—people hang on to anything and inside there is fighting and crowding. Population in Petrograd has greatly increased while the number of cars has diminished, many out of commission. No one to repair them and no new ones. During the disturbances cars running not at all or few and the situation is much worse. Also many provision stores closed and food supply reduced.

I was told that men impersonate Miliukov[9] and go to shops to stir up working men.

Exciting times on Nevsky Prospekt. As I was returning home about 4:30, I saw a company of Cossacks and another of police hurry by. When I reached Fontanka bridge the Cossacks with drawn swords lined up and closed off the street. Behind them I saw the crowd coming—then I heard shots. The crowd scattered as a company of Cossacks in full speed came charging through them. No one was hurt. Behind the Cossacks the crowd

---

[9]Pavel Nikolaevich Miliukov (1859–1943): historian, leader of the Constitutional Democratic (Kadet) party, and minister of foreign affairs in the Provisional Government from March to May 1917.

formed once more. When the Cossacks halted, the men and women gathered about them and invited them to join them. The Cossacks were cheered—they did not seem to enjoy their job and put back the sword into the scabbard—they were good natured. Their efforts to break up the crowd did not, however, succeed.

The crowd did not seem to be well organized—many men and women students, boys and girls and workmen. One or two carried red flags. One man said he had had nothing to eat for two days. The crowd seemed on good terms with the Cossacks. Heard that a police officer and an army officer were killed by a mob, also that two or three civilians were fired on and killed.

Had dinner en famille—not very edifying. After dinner grandmother smoked her cigarette. We had also the new woman. Her hair was cut and combed like a man's, she wore shirt, collar tie, vest and coat like a man's but had on petticoats—smoked cigarettes.[10]

Heard that there is bad feeling between the Cossacks and the police and that the former chased the latter off the Nevsky.

Sunday, March 11

No cars running in the city, even izvozchiks not allowed on Nevsky. Placards announce that if people gather the soldiers will shoot. City in hands of military authorities. Went to church—walked there and back. City about Nevsky in hands of the army—soldiers block the way from either side and keep people from getting on the Nevsky. That street is in the hands of the Cossacks who keep people moving—they ride in long lines across the street, including the side walk, and every living thing has to get out of the way. Heard that machine guns were fired on the people and many hurt, and killed.

Monday, March 12

Government has posters out to the effect that those who will not return to work will be sent to the front. Soldiers of one regiment nearby killed their officer.

---

[10]In the edited version, Golder writes: "Later I learned that this mother of grown up children got into her head years ago that she resembled Napoleon and ever since then she has studied that hero's dress and characteristics in order to seem more like him. The best compliment one can give her is to tell her how Napoleonesque she is."

About 4:00 returning home and at Liteinyi Prospekt there was a crowd. Leaders of working men argue against lawlessness and revolution. There must be no provocation—must be a different government. Crowd was growing larger on the Nevsky, then out soldiers came from where they had been hiding. The crowd, thinking that they were going to shoot, began to scatter. Seeing that they were not shooting, the crowd called on them to join and not to shoot. The soldiers tried to quiet them down and succeeded. The soldiers stationed themselves in the middle of the street.

Farther on toward the Nikolaevskii station there loomed up a crowd. Mr. Clare, the pastor of the British-American church, and I were walking together when we heard shooting. In a second the crowd scattered in all directions and sought shelter. The shooting came from unseen parts. After a few seconds another crowd came from around the Nikolaevskii station, among them being soldiers with drawn swords leading the crowd. Officers on foot or on horses and automobiles were stopped and their weapons taken from them. No police on the street and no one to interfere with the crowd. It is reported that the soldiers will not shoot and that they are with the people. Neither soldiers nor Cossacks on the street are against the people. Those off duty fraternize with the crowd.

Automobiles with red flags filled with soldiers with swords and guns going by and they are cheered by the people and they cheer Hurrah in turn.

Revolutionary leaders tell the people to get near the soldiers and bring them over. Stores closed—no streetcars. No school.

All the regiments have gone over to the side of the revolutionists. Political prisoners have all been freed. Arsenals seized and civilians armed.

7 P.M. On street soldiers and civilians. Girl students mix with the soldiers. Feed them bread. Sing Marseillaise.[11] Leader of one band is a student without arms. Reported that all ministers have left town and that a provisional government is being organized. Everyone is happy and believes that all has been accomplished. Bitter feeling against the Empress. I passed a crowd on the way to Duma. Cossacks have left their quarters and wander about the streets. They will soon become hungry and then?!

Tuesday, March 13

Duma organized with a "Temporary Committee to Keep Order"—twelve members from all parties. Soldiers in automobiles, no flags, drive through city and cheer and are cheered in turn. In one automobile a hooligan with a

---

[11]The call to arms of the French Revolution, which became the French national anthem and an international song of rebellion.

sword sat on the engine, about two dozen soldiers stood up in the truck and among them a girl student with a red flag. Wild shooting in the air. Excitement everywhere—streets full of people, who seemingly approve. Stores where weapons kept have been robbed. On the whole little lawlessness. Fortress of Petropavlovsk [Peter and Paul] has been seized—prisoners freed and fort made a revolutionary base.

The secret police department has also been seized and archives and papers burned and the police abused. Court house also destroyed.

No work, as the archives are closed. Crowd after police and when they get them into their hands use them harshly or do away with them altogether. More buildings on fire. Automobiles with machine guns on them; automobiles with red cross collecting the wounded. No order but little disorder. Soldiers are taking away arms from the civilians. Lot of wild shooting. Shooting from house tops supposedly by police. Sailors from Kronstadt have come over and have joined the soldiers. Only about 1000 soldiers have remained loyal.

Thousands of sailors from Kronstadt came over yesterday morning and joined soldiers. At night quiet.

Wednesday March 1/14

Cold. Police archives still burning and black paper flying about.

Great sport hunting the police. They are hooted as they are being led to prison. Also men in high political standing. This morning I saw a regiment from Tsarskoe Selo,[12] with banners and music and led by officers, marching down the Liteinyi. A little later the Izmailovskii regiment came by. Behind them thousands of sailors with band, flags and officers came from Kronstadt and down the Nevsky to Liteinyi. Other regiments also. They were cheered and they cheered in turn. Soldiers on the way to the Duma to offer their services and promise loyalty. Crowd wears red, soldiers carry red banners and everyone is excited, happy and certain of success.

About 1 o'clock there came along the Nevsky a large crowd of students, men and women from all walks of life, singing the Russian Marseillaise. They were led by a company of soldiers with red banners.

Rodzianko[13] called for the officers to come out of hiding and enter service.

Soldiers have posted bulletins calling on the soldiers to be orderly, not

---

[12]Summer palace of the royal family, south of Petrograd, later renamed Pushkin.
[13]Mikhail Vladimirovich Rodzianko (1859–1924): prominent member of the Octobrist party and president of the Third and Fourth dumas.

drink. Workmen have summoned their fellows to meet and select delegates. There is still shooting from house tops with machine guns—yesterday many killed but as a rule few get hit.

About noon several companies of soldiers with band playing came marching down the Nevsky towards the Moika [River]. When they were near the bridge machine guns from tops of the houses began shooting and, in a second, band and soldiers were hurrying for shelter and the street was clear.

Heard of soldiers taking liquor from their comrades and destroying it. On the whole very, very little lawlessness. Soldiers seem to be in earnest and eager to do what is right and help the government. On Nevsky collections taken up to feed the soldiers, etc., and people contributed generously. Today the best elements in the city have come out openly into the street—until now they have kept under cover. Many people, including soldiers, wear red—whole companies have red ribbon about their sleeves.

Thursday, March 2/15

The city is calming down—a number of stores are open. Less shooting. Have heard no shooting today. Still large crowds in the Nevsky and Liteinyi—still good order. Every one is pleased that everything went off so well, but some are a little uncertain as to the future. Not a word as to the Emperor, although numerous rumors afloat

(1) that he killed himself

(2) that he is here

(3) that he has left the country

(4) that he is under arrest

(5) that he is on the way

Rumor that there is a difference of opinion between Duma and Labor Party—latter wants a republic.[14] Former ministerial officers are being ar-

---

[14]By "Labor Party" Golder probably means the Petrograd soviet (or council) of Workers' and Soldiers' Deputies, which was formed on February 27/March 12, 1917. In later entries he refers to this body using some combination of the words "Deputies," "Council," "Workmen" (or "Working men"), and "Soldiers," frequently in abbreviated form. In later entries he begins to use the Russian word for council, *Sovet,* although this increasingly gives way to the (later common) English transliteration *Soviet.*

rested and locked up in the Duma. Rumors that other cities have joined in the movement. Cold.

11 P.M. Out in the streets crowds still gather and discuss the form of government. Students in evidence—they have done good work. Heard two ignorant women discuss the blessings of peace: "Now they can say what they like." New ministry selected—the old one in prison. The wife of the "shveitsar"[15] is afraid Russia will have a "republic."

The signs in the city that had a big N with a crown and electric bulbs are being dismantled and lights taken out. Poor Nick!!

Students and intelligent men who had lately been taken into the army as officers did the trick, so it is said.

Friday, March 3/16

Rumor last night that 300 policemen have arrived in town—women and children ran home, scared to death. Agitation for a republic is strong. Streets are crowded, especially around newspaper offices. Papers are being scattered.

Red flag flying from Winter Palace and the crowd cheers. Report that Emperor has renounced the throne for himself and his family. Grand Duke Michael[16] has refused the regency. Republic?

Some one started a report that the new regime intended a reduction in the price of butter from 3 rubles to 80 kopeks per pound. This morning long lines were waiting in front of the stores to buy butter. Some one had to explain that it was a false alarm. Crowd took it good naturedly.

Midnight. Spent the evening at home of Lappo-Danilevskii. He told me that the revolution had been planned and organized and that both sides knew it was coming. Protopopov, the Minister of Interior,[17] had a plan of the city where machine guns were placed to sweep the streets. When he was arrested this plan was found and machine guns located. The machine guns from Tsarskoe Selo are gone—no one knows where.

---

[15]"Doorman."

[16]Grand Duke Mikhail Aleksandrovich (1878–1918): brother of Nicholas II. Nicholas abdicated on March 2/15 in favor of Mikhail, who renounced the crown and called on the Russian people to support the Provisional Government; he was shot by the Bolsheviks in 1918.

[17]Aleksandr Dmitrievich Protopopov (1866–1918): vice president of the Fourth Duma and last minister of the interior. Shot by the Bolsheviks in 1918.

Saturday, March 4/17

Snow storm. Life is becoming more normal, almost what it was before the Revolution. All insignia of royalty—crests, eagles, etc.—are being taken down and curio hunters are getting their share. Question as to the form of government is under consideration. Grand Duke Michael has consented to accept throne if elected by the people. Spent the evening at Tinkham's.[18]

Sunday, March 5/18

Sunny. Newspapers out for the first time. All kinds of meetings today. People are taking advantage of the opportunity and are organizing and speaking openly. Papers are permitted to print what they please. Each house is organizing meetings of its own. New plans are made for provisioning the city. A price has been set on food products so as to stop speculation and bring food on the market.

Went to meeting this afternoon with Vernadskii. Speeches by several members of the Duma, two or three women, one of them a suffragette. Most of the speakers emphasized the need of unity and organization. Spent part of the evening at the Hollingers.

★ ★ ★

Petrograd, March 5/18, 1917

Dear Miss Eliot:[19]

A friend of mine is to start next Tuesday, 7/20 March, for America and I take this opportunity to send a line to you. He is going by the way of Siberia and Japan for it is impossible just now to go any other way.

You no doubt have read of what has transpired here during the last ten days. How fortunate for me that I came just in time to see the fun! It is only two weeks today since I reached this city and yet what a wonderful change! I did not expect it and few others did. It is unique in history. A Revolution of such importance accomplished with almost no bloodshed and with such good order. It does not seem true, but it is.

On my way across Siberia I met with many Russians, many of them army officers, and all of them bitterly criticised the government for its mismanagement of the war and with business in general. Never before had

---

[18]F.L. Tinkham of the YMCA.

[19]Henrietta Eliot, a close friend in Portland, Oregon. All Golder correspondence with the Eliot family is in the Golder collection, box 12.

I heard such open criticism. There was no concealment. When I came to the city I found the same state of affairs. In the archives where I work, which is almost under the very nose of the Imperial family, the criticism was as open and as serious as on the street. In fact, there was no exception. On the top of that, people complained because they were suffering from hunger, cold and other discomforts. During the last two years the population of Petrograd has almost doubled on account of the refugees, but no new buildings have been erected. As a result rent has gone up very much and the cost of living has jumped up so that a poor man suffers.

It is very difficult to get about. In times of peace there were many cabs at reasonable rates, but the war has reduced their number to a large extent and the few that are left will not move unless they are offered pay such as only rich people can afford. The streetcar situation is worse. Before the war there were not enough cars to take care of the crowds, but since the opening of hostilities a number of cars have broken down and there are no mechanics to repair them. The situation was this—the number of cars was greatly reduced and the population greatly increased. People jammed into the cars like herring and there was such a pushing, swearing and fighting to get out as you may imagine. I never saw anything like it. People stood on the steps, they hung on anywhere they could.

The food situation was equally serious. Russia is a great grain producing country, but lack of transportation facilities and general incompetent mismanagement have brought about a pitiful condition: whereas in southern Russia grain and flour are rotting, in northern Russia people have nothing to eat. At the same time it is well known that articles of luxury, expensive fruits, etc., do manage to reach the city, which means that those in charge of transportation manage to find cars for certain people for money.

Sugar could be obtained only by cards, flour could not be bought at all, and black bread could be had by standing in long lines in front of the bakeries. The workmen suffered the most. The well to do sent their servants and after they stood in line a couple of hours or more they came back with bread—at the worst it was only an inconvenience. The poor workman had no servants. He left home in the morning without any, or little, breakfast; when he returned at noon there was no lunch for him because the wife was standing in line waiting for bread; and when he returned in the evening there was barely enough food for supper—for not only is bread scarce, but everything else is either very scarce or not to be had at all.

The Russian people are patient and they would have put up with all that if they had had any confidence in the government—that it was doing its best for them—but all this was lacking, and what is more, the government was directly blamed and, as I am told, justly. In Petrograd—that is, in the center of the city—people managed somehow to get enough to eat. The inhabitants are fairly well to do or have a pull—but in the suburbs, where the poorer classes live, there conditions were very bad.

Early last week trouble began in the factory district. There were bread riots, cars stopped running, etc. But this is common and no one paid much attention to them. Next day, Thursday, the trouble spread to different parts of the city and crowds began to appear on the Nevsky (principal street), but it was orderly. The police kept them moving. Friday, the crowd became more bold—they marched up and down singing revolutionary songs and now and then waving a red flag—for along side the question of food there was the problem of government.

In the afternoon of Friday I was walking down the Nevsky when I saw coming down a company or more of mounted police and a large number of Cossacks. I followed in the direction they went and when I reached a certain spot I noticed that the police had disappeared and that the crowd cheered the Cossacks. I learned then that there is bad feeling between the Cossacks (the soldiers in general) and the police. On this occasion the police tried to use force and the Cossacks drove them off. The Cossacks begged the people to disperse, but the men and especially the young women students went up to them and pleaded with them: "Comrades, our cause is your cause, etc." The rough, ignorant Cossacks smiled and said, "Please, go away, go home," but it did no good. The crowd massed again and started off.

The captain of the Cossacks gathered his men and rode right into the crowd and when they were in the center they just kept turning and turning until the crowd was scattered—no roughness or anything of the kind. Another company of Cossacks formed a line across the street—from wall to wall—and swept everything before it. The people ran into stores, courtyards and other places and as soon as the horsemen passed they gathered again and cheered the Cossacks. During the night there was more of the same kind.

On Saturday the crowd was even larger, more red flags, more revolutionary songs to the tune of the Marseillaise. This time the Cossacks acted differently. When they saw the crowd coming they shot off their pistols in the air and then dashed with all speed into the mob. Woe unto him who did not get out of the way! But all did. It is wonderful how it was done—in a second there was not a person in the way. As soon as the horsemen passed the crowd gathered again and cheered the Cossacks, "Comrades, come over to us." In addition to the Cossacks there were soldiers everywhere, trying to keep the crowd moving. But the revolutionaries went up and talked to them and tried to show them that their interests were the same. The good natured soldiers were caught, they smiled, they pleaded that they had to do their duty, etc. They were in a dilemma—they were part of the people; they did not wish to hurt them, and yet they were soldiers. The day passed without bloodshed. Cars were not running, most of the stores and banks were closed, and people live largely on excitement.

During Saturday revolutionary leaders sent men to the different factories to invite the men to march on Sunday and make a great demonstration. The police knew what was coming and so did the military commander of Petrograd and he issued an order that there must be no gathering on Sunday for the soldiers would shoot to kill. This had been done before and it was no joke and many people feared to go out of their houses. The police were no longer seen, for the soldiers would not have them. Sunday morning I went to church and walked up and down the Nevsky but there was no disturbance—soldiers and Cossacks were everywhere guarding bridges and keeping the people going.

After luncheon I started out again to call on an old lady who lived quite a ways out. Not far from where I live there is a barrack and as I passed there I saw a company or more of soldiers lined up, and heard the officer give the order to load their guns, which they did and they marched off, and I went my way. In returning, I had to cross the Nevsky and found that the streets leading thither were guarded by soldiers who did not allow people on the Nevsky. However, I managed to reach the street. A couple of hours before that—i.e., about 3 o'clock—a large number of people forced their way on the street. An officer pleaded with them to disperse for they would be fired upon, but they refused. Pretty soon machine guns opened on them and a number fell and the rest scattered.

It seems that the government expected trouble, for the whole thing was well organized, and they had placed machine guns in attics and in churches and in other high places where they would command the streets and strategic points. As I came by I heard shooting in other parts of the city, but did not see anybody hit.

Early on Monday the military commander of the city posted bulletins to the effect that unless workmen returned to work they would be sent to the front. The same morning I heard that the regiment that was quartered near where I lived had killed its officer because he had ordered them to fire on the people and that the regiment itself had joined the revolutionaries. There were so many rumors afloat that I did not pay much attention to that one.

About four in the afternoon I started for home and saw the Nevsky full of people and hardly any soldiers. I was told that several regiments had revolted and that the loyal troops are besieging them and that there is a regular battle. I was joined by an English minister of one of the churches and we were discussing the situation. The day before he prayed for Emperor

Nicholas and asked God to put down the anarchists, et al. All at once the
machine guns began to talk—the crowd scattered like a flash and my
minister and I found ourselves sticking like posters against the wall. It was
my first baptism of fire and it was not at all frightful and I was exceedingly
interested to watch the effects of it on others and upon myself. When that
ceased I continued my walk and a little ways farther there came rushing out
a mob led by soldiers with drawn swords, and followed by others with such
weapons as they had, and the revolution was on.

During the day and that night, regiment after regiment joined the
"People." Those who did not join, like the Cossacks, positively refused to
shoot. I wish you could have seen the scenes that followed—it was a
Glorious Revolution!! An orderly one and I hope a successful one. I shall
have more to tell you about. It was picturesque. Just now the red flag is
everywhere in evidence, even over the Winter Palace. All signs of royalty
are being torn down and relic hunters are busy. People congratulate one
another and call each other "Comrade."

You may be interested to know something of my life here. I have a
room and board in a Russian family of the better class and seemingly well
to do. The husband is in the army and the wife and three children, 16, 14,
10 years of age, are home. I have a chance to talk Russian and I make the
most of my opportunity. It is still very cold here, snow and ice everywhere,
and, owing to the lack of coal and wood, my room is not any too warm,
but I am not complaining—it is the best that can be done.

The food problem is more serious—there is a scarcity of almost
everything. Black bread is all we have and never too much of it. In the
morning I have coffee and black bread, from now on without butter for the
city stores are out. I usually go without lunch and have dinner about six.
There is seldom anything left over. But I seem to thrive and keep well and I
think conditions will become better. The cost of living has gone up very
much recently, especially along the lines of shoes and clothing. Shoes now
cost as high as seventy-five to a hundred rubles a pair, suits of clothes 250
rubles, collars one to two rubles, and other things in proportion. Fortunately for me I brought enough things to last for a time.

Strangest thing of all there is plenty of money and many people are
becoming quite rich. It is said that never before have people spent more on
luxuries and pleasure than they do now. The streets are quite gay, the
operas and theatres quite full, and so it is difficult to get a ticket, except at
a very exorbitant price. How people can be happy when millions are
suffering at the front is a puzzle to me. But it is there and I am not able to
explain it.

Coin has almost completely gone out of circulation and we use only
paper money. Enclosed you will find a collection of this new money which

I wish you would keep. It is not as good as coin, for the paper becomes soiled from too much use and it does not look good. If I can get hold of it I shall also enclose the cards we use to get sugar and soon we will have cards for bread and butter when there is any. Milk is only for children under five and sick people.

I have not had much time to go far in my work, but I realize already there is much of it ahead of me. The few days that I have worked I have discovered some very valuable materials and I trust that I may be as fortunate from now on. My Russian friends have been very good to me and it is a pleasure to be with them again.

. . . A Russian friend of mine and I are planning to spend the two summer months at the front in the Red Cross work. It is yet too soon to say whether it will work out, but I shall try to go to the front before I return. It will not be so very difficult to bring it about, I think. If I go I shall be able to tell whether the machine guns of the Germans are worse than those of the ancien régime.

I have as yet received no letters from America and I shall be glad to receive news and friendly words. . . .

> With good wishes,
> Cordially yours,

★ ★ ★

Monday, March 6/19

Cold. Streets are normal. People still discussing and wondering how it all happened and planning new government. Question whether it is to be a republic or monarchy. Reds wish republic and would like to have election as soon as possible. All kinds of new organizations and one or two new papers. Meetings on street corners. Soldiers are spoiled and have the first say and first pick. Populace divided into "Narod, Soldaty, Rabotchie,"[20] which is not good.

Tuesday, March 7/20

A few tramways on the street for the first time. Cars decorated with red flags, on which are the words "Long Live the Coming Republic," "Long Live Liberty," etc.

Intelligent people insist that the revolution was planned by the clique

---

[20]"People, Soldiers, Workers."

near the tsar. They hoped to bring about disorder and an excuse for making a separate peace with Germany. They say that for weeks before the outbreak agents of the government came into factories and tried to get people to strike. Some of these agents impersonated Miliukov. The Hollingers left this evening for America via Siberia. Stories are being told of soldiers who say they wish a republic like England, or a republic with a Tsar. One soldier said he wanted to elect a President and when asked, "Whom would you elect?" he replied, "The Tsar." From all accounts many of the soldiers do not grasp and do not understand what the Revolution means.

★　★　★

c/o American Consulate
Petrograd, Russia,
March 7/20 the year of
the Revolution I.

Dear Friends:[21]

Just a few lines to you while I have an opportunity to send it in a way which I have reason to believe will reach you. Of course you have had newspaper reports about the Revolution, so unexpected, so orderly and so bloodless. Who would have believed it possible? In three days the whole structure of despotism fell,—I say fell, because it was not pushed over, but like a rotten tree it just fell over. At the critical moment there was not a friend to stand by it, not even to come to the funeral. Today we have Mr. and Mrs. Nicholas Romanov, somewhere in Russia. No one knows where, or cares. It is reported that the family plans to move to England and Nicholas Romanov, Esq., will spend delightful and restful days on the golf links. Even the Church has decided no longer to pray for him. It was exciting, and it is now, to hear the people shout, "Liberty," "Long Live the Revolution." The other morning I mixed with the people in the public market and heard one woman give a piece of her mind to the seller, "You can not do that now, you can not ask such prices, we have liberty now." On the same day I passed a large crowd of men and women of various stations of life, as well as soldiers, with a red banner flying and singing revolutionary songs. Two weeks ago this was impossible and it was taking one's life into one's hands to go out on the street. When I return I shall tell you of these exciting days. How fortunate for me that I came just in time to

---

[21]Addressed to Henrietta Eliot's brother Tom and his wife, Sigrid. Thomas D. Eliot was assistant professor of political and social science at Washington State College.

see it all. You can well imagine that I did not stay in the house very long and saw all that was to be seen and know what it is to be under fire. It was lots of fun. The funniest sight in Petrograd just now is to see a red flag flying over the Winter Palace. From all parts of the world, especially from Siberia, are hastening political criminals of all shades. What a gathering of freaks and patriots—they are all patriots now. I shall attend the reunion too, and see and hear.

Russia is organizing. On every street corner there are numerous posters calling on the bakers, shoemakers, school teachers, maid and men servants, et al., to organize. It is surprising to see the number of organizations. One or two newspapers have also made their appearances under such names as Truth, Liberty,[22] etc. It is hard to persuade many people that this is only the beginning of liberty and not the complete realization. There are many serious problems ahead. As it stands now the population is politically divided into "People, Workingmen, and Soldiers," a dangerous division, but I have confidence in the people and I believe that they will weather the critical times. If the war were only over! But the war will be pushed energetically. It was the vacillation of the government in the war and its German clique that helped to bring its downfall.

It is worth while being here, even if one is less comfortable than he ought to be. My work is interesting, for I find new things every day and I am sorry to see four o'clock when the archives close. I shall write you again when I have an opportunity.

With all good wishes,
From your friend,

★ ★ ★

Wednesday, March 8/21

Spent the evening at Rodichev's. Very interesting. Judge Zarudnyi[23] told how Kerensky[24] was threatened with arrest and Siberia two weeks ago and

---

[22]*Pravda, Svoboda.*

[23]Aleksandr Sergeevich Zarudnyi (1863–?): prominent prerevolutionary criminal lawyer who served as deputy minister and later, in July, as minister of justice in the Provisional Government. He resigned after Kerensky created the Directory on September 1/14 in the face of the Kornilov attack on Petrograd.

[24]Alexander Kerensky (1881–1970). Prominent attorney and member of the moderate populist Trudoviki, or "Laborites," party; minister of justice and later minister of war in the Provisional Government. On July 8/21 he became prime minister.

now he is Minister of Justice and has the former Minister under arrest. Miss Rodichev told of the darkness and ignorance in the country.

Thursday, March 9/22
Cold and quiet. Emperor and Empress arrested and kept in Tsarskoe Selo because they attempted to telegraph to each other in cipher. Form of government still topic of discussion.

Many people object to the revolution and to republic because of the Jews.

The soldiers in Petrograd who helped with the revolution are not to be sent away to the front.

Friday & Saturday, March 10, 11/23, 24
Fear in Petrograd that the Germans are preparing to break through and take the city. Minister of War[25] has publicly made the statement and has called on all to go to work and do their duty. Heard today that Deputies of Workmen and Soldiers objected and carried the point to remove soldiers from the neighborhood of Petrograd who are here. In some regiments the soldiers refuse to go to front. Reds are doing much harm and stir up discontent. Bonbons accuse the Jews of making the revolution.[26] Conditions much unsettled. Cold.

Sunday, March 12/25
According to today's Rech',[27] during the revolutionary excitement there were in Petrograd 82 killed and 173 wounded.

Among the names of spies in the employ of the ancien régime there is the editor of Pravda, the extreme radical paper.

Procession of workingmen (Petrograd arsenal) with Red flags on which are the words: "Hail 8-hour working day" and "Hail International," "Hail Russian Democratic Republic," "Hail coming direct, great election." Singing. No soldiers among them.

---

[25]This would be Aleksandr Ivanovich Guchkov (1862–1936): founder of the Octobrist party, president of the Third Duma, and minister of war and of the marine in the Provisional Government until the end of April 1917.

[26]By *bonbons* Golder probably means the well to do.

[27]*Speech:* newspaper of the Constitutional Democratic (Kadet) party.

Question of interference by soldiers and workmen[28] in the government
is serious. The extremists repudiate the government and would like to put
themselves at the head. They dictate or try to as to what should be the
policy of the government, what should be done with imperial family, who
should be foremen in the factories and whether the employees should have
any pay and how much.

Complaint by the Russians that the Russians are not patriotic that they
are trying to get out of fighting. They would rather have some one else do
that. It is true of the soldiers here. Neither they nor many of the workingmen understand "what liberty means."

Monday, March 13/26

At the embassy Mr. Wright[29] told me that during the revolutionary period
most of the Americans kept their head, including the women whose
husbands were out of the country, except five American young men who
lived together and asked for a guard.[30]

Miss Korolenko died and I went to the service at the home of Vernadskii. From there to Kniazev.[31]

Tuesday, March 14/27

This morning went to funeral of Miss Korolenko, had a cry—the first for
such a long time. Everyone in the archives busy with other things—no one
to get material for me and so nothing for me to do.

Had a visit from A.S. Lappo-Danilevskii. He told of how Grand Duke
Nikolai Mikhailovich[32] went the other day in an izvoshchik to a part of the
city that was not familiar to him. On the street stood one of the city militia

---

[28]The Petrograd soviet.

[29]Joshua Butler Wright (1877–1939): counsel at the American Embassy in Petrograd,
1916–1917.

[30]In the edited version, Golder refers to them as YMCA men.

[31]Georgii Alekseevich Kniazev (1887–1969), an officer of the Imperial Naval Archives, later director of the Archives of the Academy of Sciences of the USSR, was
a major source of archival and other historical materials for Golder, including a
typescript of his Petrograd diary for the years 1915–1922. Kniazev's remarkable
diary of the 900-day Nazi siege of Leningrad is the centerpiece of Ales Adamovich
and Daniil Granin's *Blokadnaia kniga* (Moscow, 1982).

[32]Nikolai Mikhailovich Romanov (1859–1919): military commander and historian.
Shot by the Bolsheviks in 1919.

and the Grand Duke turned to him and said, "Tovarishch"[33] tell me where such and such a number is. "I am not your tovarishch" came the reply.

"Priiatel',"[34] then said the Grand Duke, tell me, etc. In the end the militia man deigned to talk to him. The militia man had a gun which he did not know how to handle and asked the Duke, who on examining it found that the lock did not fit the gun.

Wednesday, March 15/28

Talked with one of the workmen (an old muzhik) of the Navy archives. He said it was a sin to overthrow the Emperor, since God had placed him in power. It may be that the [new] regime will help people on this earth, but they will surely pay for it in the world to come. In reply to the question why the soldiers became disloyal, he said that from boyhood they had seen how the government collectors and others took from them everything they could find—they had no pleasant thoughts about the government. The soldiers realized that if they shot the people they would be killing their own fathers and brothers.

Petrograd and Russia are full of "provokators." One day they start reports about Russian defeats, next day about victories—they keep the crowd excited and on the jump. These spies are hard to locate, but they work quietly to disorganize things. Great fear that the Germans will break through. Last night there was a meeting of the "Sovet Rabochikh i Soldat-skikh Deputatov"[35] and it unanimously passed a resolution calling on the people of the whole world to take a stand against all who have illegally seized power and bring about peace.

Thursday, March 16/29

Spent the evening at Rodichev's. Danger that the Germans will break through and take Petrograd is very great, think the Rodichevs. Government is in a bad way—no money, no support and interference by Workmen and Soldiers. Discipline in army is relaxed. Soldiers and Workmen have taken charge of the press and try to use it for themselves. At first they would not allow any papers to be published, later they permitted certain ones and now they control the supply of paper. Their deputies are ignorant and preju-diced. One soldier said he preferred a republic because it is more socialistic.

---

[33]"Comrade."

[34]"Friend."

[35]Soviet of Workers' and Soldiers' Deputies.

Finland full of spies. This is the first week that the men have gone to work. There is much discouragement and pessimism.

One man, librarian of Zoology collection of Academy of Sciences, said that the present government is bourgeoisie[36]—that the revolution has been won by the workmen and soldiers and it is their sacred duty to guard it. They can trust the men in power, but must watch over them and must keep the soldiers here for that purpose.

Friday, March 17/30

For several days regiments of soldiers with red flags and bands playing Marseillaise and lower officers have been going to the Duma where they are being praised and where they are cheered and where they shout, "Victory or Death," but at the same time many refuse to go to the front.

The intelligentsia is altogether against the social democrats and the extremists and theorists who demand that the war should be brought to an end, that Constantinople is not needed, that the present ministry is bourgeois, etc. The Deputies of Workmen and Soldiers take themselves too seriously and think they can dictate not only to Russia but to the world.

The organizations of workmen and soldiers from other parts of Russia refuse to recognize the organization in Petrograd.

Saturday, March 18/31

Soldiers still marching with bands and red banners—on one the words "In Union There Is Strength," on another "Workmen, Prepare Ammunition."

Yesterday capital punishment was abolished. Day before yesterday freedom and independence for Poland declared. Army officers are in trouble—now the soldiers themselves select the officers and many officers have been let out and they have nothing to do until some one selects them.

Much pessimism over demoralization in the army.

Sunday, March 19/April 1

An officer has just come from the Riga front and reports that the spirit of the army is very good over there. At first there was some disorder and confusion, but now it is better. Members of the government go about and

---

[36]Golder often confused the noun and adjectival forms of *bourgeois/bourgeoisie* and *proletarian/proletariat;* his usage of these terms has been left intact throughout the text.

straighten things out between officers and soldiers. He complains that there is not enough ammunition and heavy artillery on hand. He says also that many soldiers are deserting right and left, especially since the law was passed abolishing capital punishment. The officer also said that during the fights near Riga during December and January—both sides lost about 50,000 men. Neither side allowed the other to gather its dead, the snow fell on them, more [soldiers] fell until they formed a wall of protection. Now that thawing has set in conditions will be dreadful. In some places the Russian trenches are only about forty steps from the German and it is not safe to speak in a loud voice or a hand grenade will be thrown over. The officer and his family all believe in fate and that one is not going to be killed until his time comes and he will die in a certain way and no other. They quoted examples to prove their case.

Women had procession, clamoring for equal rights, etc.

Monday, March 20/April 2

Position of officers is very difficult, especially for those who have not been elected. They have nothing to do and are worried. They are embarrassed when on the street, for some soldiers salute and others do not.

Among the "Deputies of the Workingmen and Soldiers" they find many well known scoundrels who are being arrested. Although there has been a general demand for the names and occupations of these 2000 gentlemen, they have so far refused to give them.

Soldiers march on the street and sing national folk songs and they sound good.

Reports abroad that in southern Russia there is a Jewish pogrom, that in the country the peasants are burning and plundering.

Tuesday, March 21/April 3

People are getting tired of parades and red flags and are calling on soldiers and workingmen to get busy. There is also impatience with "Deputies of Workmen and Soldiers." Evening papers have it that U.S. has declared war on Germany. Jews given equal rights with Christians.

Wednesday, March 22/April 4

Mud. Part of the Nevsky is a lake of water.

Thursday, March 23/April 5

This is the day of the burial of the heroes of the revolution.[37] Stood on the Liteinyi and saw the procession from Petersburg side. First came the pall bearers, carrying the caskets, of which there were 37. Pall bearers and those in authority had a red sash across their shoulders and on sleeve. Pall bearers were workmen, soldiers, sailors. Caskets wrapped in red. After them came a fairly well trained crowd of singers who sang funeral service. Behind them came numerous organizations with banners and mottoes, some singing church music others revolutionary and "svoboda"[38] songs. There were also military bands and soldiers in the parade. It was impressive and the line was very long—thousands and thousands of people. From other parts of city also processions toward the burial ground, but I did not get to see them. I failed to reach the field because the crowd was so great.

Pessimism reigns. Conditions are serious. The working people, like a lot of children, are happy in parading and singing songs of liberty. Little work is done and ammunition is greatly needed. The "Deputies" stand in the way of the government. Government is weak and has no money, has no power, is not sure of any other support than the intelligentsia, which has no physical force. It can not threaten, it can not enforce—for the workmen might strike. Workmen themselves do not work and do not allow others to take their place. On western front Russian army badly beaten day before yesterday. What is going to become of all this? The officer who is here now says that the officers and soldiers are so worked up nervously from the long war that they can not hold out more than six months. If peace does not come soon they will lay down their arms.

c/o American Consulate
Petrograd, Russia
[March 23] April 5, 1917

Dear Professor Jameson:[39]

I am writing to you today because it seems likely that I will have an opportunity to send this letter in a few days by an American who is about to start for our west coast by way of Siberia.[40] It is not worth while sending

---

[37]On this day the bodies of 180 people who died in the February Revolution were buried in a common grave in Mars Field.

[38]"Liberty."

[39]Jameson papers, box 86, file 626.

[40]This was George M. Day of the YMCA.

it the usual way for the chances are that it will either not reach you at all or will be badly mutilated if it does come to hand.

How fortunate for me that I came just in time to see through a revolution—probably the last of its kind in the world! It was exciting and interesting and it came so quickly that it was difficult to realize what had happened. Until the emperor had abdicated I could not believe that the revolution was un fait accompli. I did not spend much time indoors while it was going on, and I know how one feels to be under fire. It was both funny and frightful, but on the whole more funny than frightful.

The really serious problems are on now. Before the present temporary government was organized a number of workingmen and soldiers formed themselves into the "Deputies of the Workingmen and Soldiers," and they wield a great deal of power, more than appears in the papers. Some of them are capable and patriotic, a few are scoundrels and demagogues and have been proven to be such, but the great majority are ignorant except for a few radical theories. There are 2000 of them in all, and you can picture to yourself the difficulty of accomplishing anything. They nearly all claim to be social-democrats (but I am sure more than half do not really know what Socialism is), and they have made use of these two words—"bourgeoisie" and "proletariat"—and use them on all occasions. They hinder the real government, they sit in judgment on it, and veto, in a quiet and effective way, its measures. They work on the theory that this revolution has been won by the proletariat and that the government as now constituted is bourgeoisie and therefore it behooves the workmen to be on their guard and keep an eye on the bourgeoisie administration. There is a still more radical faction who clamors that the war should be ended, etc. All these theories are being fed to workmen and soldiers of empty minds, and they have intoxicated them. The soldiers have relaxed discipline and prefer to remain in Petrograd to watch the bourgeoisie than to go to the front; the workmen prefer to talk than to make munition, which is badly needed at the front. Since the first days of March we have had parades and waving of red flags. The sad part of the whole thing is that the leaders, learned in the theories of the French Revolution, insist that everything should be done according to the French Revolution.

At the front a great danger threatens. The generals, officers and soldiers at the front plead with the workmen to put an end to their parades and go to work, but without much success. There is disorganization and demoralization and pessimism. Many people expect that the Germans will take Petrograd before long; some are making ready to leave. Unless the people take abrace, I do not see what is to hinder the Germans from breaking through. I am not going to run, but I am sending you whatever historical material I can lay my hands on—books, papers, etc. If anything happens to me, use them as you think best.

My work in the archives is interesting. I have found some very interesting documents on Russo-American relations during the years 1854–1855. I am now working in the year 1858 and I am collecting data on the Civil War period, and I am watching especially the opinions of the Russian minister in Washington—the evolution of his ideas. By the time this reaches you the papers will be telling you what is happening here. It is going to be a hard but valuable experience for me and will give me some new points of view. I shall probably go to the front for a month or more. Enclosed you will please find an item of historical interest, a sugar ticket, which entitles the bearer to three pounds of sugar a month. We now have a bread ticket, but not always bread. My kindest regards to Mrs. Jameson and the children and to my other friends in the office. I remember my last summer in Maine with great pleasure.

> Greetings & good wishes,
> Cordially,

★ ★ ★

Friday, Saturday, Sunday, Monday
Conditions about the same. Mud, cold, pessimism. Not much bread. Our servant girl had to stand in line since 5 A.M. and when her turn came the bread was all gone. More processions. A very big one Sunday—whole regiments, bands, banners, etc. Little work in the factories.

Tuesday, March 28/April 10
[George] Day started for America via Siberia. At the station the railroad cars were not only jammed inside but roofs were covered with soldiers.

Wednesday, March 29/April 11
Novoe vremia[41] published two letters written about six months ago by Guchkov to Gen. Alekseev[42] stating that a year or so ago when the Russian

---

[41]*New time:* conservative Petrograd newspaper, supportive of the monarchy.

[42]Mikhail Vasil'evich Alekseev (1857–1918): commander of Russian armies on the western front in 1915 and Nicholas II's chief of staff when the tsar became supreme commander late in that year. In May 1917 he was replaced as commander of the Provisional Government's armies by General Brusilov.

army needed rifles the English government offered several hundred thousand of them but the Russian War Department (Gen. Beliaev[43]) refused them.

Thursday, March 30/April 12

An officer, Vasilii Alekseevich,[44] came in and said that he had met a fellow officer from Riga who said that two divisions of infantry, about 24,000, have declined to continue to fight. Regiments of cavalry have been dismounted and put in their places. Trains from the front are full of deserters who are going home to be on hand "when the land is divided." Vasilii Alekseevich has said also that the order has been given that in case the German attack on Riga becomes too severe—the army should give up the place and retire to Pernau.

Friday, March 31/April 13

Mr. Bogoliubov[45] has met a friend of his, a colonel of the regiment to which he belonged. The colonel said that just before the Revolution he went to the Caucasus to see the Grand Duke Nikolai Nikolaevich who is at the head of the regiment. While there news came of the Revolution and N.N. called together the people and told them about it and asked them to stand with him by the new government as he was going to do. This move resulted that no harm was done, no body hurt. He asked the crowd whether they had any requests to make and they said that the governor of the district should be removed, which was done. Soon after he was called to Petrograd with the understanding that he should still be the head of the army. When he came as far as Mogilev he was told that his services were no longer wanted. His friends urged him to take power. Before he committed himself he got in touch with the four principal generals and asked them whether they would stand by him. They refused to. He gave his resignation.

Mr. Bogoliubov had also heard from good sources (?) that before the Emperor left for the front he left a number of signed blanks with the Empress to be used as occasion demanded and one of them was used in dissolving Duma.

---

[43]Mikhail Alekseevich Beliaev (1863–1918): named minister of war under Nicholas II on January 3, 1917, arrested in March by the Provisional Government, and shot in 1918 by the Bolsheviks.

[44]A friend of the family with whom Golder was living.

[45]Identity unknown.

Wednesday, April 5/18

We have had no papers since April 1 [14]. On Sunday, April 2, the mail carriers refused to deliver. April 3: Newsboys refused to sell. April 4: Printers refused to work. There seems to be better understanding among the factions. The Deputies of the Workmen and Soldiers are less aggressive. More men have gone to work although there seems to be little material with which to work. They claim there is no coal and raw material.

Germany is doing its best to bring about discord.

Mr. Lenin, an extreme radical and pacifist, has been given special permission and special facilities to come through Germany from Switzerland in order that he and his party might preach pacifism and bring about a demoralization. For the same reason Germany has proposed a separate peace.

Thursday, April 6/19

War Department is asking the citizens to return the 40,000 rifles and 30,000 revolvers which were taken from the arsenal during the first days of the revolution. Some of the soldiers sold theirs to private parties. Prof. Polievktov[46] called and he said he talked with the socialists and Deputies of the Workingmen and Soldiers and they say that much of the stuff they write and say is for public consumption and must not be taken seriously.

Until the coming of Lenin the left and right wings of the socialists were unable to unite but as soon as he came the two wings drew close together against the common danger.

Friday, April 7/20

One of the members of the committee of printers who was back of the movement not to work on Sunday, etc., has been arrested as a "provokator."

Sunday, April 9/22

Vasilii Alekseevich returned to the army. Officers not enthusiastic to be in the army under present conditions. Many would like to go to America, England, France. I heard today what seems to be true, that the two divisions which deserted at Riga have gone back—others also going back, but still a

---

[46]Mikhail Aleksandrovich Polievktov (1872–1942): historian; from 1917 professor of Russian history at Petrograd University.

great many out. Minister of War has issued a bulletin asking them to return. Today a mob wanted to attack the American Embassy and a special force of militia was called out. A stupid reason is for no reason at all. . . .

Pessimism still reigns. The Germans are expected.

Tuesday, April 11/24

Went to Embassy—it is still guarded by soldiers. It seems that an Italian is back of the movement. Hard to make out. Crowd is ready to fall in line and is easily excited.

Reports from the interior of plundering, killing, pillaging by gangs of all kinds, among them soldiers. From Simbirsk there is a telegramme to Minister of War that soldiers have taken charge of all the freight and passenger trains. Supply trains have to be side-tracked. Service disorganized and coming to a stand still.

Wednesday, April 12/25

Had dinner at Priselkov's. He is a member of the commission to put in order the papers of the imperial family. He said that the papers of Alexander III were kept in good order—he had a place for every kind of paper. Nicholas II's papers were all thrown together. Many valuable documents such as reports of Gen. Kuropatkin[47] from the front of the Russo-Japanese war and such like were never read. But they found one package in good order and on looking in it they found a note book in which Nicholas kept a daily record of all the people that were killed and executed during the Revolution of 1905. He seemed to take special delight in that. In other ways evidence is gathering to show that at bottom he was an evil man.

Priselkov tells also that at Anichkov Palace, where Alexander III lived, examinations were also made. In the apartment of Alexander III it was found that in his living room all the painting and artistic things were removed to the basement and in their place the Emperor himself pasted on the wall several hundred pictures of women which he cut out from "L'Illustration."

One of the rooms of the Empress, wife of Alexander III, was filled with postcards—all about the walls. Neither had any artistic taste, their rooms were furnished in miscellaneous ways, and their collection of curios

---

[47]Aleksei Nikolaevich Kuropatkin (1848–1925): supreme commander of the Russian army in the Far East during the Russo-Japanese War.

was most stupid and common. Nicholas II cut up Gobelins[48] if they interfered with his fire place.

In the library of Alexander III there is one book on history, literature, etc., but a few books fit for children to read—such as holy pilgrimages, lives of saints, etc.

Thursday, April 13/26

Prof. Pilenko[49] told me today that in looking over his diary he was astonished to see how for months before the Revolution it was the common talk in the best families, in the homes of generals, et al., that the Empress should be killed and gotten out of the way. It was generally expected and talked about that a revolution was coming but it was assumed that it would take place after the war. He said one of the aides-de-camp of a Grand Duke came to him, Pilenko, and said that he meditated an act of terrorism—to get someone out of the way. This aide-de-camp was a young army officer.

Dined at home of V.I. Vernadskii.[50] Met another professor who had been kicked out of University of Moscow on account of his liberal ideas, but now he and Vernadskii were both going back, while the gang that had been put in their places is dismissed. They reported that during the Revolution of 1905 the workmen insisted that geography, physics, chemistry should be taught in a democratic way.

Friday, April 14/27

During the revolution a naval officer by the name of Almquist was arrested at Kronstadt. The Admiral asked the Minister of Justice that the officer should be tried quickly and a commission was sent down a few days ago who found him not guilty and freed him. But the soldiers would not have it and they rearrested the officer and also the commission. They were released, but the officer is locked up and the government is not able to do anything.

It is rumored about that during the revolution most of the officers of the navy who were killed were engineers and others specially valuable for their technical knowledge. It is assumed that they have been picked out by

---

[48]Gobelin tapestries.

[49]Aleksandr Aleksandrovich Pilenko was professor of international law at the Aleksandrovskii Lycée.

[50]Vladimir Ivanovich Vernadskii (1863–1945): prominent scientist and thinker and father of the historian George Vernadsky.

the Germans. The men killed were inoffensive and the soldiers say they do not know why they were killed.

In Finland the Finns feel strongly against the Russians and there is a strong German agitation.

The Volynskii regiment at the front was very much thinned out and a committee was sent to Petrograd to invite the reservists of that regiment to come to the front. A number of the local agitators tried to persuade them not to go, but in the end enough of them went.

Lenin and his crowd still agitating for separate peace. It is generally believed that they are in German pay.

Situation is very discouraging. The country seems to run itself—there is no law, no sovereignty, the soldiers do as they please. The question is what will happen if the Germans begin to push on.

The Deputies of the Workmen and Soldiers have forbidden the soldiers of Petrograd to leave the city on the ground of a Counter-Revolution. Some of the soldiers are going to the front just the same.

In some parts of Russia the peasants have taken the land without leave.

Saturday, April 15/28

The socialists et al., are demanding the resignation of Miliukov as a Guizot[51] and demand that in each army in each headquarter they should have a commissar as representative. Today there was a procession of children.

Sunday, April 16/29

Today at our embassy there was a counter-demonstration to offset the one of last Sunday. The aims of this one were to show that Russia is friendly to U.S., that Russia means to persevere in the war. Crowd of thousands, largely of those injured in the war—cripples, blind—with banners, "We have done our duty," "Freedom and Victory," "War until Victory."

Report of a great deal of lawlessness. Men dressed in soldiers uniforms go everywhere. In one of the cabarets they came and cleaned it out—they rob and plunder and kill.

In Moscow elections for one of the Dumas, the socialists organized themselves into small working groups so as to be represented in that way and so secured a majority. But from among the elected they selected 3 or 4 Constitutional Democrats for the real government in order, as they say, to criticize them.

---

[51]François Guizot (1787–1874): conservative French historian and political philosopher associated with the idea of restoring the Bourbon monarchy.

Monday, April 17/30

Vasilii Alekseevich who left for the Riga front a week ago returned today. The soldiers drove him out and would not have him as an officer. He says soldiers refuse to fight and the army is all going to pieces.

Lunched with Prof. Pilenko today. Present were Lincoln Steffens,[52] Charles Crane,[53] Cresson,[54] and the Professor. He told most interesting things, first as to the death of Rasputin.

The idea first originated with Purishkevich.[55] He made a speech in the Duma (?) and got his friends together to implore the Emperor to remove Rasputin from the Court. Effort was made and Emperor flatly refused. Next Purishkevich and his friend decided to get rid of him—murder him. He looked around for help and heard of Prince Yusupov,[56] who for the sake of the dynasty was also determined to get Rasputin out of the way. Rasputin was acquainted with all the court and ladies—except the wife of Yusupov who was very beautiful. Rasputin was anxious to know her and made certain advances. This was made use of. Purishkevich and Yusupov got together. This scheme was worked out: To let it be understood that on a certain night there would be a ball at the home of Yusupov. Rasputin was invited to come about 2 A.M., when Mrs. Yusupov would come down to the ground floor to meet him. The ball was to be on the second floor.

It was planned to poison him and a doctor was called in who brought a large dose of cyanide and potassium. It was originally planned to put it in champagne but it was feared that the glasses would get mixed up. The next thing was to take small cakes—red and white—the red were poisoned. In the party were Purishkevich, Yusupov, the doctor, and Grand Duke Dmitrii Pavlovich.[57]

---

[52]Lincoln Steffens (1866–1936): American political Progressive and muckraking journalist who came to Russia in 1917 in order, as he later wrote, "to find out how a revolution is made." *The Autobiography of Lincoln Steffens* (New York, 1931), p. 747.

[53]Charles R. Crane (1858–1939): businessman, frequent visitor to Russia, and patron of Russian studies. Crane came to Russia independently, arriving in Petrograd in May 1917, although the following month he became an official member of the Root Mission, discussed below.

[54]William Penn Cresson (1873–1932): secretary of the American Embassy in Petrograd from May 1915 to August 1917.

[55]Vladimir Mitrofanovich Purishkevich (1870–1920): prominent right-wing Russian politician, one of the founders of the Union of Russian People and a Duma deputy.

[56]Feliks Yusupov (1887–1967): Russian aristocrat, reputedly the richest man in the country.

[57]Grand Duke Dmitrii Pavlovich (1891–1942): cousin of Nicholas II.

About 2 A.M. the party was on the second floor, playing the gramophone to give the appearance of a ball. In their haste there was provided only one disk and it was played over and over again. When Rasputin came he was ushered down stairs and Purishkevich and Yusupov and he drank champagne, while those upstairs waited impatiently. After about half an hour Yusupov came upstairs pale as a sheet and said, He has had all the champagne and all the cakes both the red and the white and it does not affect him in the least. The doctor fell in a faint.

After a hurried consultation it was decided to shoot him. The Grand Duke said he would do it, but Yusupov insisted, so he went down and put two bullets into Rasputin, who fell over. Yusupov came upstairs for another consultation as to what should be done with the body. They all came down and to their great fright they saw Rasputin making for the door. Purishkevich pulled his pistol and fired into Rasputin and finally killed him. This last shooting was out in the street and was hurried. The servants of Yusupov all came, but he made them swear to be silent—they did. But a policeman also came on the scene and he would not promise and through him the story came out.

After this the body was thrown into the river—clumsily done. The body hit the bridge and left a blood spot. One of his rubbers came off and gave the clue.

According to our speaker, Rasputin was not gifted mentally but had wonderful intuitive power and divined the thoughts of those with whom he came in contact, especially the women. There was a certain mysticism which appealed to them. He was different with different people. He was ignorant, coarse and dirty. He boasted of his conquests. His theory or theology was this, taken from the service: Love one another and thus confess together. It meant to the women that loving Rasputin was ipso facto a forgiveness of sin.

Pilenko said that Emperor was drugged by a Thibetan doctor.

Pilenko and wife were invited to one of the dinners given by Madame Golovine,[58] Rasputin was one of the number. Besides these two men there were a number of women. The hostess on this occasion turned to Rasputin

---

[58]Madame Golovin was the elder sister of Grand Duke Paul's wife, the Princess Paley, formerly the Countess Hohenfelsen. Madame Golovin and her two daughters were said to be "disciples" of Rasputin. (See *The Fall of the Romanoffs: How the Ex-Empress & Rasputine Caused the Russian Revolution* [London, 1918], p. 41.) According to one source, it was Madame Golovin who introduced Rasputin to Prince Yusupov, who wished to discuss "some aspects of occultism and magic which interested him." (Louis de Robien, *The Diary of a Diplomat in Russia, 1917–1918* [London, 1969], p. 28.)

and said that Prof. Pilenko was a bright man and should be made Minister of Foreign Affairs. Rasputin said yes, a wise man—but it is not so easy to make him Minister. I shall have to talk it over with the Emperor.

After dinner Rasputin went up to Pilenko and asked that Pilenko should invite him (Rasputin) to dinner. Pilenko did not commit himself. Two months later the phone rang and Pilenko's wife was called by one of the ladies of Rasputin's household. Pilenko went to the phone and the person at the other end had nothing to say. Some weeks later Pilenko's wife was again called on the phone and this time she answered and Rasputin himself came on and asked Mrs. Pilenko when he would be invited to dinner. She did not commit herself. After that Pilenko and wife were again invited to dinner at Madame Golovine's where Rasputin was also. During the meal Rasputin put his hand familiarly on Mrs. Pilenko. Pilenko jumped up and said if he did it again he would knock him down and then they left the house. This ended Pilenko's relations with Rasputin.

Tuesday, April 18/May 1

Holiday. All kinds of processions—men, women and children with all kinds of flags and with plenty of poor singing.

The Deputies of Workmen and Soldiers refuse to commit themselves on the loan question until the allies of Europe agree to their terms—no annexation and no indemnity from Germany.[59]

Spent evening at Rodichev's. He says that the demonstrations today were organized against government in favor of peace. He feels discouraged about the situation. He says the leaders of the Deputies and the socialists are stupid men who have filled their minds with German pamphlets and newspapers, with literature on socialism, and they talk like the documents. Rodichev thinks the reason the Germans do not attack is that time is working for them—Germans think that the Russian Army is going to pieces anyway and if it were attacked this might arouse a spirit of resistance.

In talking about the revolution Rodichev said that the first Saturday of the disturbances, i.e., February 25/March 10, the military commander of Petrograd gave orders not to shoot, but that night he received word from

---

[59]The "loan question" involved the so-called Liberty Loan, an internal loan issued by the Provisional Government on March 27/April 9, 1917, that essentially was a tax on the Russian people to ease the financial burden of the war on the government. The Executive Committee of the Petrograd soviet was divided over the loan issue but voted on April 22/May 5 to approve it, contingent on the Provisional Government committing itself, in a public note to the Allies, to "non-imperialist" war aims. Miliukov's handling of this note brought on the "April Crisis."

the Emperor to shoot at the crowd and to put down the disturbances at all cost. Sunday morning orders were given to shoot. The regiment that did the shooting was the Volynskii and it was so sick of its job that it refused to do it more than once, and the next day it revolted.

M[iliukov], Rodichev said, is a man of unusual gifts and he is envied even by the men of his own party and they would like to overthrow him.

Rodichev thinks that the outcome of all this revolution may be that in four or five years from now some one man will seize the reins of government and re-establish the monarchy.

Thursday, April 20/May 3

The Deputies of Workingmen and Soldiers have been demanding that the Russian government come out in a statement as to the aims of the war—such as Miliukov and Guchkov and the more conservative members think they can not in honor make and that their obligations to the allies do not permit. The Deputies have for several days demanded their resignation. Tonight they or some one else formed a big demonstration, mostly of women, servant girls, high school students, etc., who marched up and down the Nevsky, the Liteinyi, etc., crying, "Down with Miliukov, Down with war, Down with the Temporary Government." On the other hand, thousands of others cried in favor of the Temporary Government. On street corners there are assemblies discussing the questions of the day—pro and con. Most that I have heard are in favor of continuing the war, if supporting the Temporary Government and all that—but it is more in theory than in fact. They prefer to remain away from the front. As a matter of fact, they are tired of the war.

At the front conditions are bad. The poor soldiers believe everything. Since they have dismissed their officers, the Germans at the front have been fraternizing with them, they have come into the Russian trenches, have photographed Russian positions. Vasilii Alekseevich said that a German officer had come seven miles into the Russian lines and had been photographing positions before he was arrested. Today's paper says that General Brusilov[60] will not allow the Germans to come into his lines.

At the American embassy I was told some time ago that the telegram

---

[60]Aleksei Alekseevich Brusilov (1853–1926): general in the Imperial Army; in May he replaced General Alekseev as commander of the Provisional Government's armies.

sent by the American Federation of Labor to Chkheidze[61] he would not publish in his paper and that it got into the other papers through the embassy.

On May 1 the Winter Palace was decorated (and it is still there) with a banner many yards long—"Long Live the International." Other public buildings were similarly decorated.

Friday, April 21/May 4

In the demonstration last night there were cries of "Kill Miliukov." From all reports there was good order.

This morning the Walkover Shoe Store opened and when I passed (10–11 A.M.) there were several hundred people in line. At the city ticket office thousands of people waiting their turn.

Saturday, April 22/May 5

Yesterday's demonstrations resulted in loss of 5 lives and 9 wounded. The government stood its ground and when it explained its position to the Council of the Workingmen and Soldiers they too decided to back the government. This morning the Council of the Workingmen posted bulletins calling on the soldiers not to appear on the street with arms without permission of the Council—which body is solely authorized to call on them and whom the soldiers should obey.

Another placard today from the same body forbids gatherings, etc., for 2 days.

Sunday, April 23/May 6

The Sovet Rabochikh and Soldatskikh Deputies is made up of various parties, each having representatives. Sometimes these parties accept the ruling of the Sovet sometimes they do not. Each acts independently and is not bound. It would seem that although the Sovet as a whole was opposed to the demonstrations on Friday, several of the parties were in favor and hence the excitement. Not only is there no union and harmony between the

---

[61]Nikolai Semenovich Chkheidze (1864–1926): Georgian Menshevik, deputy to the Third and Fourth dumas, president of the Petrograd soviet until November 1917. The incident in question had to do with Chkheidze's refusal to publish in *Izvestiia*, the newspaper of the Petrograd soviet, a telegram, dated May 7, of sympathy and support sent by Samuel Gompers in the name of the American Federation of Labor.

Government and the Sovet, but in the Sovet itself there is disorganization. Each party in turn is divided into a right and left wing.

The military commander of the city has announced that Petrograd is in immediate danger of attack from the Germans and called on the soldiers to be ready to defend it.

During the excitement last week when Miliukov was attacked the whole ministry offered to resign and hand over the power to the Sovet, but this body would not take the responsibility and prefers to find fault.

Went to a meeting in memory of M.A. Karaulov.[62] Miliukov was one of the speakers and had a great ovation lasting several minutes.

Monday, April 24/May 7

The Sovet on Saturday took a stand in favor of the Liberty Loan. It is true that several regiments came out in favor of the Government last week.

Spent the evening with Syromiatnikov.[63] He pointed out three tactless things [Miliukov] had done. (1) At the very beginning he made a speech in which he predicted the regency of the Grand Duke Michael, (2) He talked too much about the Dardanelles and Constantinople, (3) He published his notes without consulting the Council of the Soldiers and Workingmen.

Wednesday, April 26/May 9

The question of a coalition ministry is seriously discussed. The government invites it and pressure is brought to bear on the Sovet to agree to it, but it refuses. It dodges the responsibility. In today's papers the Government gives a review of its history and asked for cooperation. It also insists that the control of the army in Petrograd is under the military commander appointed by it and not by the Ispolnitel'nyi Komitet[64] of the Sovet, as that body claims.

Thursday, April 27/May 10

Food question serious. From today only ¾ lb. of bread instead of 1 lb. The Sovet has decided to call an international conference of all the socialists of

---

[62]M.A. Karaulov (1878–1917): ataman of the Terek Cossacks, deputy to the Second and Fourth dumas, and, during February–March 1917, member of the Temporary Committee to Keep Order.

[63]Boris Ivanovich Syromiatnikov (1874–?): historian of Russian law on the juridical faculty at Moscow University.

[64]Executive Committee.

the world, of all factions of the socialists, to meet in some neutral spot. Also to send a delegation to Stockholm.

At Shlusselberg [Schlüsselburg] a committee has been organized that acclaims itself independent of the Government or any body else. Members of government there have been arrested. Shlusselberg has many powder factories and is an important point.

The division of power is disorganizing the country and no one knows the end. Party in Finland demands complete independence. Germans on front are gathering proclamations to disorganize Russian Army. The Moscow Sovet is against a Coalition Ministry.

At Moscow, Prof. Kizevetter[65] was lecturing to a large audience when soldiers sent by the Moscow Sovet broke up the meeting and arrested the speaker.

Today is the 11th anniversary of the opening of the Duma—celebrations by the Kadets. Went to a meeting in Mikhailovskii Theatre. One of the speakers, member of Duma who had been investigating the troubles in Kronstadt, said that among the 39 or 37 officers killed the first night, the soldiers remembered killing 5 or 6, but none of the other officers and what is more they say there was no reason for killing them. They say that on that night a gang of men dressed in sailors' clothing went from ship to ship killing officers—those killed were specialists either in artillery or navigation. On one ship they were not allowed to come aboard and there the officers were saved. This is a rumor which is now confirmed.

Guchkov in his speech painted conditions in dark colors. Peace at the front—war in the rear. In different parts of the country there is much lawlessness. Paper today tells of one town where 5 soldiers, pretending to be delegates of the Sovet, took charge of the town, arrested the authorities.

Saturday & Sunday, April 29, 30/May 12, 13

From the speeches in the Duma it would seem that certain members of the Sovet regard their organization as a kind of Parliament to whom the Government is responsible.

A part of the Finland Regiment stationed at Petrograd quit.

On April 27/May 10, a number of armed men, claiming to be anarchists, took possession of the palace of Herzog Lichtenberg and nothing is being done about it. The Executive Committee of the Sovet has announced that it does not approve such doings—there the matter will probably end. The palace will remain in the hands of the gang and will be plundered, etc.

---

[65] Aleksandr Aleksandrovich Kizevetter (1866–1933): historian and Kadet.

Chkheidze, head of the Executive Committee, has received a letter threatening him with death.

A number of workmen have met for the purpose of organizing a "Red Guard" to defend the workmen and the Revolution. Is the same crowd that did the shooting on April 21. Sovet is opposed. The anarchists have been temporarily driven out from the palace mentioned above but some of the property is missing.

In today's Rech' there is a report from one of the station agents telling that on the night of April 26/May 9 a number of soldiers came to the station and demanded the train which had ammunition. They killed one or two men, destroyed much property and took the train.

General Kornilov,[66] the military commander of Petrograd, has resigned because the Sovet has taken command upon itself and on April 20/May 13 soldiers wouldn't listen to him.

In today's paper Guchkov has asked soldiers to stop fraternizing at the front with the enemy.

Sovet has taken up the question of a coalition ministry. On the vote: 23 pro, 22 con, 8 refused to vote. Question to be taken up again.

Last night I saw Vernadskii, today Iochel'son.[67] They and others are much worked up and sick over the political and military situation in Russia.

                                                        Monday, May 1/14
Guchkov resigned. Mrs. Rodichev told me that Rodichev said that Guchkov is a man who never finished any job that he undertook. He goes into it in haste and with enthusiasm and quickly cools off. Rodichev thinks Guchkov did wrong in saying that the country is on the verge of destruction. Heard this evening that Protopopov and his gang planned a strike on February 14/27 with a view of forcing peace on the country. It was intended to create disturbances in order to show that Russia must bring the war to an end. To accomplish this, flour was purposely kept from the people in order by starvation to force them to acts of lawlessness, etc.

Two men told me tonight what I knew before, that Emperor was

---

[66]Lavr Georgievich Kornilov (1870–1918): commander of Petrograd's military from March 1917; chosen as supreme commander of the Russian army in July, he led an unsuccessful assault on the Provisional Government in August 1917.

[67]Vladimir Il'ich Iokhel'son (1855–1943): ethnographer and historian. The Vernadskii (Vernadsky) referred to is probably George.

double faced. Witte,[68] Sazonov,[69] et al., he told that he was pleased with them and as soon as their backs were turned he dismissed them. He made promises he never kept and never intended to keep. Could not stand to be contradicted or opposed—anyone who did that was sure to lose his good favor.

There is much pessimism and grief over the recent situation, especially thinking people fear keenly the dishonor of it all.

Crane, Steffens and I had an interview with Kerensky, Minister of War, this morning. He told us he will endeavor to persuade the allies to revise war aims. Asks support of Wilson and America. Asks America to have confidence in Russia and to believe that Russia will not sign separate peace. Peace must be based on humanity. New slogan: Freedom & Peace. Alsace-Lorraine, Belgium, Armenia will be regarded as conquered territory and each people will decide for itself.

The military commander of Moscow and all the generals-in-chief at the front have resigned because they are not obeyed and their orders are counter-manded.

★ ★ ★

c/o American Embassy
Petrograd, Russia
May 4/17, 1917

Dear Professor Jameson:[70]

. . . The bearer of this letter or the man who will mail it is Mr. Michael Karpovich, Secretary to the new Russian ambassador to the United States.[71] Mr. Karpovich is a scholar and a gentleman and intends to return to scholarship as soon as he is through with this mission. I wish you would meet him and introduce him to people of your circle. Perhaps you could

---

[68]Sergei Iul'evich Witte (1849–1915): minister of finance (1892–1903) and chairman of the Council of Ministers (1903–1906).

[69]Sergei Dmitrievich Sazonov (1861–1927): minister of foreign affairs, 1910–1916.

[70]Jameson papers, box 86, file 626.

[71]Mikhail Mikhailovich (Michael) Karpovich (1888–1959): historian and one of the founders of Russian studies in the United States. He accompanied the new Russian ambassador, Boris Bakhmetev, to the United States, where he remained after the Bolsheviks came to power. In 1927 he became a lecturer, later professor of history, at Harvard, where his seminar on Russian history was the training ground for the first generation of American professors of Russian history.

put him at the Cosmos.[72] He is worthy of any favors and attentions that you can give him. He can tell you much about Russia and the situation which is not for publication.

I am starting in a few hours for Vladivostok to meet and help the new commission which is coming here. Mr. Francis wished me to do it and I feel that it is little enough and I am glad to give part of my time.[73] I shall be gone from here about a month and then I will return to resume my investigations. I have completed nearly everything up to 1870 and the Russian government has consented to let me go on and on. For fear that something may happen here in my absence I am sending my material to you in care of Mr. Karpovich. Please take care of it for me—there is good stuff there and I shall work it up as soon as I return. My other material I left in the embassy with instructions to forward it to you in case there is danger. I suppose I will return in the fall, but I should like to remain here longer to see where this Revolution and war may lead to. I have learned a great deal of history since coming. . . .

Sincerely yours,

★ ★ ★

Thursday, May 4/17

Most of the military commanders did not quit—false report.

7:50 P.M. started for Vladivostok. On train of the Russian Mission. English classes twice a day for beginners and advanced students.

---

[72]The Cosmos Club in Washington, D.C.

[73]When Golder heard that the United States had declared war on Germany, he went to the American Embassy and offered his services. Ambassador David Francis asked Golder to go to Vladivostok and meet the American Advisory Commission of Railway Experts, better known as Stevens Railway Mission, after its chief, American engineer John F. Stevens, and escort it back to Petrograd. The purpose of the mission, which was sent by President Woodrow Wilson, was to advise the Russian government on improving the operation of the trans-Siberian railway for the war effort. Golder took a special train carrying the Russian diplomatic mission to the United States; during the journey English lessons were conducted for members of the mission.

When Golder arrived in Vladivostok, the American consul informed him that he was to be attached to a different presidential commission, the Root Mission, led by American statesman Elihu Root. Golder, however, ended up accompanying the Stevens Mission back to Petrograd, where they arrived on June 12, one day ahead of the Root Mission. (See the letter from Golder to Ernest Holland, dated May 4/17, 1917, from the office of the president: Ernest O. Holland records, 1890–1950, Washington State University Libraries, Pullman, Wash.)

Passed through Vologda—a new republic. All is quiet along the way. In one place soldiers held back our train so as to let their train go through. At another station there was a train of soldiers ahead of us and they would not give us the right of way until it was explained to them who we were.

About 10 or 12 soldiers guard our train. It was learned yesterday that the Express which left Petrograd two days ahead of us was held up by the soldiers who put out the passengers, stripped the metal and the plush from the cars and then ran off with the train leaving the passengers behind. Women are now acting as brakemen.

★ ★ ★

Sunday, May 7/20

At Omsk as in other places a lot of soldiers tried to get on. They had two weeks leave to go to Irkutsk and they had already used up one-half of that time and were still 3 or 4 days from their destination and they had no money.

Monday, May 8/21

10 A.M. Train of soldiers immediately ahead of us and will not let us pass. Our soldiers are sent to hold diplomatic conference. At every important station to which we come there are many soldiers who wish to get on the cars and move on. It takes a lot of reasoning and talking but in the end they are reasonable and say that they had no intention to use force. There is also some one—probably of the Sovet—and other cool heads to smooth things.

Wednesday, May 10/23

8 A.M. Waited more than ½ hour for a freight ahead of us. Roamed over fields and found beautiful wild tulips, yellow and blue violets and a yellow flower shaped like a rose.

Division inspectors of railway visit me in my coupé. They tell of hard winter and complain of old government. Nearly everybody socialist—but few understand what socialism is. Last speaker is always approved.

Saturday, May 13/26

Reached Vladivostok about 10 P.M. Remained on board train overnight. Took up quarters at Hotel Oriental. Vladivostok is quite gay. Plenty of everything and not very dear.

Sunday, May 14/27

A number of Russians arrived by ship from America and were met by the
local sovet with a band and speeches.

Tuesday, May 16/29

Talked today with a member of the Vladivostok Sovet. He told me that
there was a big problem in connection with the Russian immigrants. Many
went to America for reasons other than political and when amnesty was
declared and Russian Consuls and others in America were instructed to help
financially the political immigrants to return to Russia, thousands presented
themselves and demanded such help. It was extremely difficult to know
their character. The Russian political organizations in America knew them
not. When they finally got over as far as Vladivostok they asked for trains
and money to reach their destination and threatened to make trouble if they
did not get it. Many had associated with the I[ndustrial] W[orkers of the]
W[orld], and started propaganda here where lawlessness existed already.
The Vladivostok Sovet begged them to behave and finally threatened.

Thursday, May 18/31

Steamer from Tsuruga [Japan]. Immigrants singing. Flags. "Bread &
Freedom." Social Revolution—Speeches.

Disorganization of the Army. Prof. Mitinskii,[74] who came with us
from Petrograd, explained that discipline in army fell long before the
Revolution. It began in 1915, or as soon as the army realized, after its
various defeats, the incompetency of the government and the untrustwor-
thiness of the Tsar and his Tsarina. How they left the army helpless and
defenseless and when victory could be had the Tsar would not permit it.
So poorly did the government provide the army that at times there was not
more than ½-day's fuel on hand for transportation, there was no material,
even little with which to repair the rolling stock. The army at times had no
food supplies on hand and the transportation department trembled lest
something should happen to the trains and the army were left without food
altogether. When the soldiers realized all this their discipline fell—and what
happened in the Revolution was the last straw. The Professor said the
situation is much better now than it was before. Before the Revolution there

---

[74]Aleksandr Nikolaevich Mitinskii, formerly a member of the engineering council
of the Imperial Ministry of Transport, was a railway official in the Provisional
Government.

were just as many deserters but it was kept quiet. There is more work being done now and better reorganization.

* * *

Vladivostok, May 31, 1917

My dear friend [Henrietta Eliot]:

I have made a hurried trip.from Petrograd here and expect to return to the capital today or tomorrow. I came here at the request of our government to meet and help the distinguished commissions which are coming here. It was so exciting and interesting in Petrograd that I hated to leave the city, but it was a good thing I did for I did not realize how the excitement and more or less privations were affecting me. Things are in a terrible mess and I am sure the Russian people would somehow work out their salvation if the war were only out of the way. As it is, God only knows where the country is drifting to. Revolutions are not what they seem, but I suppose they are necessary. . . .

I have had three or four days here and have used them in part to get about and in part to get enough to eat. I may safely say that for two months I have not had all I needed. I have also bought a number of things to take back, among others 40 pairs of children's shoes for an orphan asylum— there are no children's shoes in Petrograd. I have bought coffee for another party, etc. This gives you an idea of the situation.

The most spiritual thing I have done is to read Tolstoy's Resurrection. It is a work of art and a great book besides.

Vladivostok is beautifully situated and just now very prosperous. Every one has work and every one has much money and the war seems to make little impression. More than other sea ports, Vladivostok seems to have specimens of every race in existence—it is a motley crowd, but it gets along quite well together.

Lincoln Steffens has been in Petrograd and he will soon have interesting papers in the magazines. We came together from Petrograd and he has come to the conclusion that I belong to the class of professors and educated people which has always blocked the progress of the world. That class contains about 99% of the educated. Strange but true, everything about the Russian Revolution seems to him so holy, even as holy as the Mexican Revolution, which, to Steffens, is the most wonderful movement of the century.

It is not interesting for you to read letters which are only half written, but I wish you to know that I think of you often and send you my best wishes and look forward to greeting you in the near future.

Sincerely,

★ ★ ★

Left Vladivostok Saturday May 20/June 2.

Reached Petrograd Monday afternoon, June 12/25.
    Petrograd as bad as ever. Socialists et al., plan to do away with opera, theatre, etc., because they are bourgeois.

June 5/18
A gang of "anarchists" seized the Russkaia volia.[75] After keeping it a day they were arrested.

★ ★ ★

Petrograd, Russia
June 5/18, 1917
Dear K:[76]
    Last week I returned from Vladivostok and found your letter of March 10 full of good and interesting news. In view of what is transpiring here and the world over what happened a week ago seems so far away. So we are in the midst of the war and God knows when the end will come. I am trying my best to make myself useful in the good cause. As you know, just now I am helping the American railway commission and I may continue with this body a while longer or I may do something else. It has been six weeks since I have done any research work. It hardly seems fair to bother with such things when thousands of good people are dying at the front.
    The situation here is most pitiful and heart breaking, for so many years the people have been kept in bondage and fear and as soon as that was removed they have gone to pieces. They (a great many at least) have no

---

[75] *Russian will*. Conservative newspaper.
[76] Not further identified but probably Harvard historian Robert J. Kerner, Golder's former fellow doctoral student.

conception of liberty. German agents with pockets full of money have been working among the soldiers to disorganize the army and they have good success. Under the cloak of socialism they preach all damnable doctrines—incite lawlessness, plunder, strikes—until no one knows what tomorrow may bring forth. No one knows whether we have an army or a mob. Here in Petrograd we have no army but a lot of lazy, good for nothing soldiers who obey orders when it pleases them to do so. The food question is serious and some of our Americans are suffering. When I returned from Vladivostok I brought two small sacks of flour and about forty pounds of sugar and people nearly fell on my neck. Prospects for next winter are not bright. We all keep hoping that the army will come back to its senses—perhaps by the time this reaches you there will be some evidence of its plans.

The Root Commission is here and housed in the Winter Palace and sleep in the beds of the royal family. Last evening I was invited to dine with them but failed to make connections. Mr. John F. Stevens of the Railway Commission is a sturdy American oak and I like him. He used to be an Indian Scout, helped build the Great Northern, knows the Palouse and the Columbia River country and is a well read man with a kindly heart. . . .

Cordially,

★ ★ ★

June 7/20

The "anarchists" propose as a means to end war to attack the capitalists and make war on them. This is seriously talked of among them, discussed in their papers and argued on the street corners. This war against capitalists is to be not only in Russia, but the world over.

Kerensky asks whether this is a Revolution of Free Citizens or an Insurrection of Slaves.

Many street meetings in which soldiers take part. Many soldiers do not wish to go to the front and when some one asks them why, they say let the other fellow go.

June 10/23

Waiters and bell boys, etc., went on strike for a short time this morning.

The anarchists planned a big demonstration—a so-called "peaceful demonstration" to overthrow the government and put themselves in power.

Lenin and his crowd are more bold than before. They are against the government and Council of Deputies. Demonstration did not come off.

★ ★ ★

Petrograd, June 12/25, 1917

My very good friend [Henrietta Eliot]:

It was so good and so cheerful to receive your letter of April 29. Petrograd is now divided into 90% pessimists and 10% who think they can see day light immediately ahead. There is only one thing the matter with the country—the soldiers will not fight. In the first place it is just to say that they are tired of the war, and in the second place the German-paid agents and extremists encourage them along these lines. The soldiers can not think for themselves and the demagogues preach the doctrine that suits best for the soldiers. We have a lot of good for nothing soldiers, who are not ashamed to live off the country but will do nothing in return. We are drifting and God knows where Russia will end up. It is pitiful and heart breaking to see how the intelligent classes suffer—but it is almost a crime to be intelligent, to be clean, etc., because you are condemned as "bourgeois." It is all so fascinating and all so dreadful. I hate to leave it and yet I feel that there is work to do and I should be something more than a spectator.

I am still with the Railway Commission, but I hope to be released this week. I can not satisfy myself that I am making the best use of my time. About all I do is drive around all day, eat expensive meals and help a bit—the help I give is the kind that anyone with much less education could do as well.

I am not going to the Russian front for there is nothing to do over there—no men fighting—and there are enough loafers without me. If I succeed in being released I shall hurry and bring my archive work to some kind of an ending and then, if I can, I may go back by way of England and France and possibly remain there, or I may come back to the States and see what I can do. You would think that in a war like this there would be some work that you could do well, but when you begin to look around, it is difficult to find.

. . . For the first time in weeks we have a rain tonight—the sky is overclouded and there is a freshness in the air and I can not help feeling and hearing the call of the woods and mountains. How sweet it would be to hear the murmur of the trees and to live in God's world. When tired, I just close my eyes and wander once more with my little pony over the desert and in the mountains and it rests me. Never supposed one could become so attached to a horse.

A Russian lady friend had just come from the village where her mother lives and has brought me a number of pieces of peasant work. You would like them. I will show you them when I come.

In the evening papers there is an article telling that the wives of the soldiers are going to the front to be with their husbands. People in Petrograd and Russia have become a bit cynical. At a meeting yesterday one of the Cossack leaders said that there seems to be a difference of opinion as to how the war should be ended—one method proposed is fighting, the other kissing, the enemy. The soldiers at the front who fraternize and sell food to the Germans are called the "Kissing Soldiers." . . .

With sincere good wishes,
Cordially yours,

★ ★ ★

Sunday, June 18/July 1

Special services in Kazan Cathedral in honor of American guests. Part of the service in English, followed by introduction to the public of American representatives—a very unusual procedure.

During the day manifestations, largely by the Bolsheviki. There was danger of a clash but nothing serious happened.

Monday, June 19/July 2

News that Russian army took the offensive near Minsk and broke through the German line in four places. A great sigh of relief and rejoicing such as has not been felt here for months. Parades and such rejoicing. Manifestations in front of the embassies of the Allies, U.S. included, at which I was present. Great day.

Wednesday, June 21/July 4

Procession—invalids, Cossacks, men decorated with cross of St. George—all bearing flags expressing confidence in government and calling on all to be loyal and patriotic and help end the war. It was very touching the way they appealed and begged.

Thursday, June 22/July 5

8 A.M. Started with Stevens Mission in special train for Moscow—cool, rainy, country green and fresh. Reached Moscow 10 P.M. Remained on train.

Friday, June 23/July 6

Circled about the city and later went into it.

Saturday

Spent the day in the city, chiefly in the Kremlin. Saw the old palace. Left Moscow 7:30.

Sunday & Monday, June 25, 26/July 8, 9

Passed through parts of southern Russia—country rolling prairies with trees here and there. Everywhere fine crops. Women at work. Crossed the Dnieper at Ekaterinoslav. Committee of railroad men came to greet the Stevens commission. Disturbances are quieting down.

Tuesday, June 27/July 10

Kiev. Automobile took us about the city. Saw St. Vladimir's Church— beautiful structure (Byzantine style). Fine view of the Dnieper.

From Kiev went to Korosten, and then on the newly built track line to Mogilev.

Wednesday, June 28/July 11

6:20 A.M. reached Mogilev.

12 P.M. [noon] went to greet General Brusilov. Left Mogilev 4 P.M. At Vitebsk Miliukov was permitted to come aboard. Great crowd to see him

off at the station. Miliukov made a speech from the window—asked the crowd to cheer for the Russian army, Kerensky and America.[77]

11 P.M. Station full of people sleeping everywhere. Remained to 1:30. Meantime a crowd gathered when it heard who had been put off. Crowd very indignant. Two places found for Miliukov and me in the International car but I could not sleep there—too stuffy.

Thursday, June 29/July 12

Reached Petrograd 2 o'clock. Went to Hotel Europe where Reading[78] informed me that I had been fired because of the Miliukov affair.[79]

Monday, July 3/16

12 P.M. [noon] Evening papers announced the resignation of all the Kadet ministers over the Ukraine question.[80] Talked with Barskov[81] from 9:30–

---

[77]In the edited version, Golder writes that his party arrived to find a large crowd at the station and Miliukov delivering a speech. A friend of Miliukov approached Golder and asked if Miliukov could be taken aboard his train. Golder asked Stevens, who gave his consent. Miliukov boarded the train, a crowd gathered outside his car, and there were calls for a speech. "We had just told him of the success of the Russian offensive," writes Golder, "and he stepped to the window and announced it to the crowd and asked for three cheers for Kerensky, the Russian army and the Allies. Miliukov came into my coupé after the train started and we got to talking. He was tired and hungry and I ordered that some food be given him. While we were engaged in conversation, the Russian officer in charge of the train called me out and informed me that in view of the fact that Miliukov's speech at the window might be classed as political and in view of the fact that he was responsible for the train, he was going to ask Miliukov to leave. I pleaded with him but in vain. I went to Stevens and he would not interfere. I then tried one more card. I told the Russian if he put off Miliukov, I would leave too. He replied that he would be sorry to see me do so, but he had to do his duty. About eleven o'clock at night when the train came to a small dark and dirty station, Miliukov was asked to leave and I got off too. The train went on and left us behind." (See also Golder to Jameson, October 15, 1917, Jameson papers, box 86, file 626.)

[78]Franklin Reading, a member of the Stevens Mission.

[79]The diary of a member of the Stevens Mission recounts this episode and offers a few interesting observations about Golder and the circumstances of his discharge from the mission. (Diary of William Lafayette Darling, pp. 15, 24, Hoover Institution Archives.)

[80]On July 2/15, the Provisional Government and members of the Ukrainian Rada signed a joint declaration recognizing the Rada's autonomy in deciding Ukrainian

11:00. He said that the common people especially in the villages are still distrustful of the intelligentsia and nobility, that serfdom was only legally abolished—socially and morally it still existed in many places. The old landed nobility is run down until it has nothing but its arrogance left. There is a great hatred and distrust towards them. The Kadet party is distrusted by the people because many of its members are of this landed nobility, capitalists, professors, et al. The Deputies of the Soldiers and Workmen really saved Russia from a great deal of bloodshed—it is trusted.

Eleven P.M. Went to Hotel de France to see Lord.[82] Streets full of people and armed automobiles full of armed soldiers and sailors running up and down the streets. There had been a big demonstration against the Provisional Government and that all the power should be in the hands of the Deputies of Soldiers and Workingmen.[83] About 11:30 a parade of soldiers—thousands of them—some had banners reading "Down with the Provisional Government." I followed them on the side walk and talked with one of the soldiers who was against the capitalists in the Ministry. Near the Mikhailovskii I heard ahead of me the discharge of a machine gun. The soldiers and the public ran for their life—the soldiers towards the Gostiinyi Dvor. Most of the public dropped flat on the ground, scared to death. Then the soldiers began to shoot, and such shooting! I started for Hotel d'Europe but was side-tracked into an open yard close by where others crowded in. Shooting lasted about 5 minutes. It was all dark. Went to Hotel d'Europe where the lights were turned out. After a bit started back on the Nevsky where the scared soldiers stood in groups. Some broke the front store windows and looted. Got back 1 A.M. but could not sleep because of the renewed demonstration on the streets.

Tuesday, July 4/17

Last night an attempt was made to arrest Kerensky and the other ministers. Failed. Today a demonstration against the government and shooting. No

---

internal affairs. Three Kadet ministers resigned in protest over this action; the remaining Kadet minister, N. Nekrasov, who supported the declaration, resigned from the Kadet party.

[81]This is no doubt Iakov Lazarevich Barskov (1863–1937), historian and assistant director of the Archives of the Ministry of Foreign Affairs.

[82]Robert H. Lord (1885–1954) was Golder's former fellow doctoral student at Harvard, where he later became professor of European history.

[83]The events Golder recounts here—the failed insurrection of July 3–5 by the radicals against the Provisional Government—have become known as the July Days.

one pays attention to the government and it has apparently lost all power. In last few days several people killed and wounded. Soldiers driving madly in automobiles and armored cars.

Today reaction in the favor of the government. Last night the bolsheviki soldiers fired and killed a number of Cossacks and their horses, which I saw lying on the Liteinyi. Government is organizing its forces and it seems as if it means business. People are indignant and are ready to support the government. Petrograd side is cut off from the city, the draws in the bridges being open. Every one excited and on the jump.

Thursday, July 6/19

City quieting down. Troops brought from the front and the disturbers are cowed and quiet. Many of the ring leaders arrested.

Friday, July 7/20

Excitement still in the air—shooting from roofs against newly arrived soldiers. About midnight Lord and I were coming from A.S. Lappo-Danilevskii's when firing commenced near the Admiralty and lasted for about ½ hour. We sought shelter in a neighboring street. Ministry is reformed and it is almost a pure socialist ministry. Scarcity of food—long waiting lines everywhere.

Saturday & Sunday, July 8, 9/21, 22

Firing almost over. More than 60,000 loyal troops from the front. Some of the disloyal regiments are disarmed and sent to the front. Bad news from the front. Russian army badly defeated. Soldiers would not obey orders and retreated and left a big opening for Germans. Food question serious.

Monday, July 10/23

Sad news from the Southwest front. Russian soldiers ran like sheep. It is said they outnumbered the Germans 5 or 6 to 1. Heavy artillery and supplies lost—thousands taken prisoner. Soldiers would not listen to officers or obey commands. Provisional Government has declared itself a dictator.

Spent the evening at Rodichev's.

Tuesday & Wednesday, July 11, 12/24, 25

Some sad news from the front—soldiers running without fighting. At the Dvinsk front soldiers took some positions and then returned to their own trenches without being forced to do so by the enemy. In some places the soldiers plundered as they retreated. Women's battalion distinguished itself, killed and took prisoners.

Thursday & Friday, July 13, 14/26, 27

Disastrous retreat continues. It is reported on good authority that the infantry killed the artillery horses so that the artillery could not be re-moved—they also killed the cavalry horses. Gloom in Petrograd and all over Russia.

Thursday, went to see Zarudnyi. He said that the present situation is due to the numerous elements that have helped to make up Russian civilization—Byzantine, Prussian, Petrine, etc. The Church was crushed by the Monarchy until a parish became nothing more than a police precinct. Church has lost its influence. German influence is greatly felt because the Jews, the intelligentsia, and the nobility got much of their training there.

He says soldiers refuse to fight because they think, "Why fight for Poland which has been declared free? Why fight for the Ukraine, which decided to become independent? At home everyone does as he pleases and land is given out." Soldiers eager to go home to get some of the land.

Evening papers announce that the government has called a meeting at Moscow for July 18 [31]. Old organized institutions to be there. Zarudnyi says that the darkest part of Russia is the part around Petrograd and Moscow where tsarism is most felt.

Friday & Saturday, July 14, 15/27, 28

Sad news of the retreat continues to come in. Army still retreating—every one is gloomy, sad and discouraged. Very tragic days indeed.

Saturday. Funeral of the Cossacks at St. Isaac's. Went to church about 9 o'clock and remained inside until 1:00. Most impressive—the metropoli-tan and the leading priests took part. The choirs of St. Isaac's, Kazan, Alexander Nevsky and of the Palace took part. It is the first event in the Revolution to which the Church was invited to participate. Kerensky, Miliukov, Rodzdianko and other prominent men were there as well as representatives of foreign governments.

After the service I went out and saw that the whole of St. Isaac's Square was filled with soldiers with their bands. The procession went by way of the Morskaia and the Nevsky. After each casket was led the horse except where the horse [had been] killed. Relatives also followed. It was sad and many people cried and I felt a tear or two. Each company of soldiers had its band playing funeral dirges. Procession lasted about an hour. Women soldiers also marched.

These are sad and tragic days for Russia and the allies.

Sunday & Monday, July 16, 17/29, 30

Sunday I saw Miliukov who explained the political situation. Heard him again Monday night. Fight between socialists and Kadets.

Tuesday–Friday, July 18/31–July 21/August 3

Discussion as to the make up of the new ministry. Kornilov commander-in-chief. Saw Prof. Ross.[84]

Increase of car fare from 10 to 15 kopeks has cut down number of passengers by 12%. According to *Birzhevye vedomosti*,[85] of July 20/August 2, 37% of streetcar passengers are soldiers who do not pay.

Friday, July 21/August 3

Ministry still not formed. Chernov is on trial.[86] Sad news from the front—soldiers retreating. Cost of living going up and winter looks bad. Many people refuse to take the ruble, which is falling in value, but prefer payment in commodities which they can exchange for other commodities; this, I am told, is true of the farmers. Returning to primitive conditions.

Saturday, July 22/August 4

Exciting times in trying to organize the new ministry. Everybody resigned, including Kerensky. The Council and the socialists insist on their own programme. In the meantime the situation is growing worse.

---

[84]Edward Alsworth Ross (1866–1951): professor of sociology at the University of Wisconsin.

[85]*Bourse gazette*.

[86]Viktor Mikhailovich Chernov (1873–1952): leader of the Socialist Revolutionary (SR) party; in 1917, vice president of the Petrograd soviet and minister of agriculture in the Provisional Government from May to August. By Chernov's "trial," Golder may mean attacks by both the right and the left on his agricultural policies; those attacks were the main reason for the resignation of Prince Lvov as prime minister, the subsequent ministerial crisis, and the split in the SR party.

Sunday & Monday, July 23, 24/August 5, 6

Bad news from the front and the interior. Every one is sad and discouraged. The Germans are having their own way and no one to stop them. It is reported that they will soon start an offensive on the Riga front. Situation is indeed tragic. No government as yet (4 P.M. Monday).

Tuesday, July 25/August 7

Ministry formed. Kerensky was given full power by all parties. He agreed that no member of the Ministry should be responsible to any organization— which means that socialists are not accountable for their actions to the Council. On the other hand he insisted that all who came into Ministry should accept the Declaration of July 8.[87]

The Kadets came in with a determination to be of service and at a sacrifice. Kerensky apparently took advantage of the offer and gave them the least important posts. He took care of his socialists, among others Chernov. The situation at the front is bad—from the regions where the Russians retreated the Germans are gathering the harvest which has already been harvested by the Russians. Food supplies are running short.

Sunday, July 30/August 12

Servant girl came from political meeting and said she could not make out what it is all about except that a certain Minimi (minimum) is to have 6 rubles and a certain Maximu (maximum) 30 rubles.

A man asked Morozov to explain to him what it meant: (1) "Tsisioli-zatsie" [sic] (socialize) the land and "natsiolizatsia" [sic] (nationalize) the soil.

Moscow elections. Each political party given a number. Kadets had ticket No 1, which socialists said belonged to people who travel in first class.

Socialist Revolutionaries had No 3 which they explained by saying that those who voted for them would get land because "3" resembles "z," for "zemlia," or "land."

Workmen and soldiers traveled 1st, 2nd, and 3rd class but not in the International because they said that those who traveled in that car were Internationalists.

---

[87]The "Declaration of Principles," published on July 8/21, pledged among other things that the Provisional Government would arrange an Allied conference for the discussion of a peace proposal and prepare for elections to a Constituent Assembly on September 7.

Tuesday, August 1/14

Left Petrograd in a special car with Messrs. Gibbs and Greiner.[88] The car was attached to the express train.

August 2/15

Train late and becoming later. Our diner caught on fire. Day pleasant. Women and children everywhere at work and at all kinds of work; few men. Grain harvested with sickles.

Learned today that Emperor is in train ahead of us, being taken to Tobolsk. His imperial party passes itself off as the "American Commission," but on the quiet the soldiers tell the people that it is the Emperor they have with them.

August 3/16

Reached Viatka at 9 A.M., which means 7 hours late. Country green and fertile, women and children at work, harvesting grain with sickle.

August 4/17

Train delayed because of lack of water and engine obliged to go to a neighboring station for water.

Country beautiful, weather delightful. About 9 P.M. we caught up with Emperor's train, which had left Tsarskoe Selo 14 hours ahead of us. There were two trains—in one the imperial family and those near to them, also guards, and in the other the servants and more guards.

We continued behind the imperial trains, which move very slowly, until midnight. When they were sided on "Sidetrack No. 18" the two trains stood side by side on two tracks as we passed them. When I looked back I saw the headlights of the two engines, I saw soldiers but not one of the imperial family. I looked at the watch and it was just midnight and we were about five or six versts from Tiumen.[89]

August 5/18

Beautiful country and delightful weather, fertile fields and numerous herds. Never saw Siberia look better.

---

[88]George Gibbs and John E. Greiner were members of the Stevens Railway Mission.

[89]Robert K. Massie, in *Nicholas and Alexandra* (New York, 1967), p. 473, writes, "Near midnight on August 17, the [tsar's] train crawled slowly into Tyumen on the Tura River."

Sunday, August 6/19

9 A.M. Came to Novo-Nikolaevsk.

Monday, August 7/20

When I got up the provodnik informed me that he had just heard that the Emperor had escaped, that the country was alarmed, that our car would be searched. When we reached Krasnoiarsk at 9 A.M. there was a strong guard—no one allowed to go in or out of the car—station guarded. Our car was searched for the Emperor. It is assumed that he is hiding with us.

So far as I can ascertain the situation is this: Yesterday a telegram from the Council of Soldiers and Workmen of Ekaterinburg reached the Council of Krasnoiarsk to the effect that the Emperor had left his quarters and was going on to Siberia. No other details except that "American Mission" was mentioned. This is the first news that any one has had and all kinds of rumors afloat. Some say that he has escaped, others say that Lenin is helping him. Soldiers who searched our car did it in name of the Council and not of the government. Council of Krasnoiarsk determined to get Emperor— the government is no government. No one had any definite plans as to what they would do when they had him. A guard was placed at the bridge just outside of the city, with instructions to blow up the bridge in case the train did not stop at Krasnoiarsk.

One of the soldiers said that Kerensky had no right to send the Emperor away without consulting the people since the government is now demo- cratic. Kerensky not the idol of the Krasnoiarskers. Every one tired of the war and ready to quit, tired of the soldiers, of the Councils, of everything.

One of the Krasnoiarsk "commissioners" went with us as far as Irkutsk and again examined our papers, although he was not always sober.

August 8/21

Irkutsk. About 2:30. Car again searched for Emperor.

August 9–11/22–24

After we passed the country near Baikal and came over the divide we ran into very beautiful and fertile valleys, rivers of which fall into the Amur. Thousands of heads of cattle, flocks of sheep, herds of horses. I do not know of any place in the world to compare with them.

JOURNEY III
1921–1923

CHAPTER THREE

VICTORS
AND VICTIMS
(September 1921–April 1922)

In the spring of 1921, several months after the end of the Russian Civil War, with the Soviet economy in ruins, Lenin and the Bolshevik leadership—under pressure from rebellious workers, peasants, and the sailors at the Kronstadt naval base— introduced the New Economic Policy (NEP), a mixed-market system that was a retreat from their program of economic centralization. The keystone of the new policy was abandoning the practice of grain requisitioning in favor of a tax. The Bolshevik reformers intended to proceed slowly and modestly, but the reforms quickly took on a life of their own, leading to a far greater degree of capitalism than had been contemplated. The party leaders struggled to keep up with the changes and to reconcile them with Marxist-Leninist ideology.

The success of these economic measures was at once threatened by the onset of a major famine, whose catastrophic proportions became clear by the summer of 1921. The famine grew out of the destruction and dislocation caused by the world war, the revolution, and the Civil War, as well as by the Bolshevik agricultural policies. In the summer of 1920 a severe drought was followed by a crop failure; with no reserves of grain to fall back on, the peasants were defenseless. By spring 1921 hunger existed in many places, and then famine broke out, centered in and beyond the Volga valley and in the southern Ukraine.

The Soviet government realized that it would need outside assistance to deal with this crisis. On July 13, Maxim Gorky (no doubt at Lenin's behest) issued an appeal "to all honest citizens" to send bread and medicine to Soviet Russia. Herbert Hoover, head of the American Relief Administration (ARA), responded with a telegram setting down the ARA's conditions for supplying aid to Russia. These conditions were quickly accepted by the Soviet government, and negotiations in Riga, Latvia, led to the signing on August 20 of the so-called Riga Agreement, the essential terms of which gave the ARA the right to control its relief operations inside Russia in exchange for a vow not to mix in Soviet politics. (See Harold H. Fisher, The Famine in Soviet Russia, 1919–1923: The Operations of the American Relief Administration *[New York, 1927].)*

The initial plan was for the ARA to feed two to three million children, but the mission rapidly expanded to include adults and medical relief as well. The major leap forward came on December 22, 1921, when President Warren Harding signed into law a congressional appropriation of $20 million for the purchase of corn and seed grain from U.S. farmers for Russian relief. To this total other government and private U.S. contributions were added (as well as a Soviet government expenditure of nearly $12 million from its gold reserve); in the end the two-year ARA program amounted to more than $60 million.

As Golder indicates in his writings from this period, relations between the ARA and the Soviet authorities were often stormy. The Bolsheviks felt humiliated about having to be rescued by American "imperialists" and uneasy about having a large independent foreign organization, with a huge local staff in its employ, operating throughout much of their country. They wondered what motive lay behind Hoover's philanthropy.

The ARA mission was headed by a career army officer, Colonel William N. Haskell, most of whose U.S. staff had served in the American Expeditionary Force. Many men had attended some of the finest U.S. colleges and universities and had had experience with the ARA in Europe. They were eager to tackle the Russian job with trademark ARA drive and efficiency and had little tolerance for Soviet inefficiency and suspicion; they especially resented the network of Red Army commissars and agents of the secret police set up to monitor their activities. There were many ARA-Soviet confrontations over issues big and small, but each was somehow resolved through diplomacy. In the end the Soviet government officially acknowledged the ARA's contribution in checking the famine and saving millions of lives.

Golder arrived in Moscow at the end of August and proceeded to the Volga region as part of an ARA investigative party. There, in the heart of the famine zone, he composed his first letter to Stanford.

Samara, Russia
September 20, 1921

Dear Professor Adams:[1]

John Gregg, William Shafroth[2] and I are down here in a special car investigating hunger conditions, which are very bad. We are held up here because we can not get in communication with Moscow. Tomorrow John Gregg is going to Moscow to see what the trouble is and I am sending this along. I am not writing a long letter because I am enclosing a copy of my diary, such as it is, without comments. While Gregg is gone Shafroth and I will proceed to Ufa and on our return here will pick up Gregg and then go to Rostov and down towards the Black Sea to look into the matter of a port. It is our plan to return to Moscow about the middle of October, after which I will give all my time to the Hoover Collection work.

I am picking up a bit of literature as I go along; there is not much worth having. It is all the same Bolo [Bolshevik] stuff and the local papers are in the hands of the government and copy what the Moscow papers publish. Intellectual life is at a low ebb and is going lower. The question that absorbs all energy and thought is how to get daily bread. It is most pitiful. But the hunger is not the main cause for the decline in the arts and sciences. I wish I could talk to you.

I am not sending anything to Hoover but if you think that he may be interested in any part of the diary you may send it to him if you like. Of course none of it is for the newspapers.

With all good wishes,

★ ★ ★

Moscow, October 3, 1921

My dear Professor Adams:

Last Wednesday morning I hurried to the railway station at Samara to help find a food train which was sent to the ARA and found not only the train but also Dr. Kellogg.[3] I did not even know he was in the country. He

---

[1]Ephraim D. Adams (1865–1930): professor of European history at Stanford University and first director of the Hoover War History Collection, the name of which was changed in 1921 to the Hoover War Library; today it is known as the Hoover Institution on War, Revolution and Peace.

[2]Famine relief workers with the ARA.

[3]Vernon Kellogg (1867–1937) in 1915–1916 was director of Herbert Hoover's American Commission for the Relief of Belgium and, from 1917 to 1919, Hoover's assistant at the U.S. Food Administration. He served with the ARA in Europe in a variety of roles and then in Russia as a special investigator in 1921, when he also became secretary of the National Research Council.

leaves again today for America and I am hurrying this letter so that he may take it along. I am also enclosing two or three additional pages of my journal. The last ten days I have been very busy with ARA activities, working from early morning until late at night, so that I have had no time to follow up my investigations.

I found on my return here with Dr. Kellogg yesterday two letters from you, one dated August 5 and the other September 7. When I reach Paris or London I will take up with you more fully the question of the courses. For the moment I should like to say that I have ready two lecture courses only, one on Russia and the other on Europe since 1825. May I suggest that course 55 as outlined in your letter be temporarily postponed until I have had a little more time to prepare. In place of it I could give a course on the Balkan states during the Nineteenth Century. When I reach Stanford we will have to go over the whole field carefully and come to some clear policy. With the Hoover Collection before us the world will expect our history people to be specialists and it is up to us to satisfy this expectation. I was talking with Coolidge[4] last night and he admits that Stanford is going to be the place for study of history since 1914.

I wish I could have a talk with you in regard to the Russian situation. The famine is bad beyond all imagination, it is the most heart breaking situation that I have ever seen. Millions of people are doomed to die and they are looking it calmly in the face. Next year millions more will die, for little planting is done, the live stock is killed off, and the population is growing weaker. To see Russia makes one wish that he were dead. One asks in vain where are the healthy men, the beautiful women, the cultural life. It is all gone and in place of it we have starving, ragged, undersized men and women who are thinking of only one thing, where the next piece of bread is coming from. This is literally true.

In regard to the work of collecting, I am beginning tomorrow and will get the work underway. It may be necessary for me to go south once more to carry on some investigations with Dr. Lincoln Hutchinson,[5] but if I do, the work will not suffer. I shall make the necessary arrangements. I am keeping the Library of Congress in mind and in view of the fact that Coolidge is here I may have to cooperate with him for he can be of aid to

---

[4]Archibald Cary Coolidge (1866–1928): professor of Russian history at Harvard University, where he had been director of the university library since 1910. He served as head of the ARA's Liaison Division in Moscow from September 1921 to January 1922.

[5]Lincoln Hutchinson (1866–1940): professor of economics at the University of California at Berkeley. Before and after the war he worked as a U.S. commercial

us. You will have to trust me in the future as you have in the past. . . .

In all these wanderings and through all the discomforts there is one blessed thought: that I have another land to go to. You have no idea how comforting it is. If I were condemned to live here always I should prefer death, and yet there are millions of men and women, as good and better than I am, who are condemned to this very thing. You see I am not very cheerful today and therefore I will close. My kindest regards to Mrs. Adams.

★ ★ ★

Moscow, October 6, 1921

Dear Lutz:[6]

The courier leaves tonight and I take this occasion to write to you, for a number of weeks will pass before I have another opportunity. It has been decided that Dr. Lincoln Hutchinson and I should strike out on an investigation trip. He has already left for Samara and I leave tomorrow to join him there and thence we proceed together in a special car. It will be difficult but interesting and when I return I will send you copies of my papers. I have decided to do this now while the weather is good for traveling. However, I have made arrangements about the work of collecting and our prospects are bright.

I called on the deputy Minister of Education, Prof. Pokrovsky,[7] an historian who knows something about me, and he received me very warmly. All the government publications since 1917 are under his control (and everything of any importance since that date has been published by the government) and he at once gave orders that two copies of every book and pamphlet should be set aside for us. One of these copies can go to the Library of Congress and the other we will keep. In addition he is going to do another thing for us. He is about as eager to please me as I am to please

---

attaché, and he served in 1918 with the ARA in Prague, where he assisted Thomas Masaryk in writing the Czecho-Slovak constitution. In the ARA Russian mission he served as a special investigator.

[6]Ralph H. Lutz (1886–1968): associate professor of European history at Stanford and a curator for the Hoover Library, where he served as chairman from 1925 to 1943.

[7]Mikhail Nikolaevich Pokrovsky (1868–1932): Marxist historian, Old Bolshevik, deputy at the People's Commissariat of Enlightenment (which Golder calls the Ministry of Education), and chairman of the presidium of the Socialist, later Communist, Academy.

him. Perhaps I told you that in 1917 when I was here I organized the Russian historians for the purpose of writing a History of Russia for English readers. Macmillan had agreed to publish it and the work was started and fell flat because of the November revolution and the death of a number of the most important scholars from starvation, etc. Professor Pokrovsky was not on the 1917 list and he is now anxious to have the work revived, and if it is, certain persons ought to be on the list.

In addition to the work of collecting that Professor Pokrovsky is having done for us, I have engaged another Russian scholar whom I know and in whom I have a great deal of confidence to make me out a list of the important things to buy and I will have him do the buying. He can more than earn his salary by the lower prices at which he will buy, for foreigners are imposed upon here as elsewhere.

I have been watching the book market and it makes my intellectual mouth water. Rare editions, beautiful bindings, heirlooms of great value are thrown on the market. I have decided to cast prudence aside and spend a part of the 2000 dollars on purchases here. Tell Wilbur, Adams, Clark[8] and all the others they might as well begin abusing me now and get done with it for they can not stop me. In a century from now when I am dead of a broken heart caused by their reproaches the scholars of the year 2000 will thank me.

Our prospects in the line of collecting are very bright. Indeed Russia is very interesting and I could spend a year here with great profit not only to myself but to Stanford. Each day I make new contacts and revive old ones and each opens up new avenues. Unfortunately I can not write you many things for so many people between my writing desk and yours have a great desire to read what I say. One has to pay for being prominent. Of course I feel greatly flattered.

I should like to call your attention to a financial matter and I wish you would bring it before Adams. My pay of 250 dollars per month is what the ARA men are getting except those in the lower positions. In addition to their monthly salary they each receive six dollars a day, primarily as subsistence, but actually as additional salary. Very few of the men spend that amount and you will note that even I with all my hotel bills and restaurant living do not spend that much. Each ARA man is able to add, by this system, from 100 to 150 dollars to his monthly pay. Is there any reason why I should not be put on the same basis? At present I am giving all my time to ARA work and at other times I am always helping out. If

---

[8]Ray Lyman Wilbur (1875–1949) was president of Stanford University from 1916 to 1943; George Clark (1862–1940) was Stanford University librarian from 1907 to 1927.

Adams can arrange it that I be put on that basis from the beginning of my engagement to the end, good and well; if not, it does not matter. It is not of any importance.

I expect to be back in Moscow by the first of November and plan to spend the two months, November and December, in Moscow and Petrograd.

Professor Coolidge and I see each other often and we talk over all the gossip.

With kindest regards, As ever,

★ ★ ★

Diary entry: October 8, 1921. Moscow.

I made plans last Monday to leave for Samara on Friday but after several days of negotiations I learned that there is no train before Saturday. . . .

Last night I was greatly surprised to receive a call from the famous revolutionist XXX [identity unknown], whom I had met many months before in another part of the world. He has recently been in Petrograd and said that the execution of the 61 men and women there has cast a gloom over the intelligentsia in that city, for most of the executed were scholars and artists.[9] The Moscow authorities were greatly displeased with Zinoviev[10] for this deed and planned to remove him in the near future and put Samarin, a Siberian, in his place. He added that in 1919, when the four Grand Dukes were executed it was also done without the approval of the central authorities in Moscow: the Cheka[11] in Petrograd hurried the execution knowing that an order was on the way or being contemplated against the deed.

XXX blamed Miliukov in part for the recent arrest of the Moscow committee . . . because of the article in his paper that in case the Bolos were

---

[9]The event referred to is the execution by firing squad on August 24, 1921, of Petrograd intellectual and political figures on charges of counterrevolutionary conspiracy.

[10]Grigorii Evseevich Zinoviev (1883–1936): head of the Bolshevik party organization in Petrograd, Politburo member, and chairman of the Communist International.

[11]That is, the All-Russian Extraordinary Commission for the Struggle Against Counterrevolution and Sabotage, Cheka or Che-Ka, from the initials of *Chrezvychainaia kommissiia*, Russian for Extraordinary Commission or Extraordinary Tribunal.

overthrown this committee could take charge of the government.[12] This article was in large part responsible for the arrest of the committee. In this connection XXX said that it is true now as it was in the time of the tsar that the émigrés, red or white, in their eagerness to talk, often made trouble for their friends in Russia.

★ ★ ★

On the Banks of the Volga, Trying to
to Get Across for the Last Two Days.
This day being the 23rd of October.

Dear Professor Adams:

Last night I went to Saratov and there found your letter of September 16, enclosing copies of the Miliukov correspondence.[13] It is about this matter I wish to write you now. The copy of my letter to Miliukov, which I enclose, will explain in large part the situation as I understand it. He never committed himself on the subject and I felt certain that Time would act in our favor. In incurring the expense for the collection I have always had in

---

[12]The reference is to the All-Russian Committee for Aid to the Hungry, established by a decree of July 21, 1921, and charged with the tasks of collecting and distributing foreign and domestic relief contributions. The committee consisted of some sixty members and included Bolshevik and Soviet officials as well as nonparty public figures, notably Maxim Gorky. The committee was chaired by Lev Borisovich Kamenev (1883–1936), Politburo member and chairman of the Moscow soviet.

Forming this committee was probably a Bolshevik attempt to make a favorable impression on world opinion at a time when the catastrophic dimensions of the famine and the need for foreign assistance to combat it had become clear. Miliukov, who was then living in Paris, was not the only voice, in or out of Russia, to wonder whether the committee might not become an alternative to Bolshevik power. This is precisely what the Bolshevik leadership feared and what motivated Lenin to dissolve it and to authorize the arrest of its leading "bourgeois" members on August 27, the very day that the first ARA party arrived in Moscow.

[13]The discussion here concerns Miliukov's personal archive of papers and books, which, in October 1920 with Miliukov's encouragement, Golder had managed to locate in a secluded barn near Terioki, Finland, and arranged to be shipped to Stanford. As Golder makes clear in this letter, Miliukov had not promised Golder to donate his collection to the Hoover Library, and when Miliukov eventually asked a price for the archive that the Hoover Library considered too high, it was bought by the University of California at Berkeley in 1928. This episode is documented in Wojciech Zalewski, *Collectors and Collections of Slavica at Stanford University* (Stanford, 1985), pp. 69–74.

mind that in case he should be unwilling to give us the collection he should reimburse us the cost. This explains why I sent you a careful account of the expense while I was in Finland. The remaining cost you have kept track of. We have saved the collection from destruction and that is a great deal and the rest depends on him.

I do not know the condition of the collection but I am convinced that if we had not come to the rescue neither he nor anyone else would ever have had the use of it. I have tried to make this point clear. For the time being it would be better to let the matter drop. If it is necessary to purchase it, and it can be obtained for a reasonable sum, I will pay for it myself so as not to have any arguments on the subject now. Should the University approve of my deal, it will reimburse me at some future time; should it disapprove it will not bankrupt me. I quite realize that this is not "business" but this is one way of acquiring a valuable collection and, thank God, I can afford to pay for a few of my fancies.

In this connection let me add that I will probably pursue the same policy in acquiring other books in Russia. I shall probably use up all the balance of the authorized money I have and some more. I hold myself personally responsible for these purchases and pay for them with my own money. We now have a very rare opportunity in Russia and I am going to take advantage of it to the full and some day scholars everywhere will come to Stanford to study and thank us. For the present I do not want to have any arguments with Wilbur and, as I said above, in going ahead on my own authority I do so at my own risk. I am not obligating the University in any way. I am not much of a business man. I let my enthusiasms run away with me, but I have never permitted them to take me beyond my means. It will be a happy day for me when I can once more return to the quiet life of a scholar and have no finances to handle other than my own poor salary.

I am not writing you a letter because I have tried to keep you informed, as much as I dared, of my movements through copies of my journal, except for a few days, which I will send when I have a good opportunity. This trip of investigation with Dr. Hutchinson is taking more time than I can well afford to give it, but I feel that I owe it to Hoover and the ARA, since one of the reasons for sending me was to investigate food conditions here. The work of the Hoover Collection I left in good hands and is not suffering and will improve when I return. My hopes for a vacation next summer are fading for I see piles of work ahead.

With all good wishes, As ever yours,

★ ★ ★

On the way to Moscow, between Tambov and Riazan
November 7, 1921

My dear Professor Adams:

Our little car is the tail end of a passenger train and the road bed is so bad that our little home rocks like a ship in a storm. I can stand even that for it brings to an end a long and not too comfortable voyage. Enclosed you will find a copy of my journal and, if you find time to look into it you will form some idea of our wanderings. Please do not get the idea that we have suffered, for we have not. We have not been as comfortable as at home and that is about all.

During the last two months I have been up and down the Volga, from Kazan to Astrakhan, that is to say, the whole famine area, and I have had the opportunity to study it a bit carefully. The result of our investigation is rather interesting. In the first place you ought to know (not the public just now) that the famine is quite local, in spots, and that on the whole it is not as bad as described. It is quite true that thousands will die of hunger this winter, yet it is equally true that right along side of them, at their very door, there is an abundance of things to eat. It is not lack of food but lack of money and poor distribution. Another interesting thing is the fact that the hunger is in the villages and not in the cities because the crop, having failed, the villager has nothing with which to buy while the man in town is on a salary and can buy where he pleases.

There are two principal reasons for the famine, which unfortunately work together this year. In the first place there was the Soviet economic and social system: the idea that the peasant should give up all his surplus to the city proletariat and the latter in return would supply him with the things he needed. It resulted in this that the peasant was completely cleaned out. Knowing that his surplus would be taken from him he planted little and had therefore little to spare for the city, but the proletariat being hungry, it took that little from him. The famine began early last spring for there was no reserve. Usually the peasant has some reserve, if not in grain then in live stock, but this year he had nothing.

On top of that came the dry summer and finished up everything. But I say again that even in the famine area the famine is local for in some villages there was rain. Professor Hutchinson has figured out that the famine area has half enough food for its needs and that an expenditure of about fifteen million dollars in Russia would secure the other half and the hunger would be reduced to a minimum and no foreign aid would be needed. This raises an interesting question: Why all this hue and cry? Why all the political capital made out of it? Perhaps you can answer this. May I repeat that without foreign aid thousands more would die than will be the case because the present government can not or at least is not taking care of the situation, though it is doing a good bit. It has been an interesting experience and I have learned something.

Our train is due in Moscow today at six o'clock, but it will probably be hours late. From tomorrow on I shall devote my whole time to the work of the collection and not allow myself to be diverted to purely ARA work. I have contributed my bit and I can now make myself more useful in other ways. I shall be near our office and be able to keep you better informed of many things. The recent speech of Lenin and Chicherin's note showing a willingness to assume the prewar debt may lead to interesting developments.[14]

It would disappoint me greatly if by the time we are through collecting we should not have one of the best Slavic, especially Russian, collections in the United States. In this collection there will be much material that the Department of Food Research at Stanford will wish to use. Would it not be a good idea if the Hoover Collection and the Department of Food Research should combine and get one person (or perhaps two) to look after the collection, as cataloguer, etc., for the former and translator and investigator for the latter? We will need someone. Europe is full of capable and highly trained men and women who would be highly pleased to get an appointment for a reasonable salary.

We could engage princes, princesses, countesses, generals, and professors of all kinds (chiefly Russians) to work for us. For example, General Golovin[15] is a highly trained man and a gentleman. He would be glad to

---

[14]Golder probably means the speech that Lenin delivered to the Moscow Provincial Party Conference on October 29, 1921, in which he spoke bluntly about the mistakes of the Bolsheviks' Civil War economic policies and of the need for a further "retreat" in their present economic program toward a further accommodation of private trade.

Georgii Vasil'evich Chicherin (1872–1936) was people's commissar of foreign affairs. The "note" referred to was his diplomatic note to the Western powers on October 2, 1921, which declared that in order to meet the wishes of the Western governments, the Soviet government was willing to assume responsibility for tsarist loans received before 1914. It made any payments, however, conditional on the willingness of the Western governments to recognize the Soviet government. It also proposed a peace conference of Soviet Russia and the major powers. See E. H. Carr, *The Bolshevik Revolution, 1917–1923*, vol. 3 (New York, 1953), pp. 355–56.

[15]Nikolai Nikolaevich Golovin (Golovine) (1875–1944): Russian military figure and historian. Golovin had been a general in the tsarist army and had fought with the White forces in Siberia in the Civil War before leaving Russia and making his way to the United States. In August 1920, aboard the *Imperator* at the start of this first collecting trip to Europe, Golder met Golovin; this was the beginning of Golovin's long association with the Hoover Library as a collector and a contributor.

come and after a year or two we could even use him to give courses on military history and tactics. He is very competent and has recently been writing articles for some American military journal on some subject relating to military history. It might be best to engage some young lady, of an ancient and honorable family but now respectably poor, knowing well five or six languages. She could be useful in many ways. A man like General Golovin should not be offered less than twenty four hundred dollars but a young woman could come for the same pay that our girls in the Library receive. Please think over the matter and let me know if I can be of service while in Europe in helping select such a person. In that case give me definite instructions.

During the last month I have become somewhat acquainted with Professor Hutchinson (not too well) and I have formed a very high idea of his ability as an economist. He is probably the leading authority on foreign trade and has had unusual experiences. I am under the impression that he is not very keen about going back to [the University of] California because of the large classes and not too many facilities, in the way of a library, for research and that Stanford and the Hoover Collection appeal to him much more. Please do not misunderstand me; he did not tell me all that, but that is the sense and the inference I have drawn from his conversation. I may be wrong. I am giving you the hint to follow up or leave. Hoover, I know, has a very high opinion of Professor Hutchinson. Enough said on this subject.

For the last three months I have given my whole time to the ARA and it seems to me that all my expenses and my salary should come out of the ARA funds and not from Hoover's pocket. It is a matter to be taken up with the ARA in New York.

Please let me know if you can get some money out of the Department of Food Research for books relating to their field which have appeared before the war and do not directly come under the Hoover Collection. Get some money from them if you can because there is much to buy for the prewar period and little money of our own.

It is too late to wish you a joyous Thanksgiving but early enough for a Merry Christmas and a Happy New Year. Kindest regards to Mrs. Adams.

Cordially yours,

★ ★ ★

Diary entry: November 15, 1921. Moscow.

Arrived here a week ago today but have been too busy to write and as usual I find very little in the city to write about. One hears much but is sure of very little. Last Saturday and Sunday I called in Russian homes and as often happens, two of the guests engaged in a discussion as to whether the mass of the Russians are patriotic and "state minded" or not and as to the future of Russia. The discussion was interesting but it led nowhere.

Last night the famous revolutionist XTZ [again, identity unknown] called and he told some interesting stories. In the first place he said that on February 9, 1917, there gathered in the office of Rodzianko a number of men, among whom was Miliukov, Guchkov, generals and Buchanan[16] (though he was not so sure of the latter), and at that meeting it was agreed to dethrone the Tsar in April by having him arrested and forcing him to abdicate in favor of his son and the regent Grand Duke Michael. When the Revolution broke out a few weeks later the high officers at the front thought that it was part of the plan, which had for some reason been hurried, and therefore they easily accepted the Revolution. They soon learned the difference. Many officers felt that they had missed their opportunity for had they themselves pulled it off they could have remained at the head, but as the soldiers did it these remained at the head. The speaker told us also that the investigations made in 1917 to discover whether the old ministers and the Empress were spies proved one interesting thing. The Empress was not a spy in the true sense of the word but at the same time she was spying for Germany in this way. Rasputin had her under his influence and when the Empress wrote to the Emperor she used to tell him that Rasputin was ready to pray for victory for the Russian forces but to make his prayer effective he must know the exact time and place of the next attack. This information would be sent to her, she gave it to Rasputin and somebody got it from him.

The question of Trotsky came up and the speaker said that Trotsky was passé and that Lenin kept him because he was useful. When the Polish campaign failed there was an attempt to oust Trotsky and the attack against him in the Soviet meeting was so hot that he offered to resign. When Lenin learned of it he called off the attack and told his friends to let up and that Trotsky could be made useful. Since then he has been kept in the background except for public occasions and his influence has been greatly reduced. In regard to Zinoviev, he has been left as a figurehead in Petrograd and two other men have been put into the city to run the show. This is meant as a punishment to Zinoviev because of the execution of 62 people in Petrograd some time back against the will of the central government.

Tonight I had another caller, a writer of note, and a friend of Kropotkin,

[16]Sir George Buchanan (1854–1924): British ambassador to Russia from 1910 to 1918.

the anarchist.[17] He told of the hardships of the old man and that it was only towards his end that the government paid any attention to him. Kropotkin was opposed to the Bolsheviks and to their methods but he never came out openly against them because he was afraid it would encourage reaction and because he hoped that something good might come out of the Revolution.

★ ★ ★

Moscow, November 16, 1921

My dear Professor Adams:

I have had a very busy week and I have accomplished something. My colleague, the deputy Minister of Education [Pokrovsky], who has to do with Universities, etc., has been very helpful. Through him I have received nearly all the publications issued by the government during the last two or three years and I expect to receive more. I have now a circular letter from him to all other departments of government asking them to give me all their publications. I started out today and find it a rather tedious job but it is worth doing. For some of the publications I have to pay but most of them I receive free and in two copies. It looks now as if our Russian collection will probably be the largest of our collections and it will be the only collection of its kind in America. I did not come any too soon but not late. I am making all kinds of contacts which I need not bother you with.

There are difficulties, however. In the first place the ARA demands a great deal of my time. I have traveled more in Russia since the ARA came in here than any other man. Of course, it is tiresome, but I should not mind it if it were not for the time it takes. When I returned a week ago I announced that I am through with traveling and would give all my time to my other work. But a letter came from London asking that Professor Hutchinson and I go down the Ukraine to make some investigations. I declined at first but the pressure became so great that I consented to go for two weeks, the original plan would have taken six. Now we are meeting new difficulties from the side of the government. It apparently does not

---

[17]Petr Alekseevich Kropotkin (1842–1921): Russian prince, anarchist thinker, and writer. A legendary figure in the history of the revolutionary movement, he had lived in exile in Western Europe since the 1870s and returned to Russia only after the February 1917 Revolution.

wish us to go there and it is putting obstacles in the way.[18] We may or may not go but in the meantime I am up in the air and can not plan my work as I should like. I shall be very happy when I shall have the collection outside of Russia and myself with it. The air is charged here and no one knows when the storm will break. The government is not too fond of the ARA. Col. Haskell[19] is not too fond of men who are not strictly under his military orders, and so we tolerate one another. The city is full of rumors of one kind or another; some have it that we ourselves are to be arrested and so on.

There is so much work ahead that I do not see how I can possibly get away from here by Christmas time. I must not go until the work is finished, notwithstanding the fact that I have one and two men helping me. It is necessary to keep my hands on the job not only in securing the material but also in seeing that it gets out of the country. I am planning to send it out by courier, box at a time. Miller of the Riga ARA has already given his consent to take care of it should I send it to him; now I must tackle Col. Haskell about sending it by courier. I have mentioned a few of the difficulties but we will overcome them. I shall have to work in Europe to

---

[18]The ARA encountered considerable difficulty in establishing its operations in the Ukraine. Initially, the central Soviet authorities in Moscow opposed the idea of the ARA feeding in the Ukraine, probably in large part out of concern that American activity there might exacerbate the unstable political and military situation in the region. Golder speculates on this below. Once Moscow gave its permission, the ARA ran into a different kind of problem in the Ukrainian capital, Kharkov, where the republic's leaders declared that ARA operations in the Ukraine could proceed only if the ARA signed a separate agreement with the Ukrainian Socialist Soviet Republic (SSR). The Riga Agreement, they maintained, was not applicable to the Ukraine, which was a separate political entity from the Russian Socialist Federation of Soviet Republics (RSFSR).

The central authorities in Moscow seem to have been caught off guard and been somewhat embarrassed by this situation, while the ARA insisted that the Riga Agreement in fact covered the Ukraine and all other Soviet republics. In the end the ARA relented and signed, on January 10, 1922, an agreement with the Ukrainian SSR almost identical to the Riga Agreement. Golder and Hutchinson were the first ARA investigators to visit the Ukraine and for a time were at the center of the controversy. See *On the Trail of the Russian Famine*, pp. 118–25.

[19]William N. Haskell (1878–1952): director of the ARA Russian mission. A West Point graduate with a distinguished military record in World War I, after the armistice he became chief of the ARA mission to Romania. In July 1919 he was named Allied high commissioner to Armenia, where he also served until late 1920 as head of all foreign relief organizations operating in Transcaucasia, including the ARA, the American Committee for Relief in the Near East, and the American Red Cross.

finish up until the very last minute and do not look for me at Stanford until the last bell of the first school day. I am a bit afraid that in the very near future our policy towards this government may change and that Hoover will ask me to remain here for a time longer. But there is no use worrying about that now.

So far about ninety per cent of the publications of the government since 1917 I have secured in two copies, one of these you may dispose of as you think best. I am going to get some very valuable material for the Department of Food Research in the line of agricultural statistics and other such material, not only for the war but for a period preceding it.

Some of the material should be bound, especially newspapers, before being shipped. I have learned that binding is very cheap, newspapers about fifty cents and ordinary books about ten cents, and I have decided to have some of this work done here.

If I am not off for the Ukraine by the time the next courier goes I will write again next week.

> With good wishes,
> Sincerely yours,

★ ★ ★

Diary entry: November 19 & 20, 1921. Moscow.

Our proposed trip to the Ukraine is being blocked by the government for one reason or another. The real reason is military. There is much restlessness down there and robber bands are at work along the Polish and Rumanian frontier as well as in the interior. Yesterday I talked with a woman who had spent many months in the Crimea and who had returned here within the last two weeks. She told me that it took her a month to reach here, that there is great hunger in the Crimea, and that robber bands are turning the country into a wilderness. A year or two ago these "Green Bands" were in control of officers of the White Armies and had a political object, but after a time the control slipped from their hands and fell into those of lawless men, especially Tartars. For a time these bands specialized on Jews and Greeks as well as other of the numerically weaker nationalities, but now the killing and robbing has become general. The hunger forces many people to travel about in search of food and when they return homeward they are waylaid, robbed and very often killed. The government is unable to handle the situation.

In the evening I had a call from a man from southern Russia who knows the Ukrainians well. He said that in the Ukraine the restless Cossack element is still a factor and as soon as it feels that the reins of government are in weak hands it is ready to run away. Then again the Ukrainian population is not only a frontier population but it is also a population that has never been disciplined as the northern Russians have. At the present time both the Poles and the Rumanians, as well as other nations, are casting longing glances on the Ukraine because of its rich resources and are encouraging revolt. In northern Russia there is a general shortage of food and dependence on the government; in the south there is food and abundance and it refuses to give it up to the government from whom it receives nothing in return. During the tsar's time the north exchanged its manufactured goods for southern bread but now there is nothing to exchange and the southern peasant refuses to part with his food, and that leads to the use of force.

From another source I learned that in many parts of the Ukraine the peasants have buried food for four years in succession and would gladly exchange it for things they need but not for paper money of the Soviet. Last year the government requisitioned grain and it led to such outcries and local revolts that it had to change its attitude and decree that in the future each farmer should pay a definite amount of his crop. From this the government hoped to collect some 160 million puds (exact amount uncertain) by December 10, but to date not more than half of that amount has been collected and the government is greatly alarmed. It is from the Ukraine that most of this grain was to come and the Ukraine refuses to give it up. There is now talk that the government is contemplating to return once more to the system of requisitioning, which means more trouble.

Ten o'clock last night I went to call at the home of M[uravev],[20] where I met many interesting people, all of whom had been in prison either under the old or the new regime. The Russian situation was discussed from many points of view, internal and external. Every one felt that changes were in the air, but no one could quite foresee what and no one could propose anything practical which the government could accept. Among other things this fact was brought out, that the present government is more severe with the socialist left-wing non-Bolsheviks than with the Kadets and those more to the right.

This Sunday morning I had a call from the son-in-law of R,[21] whom I met in 1917, who held an important position and because of his experience and special knowledge still occupies a prominent place. In fact, for a time he held three different places and received three different paioks, or rations,

---

[20]Nikolai Konstantinovich Muravev (1870–1936): well-known lawyer, defense counsel in many political trials before and after the revolution.
[21]Possibly Fedor Rodichev.

on which he and his family lived. Now he and some of his friends are trying to get forest concessions from the government and to interest foreign capital. He told some interesting things about the fuel and lumber situation, his special field of work. For this year the government proposed through his department to cut down 22 million cubic sazhen' (a sazhen' is 7 feet) of timber for fuel and other purposes but it will actually cut only 3 1/2 million; the government needs 150 million railway ties, but it will receive 5 million. Because of lack of fuel for locomotives and ties for tracks the railway situation will become worse than it is now. It is now proposed, but not yet put in force, that passenger trains should be divided into four classes: (1) to run between certain points twice a week; (2) to run once a week; (3) to run twice a month; (4) to discontinue altogether certain runs.

The government owes so much for labor, so many departments of the government have been unpaid for so long a time, that it is impossible to secure workingmen for government work. The much talked of "mobilized" labor has turned out to be a joke. After the downfall of Kolchak,[22] Trotsky demobilized certain regiments from military service and mobilized them into labor regiments. Some of these were put to work in the Urals to prepare timber and under his system 82 men prepared a cubic sazhen' of wood which under normal times is done by 2 men. The scheme of mobilized labor has completely broken down and the government is abandoning it in favor of the old system, but the old system of industry needs capital and freedom, which the government can not and is not ready to give.

Industry is at a standstill for the present. The burden of supporting a mobilized labor army, which does not labor but which expects to be supported, has become so heavy that the government is unable to carry it. Consequently, during the last few months many departments have been closed down and others are closing, throwing thousands of people out of work at a time when private industry is dead. The army is also being demobilized and that throws another lot of unemployed on the market. Many of those who are retained in the government service have not been paid for months and their bread rations have not been handed out to them.

This pitiful situation is creating much discontent and is forcing the government to make concessions to the right and to invite foreign capital to come in and do something, and as that invitation is not being accepted, the government has gone so far as to offer to assume the old tsarist debt, and is willing to go even farther. Whether the foreign governments will be

---

[22]Aleksandr Vasil'evich Kolchak (1873–1920): Russian admiral and a leader of the White forces in the Russian Civil War; his regime at Omsk was crushed by the Red Army in November 1919, and he was shot by the Bolsheviks in February 1920.

satisfied with these promises, whether they will demand impossible guarantees, whether they will insist on political surrender of power on the part of the Communists will be decided in the very near future. Among the Communists there is much disagreement. Lenin and his followers are ready to go to the limit in economic concessions, but how far he is ready to give up political power is not clear. In a speech some time ago he said that his party ought to retreat as long as it is attacked and is unable to defend itself, to stop when the offensive stops, and to advance when it is in position to attack again. Whether it retreats one mile or a thousand is of no consequence. Enemies of Lenin are "die-in-the-ditch-men" who rather than give up their principles would like to be crushed with Russia on the top of them.

★ ★ ★

Moscow, Thanksgiving Morning. 1 A.M.

My dear Lutz:

A little while ago I received your letter . . . and I have been trying this evening to answer it and I am going to try to do it now, if I can. Our ARA army officer crowd decided to give a Thanksgiving party and we have a lot of ballet dancers and other females of that kind and all the men and women are more than half full of booze and we are having a happy time. I hear the music going now and I wish I were quietly asleep. The prize guest is Isadora Duncan and the woman is either drunk or crazy, perhaps both. She is half dressed and calls to the boys to pull down her chimies, I think that this is the way they are called. The poor ballet dancers have eaten and drunken everything in sight and they are still hungry. We are a happy crowd, particularly Professor Hutchinson and Coolidge and I. They have just gone into my neighbor's room asking for cognac, I mean the ballet dancers. What may happen before morning I do not know. The pitiful part of it all is that we are housed in a museum where there are many rare and beautiful things, finest furniture, and the pigs are crawling all over it, throwing cigarettes around and more like that.[23] But enough of this.

---

[23]Golder lived in the ARA residence at Bol'shoi znamenskoi pereulok No. 8, which had been formerly the private home of the Moscow merchant and art collector Sergei Ivanovich Shchukin and a state museum since 1918. Shchukin, who was allowed to remain with his collection, lived in the attic. Initially, the idea of the ARA occupying the house met stiff resistance from Madame Trotsky, the head of the Department of Museums, but it was decided to turn the house over to the ARA if it would guarantee the safety of the art collection, which it agreed to do. It was dubbed the Pink House because of its pink borders and trimmings.

Now to business. Tomorrow I have to go to the Ukraine. After much persuasion the government has consented. I am hoping I shall not be gone more than two weeks but I can not tell. The work of the collection suffers. The man I have engaged to work during my absence has not proved the success I had hoped. But I stopped him in time. He was so excited over the fact that books are cheap that he bought many things that we can do without. Some of these things I am returning. He has not done much damage. I have told him to stop buying until I return and have sent him to work to catalogue what we have. Some of the stuff will prove too expensive to catalogue at home and a rough catalogue will do. But I am making the catalogue largely with the view of avoiding buying duplicates and not to anticipate your work.

From the government offices I am getting much material which will be unique in America. Its value is not great, but like a good deal of other war material it is needed for the collection. I feel confident that so far as the Russian collection is concerned it will be the largest we have and the only one of its kind in America. But much water will pass before it reaches you. With this government things are not done off hand. I have yet to get a permit and a dozen other things. Today I went to see my friend the deputy Minister of Education who assured me that only he had the right to issue permits and that he would issue mine, but another department informs me that it is not so. Of course I have to give up the idea of coming out at Christmas time and I am now planning for the end of January. Petrograd is still before me. I should not be surprised if our collection will count fifty or sixty boxes.

. . . I can not write any more tonight because of the noise. If I find a minute tomorrow I will continue.

★ ★ ★

Diary entry: November 24, 1921. Moscow.

After a rather hilarious night of celebration at the Pink House the porter this morning asked me what kind of a "prazdnik" [holiday] we are having. "It can not be Christmas," said he, "because that comes in December. Some say it is the anniversary of the day when you became independent of France, and others tell me that it is in memory of the time when you threw off the yoke of Spain. But it can not be the latter because that happened about twenty years ago." Such is the knowledge the average Russian has of us.

Diary entry: November 25, 1921. Aboard a train, Moscow-Ukraine.

After ten days of negotiations about going down the Ukraine and after having been refused once, the Soviet government finally agreed to it last Monday. I have just learned confidentially that it had been reported that I had been with Kolchak and that I had spoken against the Soviet government and that was one reason for the delay, or perhaps it was an excuse. Professor Coolidge proved that I had not been with Kolchak because all during that time I was with the Colonel House Commission of Inquiry and that the other charge was equally untrue. Anyway, the negotiations dragged on, but as soon as the permission to proceed was given, Professor Hutchinson and I commenced to prepare.

It was decided that our car would be attached to the weekly Kiev express, which leaves every Thursday. Twice yesterday we tried to see the car but could not. Finally at five o'clock we came to the station with all our baggage and were told that the car was not yet backed in and were asked to unload our things on a certain platform. The representative of the Soviet government had assured us that two government representatives would accompany us and that another important personage would be at the station to see that we got off all right, but no one was there except at the very last minute as the train was already pulling out one representative got on the car. The train was to start at 5:40, but at that time no car was in sight. The station master held the train and went in search of the car. He returned and said that we should move our baggage and provisions to another place, which we did. After waiting there another hour the car was backed in. It is a small second class car, having two coupés, one occupied by the two porters and the other by the Soviet liaison officer. In addition to these coupés there is a semi-open space with cushioned seats which the three of us, Hutchinson, Smith of the AP,[24] and I have taken for our quarters. Two of the car windows are smashed and boarded but on the whole the car is comfortable and warm.

This morning Professor Hutchinson made a table and that helped. In addition to our car being the last one it has also a flat wheel just under our table and we find some difficulty in adjusting the cups to the lips for the liquid either splashes into our faces or fails to reach our lips as the flat wheel makes its revolutions and as the car swings. However, that is not a matter of importance.

The country we are passing today does not seem as fertile as the Volga valley. A thin layer of snow covers the ground, just enough to encourage sledding. There is a good deal of small timber and many of the people are

---

[24]Charles Stevenson Smith of the Associated Press.

engaged in hauling fire wood to the stations. At three o'clock we reached the station in Briansk and there was hooked on in the rear of us a prison car to keep us company and steady. Thanks for little favors. We remained at this station for a half hour or more to change engines and buy supplies. Bread (black) is only 3000 the pound.

Diary entry: December 6, 1921. Aboard a train, Kharkov-Moscow.

Yesterday morning at 10 o'clock we left Kharkov for Moscow and this morning at the same hour we are at Tula, hoping to reach our destination sometime today. Our invasion of the Ukraine was not altogether a success and like the armies of the Central Powers we have learned that the riches of the Ukraine are mostly underground. The stories which we had heard of the great abundance of food in the Ukraine we found to be untrue. Kiev, Volhynia, Podolia, Chernigov and Poltava had harvests varying from fair to very good, but the other governments of the Ukraine had harvests varying from poor to almost nothing. This is especially true of the governments along the shores of the Black Sea. Taking the Ukraine as a whole, there is enough food to feed every person in that republic under normal conditions. But normal conditions do not exist here and consequently millions of people will be hungry this year and thousands will starve.

The blame for this must be laid at the door of the communist economic policy. Under the capitalistic system the laws of supply and demand were not interfered with and bread was sent to places where it was needed and in this way the distribution of food was fairly equal all over the country both in quantity and in price. Each farmer tried to produce a surplus so that he would have something to sell and with the money received buy things he needed. In order to do away with the capitalistic class the Communists abolished trade and money; they nationalized industry and agriculture. They took the surplus bread from the farmer and gave it to the city proletariat, planning to give to the farmer the produce of the city proletariat.

The system of nationalization forced the government to take into its service thousands and thousands of employees who were formerly engaged in private industry of some kind or other. All these employees, from the trained doctor to the doorkeeper, were treated alike as far as pay was concerned—each was given a "paiok," or ration. Realizing that their paiok was assured, regardless of the amount of work accomplished, the employees in the factories and in the bureaus loafed on their jobs, some sabotaged because they were opposed to the government. Consequently there was not much produced for the farmer and he received little for the supplies which were taken from him. He, too, began to loaf, planting no more than he needed for his own use. But the city proletariat and army had to be fed and therefore the government in 1919 and 1920 was obliged to adopt a policy of requisitioning and confiscating.

Gangs of soldiers or factory workmen were sent into the country to demand that the peasants turn over the grain to the government. When they refused the third degree was applied until the man indicated just where he hid the grain. When found, it was confiscated. Some peasants were shot. In many parts of Russia the peasants were cleaned out of food almost a year ago, not having enough grain even for seeding this last spring. In the spring so many peasants in so many different parts of the country rose in revolt that Lenin saw the wisdom of giving up the system of requisitioning and putting in its place a definite grain tax, so much per acre and family. This quieted the farmer, but it was too late. There was no reserve of grain in the land. Had the crop been fairly good the country might have pulled out, but unfortunately there was neither a reserve of food to draw upon nor a crop, and consequently there was hunger over a great area of Russia.

The present situation is this: In some parts of Russia there is a surplus of food as before. But while before the peasant was ready to sell it to the trader for money he now refuses to part with it because there is no money. The paper stuff which serves as a medium of exchange he is unwilling to accept because he realizes that it has little value.

A man who has recently returned from Smolensk tells me that in that part of Russia the standard of value is a pud of flour—a horse is worth so many puds, a pair of shoes so many, etc., even a ticket to Moscow means a pud of rye flour—that is, giving the ticket agent the flour and he somehow fixes it. The paper stuff which passes for money has lost its function. A peasant will trade his rye flour for shoes, clothing and such articles. As a result of this situation and the breaking down of the transportation system, one sees everywhere men and women with baskets and sacks on their way to trade clothing, axes, saws, for flour. Our porters are taking from Kharkov to Moscow sugar, the conductor is carrying kerosene from Kharkov to Kursk, etc. These people with sacks and baskets are a pitiful sight. The trains are so few and so overcrowded that people can not get in even with tickets. They are therefore obliged to ride on the top of freight cars, on the steps of passenger cars and even on the bumpers. Every time our train comes to a station there is a mad rush of these sackers to get on but the police and the porters are at the doors to keep them back. There is crying, wailing, bribing, swearing but only few get on for there is no room in those stuffy, ill-smelling cars.

Some of these men and women have been a week or more from home, some have left their jobs without permission and will be arrested on their return, some have left little children at home, but they are all on the go for the hunger is driving them. All of Russia is on the move and in search of bread, it thinks of nothing else, it talks of nothing else. Out of this misery some people are growing wealthy. A new class of trader has come to the front, the new bourgeoisie. It has acquired by various means, mostly by trading in war plunder and revolutionary confiscation, a large amount of money with which it buys goods in the cities, takes them to the country districts to trade for bread, which it brings to the cities to exchange for manufactured goods and in this way grows richer. It bribes where it must and gets privileges on railways and in other places. Where people are starving, bribing is easy. Many of these new rich are Communists and the government became so ashamed of them that it has had a party cleaning and forced many to leave.

The nervous strain of recent years is beginning to manifest itself in peculiar forms in the country places. Reports come from many places that many sects are coming to the front, or old fanatical sects are becoming active. A friend who has recently returned from White Russia says that in the village where he was the Baptists (not the same as our Baptists) have taken to smashing ikons in the churches and doing such things. Recently they interrupted a religious procession which led to a fight resulting in the death of two men.

If conditions do not change for the better, the future, at least the immediate future, is really dark. The prospects for a good crop for next year are not very bright. This fall less land was seeded than usual. For some reason there has been a very light snow fall thus far and considerable cold and there is great danger that the seed which has come up will freeze. Much has been hoped for from the grain tax but only about half the amount expected has been collected. The peasants refuse to part with their grain on general principles for they do not have too much. They refuse to part with it because they are not particularly fond of the government and the city proletariat. They refuse to part with it because they say the commissars get it. Many of the grain store houses have been burned and this has led to charges and countercharges. The commissars say the banditi did it; the peasants declare the commissars did it to hide their misdeeds.

The Soviet government is trying its best to adjust itself to the changed conditions but without much success. It is closing down certain bureaus, reducing the number of employees in others, cutting down the rations of thousands, and taking it away altogether from tens of thousands, among this last class are teachers and students. These unemployed and underfed can find no other work, for private industry is dead and all these fine speeches and new economic policies have not been able, as yet, to put it on its feet. The cost of living is daily going higher, it had doubled since our coming and now seems to go in bounds. One can merely guess what will become of thousands and millions of Russian people this winter. During the last two or three years diseases of many kinds have found a fertile field in Russia, the death rate is going ahead of the birth rate. Every one is asking the question, "Where is the end?" but no one can give the answer. Many Russians insist that only America can save the country, rumors are even about that America will, but when I ask what can America do, there is nothing definite to propose. The ARA finds great difficulty in working with the government, our experience in the Ukraine shows some of the problems and difficulties business men will have to encounter in dealing with petty politicians.

★ ★ ★

Moscow, December 8, 1921

My dear Professor Adams:

I returned to Moscow Tuesday night. Our experiences in the Ukraine you will find written up in my journal which I enclose. Since my last letter to you about two weeks ago, many things have happened. You will note from the journal that the secret service, the so-called Che-Ka, is on my trail and after my scalp. It is on the wrong trail: that I was with Kolchak; the other complaint, that I speak against the government, is so vague that it can not make an issue of it. Of course, I am careful, not so much for my sake as for the sake of Hoover and the ARA. My great crime is that I understand the language and talk with people, something that most of the ARA men can not do. They can get nothing on me because there is nothing. Just the same, I walk around as if a sword hung over me. The relation between the ARA and the Soviet government is not as friendly as it might be and some of the treatment the organization receives here it would not put up with anywhere else, but most of us realize that we have to put it through somehow.

I hope that now I can be let alone for a time and not be obliged to go on the road again. I think that most likely I will be. During my absence the Hoover collection has suffered and I have a tale of woe to tell. When I returned to Moscow at the end of September and realized that I had to go again I engaged one of the learned men here who knew books quite well and was quite honest, to buy books for us. In his credit I placed with the accountant of the ARA nine hundred dollars. Unfortunately for us the accountant exchanged all that money into rubles at the rate of 100,000 to the dollar. Since then the value of the ruble has fallen until now it is somewhere from 250,000 to twice that amount. The man I engaged to work has not been a brilliant success. He has bought a number of very valuable books at a very low rate but he has also purchased many things that we do not need at all and which I have to sell back. Like so many other Russians he has spent much time on organization, etc., to no purpose. To make a long story short, my roaming over different parts of Russia will cost the Hoover Collection somewhere about 300 dollars. There is a bit of money compensation for that. During the last three months, as well as this month I shall not cost the Hoover Collection any money for living expenses, for I have been put on ARA subsistence. It would be right if my salary were paid wholly by the ARA during this period of time.

The collection has not suffered in quantity or quality. We are getting most or nearly everything strictly Hoover Collection. I have decided in view of the delays not to bind anything but send the boxes out as quickly as I can. Much of the material is not worth binding, some of it even cataloguing, but that is true of all other collections. We have many duplicates of the new material which we secured for nothing or for very little cost. I assumed that these duplicates would go to the Library of Congress but I learned yesterday that Putnam[25] has an agent, one of his staff on the ground [in Russia]. This need not worry us for we will have no difficulty with the duplicates.

My immediate plans are to remain in Moscow until the end of this month in order to wind up affairs here and get the stuff out. Next month I will go to Petrograd and get what material is there. I hope by the end of January to leave and to take up my other work in other lands. I am way late in my schedule but it is not my fault, as you know.

I do not hear very often from America. My last week's mail was sent to Odessa to wait for me when I should reach there, which I am not going to do very soon. Yesterday's mail is not due until today, and so it goes. Brown[26] of London was here about a week ago but I was away and did not see him. Professor Hutchinson is here and from now on he will see the world without my cheerful? company.

May you and yours have a very Merry Christmas and a Happy New Year. I wish I were near to make a New Year's call and to see Mrs. Adams and the children. I long to touch once more a clean healthy child that is not hungry.

With all good wishes, Cordially yours,

---

[25]Herbert Putnam (1861–1955): librarian of Congress from 1899 to 1939.
[26]Walter Lyman Brown was ARA director for Europe.

Diary entry: December 10, 1921. Moscow.

Called at the home of X[27] where there was the usual number of intellectuals discussing and criticizing affairs of state. Nearly every one of those present is occupying some important posts in the government service. Not one of them is a Communist and all, with one exception, are bitterly opposed to the Soviet form of government. Many interesting things came out in the discussion. Among others we learned that there is a joint committee of the Ministry of Finance and Ministry of Foreign Affairs working on the question of counter-claims against the Allies in case the question of the tsar's debts comes up for a conference. The Soviet government is going to claim damages from the Allies for their interference in the Civil War and plan to make use of the Alabama claims[28] as a precedent. The committee had estimated the damages as amounting to 92 billions of dollars, but that seemed so large that it has been cut down to 42 billions. The claims of the Allies against Russia are estimated at 22 billions, which leaves a balance in favor of Russia. Of course the Soviet government does not really expect to get any money, but it looks on the counter-claims as excellent propaganda and ammunition against the bourgeois allies.

Diary entry: December 11, 1921. Moscow.

Professor Coolidge and I were given two tickets to a concert given by the Stradivarius quartet to be preceded by an address by Lunacharsky.[29] The program was to begin at eight but it was almost an hour later before it really started. The concert was given in honor of the strangers, mostly members of the diplomatic corps and relief missions. Many of the guests were dressed up, more than half had stiff collars, and a few wore evening clothes and Prince Alberts. Lunacharsky made his speech in French, which was as cramped as the French description of the quartet which appeared on the written program. I was disappointed for I had heard so much about his linguistic ability. Among other things he said that in the spring the violinists

---

[27]This is once again Muravev.

[28]The Alabama Claims concerned American grievances against Great Britain for its intervention in the U.S. Civil War, chiefly building and arming Confederate warships, despite its declared neutrality. The case became known as the "Alabama Claims" because the major Union losses had been inflicted by the Confederate warship *Alabama*. A settlement was finally reached in 1872, when international arbitrators awarded the United States $15,500,000 in gold for damages.

[29]Anatolii Vasil'evich Lunacharsky (1875–1933): people's commissar of enlightenment.

in Russia would be invited to Moscow to compete for the use of the Stradivarius violins. Each competitor will first play for the general public and then for a special public. The best players will be given the use of a Stradivarius for three years. During that time they will engage themselves to play before the masses for nothing or for very low pay. At the end of the three years another contest will be held along the same lines in order to give the new blood a chance. This will go on indefinitely. The whole thing reminded me of a high school essay or athletic contest.

★ ★ ★

Moscow, December 15, 1921

My dear Lutz:

Another courier day. I have not heard from Adams or you for a long time, but that is due no doubt to the fact that the mail is either following me around or you are having difficulty in following me around the map. The first thing I wish to tell you is that I managed for the time being to shake loose from the regular ARA work to do the Hoover Collection work. Poor Doctor Hutchinson had to go alone and my best wishes went with him. It is hard work, especially because of the suffering. It is getting my goat, as the boys say. The country is in ruins and I wish I could see sunshine ahead. So much suffering, so much talking, so much arresting, so much stealing, so much demoralization one finds nowhere else and while Rome burns the leaders fiddle.

In regard to our own work. As I wrote Adams last week, my absence and poor choice of a man is going to cost somebody about three hundred dollars. But I do not wish to have this spoil the pleasure that we are to have a very good collection, both for the Hoover Collection and for the University, for a lot of the stuff bought is specially good for the University Library. Queer thing about the book market is that it has been almost altogether cleaned out. When we came here book shops were just opening and the few professors who had books put them on the market and used the money to buy bread. These books have been bought up and there are no others. The price of books has gone up several hundred per cent. The books which I am selling back will bring me in rubles two or three times what we paid for them, but, of course, the exchange has fallen. We got what books we need and all I am worrying about now is getting them out and I am working hard on that problem. I am still going through the government offices and making as complete a collection of official documents as I can. Next month I will go to Petrograd and clean up things there.

Winter is on us and it is cold. I came without much preparation, as you know, and did not bring much winter clothing. When in Riga I had the Red Cross present me with a couple of suits of heavy underwear and a greasy chauffeurs coat and with these, and a fur cap that I have bought, I have managed to keep warm and to look like a real proletariat. Most of the other men have gone in for fur coats, but I passed it up. We have managed to be very very comfortable, there is plenty of fuel for the present, an abundance of food and no shortage of drinks.

Socially I meet a number of interesting people. Professor Coolidge and I play together. On Saturday we meet Radek[30] and some other Bolos. Most of the time, however, we hobnob with the Reds because they hobnob with us. We pick up a great deal of interesting information of one kind and another. For example, we have recently learned that in the expectation that a conference to discuss the Russian debts would take place soon our friends the Bolos have organized a commission to study counter-claims against the allies for their interference in the civil war, and the counter-claims are twice what the claims are. Interestingly enough, the Alabama Claims are going to be used as a precedent in arguing the counter-claims.

With all good wishes,

★ ★ ★

Diary entry: December 17, 1921. Moscow.

This morning I called on my friend, the assistant Minister of Education and director of all the archives. He told me that in the imperial archives, or rather in the archives of the imperial family, have been discovered a number of valuable papers, many of the diaries of the emperors, including those of Nicholas II. These are all to be published soon.

At six o'clock, Professor Coolidge and I, guided by our good friend S.,[31] went to call on Karl Radek at the Kremlin. To get into the Kremlin is

---

[30]Karl Radek (1885–1939): Bolshevik journalist, member of the party's Central Committee and of the Executive Committee of the Communist International.

[31]This is probably N. D. Sokolov (1870–1928), the well-known political trial lawyer and friend of Muravev. In 1909, in supplementary elections to the Third Duma in Petrograd, Sokolov ran as a candidate of the Russian Social Democratic Labor party. According to a Soviet source, he was at this time "sympathetic to the Bolsheviks." V. I. Lenin, *Polnoe sobranie sochinenii*, 5th edition, 55 vols. (Moscow, 1958–70), vol. 48, p. 514. After the February Revolution he was a member of the Executive Committee of the Petrograd soviet, at which time he was, according to the editors of Lenin's works, "in favor of coalition with the bourgeoisie." Ibid., vol. 19, p. 588.

not an easy task, for all gates are guarded and one must get a special permit. We got in because Radek telephoned to let us in. The engagement with him was at his own request. He received us in his study, which was full of books, many of them of recent European and American publication. He is a little man, has a beard and long hair, big eyes with spectacles, and is simply dressed.

He started in by talking German which had a distinct Yiddish accent; later he switched to Russian which had a marked Polish accent and was not very good. He admitted that he was no Russian, had nothing in common with the Russian muzhik, and would much prefer to be in Western Europe doing propaganda work than to remain in Russia. He started the conversation (he did most of the talking all the time we were with him) by complaining of the difficulties of understanding America, the difference between our leading political parties, and the lack of a well defined foreign policy. As he continued talking American affairs it became clear that he had a better grasp of things American than he was ready to admit.

He brought up the question of Russo-American relations and pointed out that America's interests in the future are in the Far East, China and Russia, the two countries yet to be exploited. Russia, too, is turning her attention in that direction. She is not afraid of Japan. From now on Russia is going to strengthen her military forces in the Far East and develop that part of the world. She would rather stand with America against Japan but if America should show herself unwilling to play with Russia then the latter will make friends with Japan. America refuses to recognize the Soviet government not because it is not democratic (did she not have relations with the tsar's government?), but because of the economic situation. If Russia had commerce, America would come quickly enough.

A democracy in the American sense is now impossible in Russia—the ignorance of the population, the vastness of the territory, the break down of the transportation system are a few of the reasons why. It would be easy enough to make a bluff at it. The Soviet government is keeping very closely in touch with the peasants and its whole strength is based on the assumption that they are standing behind the Soviet. Every Red Army soldier goes to his home a Communist. Russia has two possibilities of getting out of the

---

Sokolov accompanied Golder to a number of high-level meetings with Bolshevik and Soviet officials in 1921 and 1922, and he seems to have been intent on trying to bring the Soviet and American sides to a rapprochement. Golder wrote to Coolidge on June 10, 1922: "Sokolov plays the role of mediator with his usual success—gets kicked from both parties." Coolidge papers, file: Correspondence, A–Z 1922/23—A–Winship 1923/4. For Sokolov's reminiscences of the Russian Revolution, see Golder's Conversations with Sokolov in the Golder collection, box 35.

poor economic situation. First, through the aid of the European powers and America. If they come to the rescue in an economic way then the development will come quickly; if they refuse then Russia will drop back into mediaevalism for a time and in the end will help herself.

His views were very intelligent and interesting. He was not easy to follow because of his poor Russian and German as well as the skipping about from topic to topic. He showed himself friendly and made no attempt to whitewash. He expressed a desire to get closer to America through other channels than diplomatic (for the diplomatic negotiations with England have led to no good results), but through social intercourse. He offered to introduce us to other Bolos and asked us to call on him at any time.

About nine o'clock we paid our usual Saturday evening call at the home of M[uravev]. Various subjects were discussed, but the most interesting was the question of whether the Russian Revolution was more bloody than the French. One man, giving as his authority Prince Kropotkin, said that the French was more bloody relatively, and if the Russian followed the French it would have to have 15 million victims. The others insisted that the Russian was already more bloody and each recited case after case where thousands were shot down in cold blood.

★ ★ ★

December 22, 1921

My dear Professor Adams:

This is mail day again and I hasten to drop you a note and to send you a few odds and ends of more or less interest. I have now more than twenty boxes of good size full of books for the period from 1917. For the three to four years preceding I will have to go to Petrograd which I hope to do next week. I am now making an effort to get the permit to send them out but I have not yet succeeded. There is going to be no difficulty about it but the usual delay.

This week the Bolos are having their big Powwow and it is difficult to get them to pay attention to anything practical.[32] They are all discussing the theory of Marx and trying to harmonize the new economic policy with it. All kind of rumors are in the street as to what will be the outcome of this session. While they are talking, hunger and disease are spreading over the land in a frightful way. Our agents in the field report that in their districts from 50 to 75% of the horses have already fallen and it is hard to transport

---

[32]This was the Eleventh All-Russian Party Conference, December 19–22.

food to the villages, some of these places have no one left in them. But all that is a matter of no importance to people who have theories to work out.

I have not received any mail, but I am now going to the office to see if there is anything there. I am falling behind in my programme but I can not help it.

With all good wishes to all good friends,

Sincerely yours,

★ ★ ★

December 29, 1921

My dear Professor Adams:

. . . The excitement of the week has been the All-Russian Soviet meeting.[33] Through friends I secured a ticket of admission but I have been so busy that I could attend two meetings only, and these two were not the most interesting. The Soviet has a well oiled political machine and there is no delay in getting through. In less than a week all the business was finished and today the delegates are on their way home. The Executive Committee does all the work and the delegates are called together to say Amen. Motions are put in the affirmative: "All in favor will please hold up their hands (or rather their red cards), all opposed do the same. There is no opposition, therefore the motion is carried. Tovarishch X asks to discuss the motion. Is it your pleasure that he should discuss it?" Shouts of "No!" from the audience. "There is going to be no discussion."

The Soviet meeting suggested a bit a Hobo Convention. People were there in all kinds of clothing, hats on, hats off, coats on and off, people sat everywhere. At each meeting one of the Commissars made a report on his department. These reports were long and tiresome. Only two reports attracted attention—Lenin's and Trotsky's. The others were listened to. I was interested to listen to these Commissars as they glibly quoted figures. From their reports one could have imagined that Russia was in a normal state of affairs instead of suffering hunger and pestilence and facing, as the Russians say, a catastrophe.

Much was expected from this Soviet; it was supposed that a new policy, leaning more to the right would be announced, but nothing happened. It may be that some declaration may be made soon by the Commissars. After each lengthy report there followed much short discussion. All those who

[33]This was the Ninth All-Russian Congress of Soviets, December 23–28.

wished to discuss threw their names on the platform where they were handed to the chairman and he called on them or some of them. These five minute discussions were very interesting and it was astonishing how freely the government was criticized. The government watches these discussions for it gives an idea the way the wind blows. The building where the Soviet met was surrounded by Red Guards, inside and out, and tickets were carefully examined.

Last night was the last session and Professor Coolidge and I went. Elections went through in a hurry, there was no discussion, not even nomination, for the nominations were made in the corridors. The candidates were put up and unanimously elected. Nevertheless there are many of the less intelligent Communists and reds in the army who have an idea that they really have self government.

After the election the session was declared closed and then the whole audience of several thousand stood up and sang the International. It was well done and made a very deep impression. I could not but help thinking that no matter what happens in a government way to Russia the Communist Revolution will not be easily forgotten and that the propaganda work will go on and on. The Communists have succeeded in developing class hatred and the capitalists who may come in here to do business in the future must take that into account. If the tsarists have an idea that the Russian people would like to have them back they are mistaken. Just now the mass of the people is hungry and sick and it does not care who rules over them but as soon as they recover they will assert themselves. The Revolution has done a great work which can not be undone, and the good and evil will go on.

When we came outside a band was playing and an outdoor movie was going on, showing how much superior tractors are to plows. This was for the benefit of the peasants. Tractors and electrification are two great hobbies of the Communists. No one knows just where the money is to come from but no matter. Everyone expects America to come to the rescue. The cry now is that Europe and America can not get along without Russia, therefore they will come to the aid. One man was in to see me this morning to ask what I could do to establish trade relations between America and Russia and to persuade Hoover to send grain ships. When I asked what the Russians would pay he said "of course, in our paper money. Perhaps it is not very profitable for America but for the sake of future trade it is important to make a sacrifice." Russia is full of dreamers.

I must not close this letter without calling to your attention two movements to the right which the Soviet government has made at this session. One is the limitation of the Che-Ka or Extraordinary Commission, which arrested, condemned and executed people without the ordinary legal processes. Lenin announced that in the future this Commission would have police power but not judicial. Whether this will be carried out in practice remains to be seen. The other advance to the right was the admission of non-Communists to important offices in the Executive Committees. In practice it will make little difference for they will be hand picked, but the principle is a step in advance.

Colonel Haskell is now in London talking over with Brown the work ahead of the ARA, especially in view of the new Congressional appropriation.[34] For the life of me I do not see how the transportation is going to take care of all the grain that may come in.

With all good wishes,

★ ★ ★

Moscow, December 30, 1921

My dear Professor Adams:

. . . The situation here is about the same. Just now we are excited about the Congressional appropriation and we are wondering how the food is going to be taken care of. Our friends in New York are rushing things a bit. Yesterday or the day before a telegram came that ships with grain are on the way or about to start. No arrangements have been made for unloading or for transportation, no arrangements have been made for milling, for sacking, for a dozen and one things and it is a serious question whether the grain can be milled and so on. It sounds good in the papers that the next day after Congress appropriated the money the grain was shipped.

This Soviet government does not show itself particularly appreciative. A few days ago a special vote of thanks was passed by the All-Russian Soviet to Doctor Nansen[35] and it featured in the paper while the ARA was

---

[34]That is, the congressional appropriation of $20 million for famine relief in Russia, signed on December 22.

[35]Fridtjof Nansen (1861–1930): Norwegian explorer and humanitarian and the League of Nations high commissioner for famine relief in Russia since 1921. His mission represented numerous governments, national Red Cross societies, and various political and humanitarian organizations. In the end Nansen's efforts brought into Soviet Russia several million dollars in food aid. This was far less than the $60 million behind the ARA mission, but the Bolsheviks found it easier to praise Nansen publicly because he represented no single government or country and also because his relief arrangements with the Soviet authorities, unlike the ARA's Riga Agreement, placed the distribution of relief supplies in the government's hands. On top of this, Nansen was an attractive figure, big-hearted and courageous, who had

attacked openly. In some corner of the papers something was said about a vote of thanks to us, yet Nansen does hardly anything and the ARA does very much. Of course Nansen works through the Soviet and we do not. Little by little, however, they are taking us into camp and running our show. In a thousand and one ways they worry us, they arrest the Russians who work for us, they block us here and side track us there. I dare say that nowhere in Europe have our people suffered so many humiliations and have been appreciated so little as here. Were it not for the fact that all realize that the honor of the ARA and of Hoover are mixed up with this work many of our men would not remain here. As it is, we all say we have got to see this thing through somehow.

Let me give you an instance of their treatment that happened today. Yesterday a telegram was received from Hoover about the Congressional appropriation. Of course they know all our telegrams and their liaison officer asked that he might see a copy of it which was shown him. Today the telegram appeared in the Izvestiia as a telegram from Hoover to this liaison officer. When asked about it he said that it was a mistake. The impression they are trying to give is that the Soviet is running the ARA. This is just one illustration. The Soviet keeps a list of all those who receive our food packages and it can, of course, arrest anyone it pleases if we should pay no attention to its request not to hand out packages to people whom it dislikes. Life is hard, very hard, and it makes one's heart ache at the misery and suffering, needless suffering.

When I was here in 1914 I made the acquaintance of a family whose name I will not give for I do not know who may read this letter before it gets to you. The family was wealthy and very cultured and very kindly and had nothing snobbish about it. There were eight children who were being educated and trained to be useful citizens. When I was ill here, they came to see me, especially one of the boys about 17 of whom I was very fond. When the revolution came everything was lost. The father told me that a few days after the outbreak of the Revolution there was a family council as to what should be done. The children all voted to leave the country and the

---

been since 1898 an honorary member of the Russian Academy of Sciences and thus widely known in European Russia before the revolution. His visits to Soviet Russia were marked by public ceremonies in his honor and official gestures of gratitude (including an honorary membership in the Moscow soviet), much to the irritation of the ARA. The ARA men also disliked the considerable fanfare in Europe over what the ARA regarded as the Nansen mission's marginal contribution to Russian relief, while the huge ARA effort was downplayed. For his humanitarian work Nansen won the 1922 Nobel Peace Prize.

father agreed to it but during the night he thought it over and decided that with such a large family it would not be safe to move and they remained.

During the Civil War that followed one son disappeared, one was exiled, a daughter and her husband were driven out and they are now beggars in Constantinople, and one son, the boy who used to come to see me, was taken ill. When I reached here I looked up the family and I am glad to have been able to do a little for them. Yesterday I went to call on them and found the boy very ill and the family frantic because they were unable to get him the necessary medicine. I returned home and told our doctor who promised to give them something but during the night the boy died. In this way some of the finest people are dropping off one at a time and that fanatic crowd rejoices because the bourgeois are going. It is heart breaking. Yesterday I received a letter from a Russian professor of international reputation begging that I should do something for him. He was kept in prison until his health broke and now they have let him loose to end his days in misery. But why prolong this tale?

Pardon me for dwelling on it but I think you ought to know.

Sincerely,

★ ★ ★

Petrograd, New Year's Day, 1922

Dear Lutz:

I reached here yesterday about noon. I was very eager to see this city and to note the effect the last four years have had. On the Nevsky Prospekt there is still some life but the other streets are distinctly deserted. This was especially noticeable this morning when I started out to find some people whom I used to know. I knocked on a number of doors and received in reply a hollow, dead sound—no one there. After some difficulty I located some of my people. Here is the history of the family with whom I used to live.

The strain of the war and the Revolution has demoralized the family, husband and wife are not living together, the oldest girl has married a worthless fellow, and the mother and two boys, one of whom has been arrested a number of times and finally put into the red army, are occupying two small dark overcrowded rooms near the roof of the building. Before the Revolution they had a beautiful home and considerable wealth. Of course the family is in the greatest poverty.

The family of Professor Lappo-Danilevsky is as low down as possible. Professor L-D was a great historian. He lectured in Cambridge University in 1916 and had some kind of a degree conferred upon him. In 1917 Lowell of Harvard invited him to deliver the Lowell Institute Lectures but before the invitation reached him he died of hunger. Of his two sons, the more talented died of hunger and typhus, the less talented has degenerated into a worthless bum, and the poor wife is left all alone and is now living in a garret. I climbed up several dirty stairs but could not find her. I could go on with this but all the stories are alike, more or less misery, death, demoralization.

New Year's Eve was celebrated by the local soviet in a joyous manner. Until now our people have been afraid to go near anything red but I persuaded Walker[36] that we ought to go. He notified the Soviet representative and he secured us tickets for the Opera house, the place of festivities. I have not been in that place for seven years and I was interested to see what it looked like. As soon as I entered I was greeted by the guard which was dressed in the uniform of the old Imperial Guard. Why this relic is preserved I do not know. The uniform hung on these poor peasant soldiers and they behaved like farmers, smoking cigarettes on duty, but the uniform was there. We had three tickets, one for Walker, one for me, and one for the representative of the government, for even here we are followed and looked after. There is only one place where we can go alone but I will not name it.

We had places in one of the best loges, where formerly the Grand Dukes and their fair ladies sat. But we were there only a few minutes when the director of the opera came and announced that these places were not good enough for us and that he had reserved three better places in the loge of the tsar. Sure enough in the front row of the balcony, seats were waiting for us. I thought how unfit for such plebeians as we two to sit there until I looked around and saw our companions the Communists. After all we were bourgeois and in that respect more closely related to the tsar than any of the others. The opera was full of members of the Soviet and their families, so it was all red.

The performance was to begin at seven but it was eight before the curtain rose and displayed on the stage a long table besat on three sides (the side to the public being unoccupied). In the center was Zinoviev and around him were dignitaries of one kind and another. It seems sacrilege to say it but the scene recalled to me an Italian picture of the Last Supper. The programme opened by the playing of the International during which we all stood up. It was not well played, it was not sung at all, and it dragged. When I heard it in Moscow it was really stirring. When that was over Zinoviev stood up to make his report on the IX Session of the All-Russian Soviet just ended at Moscow. His voice is squeaky and tiresome, but this

---

[36]Herschel Walker of the ARA.

was just at first; as he went along he became quite eloquent and I listened to him with much interest.

He began with a eulogy of Korolenko,[37] the great Russian writer, who died a few days ago, and announced that a street and a university would be named after him. When he buried him and had placed a wreath on his tomb he proceeded with the result of the IX Session. I will report only on the things which may interest you most.

First as to the hunger. He said that when the world learned of the Russian famine some of the capitalistic governments thought that it was the opportunity they needed to crush the soviets. Small military bands from here and there began to invade the territory; some of the powers proposed to send in committees to investigate and to spy but nothing came of that. Other capitalistic powers (U.S.?) saw in it a chance to develop commerce and proposed to help. The Soviet government accepted the offer for it regarded it as a great moral victory on its part that the capitalists made such an offer. (Who is playing politics now?) More recently the American government through Hoover proposed that (please note the order of the procedure) the Soviet government should spend ten million dollars in America purchasing food for the famine region. In addition the American government proposed to spend twenty million more for the same purpose. This offer was made while the Soviet was in session (intimating that our Congress planned it as a Soviet greeting for the occasion) and the offer was accepted.

He then went on to say that the year 1921 will be memorable in history because in that year in capitalistic countries grain was being burned as fuel (Soviet papers had it announced some time ago that in the U.S. the farmers were using grain as fuel), while millions of the Russian proletariat are dying of hunger. It is the crumbs that the bourgeois give to the proletariat. There was not a word of gratitude and appreciation, nothing to show that we did it out of purely human kindness, nothing like that. No matter what we do we are nothing more than capitalists who are trying to crush the life out of the proletariat.

He then went on to talk of the Che-Ka, that is the Extraordinary Tribunal. He said that the Soviet is very eager to establish international trade and international diplomatic relations and therefore it is necessary to show them that they have nothing to fear in Russia. With that in view the power of the Che-Ka is to be limited and its judicial power taken from it.[38]

---

[37]Vladimir Galaktionovich Korolenko (1853–1921): famous Russian writer, widely considered to be the conscience of the radical intelligentsia.

[38]The Cheka was abolished on February 6, 1922, at which time the State Political

On the program of the IX Session there was to be an evening devoted to International Relations. But it was not discussed because he said there was little to be said on the subject. It was hardly worth while to waste time to discuss whether the capitalistic powers would or would not recognize the government of the soldiers, peasants and workingmen. As a matter of fact they have already recognized us by their acts, by their trade relations, so the diplomatic papers did not matter. After all, we are here and we have been here for five years. The Soviet government (meaning the ministry) has been in office longer than any other European government and that is enough to prove its strength. Let the bourgeois recognize us or not; it is a matter of indifference to us.

At the session of the Soviet in Moscow, he went on to say, little was said about World Revolution. Facts, however, speak louder than words. While we were in session we heard that revolutions had broken out in India and in Egypt and in other places. History works for us.

We learned at the Session that the Japanese seized Khabarovsk. By a strange coincidence there was present at the Session a Japanese delegate, an old worker in the cause of the proletariat, and he said that such a deed made him ashamed that he was a Japanese. From this, you see, tovarishchi, that the best people the world over are on our side and our side is the best side.

The bourgeois, when they attack us, say that they do so because we are not democratic and so on. Why did Japan attack the Far Eastern Republic? It is democratic according to the understanding of the capitalists and yet they do not leave it alone. It merely shows the hypocrisy of the whole system.

This in substance is the speech which I heard in the tsar's loge as it was delivered by the Communist Zinoviev. It will help you to understand their point of view, at least the point of view they are trying to spread.

After his speech came the musical concert. I am afraid you may think that I am trying to find fault, but I really am not. You have heard and I have heard how much the Revolution has done to spread culture among the masses. If it has, and it probably has, it does not yet show itself. In the first place the audience does not know how to behave. Some of the men have their hats and coats on and others off, some read the papers, some talk, and others come and go. The orchestra played well but the members behaved badly, they lounged, they talked and distracted attention. It was a mixed

---

Administration, known as the *Gosudarstvennoe politicheskoe upravlenie* (GPU), took over its police functions and to a great extent its staff and premises. Golder generally followed the local practice, continuing to use the word *Cheka* for the state police.

program, good music and light stuff. The latter appealed much more and I concluded that it was a vaudeville audience rather than an opera crowd.

The first time I was in this opera house was early in 1914, that is, before the war. One of the Russian semi-oriental ballets was played and to the color of the staging and the soft oriental music was added the brilliance of the audience, the military uniforms, the gorgeously dressed women in their beautiful evening gowns displaying beautiful necks and arms. The whole scene was a page from the Arabian nights and I remember being greatly moved by it all. Now there was below me in the audience short haired women and long nosed men, dressed in proletariat clothes and thinking how much superior they are to the rest of the world. I am afraid I am becoming pessimistic and sour and that is not a good way to start the new year.

Your dam—d bourgeois friend

January 2

Went to the ballet last night and found quite a different audience from the night before. This one was very much bourgeois, many were well dressed, some wearing evening clothes. It looked just a bit like old times. I questioned those near me how these people in the audience found the means of dressing so well and they answered "speculation." The ballet was fairly good.

Looked up today some people whom I used to know before the Revolution and found them in rags, broken in spirit and in health. One of the archivists whom I ran across grabbed my hands and almost went down on his knees begging my pardon. I looked on with wonder not knowing what he had done to me. When he had quieted down he told me that in 1917 when I had worked in the archives he had failed to give me two documents by mistake. Soon after I left he found them and they have been on his conscience ever since.

In the course of the day I learned that some time ago Krassin[39] while in London offered to English companies certain concessions. Before accepting them they asked permission to send agents on the spot to examine the conditions. Soon after reaching Russia they were arrested by the Che-Ka. When Krassin heard of this he sent his man to Moscow to tell the government that if the Che-Ka were like that he was through and coming home. This explains the new policy towards the Che-Ka.

---

[39]Leonid Borisovich Krassin (1870–1926). Old Bolshevik, Soviet diplomat, and people's commissar of foreign trade.

Took an old man, a friend of former days, to the Dom iskusstva (Home of Art) to dine. The artists of the city gather there. Formerly it was the home of a wealthy merchant. The dining room is nicely fixed up and the meals good and, from the American point of view, cheap. Dinner for two, consisting of a plate of soup, meat and potatoes, dessert and tea, costs 68,000 rubles, or the equivalent according to the present rate of exchange, of about fifty cents.

★ ★ ★

Petrograd, January 4, 1922

Dear Lutz:

The courier leaves here tomorrow for Moscow and will take with him this letter where it will rest a week and then start for Riga and sometime in February will reach you.

I should like to say a word about our prospects here. There is a Revolutionary Museum here and I have made contacts with it. The men in charge have promised me a large and complete list of the revolutionary papers for 1917–18, which will supplement my collection of 1919–22 papers that I have secured in Moscow. They promise and have already selected a very large collection of posters and this will supplement the collection made in Moscow. Our poster collection of the revolution will be large and unique. The government printing office has promised one or two copies of each of its publications that still remain. Another government publishing house is going to give me carte blanche to its stacks tomorrow.

The Academy of Sciences and other learned bodies where I am a bit known offer me everything they have. Among the learned circles I am fairly well known and just this week there has come out a review of the Guide to the Russian Archives which was published in 1917. It happens to be favorable and it has given me quite a boost.[40] I also discovered that an article that I wrote for a publishing house in 1917 was translated into Russian and published as a pamphlet and has had quite a success.[41] All these things help. Books are cheap here, much cheaper than in Moscow, and I shall supplement our wants by purchase for I receive most of the government things for a very small price or for nothing. I have promised the Revolutionary

[40]Golder may be referring to the review by A. N. Makarov in the journal *Dela i dni (Works and days)*, no. 1 (1920): 206–12, whose inaugural issue seems to have appeared well after its official date of publication.

[41]*Svobodnaia shkola v svobodnoi strane (Free education in a free country)* (Petrograd, 1917).

Museum that we would send them what things have appeared in America on the Russian Revolution. Please collect your duplicates. Next week I will write more. How long my stay will be in Petrograd I can not now say. On one thing I have made up my mind—the books go with me out of Russia and I shall remain until they are out.

Enclosed you will please find additional archive material on various phases of the revolution. More next week.

As ever,

★ ★ ★

Petrograd, January 8, 1922

Dear Lutz:

I run around so much every day and shift so much from one thing to another that I find it difficult to keep a diary, but in the course of the day I pick up quite a few bits of interesting news, some of which I am going to unload on you.

You may be astonished to know that the Professors of Modern History have not yet read the treaty of Versailles or any of the other treaties that followed, that they have very little idea of what has been published or what is going on and no way of finding out. Queerly enough, this information and these books are in Moscow and Petrograd but for the use of the elect only, and the elect do not care to use them. To many people here I seem to be a man from Mars and they take off enough time from bread hunting to ask all kinds of questions which are old stories to us. For the little that I'd do for them they repay me ten fold by telling me of what is going on here, and which to them seems common place.

It is generally agreed that the worst years for Petrograd and Moscow were 1919 and 1920. Then people died of hunger in the streets. Because people can buy and sell now makes living more possible. During the lean years stores were closed and trading was prohibited. At the same time the government did not ration out enough food to keep body and soul together. The streets were not lighted, the houses were not warmed, the electric lights did not burn. It became necessary for the family to crowd into one room and sleep as close together as possible to keep warm. Abe Lincoln is not the only one who used pine knots, but he had plenty of them while these people had splinters only. When it became dark some member of the family would sneak out of the house with some valuable hidden about his person in search of a speculator or a soldier to exchange food with. The time of his absence dragged unmercifully, for the family did not know whether he succeeded in his mission or was captured together with the speculator and dragged into prison.

Those prisons! The prisoners were fed on thin soup and the members of the prisoner's family had to bring food to him. Sometimes the hunger became so great that people came out to the accustomed places to trade. Then the police swooped down upon them, took their things away, which they never saw again, and locked up those who could not escape. But worst of all were the night searches. For weeks at a time families went to bed with their clothes on and laid there hourly expecting the dreaded knock and search. Dirty soldiers would turn things upside down in search of valuables and incriminating papers, a letter from abroad, a bit of newspaper was enough to put you up against the wall and bang, out went the soul through a little bullet hole. Yet, all the terrors have not been able to drag out all the jewels and valuables and today when there is free trade there are all kinds of precious stones on the market.

This last week has been soviet week—all the theatres have been open for soviet people only and tonight is the grand finale—a masquerade ball. I have been invited to go but I have refused and I know that some of the royal and court pearls and diamonds will adorn the beautiful necks of the Red Rich. There is a new rich, less cultured than the old, less gentlemanly, less White, but it is here and that is the new bourgeois of Russia. The new rich have made their money by speculating, by robbing, and now they are investing it in more jewels and valuables for they realize that these things have a standard value, while the paper stuff has none. People pay high prices for everything, even books. The old prewar editions are scarce, so many have been used for fuel and cigarette paper, and they will soon command high prices. Therefore the Red rich are buying them for speculation. Let them do their worst in so far as we are concerned; we are provided for.

I spoke to you of the advantages of free trade but I ought to tell something of the other side of the story. During the period of nationalization, all those who worked for the government, and nearly every one did, were not obliged to pay rent, or light if they had it, or car fare if they could get in. Now the same people, on the theory that they are receiving salaries, are obliged to pay house rent, etc. A friend of mine, a professor, tells me that he lectures all day on all kinds of subjects and in all kinds of places and for his work he receives 108,000 rubles, the equivalent of about a dollar a month, but he does not even receive that regularly. His November salary is yet unpaid. The porter of his house gets 400,000 rubles a month. The professor receives, or rather is supposed to receive, a small paiok of food which is quite inadequate to feed his wife and four children.

Very few homes in Petrograd have their front doors open and since coming here I have been climbing back stairs. When you stop and think that these stairs are used for chopping wood, for sweeping dirt into them, and that they are not lighted, you can imagine their condition. It has all the back stairs smells except one—of the cat—during the lean years poor pussy was made into sausage. People use the back stairs because they live in one kitchen to keep warm and because it reduces the opportunities for stealing. Stealing, stealing, everybody is stealing in one form or another. The people here who have lived through the lean years of 1919 and 1920 divide them into periods: the period of millet, the period of frozen potatoes, the period of salt herring, all depending on the principal food of that time. Bad as conditions are now, and they are very bad, they are so much better than they were, that people look back to those days and talk about them now with, shall I say, tears of joy that they are passed. How horrible!

The sufferings of these years are beginning to tell on the physical and mental health of the inhabitants. The younger people are suffering from tuberculosis and the older from heart trouble and nervous break down. I have been told that in former days the judges and military officers who had to condemn people to death, or Siberia, sooner or later broke down mentally. The same phenomenon is taking place now among the Bolsheviki, especially among the women. The theory is, as you know, that the Revolution demands sacrifices, that the bourgeois and counterrevolutionists are serpents that must be destroyed, and therefore many of the Bolsheviks have hardened their hearts to the suffering. I have heard of noble and misguided women who have asked for the hardest tasks, dodging nothing and doing everything, but in the end the strain was too much and ended in an asylum. They could not remain indifferent to the suffering of these poor helpless bourgeois. There is a cry all over the land to let up for God's sake, let up. Human nature can bear it no longer. The Bolsheviki themselves are tired of all the bloodshed and even the most bloody are satisfied. There is no more enthusiasm for communism. Don't you see how the French Revolution is repeating itself? The persecutions are ceasing gradually but the old fear is still on. Since coming here I have been trying to find the sister of a Russian lady in London but have not been able to see her. The poor woman fears that the Bolos are after her and she is like a hunted animal trying to hide her trail.

A moment ago I said something about the festivities that are going on, of the masquerade balls, and of the champagne suppers. All this is merely additional evidence of the reaction from the horror of the year just passed. As to the Che-Ka, I have already told you what the head of that organization told a friend of mine: the Che-Ka is going to be "Scotland-Yardized" and the first steps have already been taken. It was recently published in the papers that a person arrested has the right to know within two days the reason of his arrest and within two weeks to demand a trial. This sounds well but much water will be spilt before it will have practical value. Nevertheless it is a point gained. As Zinoviev said in his speech Russia must have foreign capital and foreign relations and it can not have them until foreigners have more confidence in the Russian government. The poor Bolos are up against it. They have used up their resources, their gold, their propaganda, their tricks; they can no longer play off one foreign power against the other. They can not even appeal to the proletariat to rise and shake off the yoke of the capitalists, for they themselves are now putting on that coat.

Lenin, we hear, has been invited to an economic conference at Genoa.[42] You may be interested to know the reaction of some of the Russians. They tell me that Lenin will not go because he refuses to sit at the same table with bourgeois. They tell me also that the reason for Chicherin's desire to have the conference at London was to have a bigger field for propaganda. If I remember correctly, I told you something of the counter-claims which the Soviet is preparing for the time when the question of the debts comes up. Today I have been informed by good authority that one of the counter-claims is based on the failure of the allies to give Constantinople to Russia as promised.

Today I had a rather interesting experience. I called at a home where the family is composed of one old lady and two bachelor ladies of an uncertain age. All three were dames de la cour. The old lady could not walk so she sat in her chair dressed in the few bits of finery left over and which will soon have to be sold for food. She told me of the court and recalled the fact that she once danced with our minister Cassius Clay. Now Cassius was here in the Civil War period. But the event in her life which she recalled with most pleasure was one day when she was at court and the Empress introduced her to the Emperor, who in the course of the afternoon talked to her twice. When he asked her about her family, she replied, "My ancestors served your ancestors." This pleased him so much that he sent her a telegram the following day thanking her for her loyalty to the throne and this telegram she has kept and is going to have it buried with her. "Il était si gentil, mon empereur."

While she was relating her great happiness other dames de la cour entered and talked of old days and occasionally of the new. One good lady was so proud that she had never worked for the Bolsheviki, that was still left to her, and her wish and prayer is that she may die rather than be obliged to do so. As I sat there among these dowagers one scene after

---

[42]The Genoa Conference of European powers took place from April 10 to May 19, 1922; the U. S. government was not an official participant.

another of the French Revolution and Restoration came to me and I understood history and felt it as never before. The room was cold and dark, we sat with our coats and overshoes on us, most of them were hungry and some of them were selling their last bits of the old regime, but we forgot all that. They were living through happiest moments and for once they forgot their troubles and thought of mon empereur, mon empereur, and once again we took the oath of loyalty and vowed never, never to compromise with the revolution.

Russia is divided in two camps, "we" and "they." "They" are few in number but in power are strong, but "we" are going to have our day. Between the Bolsheviki and others there is no social intercourse, no relations of one kind and another, no more than there is between negroes and whites in the South. The only difference is that there one calls the other "nigger." Before I leave this subject let me return once more to my dear old ladies whom I am going to see again Sunday. They were greatly worried over one thing. In the French Revolution the nobility stood by the king to the last, while in Russia the nobility gave up without making a great struggle. Of course, we talked French, any other language would have been quite improper.

In speaking of the empereur let me tell you that I saw a day or two ago a copy of his diary which he kept during the war (and which I hope to secure for our collection). It is of great interest because it is so uninteresting. At a time when the world was in turmoil he merely notes in his journal the state of the weather, whether it was too warm to be out in the sun, the exact hour and minute when this one or that one came to see him, and usually winds up the day's work with a phrase like "and in the evening I pasted post cards in the albums," or "I pasted more cards in the album," or "after Grigorii [Rasputin] left I played dominoes." Il était si gentil, il était si bon enfant, but I would not deprive my dowagers of their delights. Poor old souls. How my heart aches for them. They told me of their hardships and disappointments. How they had looked for deliverance to Kolchak, Denikin, Iudenich, Wrangel,[43] and how one by one their hopes like their jewels went. Finally they came to the conclusion that Russia could be saved only by an uprising from within. Great was their joy when they heard the guns of Kronstadt boom. They crawled out from their dark corners and went out into the street, and when they passed one of their own kind they passed a smile of understanding between them, and when they met in private they embraced. But alas! nothing came of that. "La

---

[43]Anton Ivanovich Denikin (1872–1947), Nikolai Nikolaevich Iudenich (1862–1933), and Petr Nikolaevich Wrangel (1878–1928) were all White Army leaders during the Russian Civil War.

Russie est morte, il ne reste que mourir avec le télégramme de l'empereur aux mains." God bless them.

★ ★ ★

Petrograd, January 10, 1922

Dear Lutz:

I have at last found the woman I have been looking for and she has had a most interesting and pitiful story to tell. During the last four years she has lost her father, mother, husband, one child and another child that has disappeared. Here is the story of her father.

The old man had been a general in the army but the revolutionists compelled him to take off his shoulder straps, but, like other officers, he was permitted to wear his coat. He was old and deaf and one day as he was walking along the street two soldiers bumped into him and knocked him so that he hurt his foot. Blood poison set in and killed him. For ten days the body was kept because no one could be persuaded to bury him because he was a general. Finally enough people were bribed to sell a plot of land. The next problem was to buy a coffin and in the end a box had to be used. A woman found an old plug and a cart and on this the box was loaded and the woman led the horse while the mother followed through the rain and sleet of the late fall to the cemetery. There the grave diggers struck because they had no bread and some one had to go and secure food for them and then they lowered the coffin and covered it.

This left the old lady and the daughter, the latter acted as nurse in a hospital. The mother was all alone. One day a man came to her and asked if she had diamonds to sell. She replied that she did not because there was a law against buying and selling. The man left threatening to get even with her. Later in the day two men came to the hungry woman and offered to trade flour and other eatables for diamonds. The poor old lady was so hungry that she consented. The two men went in search of the food and returned with the man who had been there in the morning and between them they arrested the woman for "speculating," searched the house and secured whatever valuables they could lay their hands on. The old lady remained in prison and then was released.

When she came out she was deathly scared of selling anything and yet she was very hungry. Another man came to her and offered to give her some money. In an evil moment she accepted and from that time on he had her make over and hand over such lands and movables as she had. The old lady's health began to fail and she decided to make one grand effort to escape. She offered an Esthonian? sailor some jewels to marry her and take her out of the country. The sailor was a rough customer and kept his bargain as far as marrying the woman was concerned. He packed her into a cattle car with a lot of other human beings and started with her for Reval. There she died.

The woman I saw today was left alone. When she saw how her mother was treated she went back to her room and took poison but she did not have enough to kill her. She recovered only to catch cold on her lungs and now her lungs are in very bad order. The fear of being arrested haunts her and she lives in hiding and I hear it is beginning to affect her mind. She has no money but a lot of valuables and that frightens her. At different times she went to the Bolsheviks and told them all about her ancestors and their reactionary deeds in the hope that they would shoot her but they refused. She now desires to become a nun and build a convent. What she really needs is food, rest and peace of mind. It is a most pitiful story. The woman is only 32, accomplished, from one of the most aristocratic families in Russia. She has served as a Red Cross nurse during the war, loves her country, and now she is hunted, or rather haunted. If she is not taken from here soon she will go mad. One feels so helpless and so discouraged and wishes that he were dead.

★ ★ ★

Diary entry: January 13, 1922. Petrograd.

Had as visitors tonight A.N.B. and S.M.Z.[44] They agreed: that the revolution began when Miliukov and other members of the Duma made their famous speeches in the Duma, when Rasputin was killed by Yusupov and the Grand Duke; that the army was demoralized before the Revolution and Prikaz No. 1;[45] that England was backing the liberals in their warlike and, if necessary, anti-dynastic attitude; that the coalition government was a mistake; that the Kadets should have left the ministry when Miliukov quit; that Rasputin had a good deal of ability and that like a common peasant he felt that the soldier did not want any more war; that the land question was behind the revolution.

In regard to Gorky. It seems that Gorky regarded himself as the

---

[44]The first is Aleksandr Nikolaevich Benois (Benua) (1870–1960), a Russian painter, illustrator, theatrical designer, and leading art historian and critic.

[45]Order No. 1 was issued by the Petrograd soviet on March 1/14, 1917. Among other things it declared that the Russian army should obey only those orders of the Provisional Government that did not contradict those of the soviet.

successor of Tolstoy, as the embodiment of Russian art and culture; that he helped to a certain extent the intelligentsiia, but he was always coarse and domineering and turned people against him; that he played a double role, siding at times with the Bolos and other times against them without there being any principle involved. The intelligentsiia does not feel any gratitude towards him, but feel that he made a funny, or rather a pathetic, figure as he tried to wear Tolstoy's boots.

★ ★ ★

Petrograd, January 15, 1922

Dear Lutz:

It is almost midnight and before retiring I am going to tell you something of my activities during the last twenty four hours.

Last evening I went to return a call on a well known scientist who has made some studies in radium and he thinks he has made some great discoveries, and probably has. If his discoveries are what he thinks they are, they are great weapons for destruction and he is greatly troubled as to whether as a man and a lover of his kind he ought to make his discoveries known. The last war has shown how science was used to ruin mankind, so that the dear old man is in great trouble. He sees wonderful possibilities but he says that so long as scientists have so little to say in matters of government it behooves them to keep their secrets to themselves and not to hand them over to irresponsible persons. His remedy is to have the government in the hands of learned men who will use science for the uplifting and not for the destruction of mankind. I am "agin" any clique of any kind. We have now in Russia God's chosen people and they have made a mess of it.

This morning I left the house early and went to service in St. Isaac's Cathedral. When I was there years ago, 1917, it had thousands of worshippers, today it had a mere handful. The same two classes were present as then, the common peasant and the nobility, but since that time they have changed places, the nobility keeps in the background to hide its old clothes and torn shoes. Since the revolution women have entered the church choir in larger numbers than before and their voices are not very suitable for the Russian church music and it rather repelled. The whole service was rather pitiful and I felt so sorry for Russia. Thinking that perhaps in the other churches conditions are different I walked over to the Kazan Cathedral, but there I saw the same pitiful conditions and I did not remain long.

I continued my way to call on the lady about whom I wrote you last week who has lost her parents and her children and her worthless husband. She had been in church for many hours but reached home a few minutes after I reached her cold room which had not been heated this cold winter. A letter was on the table and she asked me to excuse her while she read it. It was from a woman who had robbed the woman on whom I was calling of all her jewels. In this letter the woman asked for pardon and forgiveness and on this ground: she had a lover who is twenty years younger than herself who has a young woman as a mistress, therefore the old mistress had to steal to give her lover money to support his young mistress. Not bad. After my lady friend finished the letter she stood for a moment debating the question, "Shall I forgive her? Yes, I will forgive her because she has confessed and because I know when I was married my husband was in love with another woman and I had to give him money to buy her presents. Yes, I will forgive her. If I do not and have her arrested, they will arrest me too and the police will come and search my house and take from me what little I have left. Yes, I will forgive her." Saying this she crossed herself and thanked God that she had one worry less.

I took this once rich, now poor woman to lunch and she insisted on going to the place where she usually eats and where are gathered all odds and ends of humanity. We had lunch for two which consisted of big plates of soup followed by a plate of chopped up meat and two vegetables and black bread. Later we had tea. The two lunches cost 50,000 rubles or something like 25 cents. There was plenty of food and I have not felt any evil effects. What puzzles me is this. At the ARA mess we pay from twenty five to fifty cents for a pound of meat, sugar in the city costs about seventy cents a pound, flour is very expensive and everything else is in proportion. How then can the restaurants afford to put up such a meal for such a price? I can not answer the question.

After luncheon I went to see a professor friend of mine who had nothing very cheering to relate. "Let the end come as soon as it will. I have nothing more to live for. Some day Russia may be a happier place to live in, today death is preferable."

From him I went to see my dowagers and we talked of royalty and if I continue making my calls at this house I will be able to tell you the genealogy of every royal house, naming the "fils naturel" as well as the other members. I must not forget to tell you that the other morning I had a call from a "fils naturel d'Alexandre III." I did not know whether to pity him or to congratulate him when I thought of the fils (unnaturel) of the same tsar.

Guess where I went from there? To the Hotel Astoria, the headquarters of the Bolos. So far as I know it is the only building in the city that still has an elevator, the rooms are still nicely furnished, and the accommodations are better than any other building in the city. The Bolos are better housed than my bourgeois friends. I went there to call on an old lady Bolo, an old war horse, to hear something of Bolshevism.

. . . From my Bolo lady I marched straight to the opera house to see the ballet. After the first part the director or assistant director came into our box, there were three of us Americans there, to invite us behind the scenes and to offer us any other honor or courtesy in his power. I was in the same opera house just eight years ago and then it was the grand dukes, the young military officers of noble birth who were invited behind the scenes to chuckle the girls under the chins, to take them out to champagne suppers, and today three plebeian Americans of no importance at home but looming up big here because they are feeding hungry people have the place of honor. I pointed out to our men that we could not accept these honors without obligating ourselves very deeply and young America spoke up: "Then we will invite the girls home and give them a square [meal]." I am sure that you will see with me the comedy and the tragedy of the whole thing.

The opera house was cold but full of all kinds of people (and an unusually large number of children), mostly Bolos and the red rich speculators. In this connection let me call your attention to the hatred that is spreading among the Russians against the Jews. You probably know that in northern Russia there was comparatively little anti-semitism but now it is smouldering and when it breaks out there will be rivers of Jewish blood flowing. It is their active part in the government that is bringing down the wrath on them.[46]

Here endeth my bloody page. Monday morning 1 A.M.

Diary entry: January 19, 1922. Petrograd.

Alexander N. Benois, the artist, and his wife invited us to the Malyi Theatre to see Molière's "Les Précieuses Ridicules" and "Le Médecin

---

[46]The number of Jews in the ranks of the Bolshevik party and in the Soviet government was disproportionately high, notably among the party's top leadership (Trotsky, Zinoviev, and Kamenev were Jews) and the Cheka. This fed the traditionally strong anti-Semitic sentiment among the people of Russia, many of whom blamed the revolution (or its unfortunate outcome) on the Jews. There was a general tendency even among the most sophisticated Russians to exaggerate both the actual number of Bolshevik Jews (Lenin, a non-Jew, was sometimes counted among them) and the significance of their presence (e.g., as the inspiration for the Bolshevik party's stated internationalism). See Leonard Schapiro, "The Role of the Jews in the Russian Revolutionary Movement," *Slavonic and East European Review* 40, no. 24 (1961): 148–67.

Malgré Lui." One of the reasons why the invitation came for this evening was because Benois's son did the scenic decorations and be it said to his credit that he did them well and quite in harmony with the play. Whenever before I had the opportunity to see Molière it was always in Paris and I was interested to see how the Russians did it. After seeing it I have almost come to the conclusion that Molière is probably played in the same style everywhere. It reminded me very much of the Comédie Française. The acting was very good and a credit to the Russian stage. Our hosts were most charming and introduced us to the principal actors who were very gracious. We had the loge of honor and have been invited to come next Tuesday to the "The Merchant of Venice."

I raised the question with the actors how they like playing for a proletariat audience. Those I talked with said that they were not very enthusiastic, but taking it all in all the proletariats are no worse than the bourgeois audiences before the war who came not for the sake of the play but for the purpose of showing off. One actress said that at times she even preferred the proletariats because of their naiveté and the pleasure they showed at simple things. The audience tonight was a trade union audience— it was their night. There were also many soldiers. They enjoyed the funny parts and it should be said to the credit of the Soviets that they have given the masses a taste for good things and they have raised their ideals of art which will survive them. Unfortunately the day of the proletariat in Russia is on the wane. Nearly every day some of the privileges which he has enjoyed until now are being taken from him and he will soon return to his humble position which is a pity. It is going from one extreme to another, just like the audiences of former days and today.

During the entreacts Benois took us to one of the studios, the director's, where tea was served. People of literary and artistic distinction were called in to meet us and we were treated like Grand Dukes or persons of note, "our friends from America." There is great interest in America and so many people are learning English who formerly studied French or German.

Visited Dom uchenykh,[47] the central place for the scholars of Petrograd. It was filled by men, women, children and servants waiting in line for their turn to receive the akademicheskii paiok, the food ration which the government hands out to the scholars. Occasionally it gives out clothing but most of that comes from foreign contributions. Recently the Czecho-Slovaks brought shoes and other things which are being distributed and I was shown one warm shawl that came from them. In the building of the Dom

---

[47]House of Scholars.

uchenykh, formerly a palace of one of the Grand Dukes, there is also a reading room and a tea room which serves a glass of tea and a bite of bread for a reasonable sum. The scholars are afraid that their paiok may soon come to an end and should this happen they do not know where to turn. Just now every department of the government is reducing its forces to one fourth and even less of its personnel and those thrown out are literally thrown out on the street and into the cold for there is no other work to do, for private industry does not yet exist.

January 21

The man who translated Hoover's telegrams to Gorky[48] and wrote the replies to them told me today that when the Bolos published these despatches they changed them to make them read as if Hoover had telegraphed to the Soviet government. This matter was called to Kamenev's attention at a meeting where my informant was present and Kamenev replied, "There must be some misunderstanding," and dropped the matter.

Sunday Night

I went to the ballet and saw there one of the finest displays of parvenueism that I have ever seen. In the box next to us were well known speculators who are making their money in buying diamonds and other precious things from the starving White bourgeois and selling them at very high prices, as well as speculating in sugar and other necessities of life. The lady in the box was dressed in costly raiment and had on very precious jewels. But the crowning evidence of the newly acquired wealth was this. They displayed a beautiful box of delicious sweets and in the presence of the audience they peeled a very fragrant orange (oranges are as scarce in Petrograd as bananas in the Arctic circle; this is the first one I have seen here) which they put on the top of the box so that every body could see it and then they left it all in sight of the audience while they went out. Can you beat that? When the ballet was over and I remained for a moment to cheer I noticed that they had left part of the sweets in the box as if it were something which was of no value. This beats the old White rich. Hurrah for the Red rich!

The audience was very ordinary and among those present there were one or two in frock coats. A lady with whom I was talking told me that

[48]There was only one telegram from Hoover to Gorky, that of July 23, 1921, responding to Gorky's published appeal to Europe and America for famine relief.

during the hard times many men sold the trousers of their dress suits to the sailors who wore them as part of their uniform, but they could not dispose of their frock coats. As a result, many men in the city have frock coats but have no trousers to go with them.

January 24

Went to the Little [Malyi] Theatre on the Fontanka to see "The Merchant of Venice," which was fairly well done, not as well as Molière. I learned one or two interesting things. Since the Revolution, the Hermitage and other art museums have accepted precious and artistic things for safe keeping which they promised to return when the owner claimed them. Today an order was received that such things should not be returned to their owners, that all silver in the Yusupov Palace should be brought to the Hermitage, and that Trotsky has been put at the head of a commission to take stock of these precious things. All these things indicate that there is a movement on foot to sell some of the art things in order to realize some money. This threat has been in the air for some time and it is likely to be carried out. The fact that Trotsky has been put at the head looks bad, for whenever he is put in charge it means that an important piece of work has to be done and that he is the one to do it.

★ ★ ★

Moscow, January 30, 1922

My dear Professor Adams:

I returned here today and am making ready to leave tomorrow. Before this letter comes to your hand a telegram will have informed you that Dr. Hutchinson and I have departed for the Caucasus, Armenia and way stations. Last week I received urgent telegrams from Colonel Haskell and Professor Hutchinson that I should go on a special mission with the latter. It is in connection with the Congressional appropriation and it is Hoover's special request that certain investigations take place, and the work falls on the two of us because there seems to be no one else to do it. I agreed to do it because the cause demanded it; the reputation of the ARA, Hoover and America are deeply involved in what is going on in Russia. I consented also because the work of the Russian collection is practically finished; the books (about 50 boxes) are packed. I had, of course, the choice, but I did not feel justified in refusing. I wish this were the last time and when I return I will be free to leave. I hope that you have had a conference with President Wilbur and Mr. Hoover on this subject as you intimated in your letter of

December 23 that you might have. My plan is still to come back in time for the fall teaching. In the course of the summer I will visit the countries that still need to be worked and get things started and if necessary return a year later and finish up in the course of a summer.

Now with regard to the Russian collection. It is a good one and I am pleased with it. We have some of the best things that have appeared in Russia since 1914 and we have practically the only collection of its kind in America. Professor Coolidge has not touched this period though he has bought much on the period preceding the war. For that period we have also the more important things, in good condition, and some in most artistic bindings, and for a very reasonable price. My Petrograd visit was quite successful for I had the benefit of the exchange and a cheap market. Books that cost fifty and sixty dollars before the war I bought for a dollar or two. I bought on my own account, if the University does not want it, a splendid collection in fine bindings of numismatica for five English pounds. I had given me nearly complete sets of all the revolutionary papers from 1917 and 1918 and in Moscow I was given the period following. I have promised to buy a collection of newspapers for the periods 1913–1917 which will complete our newspaper files for Russia. My numerous friends in Petrograd in the archives loaded me down with sets of publications until I was ashamed to take them, but I took. I should like to tell you something about the manuscripts that were given me but it is not wise. I am telling you all this not to praise my work, for I have made many mistakes, but to explain what we have for it will please you. On this trip I will be in a position to pick up a number of things which never reached me last year and a number of new things.

Professor Hutchinson assures me that we will be back in a month but I doubt it. I doubt very much whether I will be able to leave Russia before the end of March. The problem of getting the books out is still before me but I am not anticipating great trouble, though it may not be easy sailing because somebody will want to play politics. I will not leave without them and I shall be so happy when I get them on board the ship and happier still when I learn that they have reached you in good condition.

Professor Coolidge is making ready to leave in a month. Quinn[49] is here. The situation in Russia is not improving. The hunger area is spreading and the big cities including Petrograd and Moscow are threatened. In October the price of bread was 4000 a pound and today it is six times that amount and going up daily. At the same time, thousands of people are discharged from the government shops and no other places are open to

---

[49]Cyril J. C. Quinn: assistant director of the ARA Russia mission.

them. The transportation system is unable to stand up under the transportation and I wonder how in the world the food supplies which our [ARA] friends in New York are hurrying here are going to be handled. Typhus is raging and some of our ARA men are caught. I have managed to keep in condition and I trust to continue to do so, but I am tired and without clothes. I have had the same suit of clothes on me ever since September and the wind is beginning to find openings, my overcoat is a second hand chauffeur's coat that the American Red Cross in Riga gave me, and my fur cap is the kind the muzhiks wear. It has advantages for I look quite like a Bolo and the highwaymen let me pass.

I am living through a tremendously interesting period, which I am just beginning to understand a bit. What I need now is a little rest and a little time for thinking. Will it ever come?

It is getting to be very late and my mind does not work clearly any more. I need some sleep. Thereby hangs a story. The Soviet government is obliged to provide the ARA men with the best traveling accommodation possible. It promised a coupé in the Wagon Lit which it runs between Petrograd and Moscow. On the appointed day, Saturday, it notified us that it could not give us the coupé because all the important Bolos in Petrograd had to go to Moscow to attend the meeting in connection with the Genoa Conference, but I was promised a nice clean comfortable coupé in another car. I agreed. When I reached the station and looked into the car I discovered that the coupé was occupied by several others and that I had merely a seat, and that in addition the coupé was dirty, cold, and unsanitary. I refused to go and returned to the office and made a fuss. The Soviet officials apologized and became at once active and assured me that I would surely have a coupé in the Wagon Lit on Sunday. They failed me again and at the last minute gave me a cold dirty coupé in another car. I had to reach here today and had no choice and passed a cold night in a cold car but I got here and I hope without having been bitten by a typhus carrier.

Three of the ARA men are lost. They departed for their destinations days ago and no word has been heard from them. Life in Russia is not dull. Oh, yes! I must not forget to tell you that the Moscow University professors are on strike because they have not received any pay for months. Aside from the schools for poets, for propagandists and such like, education is practically at a stand still in Russia.

With all good wishes,
Sincerely yours,

★ ★ ★

Moscow, February 1, 1922

Dear Lutz:

. . . Today brought forth interesting developments. As you remember we were to start yesterday for the Caucasus but were told that there was trouble on the line and our journey had to be postponed for a day. Today Professor Hutchinson and I started for the station in two cars, one carrying our baggage and supplies and the other ourselves. We were told that our car might be in one of three stations and that we should try one and then the other until we located it. We came to the Kazan station and learned that sure enough a train was due to depart for Rostov at the hour when we were to go. No one knew exactly where our car was but after some search we located it on a side track. We tried to get in but found it locked. However, we came across a man who told us that the car was damaged and would not go. Along side of it was another car in which Professor Coolidge and Quinn were to go and it too was damaged and could not leave tonight. The station agent whom we went to see told the same story. It seems that last night in moving the cars from one station to another some one conceived the idea of forcing the cars to run on two switches at the same time with the expected result.

After wasting an hour or two we returned to the office and reported. Col. Haskell was mad and he went to talk to the representative of the Soviet government and, though I did not hear his language, yet, from reports that have come to me, I dare say it was picturesque. The Colonel demanded a special engine and car to send us on our way until we caught up with the main train. He did not get it but received many apologies and promises that we surely would depart tomorrow. I remained in the building to see what might happen.

About five o'clock a telephone call came that car 1021 at Briansk station had been assigned to us for tomorrow. I hurried immediately to look at it. Imagine what I found: a car as large as the largest of our Pullmans (this for two people), no accommodations for cooking, but worst of all—this car had been used until within the last few days to transport typhus patients and since then had not been fumigated, had not been cleaned or aired and the atmosphere and odor were rather sickening. I left it and came back to report. The last word I have had until now (eight in the evening) is that we would have another car, not a typhus car, for tomorrow. Qui vivra verra.

Now to return to Quinn and Coolidge. When they learned from us that their car was unfit for travel they reported to headquarters with the result that another car has been assigned to them. They had not been down to see it but they are terribly scared it is a typhus car. About half an hour ago they started for the station and I should not be surprised if they report back within the next hour.

I am telling you these things to give you some idea of what is going on here, of the economic and transportation situation, as well as the moral atmosphere we have to live in.

A demain

P.S. An economist friend just came in to see me and reports that he and two of his colleagues have been asked to go to the Genoa Conference as experts and that they had declined because, he said, they decided that they would not be the tools of the Bolo politicians and that they would not furnish them with material to be used for propaganda.

In discussing with him the shocking situation in Russia where millions of people die of hunger while hundreds of others waste their money in riotous living, he said that many of those who have been borrowing millions from the government banks for the purpose of developing industries have invested large sums of the money in jewels and precious stones. With each day the value of the ruble goes down and consequently the selling price of jewels goes up. The difference between the selling and buying price is the real profit in paper money of the investor. It is from this source rather than from the development of the industries that the profit comes.

Last night an editor whom I have known for some time came to see me. He said that in 1918 the Soviet government had confiscated all his printing paper but left it in the printing shops. The new economic policy made it possible for him to buy it back from the government by borrowing from the government bank at the rate of 12% a month. The bank pays 3% a month on deposits.

★ ★ ★

Moscow, March 16, 1922

My dear Professor Adams:

. . . The paper money situation is comic and tragic. When I left Moscow six weeks ago one dollar bought nearly 300,000 rubles, by the time I came to Tiflis[50] it was worth about 900,000 and now it is sold for 1,800,000 on the curb and it is going fast, faster than the trains, for as you see I have not been able to keep up with it. The cost of everything is going up in proportion except wages and poor people have a hard time of it. A group of professors' wives, I heard last night, are baking bread and selling it to make ends meet.

I called on Professor Pokrovsky, the [deputy] Minister of Education,

---

[50]Tiflis (Tbilisi), the capital of Georgia.

and he was pleased to see me and asked me to have a conference with him. I called on him in regard to a permit for shipping out our books and he assured me that I could have it any time. The matter is now in the hands of the Soviet representative in the ARA and if he makes trouble I will carry it further. But I do not expect any trouble. Next week I will begin the shipping. Our number of boxes is passing fifty and I am not trying to keep it down. Everything is cheap except food. Today I bought a collection of Russian coins, very old, for 23 millions, which is the equivalent of about fifteen dollars. It is an unusual collection. All these fancies I buy for myself but the University may have them if it so desires.

The political situation is very much disturbed and the Bolos are having a little squabble among themselves regarding the course concessions have taken. A group of 22 Bolos not long ago came out strongly against Lenin because he was moving too far towards capitalism.[51] They were quieted, but I have noticed that since then Lenin has come out in a speech warning the European powers that the Soviet has come to the end of its concessions and that he would tell them so at the Genoa Conference. The question is, of course, whether there will be any conference. Here in Russia there are all kinds of war rumors and the question is who wants war? Among the more intelligent people with whom I talk there is a conviction that there is a strong element among the Bolos which favors foreign war. At the head of this group is Trotsky and the left wing is with him. The reason, so it is said, is that in case of victory they can undo all the concessions made by Lenin. Then again there is strong pressure to reduce the army and reduce the expense, but, say the Lefts, if we reduce the army which supports the Communists, what is going to become of us? What is true and what is false in all this I can not tell you. By the time this reaches you the situation may change. I hear from good authority that mobilization is going on.

For some reason or other it seems to be the official policy of the government to pull the feathers out of the American eagle, perhaps in the hope of making him say something. The ARA is praised by one man while the other questions and suspects its motives. Whenever a good word is said for the ARA the name of Nansen is mentioned along side and the ARA

---

[51]Golder refers to the appeal in February 1922 of twenty-two Bolshevik supporters of an internal party faction, the Workers' Opposition, addressed to the Executive Committee of the Communist International. The appeal, which became known as the Declaration of the Twenty-Two, criticized the increasingly nonproletarian composition of the party and its complete dominance over the trade unions. The Executive Committee voted to condemn the declaration. See Leonard Schapiro, *The Origin of the Communist Autocracy* (Cambridge, Mass., 1956) pp. 332–34.

looks cheap. The ARA is doing good work nevertheless and will manage the hunger and keep it down.

   . . . Quinn remembers you with great pleasure.

With all kinds of good wishes,
Cordially yours,

★ ★ ★

Diary entry: Sunday, March 19, 1922. Moscow.

   Went last night to the home of M[uravev] where there was the usual interesting crowd. During the last two or three years a number of popular legends have arisen in regard to the Emperor and Church. One of the latest is this. When the Bolos seized the Troitse-Sergieva Monastery,[52] a guard was put in for the night. About midnight the church bell overhead the guard rang. The guard jumped up and shouted up the belfry to ask who the scoundrel was. When no reply came one of the soldiers said, "I will go up and will throw that d—— fool down headforemost." He started up and a few minutes later he came down headfirst and dead. Another soldier gave a mighty oath and started up the ladder to cut the throat of the intruder and the second soldier also came down, and with his throat cut. A third and fourth did the same thing and each came down, having died in the manner by which he threatened to kill the ringer of the bell. At last one soldier said that he would go up without any arms or threats. Crossing himself he climbed up. When he came to where the bells were, he saw an old man with a white beard who asked him why he came and whether he too had murder in his heart. The soldier said he did not. Then the old man took him by the hand and led him to where he could look out and there he saw conflagration of cities and villages, from this scene he was led to another where war was going on, where one Russian massacred his brother, the third scene showed parched fields, hunger, pestilence, and the fourth scene human beings reverting to savagery and idolatry. After showing him all this the old man told the soldier that what he saw was the fate of Russia under the Bolsheviki and asked him to go and tell them to desist. The soldier climbed down and told his fellows what he saw.

   One of the men present, a prominent lawyer, who is now engaged in an important trial where many Bolos and others are accused of graft, made the charge that never was Russia so demoralized, never before were there so

---

[52]The Troitse-Sergieva Lavra is located some 70 kilometers north of Moscow in what today is the town of Zagorsk.

many men without principles, men who feared neither God nor the devil, who had no sense of honor, who did not hesitate to commit perjury or any other dishonest act, and for this condition of affairs he blamed the Bolos. Most of those present, though they agreed that moral conditions are bad, were yet unwilling to lay the blame on the Bolos, and pointed out that, at least as far as the peasants were concerned, demoralization had begun even under the old regime, that the old regime had prepared the soil for the evil seeds of the Bolos. Religion was already losing its hold in the time of the tsar and it failed to have much influence. On the other hand, they said, there is now a real awakening among the masses and some are doing some real thinking, many more than formerly, and great good is bound to come out of all this misery in the future.

The question of war and peace was discussed. Everyone had some bit of news to report, pointing to war preparations but no one could see a good reason for war, nevertheless all were apprehensive. All present commented on the seriousness of the economic situation and wondered how Russia would work out of the terrible conditions that awaited her.

★ ★ ★

Moscow, March 28, 1922

My dear Professor Adams:

. . . During the two months that I have been away from Petrograd the situation has grown worse. The fall of the ruble and the rise in prices is crushing many people and conditions are bad. Then in addition there is the government oppression. I had a talk with Professor Pavlov, the noted physiologist, of whom Wells wrote much nonsense.[53] Pavlov is now past seventy but still mentally vigorous. He told me this pitiful story.

During the last four months and a half he has petitioned for a permit to go to Finland for a month to read up on his speciality. At last it was granted. Then he had to wait for tickets, then for money. When he got all that, the Soviet government asked of him 16 millions for his visa and the Finnish government asked for an equal amount. His monthly pay is about 6 or 7 million, the equivalent of 3 dollars. When the Finnish government learned the real situation it dropped the charge for the visa and later the Soviet government did the same. But now he is waiting for a train, which is promised and does not materialize. His visa expires April 14.

---

[53]Ivan Petrovich Pavlov (1839–1946). Golder must be referring to something that H. G. Wells had published in the periodical press after his 1920 visit to Russia.

Other scholars have more or less the same difficulties and they become discouraged to the point of nervous exhaustion. One of the finest Russian scholars and cultured gentlemen that I have ever met, Professor S. F. Oldenburg, Secretary of the Academy of Sciences,[54] who has done all that he could to keep the Academy going and the Academicians alive, is now very sick. He sent for me and I had a long talk with him and as I left him I felt as if I would never see him again. It is so pitiful and so heart breaking that it completely upsets me. It is not only among the scholars but among every class that I come in contact with.

The Soviet government has raised a hornet's nest about its ears lately in trying to confiscate the gold and silver in the churches for the use of the hungry.[55] The leaders of the Church have come out against the decree and the people are supporting the Church men. Of course the government has the papers and carries on propaganda but the great mass of the people do not read the papers so all its cries fail to reach. Yesterday I noticed on the walls of the city posters by the Communists denouncing the Church leaders but I doubt whether that will change the opinion of the masses who have confidence neither in the Communists nor in the government.

Two Communists told me that when commissars went to churches in Petrograd to take charge of valuables they found the church surrounded by a human wall and had to give it up. Reports come that in some places commissars were killed for trying to take the church property. It is not so much that the Church refuses to give up its gold and silver as the fact that it refuses to give it up to the Communists in whom the Church and the people have no confidence and it is even questioned by them whether the wealth will go for the hungry.

Here in Russia rumor goes much faster and carries much more strength

---

[54]Sergei Fedorovich Oldenburg (1863–1934): orientalist who served as permanent secretary of the Academy of Sciences from 1904 to 1929.

[55]On February 23, the All-Russian Central Executive Committee of the Soviet decreed that all valuables containing gold, silver, or precious stones be removed from all religious establishments and given to a special famine fund within one month. Patriarch Tikhon protested on March 2 against the seizure of consecrated vessels. There followed some incidents of physical resistance to the taking of church treasures, as a result of which a number of priests and laypeople were arrested and imprisoned. Several criminal trials followed in the spring and summer during the course of which Tikhon was arrested for inspiring the resistance to the removal of the treasures. Golder refers to these developments in the pages below. Tikhon's case never came to trial. In June 1923 he confessed his guilt and swore an oath of loyalty to the Soviet government, which led to his release. See John Shelton Curtiss, *The Russian Church and the Soviet State, 1917–1950* (Boston, 1953), chap. 6.

than the newspapers, especially if these rumors are against the government. I have reached the point where I do not accept half the rumors that I hear and more than half of them against the government are unjust but the masses revel in them. The position of the government is slowly being undermined partly through these rumors. Government prestige is low and even fear of it is less than it used to be. The poor Soviet is in a deuce of a fix: from foreign countries comes pressure for personal freedom and all that, but the poor government is afraid to open the box of freedom for it does not know where the devil locked up in it will go. Uneasy lies the head that wears a crown. I had recently a talk with Bolos and they were of the opinion that the Soviet will make concessions, and make concessions, and if necessary will even go so far as a coalition government. Strangely enough, although America is taking the most outspoken stand against the Soviet, yet the position of America is respected because it is open and clear. Hughes's last note[56] was accepted with joy by the Whites and without bitterness by the Reds. Some of the Reds would rather concede to the American point of view than to yield to the English and French, who after all have no regard for Russia and the Russians and are thinking of themselves. It seems to me that our policy of helping the Russian people as we are doing from the point of view of humanity and at the same time taking an honest position in regard to the government is praiseworthy.

March 29

I wrote you yesterday morning about the church disturbances before I had a chance to read the papers. It appears that in one place near Moscow the soldiers were called upon to fire on a mass of people who guarded the church and about ten people were killed. In another place the soldiers refused to fire and therefore the Young Communists, a kind of Young People's Christian Union, were called out and they fired. The papers tell these stories to show that the priesthood is the cause of this blood shed. Many bishops and others have been arrested and a report has it that the

[56]The reference is to Secretary of State Charles Evans Hughes's diplomatic note of March 25, 1921, rebuffing a Soviet appeal to the incoming Harding administration to reconsider American policy toward Soviet Russia. Hughes's note declared that the U.S. government could not consider initiating trade relations with Soviet Russia until it was assured that there had been established in Russia "conditions essential to the maintenance of commerce," including "the safety of life, the recognition of firm guarantees of private property, the sanctity of contracts and the rights of free labor." Frederick Lewis Schuman, *American Policy toward Russia since 1917* (New York, 1928), pp. 201–2.

Patriarch himself is on that list. I have just come in from the street and have noticed new posters pointing out the number of starving people the wealth of the Church would feed. There is also a colored poster showing the famishing asking for bread and the Church refusing it. It is becoming exciting.

Yesterday I called on some of the Whites and had a talk with them about conditions here. They are most pessimistic. I took up the question of a coalition government which, it seems to me, is the only safe way out just now. But my friends the Whites would not hear of it. "What, coalition with these robbers, thieves, cutthroats? Never." They admitted that it was impossible to overthrow the Reds, that conditions could not go on as they are now, that death and starvation were staring Russians in the face, and yet, they regarded themselves as too pure to cooperate. What can you do when you have a lot of abnormal, hungry fanatics, Red and White, who rather than yield a point of pride prefer to see the whole country go to the dogs?

5 P.M. Professor Hutchinson and I had an interview with Krassin today. It is the first time since September 1920 that I have seen him.[57] During that time he has greatly improved in his English and the conversation was carried on in that tongue. In discussing the foreign trade situation he said that the Soviet insisted on two things. First, that it control the trade and for these reasons. Under the present rate of exchange merchants with dollars or pounds or any of the other standard moneys could come in and buy up all the valuables in Russia and take them out; also, it is necessary to regulate Russia's imports so that too many luxuries not be brought in.

The second thing the Soviet demanded is that it should be a partner in all business undertakings and share in their profits. His arguments sounded reasonable but they were not especially convincing. The real reason seems to be the desire to control and mix in everything. We did not push our questions beyond the point he wished to go. Owing to the fact that he was busy in getting ready to go to the Genoa Conference we did not remain long.

It was interesting to watch the kind of people who waited in the anteroom to see him. Most of them looked like cheap business men without capital and without big ideas, men whom I would not trust very far. To go

---

[57]In September 1920 the ARA arranged for Golder to meet with Krassin, who was then head of the Russian Trade Delegation in London, in an attempt to obtain permission for Golder to enter Soviet Russia, both to collect historical documents for Stanford and to make a study of the food situation for the ARA. This was part of an initial, and unsuccessful, effort by the ARA to establish operations inside Soviet Russia.

through the Russian ministries of today and to observe the insignificant looking men and women who occupy responsible positions makes one very discouraged as to the future of Russia.

Moscow, April 1, 1922

Dear Professor Adams:

Midnight Saturday.

. . . Something has happened tonight that President Wilbur, Lutz, and you ought to know because, I think, it is important. A year ago when I was in Tiflis I met the Soviet representative, Mr. Sheinman,[58] who is now the head of the Russian bank. During these busy months of running around I had no time to look him up and therefore I invited him to dine with me last night. Before he could accept he had to ask the permission of some one, the government, I suppose, and that made his coming somewhat official. Before sitting down to dinner he said a few things about commerce with America which made it clear that he came officially loaded. After dinner we, Governor Goodrich,[59] Professor Hutchinson, Quinn, Sheinman, a Russian by the name of Sokolov, and I met again and Sheinman lost no time getting to his points.

He started the conversation by pointing out that the Russian government is very eager to make large bread purchases in America for next year but that this transaction was difficult to bring about because of a lack of banking connections. At the present time the American people do business with Russia through German and Polish banks, countries of cheap money, which is harmful both for Russia and America. It would be much better if direct banking connections be established between Russia and America, but for some reason the U.S. government is opposed to it. Some time ago he, Sheinman, went to Berlin to take up the question of banking relations with Mr. Cooper of the Equitable Trust Co. and an agreement was reached and signed. About the same time, Krassin in London discussed a similar arrangement with the Guarantee Trust Co. The Irving Street National Bank of New York was also ready to enter into conversations, but of all this talk there are no results to show because, according to reports, the American government notified the said banks to have nothing to do with Russia.

---

[58] Aaron L. Sheinman (Scheinmann) (1886–?): Old Bolshevik, a staff member of the People's Commissariats of Finance, Food Supply, and Foreign Trade since 1918, and director of the newly created State Bank since October 1921.

[59] James P. Goodrich (1864–1940): former republican governor of Indiana and ARA special investigator in Russia.

Of course, the American government is strong enough to forbid big banks from entering into business relations with Russia, but it can not prevent the American people from doing the same. As it stands today millions of dollars are transmitted from America to Russia through foreign banks. If direct banking business were established all these millions of dollars could remain in the States, for Russia would spend them in buying machinery, food, etc. Sheinman said that he felt sure that if he were permitted to go to the States to have a talk with American bankers he could easily persuade them to enter into business relations with the Russian banks. But to go to America a visa is necessary and he, as a representative of the Russian banks, could not humiliate himself to ask for a visa without knowing that it would be granted. But neither visa nor visit would do any good if the American government insisted on dictating to the bankers what they should and should not do. If the government allowed the banks free action he was sure that he could convince them of the need of entering into relations. He could promise that all the money which would be sent from America to Russia would remain in America to be used as a fund for the purchase of goods for Russia. Without such banking facilities business in America is impossible. He then mentioned the cases of two business firms, one engaged in pig bristles and the other in ferum manganese, that could not put through the deal because of lack of banking facilities.

We followed his conversation sympathetically and agreed to all that he said. Governor Goodrich in particular expressed his eagerness to see business relations established but he pointed out several reasons the matter was delayed. In the first place was the case of the National City Bank, which had its money and books confiscated and all its efforts to get possession of the books have been in vain. Then there is the systematic attack by the officials of the Soviet government, Trotsky and others, on America, their insinuations that the welfare work which the ARA is doing is prompted by selfish motives, the praise which is everlastingly showered on Nansen, who does hardly anything, and the damning praise which the ARA receives. Thirdly, there is the case of Dubrovsky,[60] representative of the Russian Red

---

[60] D. H. Dubrovsky: collegium member of the American Bureau of the Red Cross Society of the Russian Soviet Republic. In February 1921, when Ludwig Martens was deported from the United States, Dubrovsky was named RSFSR representative in the United States, although as official relations between the two countries did not exist, his status was not recognized by the U.S. State Department. Dubrovsky's behavior became a sore point in U.S.-Soviet unofficial relations, the United States' accusing him of carrying on Bolshevik propaganda in America and of involving himself in some questionable Russian relief efforts conducted by American radical groups. Golder has more to say about his background, below on pp. 194–95.

Cross, a Soviet organization, who is abusing Hoover and the ARA, and discredits their efforts. These and other such acts on the part of the Soviet government alienate American public opinion and make it difficult for the friends of the Soviet to bring about the desired business relations between Russia and the United States.

In reply Sheinman pleaded that he was neither a diplomat nor a politician, but a banker. He knew nothing about the matters referred to by the Governor and was not interested in them. As a banker he desired to see banking relations established between the two countries on a purely business basis. In other words, he dodged the issues raised. We came back by saying that the matter was not quite so simple, that in America we had to consider the wishes of the people. "Why talk about the people?" he cynically said. "They have nothing to do with the matter. It is the government that is against us and not the people." We vehemently protested.

He next remarked that the conversation interested him greatly for he had not before realized to what extent the banks influenced the administration, that because of the books of the National City Bank the United States government refuses to allow the establishment of trade relations which would benefit the mass of the people in Russia and America. We gave it to him good and strong that it was not a question of the bank, but whether the Soviet is ready to do the honest thing, whether it is a government on which one could depend. Governor Goodrich said that when he was last in America he made a speech in which he almost came out openly for recognition of the Soviet and the next morning the papers attacked him on the ground that so long as the Soviet was unwilling to do the honest thing with the National City Bank it was not worthy of recognition. To this statement Sheinman said in a sneering manner that in America the papers were political tools of one party or another and that they probably attacked the Governor not because he favored recognition but because he was of a different political faith from the editors.

We drifted to the question of Dubrovsky and his activities and pointed out how difficult he and his cohorts were making it for the friends of the Soviet to accomplish anything. "If the American government does not like him why does it not send him out as it did Martens?"[61] asked Sheinman. "Because," we replied, "in America free speech is permitted and that so

---

[61]Ludwig Christian Alexander Karlovich Martens (1875–1948): Russian revolutionary who moved to the United States in 1916 and joined the American Socialist party. When Maxim Litvinov's credentials as ambassador to the U.S. were not accepted by the State Department, Chicherin appointed Martens, on January 2, 1919, as plenipotentiary representative of Soviet Russia to the United States. He left the United States in January 1921 to avoid formal deportation.

long as Dubrovsky does not violate laws, no action can be taken against him." "If the government is so careful about free speech why does it not permit free action, why does it not allow the Equitable Trust Co. to do business in Russia?" Governor Goodrich told him that he was missing the point, that our government did not give a hang what Dubrovsky said either as an individual or as representative of the Soviet. All that we wished to bring out is that the tactics of the Soviet were making enemies, were playing into the hand of its enemies and were making it impossible for its friends to bring about the very relations which the Soviet was eager to bring about. That as to the case of the Equitable Trust Co., our government had no reassurance that the Soviet would act any more fairly with it than it did with the National city Bank.

Sheinman replied that if the U.S. government did not like the tactics of the Soviet government the matter could be arranged very satisfactorily and easily by the American government asking the Soviet to return the books of the bank, to make Trotsky stop calling the U.S. names, to call off Dubrovsky and his cohorts and promising in return to make a loan to the Soviet, to treat it as an equal, etc. To make quite sure of his meaning we put it up to him whether he really meant to say that unless the Soviet was recognized it would continue to abuse us and to pursue the same policy of insinuation and slur. He hedged, as we expected, but said that were he Chicherin, he would reject the American ultimatum. What he meant by ultimatum he did not make clear, but I suppose he meant the conditions which the U.S. government has at various times laid down as a sine qua non to even preliminaries for Russian recognition.

We also became quite hot and Governor Goodrich made it clear that so long as the Soviet pursued that kind of a policy the American government would never recognize it, that America could get along without Russia, that if in the face of the suffering of the Russian people the Soviet enjoyed playing such petty politics and such childish games he was through with them.

Sokolov broke in by saying that just a year ago Sheinman, then Soviet representative in Georgia, said exactly the same thing to the Georgian government, that Russia could do without Georgia, etc. Sheinman interrupted by remarking that this was not quite so because he added to the above statement that if the Georgian government would accept the conditions of the Soviet the latter would give it supplies of food and other things, while the American government as yet has made no such promises.

I am glad that we had this opportunity to see clearly the Soviet game. Most of us had already suspected that the Communists were purposely pursuing a policy of baiting the American government, of throwing slurs on Hoover and the ARA in the hope of bringing us to our knees in prayer to them to stop. We are now convinced that this is so. This explains many things—why Dubrovsky is in America, why Trotsky calls us names, why the official papers throw mud on us, why the ARA has to face such difficulties in carrying on its humanitarian work.

Three months ago Governor Goodrich was in favor of recognition but he has now lost much of his enthusiasm. Six months ago I regarded the Bolo leaders as real statesmen, but today I see in them cheap east side politicians and shopkeepers. They think they can buy the American people by tempting with the pig bristle trade; they think they can bully us until we are ready to buy them off by the offer of a loan or recognition; they think they can make it so hard for the ARA that its leaders will commit some faux pas which will play into the hands of the Bolsheviks. They do hundreds of things which men of honor would not do, which statesmen would not do because it does not pay. They do all these things at a time when Russia is bleeding to death and rather than draw out the dagger they prefer to let her die and thereby save their face. They treat Russia as a white slaver treats his victim. They beat her, they hold a knife over her head, they dispose of her body, they try in every way to enslave her mind and soul. But it is in vain. Russia hates the Communists with the hate of a wronged woman and when the time comes she will stick a poignard into the heart of the white slaver. He knows it too, and never goes to bed without locking his door and leaving a military guard outside.

I have no time to tell you of my visit last evening in the company of the Governor with the head of the CheKa, who is also the head of the railway service. Dzerzhinsky[62] is a thoroughly honest, conscientious fanatic who has formed his ideas during the ten years that he has spent [in prison] in Siberia. He is about as fitted to run a railway as I am, but he is better qualified merely because he is a Communist. He is like an inquisitor of old; he regards Communism as a religion and those who disagree with him are heretics to be rooted out.

The confiscation of the Church wealth is creating a great deal of excitement and some trouble. In numerous places the Chekists and the masses have come to blows. The papers pursue a policy of abuse of the clergy, the walls are plastered over with posters discrediting the Church, Communists outrage the faithful by going into sacred places and sending women behind the altar. There is no lack of excitement and wild rumors.

---

[62]Feliks Edmundovich Dzerzhinskii (1877–1926): head of the Cheka (later the GPU) and people's commissar of internal affairs (NKVD). On April 14, 1921, he was made people's commissar of transport, charged with bringing some life to the country's crippled railroad system.

In concluding this Sunday morning letter let me tell you that I have recently lost 300,000 rubles to Quinn and the Governor in a poker game.

Sunday morning.

. . . When I was in Petrograd a week ago my good friend Professor Oldenburg, Permanent Secretary of the Academy of Sciences, sent for me. I found the man sick in bed, suffering from what so many Russian men of culture suffer, nerves and a weak heart. I wish you could meet him for he is one of the most scholarly, cultured and kindly men that I have ever met. He reminds me so much of Burr of Cornell.[63] During the last four years he has worked like a giant trying to keep up the Academy, trying to find something to eat for the academicians, trying to keep on good terms with the Bolsheviki and not to alienate the antibolsheviks. As a result he has been abused by all. In addition to his public work he has been trying to support his own family, the orphan children of his brother, the wife and children of his son, and all these people have to be supported on a salary of about 9,000,000 rubles or the equivalent of about five dollars. One of the members of his family told me that the family as a whole ate bread four days each month and only the children had bread every day in the month. Life is one nightmare to these people and they are breaking under it. When I took leave of Professor Oldenburg I felt that I would never see him again, that he was on his way to join Lappo-Danilevskii, Shakhmatov, and the other 21 academicians who have died during the last four years from disease and underfeeding. A friend of mine told me of visiting one of these late academicians during his illness. The poor man was quite weak and on the table near him were a few white bits of toast and every now and then the sick man's hand would reach for them and after a little effort to chew them he would put them back.

In the Crimea there is much hunger and yet for some reason or another the ARA has not been asked to go down there. Lately some of the professors from the Crimea appealed to their colleagues in Moscow and Petrograd to do something for them. One of the local professors called on the representative of the Crimean government (Crimea is an autonomous Republic) in Moscow. The representative is a young female Communist and when the professor said that the professors in the Crimea were dying of hunger she said, "What of it, let them die!"

I am taking leave of Russia with a sad heart, knowing that thousands of

---

[63]George Lincoln Burr (1857–1938): librarian and professor of history at Cornell University.

the best minds and hearts will die in the near future, and that we are helpless to do much under present conditions. In some ways I wish I could remain here a time longer and study conditions more thoroughly. Somehow I feel as if I had merely a traveler's impressions and nothing more.

As ever cordially yours,

★ ★ ★

Paris, Easter Sunday [April 16] 1922

My dear Professor Coolidge:

Governor Goodrich and I left Moscow April 3 and reached London April 11. He left for New York on the 13th and before this reaches you he may have seen you for he said he would try to do so. I hope he did for I am eager that you should know what is going on. The relations between the Soviet and the ARA are becoming more and more strained and I sometimes wonder how it will end. The internal organization of the ARA has improved wonderfully since the coming of Quinn.

Our books left Moscow for Riga on April 6 and a convoy was to look after them as far as the Latvian border. The ARA men in Riga promised to take charge of them there and ship them out. We still have some books in Petrograd which will probably be sent out by some boat directly to New York.

It is quite likely that I shall go in again in June and do some of the things I left undone. It is barely possible that I shall go out by way of Siberia, but there is nothing definite on that point.

I took leave of our many friends in Moscow with much regret and sorrow. Conditions of living are becoming more and more difficult and the resources are exhausted. The ruble is 2 millions a dollar and the cost of living is in proportion. I do not see how the handful of intelligentsiia can survive much longer. I have been interested in comparing the conversations at Muravev's with those at Bakhrushin's[64] and I am deeply disappointed with the Professor crowd. I wonder if all professors are like that crowd. God help us!

Since reaching civilized lands again, I have taken a peep into the New York Nation and glanced over its comments on Russia, on Hoover, etc. How asinine! Is it on this kind of food that the radicals in America are fed? God help them too!

---

[64]Sergei Vladimirovich Bakhrushin (1882–1950): professor of Russian history at Moscow University.

I have come away from Russia deeply disappointed with the Reds. They are clever, devilishly clever, but they are crooked. I am convinced (I do not think that you will agree with me) that they have adopted a policy of pin-sticking the ARA and Hoover to force the latter to bring about recognition. They did something similar to England in India, and they are doing it to the ARA because, just now, this is the only way they can come in contact with America. Some of the Red leaders have intimated as much. Kamenev told us that the ARA could have no freedom of action until America had a representative. Krassin said that if Russia had a representative in America, Dubrovsky in the U.S. would never do what he is doing. I can multiply such evidence—all of which you would probably throw out of the case.

I have reached Europe at the wrong time of the year—Easter season. The few friends I have on this side are away and I am starting too. I expect to leave Wednesday for Italy and work my way back to Paris by way of Switzerland, Austria, and Germany.

I am still hoping to return to teaching in the fall and probably will.

With kindest regards,
Sincerely yours,

P.S. I have brought out with me copies of the letters of Nicholas to Stolypin from 1906–11(?). Would the American Historical Review be interested in them, or shall I get them published in Europe? They need editing. (Confidential)

CHAPTER FOUR

BETWEEN WAR AND PEACE
(June–November 1922)

Golder reentered Soviet Russia in the first days of June after two months of collecting books and documents in Europe. His return marked a new phase in his Russian activities, one dominated by discussions with Soviet officials concerning the prospects for U.S.-Soviet relations. Beginning in mid-July Golder reported on the substance of these conversations in weekly letters to Christian Herter that were also meant for Herbert Hoover's eyes.

The Soviet government, intent on breaking out of its diplomatic and commercial isolation, had placed much hope in the Genoa Conference of thirty-four nations, which met from April 10 to May 19, 1992, to deal with the Russian question, a large piece of unfinished business from the Versailles Peace Conference. The conference at Genoa broke down owing to a fundamental disagreement: The Allies insisted that Soviet Russia had to recognize its foreign debts and its obligation to compensate foreign nationals for destroyed or confiscated property before any discussion of Western loans to Russia could take place; the Soviet delegation, with equal insistence, demanded compensation for material damage caused by Allied intervention in the Russian Civil War and declared that guarantees of future loans and credits would have to precede any Soviet compromise on the debt question. One month later, the Hague Conference (June 15–July 20) convened for the purpose of seeking a way out of the circular arguments regarding debts, property claims, loans, and credits, but it too was unable to find a solution.

The Harding administration, wary of all European entanglements, kept its diplomats from officially participating in the Genoa and Hague conferences, which further disappointed the Soviet leaders, who were keen on drawing the Americans into trade and official relations and who believed that the presence of the ARA mission in Soviet Russia put those relations within reach. However, as Golder's account demonstrates, despite its isolationism, the U.S. government had opened its own indirect lines of contact to the Kremlin, one of which was through the ARA. When Golder reentered Soviet Russia he was accompanied by Governor James Goodrich, who was returning from a visit to Washington with instructions from President Harding and Secretary Hughes to feel out the Soviet leadership on the obstacles impeding U.S. trade relations and recognition. Goodrich received Hoover's permission to draw on Golder's services as an adviser and translator.

★ ★ ★

Interview with Karl Radek, Thursday Night, June 8, 1922, Moscow

When yesterday at noon (June 8) Governor Goodrich and I were scheming how to bring about a meeting with Radek and Kamenev without taking the first steps, Volodin, the aide of Eiduk,[1] the representative of the Soviet government in the ARA, walked up to us and said that Radek had invited the Governor to take tea at his home at ten o'clock at night. The Governor accepted but asked that I should also be invited, which was done later in the day. Towards 9:30 in the evening, Eiduk in his ARA car drove up to the Governor's residence and a quarter of an hour later we started for the Kremlin and, after passing the guards and giving the necessary certificates, we were admitted to the inner temple. Mrs. Radek received us and at once telegraphed somewhere for Radek who was attending a Communist meeting where the high priest Trotsky was preaching.

In a few minutes Radek appeared and after passing the time of day he launched into politics by stating that America is Russia's bitterest enemy and was backing France in her hostile attitude towards the Soviet government. Governor Goodrich took issue with him on this and made it clear to

---

[1] Aleksandr Vladimirovich Eiduk (1886–1941) was an Old Bolshevik, a former member of the Latvian Rifle Battalion, and, since 1919, a collegium member of the Cheka. From October 1921 to June 1922 he was plenipotentiary representative of the Soviet government to the ARA. His ostensible job was to act as liaison between the ARA and all government departments; however, one of his main functions was to be the "minder" of the ARA. As Golder makes clear, Eiduk's was not the kind of company he and the governor liked to keep. V. E. Volodin, a Russian Jew who settled in America, was subsequently deported for radical activities. He worked in the People's Commissariat of Foreign Affairs and was Eiduk's assistant as ARA liaison.

him that if the policies of the two countries seemed to coincide it was not because the United States is backing France, but because the latter takes her cue from the former and made it appear as if the two were working together.

Radek next took issue with Hoover's recent speech in which he said that America had little to hope for from Russian commerce because even before the war Russia took only one percent of America's export. The truth is, remarked Radek, that America can not be prosperous as long as England and Germany are not, and these two countries can not thrive as long as Russia is down and out. It follows therefore that America can not be prosperous as long as Russia is in misery. With this the Governor agreed and admitted the weakness in Hoover's argument.

From this the question drifted to the subject of protection of private property. Radek thought that much was made of this rather academic question. Russia has not passed the required legislation on that subject because there is as yet no private property to protect, but just as soon as commerce and industry were developed to the point where such legislation were needed it would be forthcoming, for the Soviet government would be most deeply interested in protecting these channels of national life. The other argument which was made against the Soviet, that it tries to keep its hand on commerce and industry, was not well taken, for in a country ruined as Russia is, only a strong government can function. Just now there is no other government that could function—the Social Revolutionists[2] are incompetent, they are men of words and not of deeds. Kolchak tried to work with them and had to drive them away in the end.

Radek wandered back to America. In the end, said he, it will be a political and not an economic bridge that will bring America and Russia together. When the time shall come, and it is not far off, when Russia shall have a strong army in the Far East and shall have it in her power to ally herself with or against Japan, then America will be eager enough to make friends with Russia. Personally, said Radek, he would be very happy to see the two countries come together, and so would the Russian people, for the ARA has made a very favorable impression in Russia, but unfortunately the attitude of the State Department made this rapprochement impossible.

Governor Goodrich managed to break into his speech by saying that the American people and the American government were most eager to come to the help of Russia and were not opposed to coming to an understanding with the Soviet government, though they took no stock in

---

[2]The correct English rendition would be "Socialist Revolutionaries," but "Social Revolutionaries" and "Social Revolutionists" were the commonly used, if incorrect, translations at the time.

its communistic ideas, but they could do that only on certain conditions which are very simple and very just. America demands that the Soviet government should recognize its debts to the American government, that it should recognize its obligations to American nationals whose property it has confiscated, and that it should either restore the property or compensate for it. That is all. The amount of the debt, the terms of payment could be arranged satisfactorily later.

Radek replied that he agreed with this and had in fact urged this view on his comrades but without success. They held, especially Lenin, that the promise of bankrupt Russia to pay debts would have no weight and would be a waste of words. There is no use making such promises until the Soviet knew how much debt it had to pay, how much time it had in which to pay, what terms it had, and, most important of all, until it knew where the money with which to pay came from. That explains the attitude of the Soviet delegation in Genoa. Before it committed itself on the question of the debts it wished to know what financial help it could have for reconstructing the country and for securing the necessary money for payment. At the Hague, the Russian delegation will be instructed to demand to know just how much the amount of the debt is and the terms of payment. Little can be expected from the Hague. For the time being, Russia will have to go along the best way she can. After a few years she will get on her feet again and then she can be in a position to make promises which will be believed and accepted.

Governor Goodrich took pains to show to Radek that the importance of making the promises lay not so much in the fact of promises of payment, for no one expected Russia to pay at once, no more than France was expected to make immediate payments, but in the fact that it reestablished Russia's moral credit which the Bolsheviks had ruined by repudiating these very debts. Russia could secure help only through loans and no one would invest or lend a cent to Russia so long as she refused to acknowledge her former debts. If Russia should now say that she would pay her debt and make compensation for private property, the American people would accept these promises in good faith and be ready to help her financially. The amount of the payment and all questions relating to that and compensation could be adjusted to the satisfaction of all parties at some later time.

Radek then raised the question of the exploitation of Russia's resources. Three plans had presented themselves: (1) government ownership and control; (2) private ownership and control; (3) government and private ownership and control combined. The Soviet government had decided on plan (3) because, among other things, if there were complete private ownership and control of the mines the government could not be certain of its needed supply of coal to run the railways. Governor Goodrich pointed out numerous other ways, such as taxation and the right of eminent domain, by which the government could handle the situation and yet leave the management of the resources to private parties. Mines and public utilities, said the Governor, are run more efficiently under private management than under government control. With this Radek agreed and remarked that the question of control is not serious and would not be a serious obstacle in the way of coming to an understanding.

After this the conversation drifted into general European politics. Radek thought that in the future England and the United States, two natural trade rivals, would be working against one another and using France as a pawn. But, added he, if the two could combine, they could not only control Germany and Russia, but they could dictate to the world. Governor Goodrich assured Radek that the relations between the two Anglo-Saxon states were daily growing better, that neither took any very important international step without first consulting the other, and that there is every reason to believe that this would continue to be the case in the future. The true internationalists, said the Governor, are the bankers and not the Internationalists, who are daily becoming more nationalist. Radek accepted this remark with a smile. In discussing the diplomats and their fellows at these conferences Radek said that no good could be expected from them for they were always playing to the galleries and that a half dozen bankers could settle most of these world problems and do it with little fuss.

The part Hoover played in the Hungarian revolution was touched upon.[3] Radek said that he had read Gregory's story and had attached no importance to it because it sounded too romantic, but many of the Russian Communists believed in it and became suspicious, even Lenin. When it became known that Congress had voted twenty millions of dollars to feed the hungry, Lenin telephoned to Radek to ask him to explain the motives that were back of it. Radek tried to explain it on humanitarian grounds but Lenin was not convinced. Governor Goodrich assured Radek that Hoover had no part in putting down the Hungarian revolution, that there was a letter in the State Department which Hoover wrote to Wilson in which he came out against intervention in Hungary.

---

[3]This refers to the role of the ARA in the Hungarian revolution of 1919, specifically the events leading to the overthrow of the Bela Kun regime. At the time the ARA, then an official U.S. government agency, was providing food relief to Hungary under the direction of Thomas T. C. Gregory. After the events, Gregory wrote a series of articles, "Stemming the Red Tide," that gave the impression that Gregory and Hoover had been instrumental in the fall of Bela Kun on August 1, 1919. These articles appeared in *World's Work* in April, May, and June 1921, the eve of the negotiations in Riga between the ARA and the Soviet government.

Before the party (consisting of Radek, Mrs. Radek, Governor Good-rich, Eiduk, and Golder) broke up, Radek said that if a declaration on the part of the Soviet government of its willingness to pay its debts would help to bring about an understanding he was sure that it would be made and he urged that the Governor should see Kamenev and the other comrades. Eiduk broke in by offering to make the necessary arrangements, which was not part of our plan, but we had to leave it there for the time being.

★ ★ ★

Moscow, June 10, 1922

Dear Professor Adams:

Governor and Mrs. Goodrich, Miss Moorman, a friend of the Goodrich family, Walter Duranty of The New York Times, and I left Riga in a special car which Col. Haskell sent out for us, on Monday night June 5. We crossed the border late on the sixth and found ourselves in Russia once more. As we neared Moscow we ran into beggars and people with sacks and people with pessimism. Notwithstanding the fact that the crops looked good, the peasants with whom I had an opportunity to talk complained that the crop would be a failure and that hunger stared them in the face once more. There is, however, little reason for accepting this statement, at least for the region which we traversed. The reason for the complaint is two fold: one is the usual hard luck story of the farmer and the desire to avoid paying heavy taxes and the other is the psychology of the people. They are thoroughly discouraged and expect the worst.

Late in the afternoon of the seventh we came into Moscow and found the city as usual on the surface. But as soon as I had time to make a few calls many differences were called to my attention. The topic of greatest importance was the health of Lenin. There is very little doubt but that he is a very sick man and though it is possible that he may pull through it is not probable that he will in the future play a big political role. Naturally the question is, Who will succeed him? By the time this reaches you the points which I discuss in my letter may no longer have a value but I think I will take them up anyway and record them.

It may probably be known to you that the running of the Soviet government was done by a group of five men—Lenin, Trotsky, Zinoviev, Kamenev, and Stalin. More recently two others have been counted in this group, namely Tomskii[4] and Rykov,[5] making seven in all. Lenin has been ill for some months, off and on, and during the time that he could not attend to his official duties two men, Rykov and Tsiurupa,[6] take his place and preside for him in turn. These two are now performing his duties, but behind them there is a struggle of cliques to get them in control. It is going to be an interesting intrigue and should I remain here long enough I will keep you informed as to its progress.

The next topic of importance is the trial of the Social Revolutionists, the friends of Kerensky, Savinkov, et al.[7] These men are charged with inciting revolt and conspiring against the lives of the Soviet [leaders] and so far as is known no evidence has been offered which was not known more than a year ago, and just why the Bolos are pulling off the trial just now is not quite clear. Some would have it that it is the purpose to discredit the Social Revolutionists, who still have a large following among the working-men, by showing that their plots have cost the lives of hundreds of the proletariat. Others say that it is a part of the game to keep themselves prominently before the public and as saviors of the patria and the working classes. When it became known abroad that these men would be tried the Russian Social Revolutionists abroad raised a howl and appealed to the socialists of Western Europe to intercede for the brethren. Last month, at the meeting of the International in Berlin, the question of the trial of these men came up for discussion. Comrades Radek and Bukharin,[8] who were authorized delegates of the Communists, assured the assembled body that

---

[4]Mikhail Pavlovich Tomskii (1880–1936) was an Old Bolshevik and chairman of the All-Russian Central Council of Trade Unions.

[5]Aleksei Ivanovich Rykov (1881–1938) was a leading party and government official; during the Civil War he was director of the Supreme Economic Council. Since 1921 he had been deputy chairman of both the Council of Labor and Defense (STO) and the Council of People's Commissars.

[6]Aleksandr Dmitrievich Tsiurupa (1870–1928) from 1918 to 1921 was people's commissar of food supply; from 1921 he was deputy chairman of both STO and the Council of People's Commissars.

[7]The trial of the Socialist Revolutionaries (SRs) opened in Moscow on June 8. In the dock were thirty-four SR leaders accused of terrorism and counterrevolutionary activity. The judge, who announced his verdict on August 7, found most defendants guilty as charged and sentenced fifteen of them to death, but these sentences were commuted. Boris Viktorovich Savinkov (1879–1925) was a former SR leader living in Paris.

[8]Nikolai Ivanovich Bukharin (1888–1938) was editor of *Pravda* and a member of the Executive Committee of the Comintern.

the accused would have a fair trial, that even if found guilty no capital punishment would be inflicted, that they would be allowed legal defenders, and invited foreign counsel.[9] Emile Vandervelde, the well known Belgian socialist and at one time Minister of Justice, Kurt Rosenfeld, one time Minister of Justice in Prussia, and Theodor Liebknecht (brother of Karl) volunteered their services and came. Imagine their shock, when on reaching the Moscow station a howling and jeering mob headed by the same Bukharin who had promised them fair treatment, greeted them. Since then the papers have been full of abuse of these men. Just now there is a strong agitation among the Communists to free the judges from the promises made by Radek and Bukharin and let justice take its course. It is planned to have a demonstration in a few days which should demand the death penalty for the accused.

Now as to the trial and the judges. The case is tried before the Revolutionary Tribunal at the head of which is the famous Krylenko,[10] the first commander-in-chief of the Red army, and well known for his bloody deeds. In this case Krylenko is acting as prosecuting attorney. Mrs. Krylenko has prepared the case; Mrs. Krylenko's brother-in-law is chief judge. The Pravda of June 9 gives a biographical sketch of the three judges (Piatakov, Karklin, and Galkin)[11] and there is nothing to indicate that a single one of them has had any kind of legal training. These sketches lay emphasis on the fact that all three have served many years in prison, penitentiary, and exile, for political offenses, I assume. It is a political trial and nothing more and the Communists sit there as accusers and as judges. The hall is packed with partisans—or as the Russians say, with "blacks" (Jews)—who demonstrate at intervals.

From our point of view the trial is a farce. When the other morning Rosenfeld protested at certain illegalities, Krylenko said: "In reply to citizen Rosenfeld I ought to say that if he came to the Soviet Republic to establish what he regards as proper procedure then he came here for the wrong purpose. It is not for citizen Rosenfeld, representative of a capitalist country, to tell us what to do. We have our own laws and have a right to insist that they be recognized and not those of the Berlin courts which tried the murderers of Luxemburg and Liebknecht." The trial is a mockery from

---

[9]Lenin was infuriated by the arrangement that Radek and Bukharin had made in Berlin but publicly vowed to abide by their agreement.

[10]Nikolai Vasil'evich Krylenko (1885–1938) in 1922 was appointed assistant prosecutor of the RSFSR.

[11]Georgii Leonidovich Piatakov (1890–1937), Otto Ia. Karklin (1875–1937), Aleksandr Vladimirovich Galkin (1876–?).

other points of view. Last week the prisoners protested that they were not getting a fair deal, refused to be tried by making much noise, and forced the judge to give them a recess to consult with their lawyers.

Many people are being arrested and no one knows the reasons. Among those who are locked up is a book dealer from whom we made many purchases. The situation is a bit discouraging.

A third exciting subject is the Church. In the near future I hope to be able to send you a long paper on that topic, but for the present I will give you an outline. With the decree to confiscate the Church treasures for the benefit of the hungry and with the protest of the Patriarch and the clergy to the measure you are already familiar. The clergy did not believe, does not believe, that this Church wealth will go to the starving and in this opinion they are by no means alone. The Patriarch was ready to agree that as much of the Church treasures as were not needed for sacred services should be taken but the Soviet demanded all and proceeded to collect it. Here it came in contact with forced resistance which led to bloodshed. In the course of the investigations the accused peasants said they had obeyed the priests, the priests shifted the blame to the bishops and the bishops to the Patriarch.

The Soviet government raised the very naive question by what right the Church organization existed, that is, by what legal right. The decree separating Church and State is copied largely from the French law but with this difference: The French law neither recognizes nor ignores the Church Organization, it merely does not concern itself with it; on the other hand the Soviet decree is hostile to the Organization. But this point, though it plays a part in the prosecution, is not pushed too hard for fear of arousing the ire of other Church organizations—Catholic, Moslem, etc.—but it figures in the proceedings. Of course, the principal charge is violation of the decrees and incitement to revolt which led to bloodshed and death. Eleven prominent clergymen were brought to trial and all condemned to death, of whom five were actually executed about ten days ago, and the other six are for the time being spared.

The Patriarch was put under arrest and kept in seclusion, at first in his home but now in the Kremlin. While he was at his home there came to him one night a group of clergymen of Soviet leaning and threatened him that unless he handed over his power to some one to carry on the Church functions during his arrest, the eleven accused priests, above mentioned, would be immediately executed. In a few days I will have a copy of the exact letter of the Patriarch and will send it to you. The Patriarch expected such a move and was ready for it. He wrote a letter in which he appointed some high Church dignitary of Iaroslavl to act in his place. With this letter in hand the Soviet clergy hastened to Iaroslavl and informed the regent of his new duties. He accepted. Immediately the group demanded that as Patriarch he should sign a paper charging the Patriarch and a number of clergymen with certain crimes and bring them to trial. This he refused to do and was placed under arrest. There being no one to act in the place of the Patriarch this small junta of clergy is performing that office on the legal ground that the patriarchate is vacant. The Patriarch by handing over his power to some other person had ipso facto abdicated. This is a point in canon law which I leave to you to settle.

Under the guidance of this new group the Church is being reorganized and broken up.[12] Interestingly enough and cunningly enough it is made to appear as if this were done because of a great religious reform movement. The cry is let us return to the primitive Church, the Church of the Fathers. At that time there was no Church hierarchy, let there be no hierarchy now; at that time the Church was subject to Caesar, let it be subject to Caesar now. Let there be no Church organization, but let each Church community be a distinct unit and deal directly with Caesar.

But the reform of the Church is not only in matter of organization, but also in ritual. It may not be known to you that in the Orthodox Church the Consecration of the Host takes place behind the altar and out of sight of the faithful, and in this respect it is different from the Catholic Church. In the Red Church (as the new movement is called here) the altar is being removed. This raises the interesting question of whether this means a rapprochement with Catholicism. The Russians with whom I have talked are at a loss to explain what it all means. They are, however, agreed that there is a great schism in the Church and that the expected as well as the unexpected may happen. That the Soviet will allow the Catholic Church to get a strong hold here they do not believe, but they think it is very possible that a great many

---

[12]The controversy surrounding the Soviet government's drive to confiscate the church treasures, especially the arrest of the Patriarch Tikhon, moved a group of "progressive" clergy to establish the so-called Living church, and it is these events to which Golder refers. The Living church, also called the Renewal (*Obnovlenie*), backed confiscating the treasures and for a time appeared to enjoy some measure of support from the government; thus, it was popularly known as the Red church. The *obnovlentsy* called for extensive church reform, including the replacement of the patriarchate by a collegiate administration. When Tikhon's confession of guilt and oath of allegiance to the Soviet government led to his release from prison in June 1923, government support of the Living church waned. The letter of Tikhon that Golder discusses was written to Metropolitan Agafangel of Iaroslavl, who was indeed arrested shortly afterward. See Curtiss, *The Russian Church and the Soviet State, 1917–1950*, chap. 7.

of the intellectuals, even members of the white clergy,[13] will turn their faces towards Rome rather than submit to the humiliations of the Kremlin. At the same time they seem to be certain that the peasant will never change and they mention the obstinacy of the ignorant peasants and their martyrdom in times whenever their Church rights were touched upon. If the peasant can not have his Church he will turn not to the Catholic dogmas but to sectarianism. This has been pretty much the history of the religious movements of Russia.

In talking with a churchman this morning he complained of additional troubles which the Russian émigrés are making for those Whites who have remained at home. For example he said that not long ago the Russian émigrés in Belgrade gathered in the Cathedral to protest against the mistreatment of the Patriarch and clergy, but before they dispersed they came out in favor of a monarchy in Russia. Of course, the Soviet authorities have made use of that incident to their own advantage.

The economic situation is also full of interest. Food is now more abundant and costs less than two months ago. There are two or three explanations. It is quite possible that peasants and speculators have been hoarding large quantities of food and now that the new harvest is almost on them and promises to be good, they are unloading on the market. Some say that the government is unloading. Another important reason for the cheaper food is undoubtedly the ARA food packages.[14] So many have come in that they have affected the market. Our people have followed this movement. Just now one can buy for ten dollars as much food in Moscow as he can get in a food package. Some months back the equivalent of an ARA food package cost thirty dollars.

But aside from food other things have gone up in price. I have priced books and they have gone up out of all proportion and have become practically prohibitive. Yesterday I saw in a window a set of books which I bought some months back for five millions or for about ten dollars. This time I was asked six hundred millions, or two hundred dollars. A pamphlet which a few months ago cost a cent or two sells now for fifty cents or more. There is no relation between the price of food and other commodities. Merchants have become so accustomed to increasing prices that they continue doing it without reason. Of course as a result sales have decreased

---

[13]That is, the married parish priests as opposed to the "black" or monastic clergy.

[14]One of ARA's supplementary operations was its food remittance system, whereby people outside Soviet Russia could, for $10, have the ARA deliver a food package to a loved one or relative inside the country. The typical food package consisted of flour, rice, lard, sugar, tea, and milk and weighed 117 pounds.

and sooner or later there will be a big slump and prices will come down, but in the meanwhile the situation is bad and taxation is high.

I am so glad we bought our books when we did and at the prices we did. It is out of the question to acquire more at the present prices. I am picking up the newer things for the Hoover War Library and pass up everything else. I am buying few duplicates for those with whom we might exchange might think that we are robbing them if we asked from them the prices they cost. So far as we are concerned we have a well rounded collection and the prices can mount as much as they like. By the time this reaches you the Russian collection should be not far from you. You know, of course, that we have an important shipment from Petrograd. I have not yet learned whether it has gone or not.

In order to raise the value of the ruble the Soviet government has slowed down the printing presses and has issued a Bread Loan. A consequence of the first step is that there is a scarcity of the medium of exchange, especially in the provinces. It will be interesting to watch the working out of this experiment. The Bread Loan is very interesting. The Soviet government asks for an immediate loan (each bond having the value of 3,800,000 rubles) for which it promises to pay a pud of rye flour between December 1 and January 31. I have made inquiries as to support of this loan and usually get this story. "No one with any sense subscribes. People in government service are obliged to take the bonds as wages." I can not understand why people should subscribe. The price of the bond is sufficient to buy a pud of flour in today's market. Why should a person take a chance of getting or not getting his flour months hence when he can get it now? . . .

June 11

On Thursday night at Radek's home, it was agreed that Radek and Kamenev should have dinner with the Governor either Friday or Sunday evening. This did not please Eiduk for he wished to be in on everything. He saw him and brought it about that Kamenev asked the Governor to come to his office on Saturday afternoon at two o'clock. This meant that Eiduk would go along. After thinking over the matter the Governor excused himself for it was realized that sooner or later Eiduk had to be shaken.

In the meantime I tried to get in touch with Radek and finally last evening I made an appointment with him for today, Sunday, at eleven o'clock. I was there on time and told him that in view of the fact that he had expressed a desire that the Governor should meet Kamenev and the other comrades, the Governor is quite willing to do it in the hope that the misunderstandings which now exist between America and Soviet Russia might be talked over. But the Governor did not wish any one connected with the ARA, either Russian or American (except he and I) to be mixed up in this and therefore he hoped that if Radek wished to continue discussions then he should take the direction of the matter in his own hands. Radek replied that he had little hope from discussions in view of the fact that the Allies demanded promises and refused to advance a loan, the only basis on which the comrades were willing to carry on negotiations. However, he would see Zinoviev today and tomorrow, and Kamenev tomorrow morning, and between them the matter would be discussed and a meeting arranged. He suggested that Litvinov,[15] a man of action and not words, should also be a party. I assured him that the Governor would be glad to meet and talk with any officials of the government who might wish to see him.

He next launched out a little more into his theoretical international political situation. Russia could reach France only through England, and America through France, and therefore, he intimated, separate discussion would lead nowhere. Without entering with him into the discussion I begged to take issue with him on that point and pointed out to him that there was a great difference between the American and the French case and that he and his comrades had now an unusual opportunity through the Governor to inform themselves authoritatively of what the American point of view is. With this we parted with the understanding that I was to call him up tomorrow, Monday, at eleven o'clock in the morning.

★ ★ ★

Moscow, June 24, 1922

My dear Professor Adams:

In my last letter I told you that something important was going to happen in a day or two. I had in mind the interview between Governor Goodrich and the leading members of the Soviet government. At this interview I was present and a report of it I sent to you a few days ago.[16] The day after the interview Governor Goodrich and I attended the trial of the Social Revolutionists.

At twelve o'clock some one announced that the judges were coming and all, except the prisoners, rose to do them honor. There were five judges in all, three in charge of the case and two in reserve. The chief justice had

---

[15]Maksim Maksimovich Litvinov (1876–1951) was the deputy people's commissar of foreign affairs.

[16]For Golder's report on this June 19 conference, see the appendix, pp. 345–50.

the appearance of an intellectual and the other two looked and were dressed like coal miners or dock workers. On the right of the judges were 34 prisoners, divided in two groups. In one were about 22 or 24 who were and are Social Revolutionists and the other group were men who had been SRs and had become Communists and are now giving evidence against their former comrades. In front of the prisoners sat their attorneys and opposite to them the accusers and the prosecuting attorney. One of the prisoners was given the word and for three quarters of an hour stated his case, after which he was cross examined by Krylenko, the prosecuting attorney, and the chief justice. On the platform were also a number of prominent Communists, the most conspicuous being Bukharin, who was dressed in a dark blue flannel shirt open at the throat. Just below, near the platform of the prisoners, sat the female relatives of the prisoners. The court room was only about half full, for the Communist crowd that usually attends was outside preparing for the demonstration of the afternoon.

Did I tell you in my letter that the Communists planned a big demonstration for June 20, the anniversary of the death of one of the comrades, Volodarsky?[17] The real purpose, however, was to create a public opinion in favor of the death penalty for the accused SRs. In the interview with the leading Communists the day before, Governor Goodrich raised the question of the demonstration and Kamenev replied that "Russia is a free country and if the workmen wish to demonstrate they have a right to, but I can assure you that there will be no LYNCHING." Needless to say that the workmen were asked to parade and whoever employed them paid their wages for the day of the parade just as if they had worked.

We passed a number of these demonstrators, tired men and women and children, who had about as much heart in it as I had. Each group carried one or more banners demanding death for the Social Revolutionists. This is the kind of cultural training the proletariat is getting. The paraders marched through the Red Square in front of many prominent Communists, among whom was the prosecuting attorney, Krylenko, and the chief justice. As the crowd marched by it saluted the dignitaries and stopped for a speech. The prosecuting attorney called to them, "Shall we inflict the death penalty on the prisoners?" to which he received a shout which translated into good American meant, "Give them hell, shoot them!" etc. The judge also made a speech in which he assured his auditors that the accused would receive all that is coming to them. Many of the demonstrators asked to be permitted

---

[17]V. Volodarskii (1891–1918) was a Bolshevik party official assassinated by a Left SR on June 20, 1918.

to submit petitions on that subject, which petition the judge granted and received the petition.

When that same evening the court met again the judge asked the opinion of the prosecuting attorney whether the petitions should be read into the case and whether he should receive a deputation which was waiting outside and wished to be heard. The prosecuting attorney ruled that in view of the fact that the Soviet government is a government of the masses, the masses should be allowed to come in. The mob came in, a few of them drunk, and for two and a half hours it stood there abusing the prisoners and accusing them of all sorts of crimes. Later the prosecuting attorney told the judge that the scene reminded him of the French Revolution when the crowd broke into the court room to demand the head of Louis XVI. Before the mob scattered they were photographed and thanked by the judge for their public spirit and for the valuable evidence presented.

The next day, Wednesday, June 21, the lawyer for the defense addressed the court on the illegal proceedings of the evening before and pointed out that according to Soviet law the prisoners were entitled to a new trial and to new judges. While he was speaking the Communist crowd in the audience hooted him until he lost patience and shouted, "Woe to the nation that breaks the laws which it has made." This made the judge angry and he accused the lawyer of insulting the Russian people, and of being an ignoramus and unfit to conduct the trial, etc. The question of whether to go on with the case was debated by the prisoners and their attorneys and they concluded that it was no use, since the court refused to follow even Soviet law and was guided entirely by the rulings of Krylenko, the prosecuting attorney (and the brother-in-law of the judge).

On Saturday night (June 23) the prisoners told the court that they of their own free will would ask their attorneys, in whom they have great confidence, to withdraw from the case because the judge has insulted them and because of the court's rulings in the matter of evidence. This is how the matter stands today, Monday. As you remember, two weeks ago Vandervelde and his German associates withdrew from the case, and Saturday the Russian lawyers followed. It is quite likely that in a few days more the prisoners themselves will withdraw by refusing to plead and to answer questions. That the prisoners will be found guilty there is no question; that they will be executed is doubtful. I can not imagine the Communists committing such a stupid act which will arouse against them the socialists the world over, not to say of the more conservative public opinion. But then, it is hard to tell. They do so many other stupid things.

Tuesday night, Rickard,[18] Brown, Goodrich, Herter,[19] Haskell, Hutch-

---

[18] Edgar Rickard (1874–1951) was the director general of the ARA.

[19] Christian A. Herter (1895–1967) was an assistant to Hoover at the Department of

inson, and others started for the Volga while I left for Petrograd, from where I have just returned. We have there something like twenty boxes of books which should have been sent out but have not been. I am attending to that matter now and will report more fully later.

In Moscow the government attracts all the attention and one does not notice the undercurrents as much as in Petrograd. I always come back from the former Russian capital with an aching heart because of the suffering I witness there. Six months ago I wrote to Lutz about a certain young woman, the sister of a lady in London whom I know and who asked me to look her up. This young woman has lost her father, her mother, her husband, one child by death, and the other by disappearance; her sister and brother have emigrated and the poor thing was all alone and suffering. She was a Red Cross sister, and lived in a convent but had to leave both places because of ill health. When I first met her she was giving herself to prayer and devotion. I tried to get her out of Russia to join her sister but she told me she could not leave until after Lent. When I left her in April she was in the hospital and since then she has had to undergo a serious operation.

When I reached Petrograd I went to the hospital and learned that she was in prison, but fortunately she was released that same day. When I saw her the next day she told me the following story. She was greatly worried about the trial of the clergy and just as soon as she was able to leave her bed she went to the trial and at the end of the trial, as the Metropolitan was being taken to the car to be removed to his cell, she with a number of others followed him and threw flowers. The police rounded up the whole crowd of more than 2000 people and took them all to prison. They were kept in the court yard the first half of the night, until a commissar appeared and asked for all the Communists to go into one corner, all the government employees to another, and all students into a third. These three groups were released, which left 538 to be dealt with. The woman in question, whom I will call Mrs. X, was put into a cell with four others and there she spent the remainder of the night. Next day she was put in with forty others, most of them criminals and the dirt and vermin were so bad that she just walked the floor.

When the prison doctor came through she begged him to take her out of there and when he realized what a sick woman she was he used his influence to have her removed and put into another cell where there was one other woman. This cell was clean, and admitted some light, but it had

Commerce; he later served as governor of Massachusetts (1953–57) and secretary of state in the Eisenhower administration (1959–1961).

no other bed than a board. Each morning she was given hot water and a small portion of bread for the whole day. At noon she was given soup made out of herring heads, which she could not eat, and in the evening hot water was once more put before her. Had it not been for the nurses of the hospital who were permitted to bring her something to eat on Mondays and Fridays she would have starved. Once a day she was allowed in the open air for twenty minutes. She was obliged to scrub floors and do other menial work. After she had been there nine days she was released because the doctor realized how ill she was.

It was a shock to me to see her. Two months ago she had color in her face and her bones were covered with a sufficient amount of flesh, now she is a skeleton, her clothes hang on her, her face is full of blotches, she spits blood and suffers from asthma. All this because she was in the crowd which demanded "No death for the priests." Had she been in the crowd which called for "Death to the Social Revolutionists," she would have been honored and rewarded with a day's wages. This is not all of the sad story. The poor woman's mind is becoming affected by this suffering. She glows in her martyrdom and is eager to repeat her performance in order to be locked up again. I got her something to eat and then persuaded her to leave Russia and join her sister. Next day, that is yesterday morning, Saturday, I took her to the Foreign Office, where a Communist friend of mine promised to help her get the necessary papers. But when she reached there she insisted on telling him that she was for the Church and the priests, etc., and I am afraid that she will spoil everything. Can't you see what a mad house we are in, and how helpless one is before this terrible tragedy?

While in Petrograd I called on one of the archivists whom I had known in [his] better days when I was collecting material for the Carnegie Institution.[20] This poor man has to support a wife and an old father and mother and here is what the government pays him: he has not received a full month's pay since January. Since the first of the year he has received altogether about 10 million rubles, but the little he receives is of not much help. He received in May a part of his January salary at the rate of wages paid in January, when a pound of bread was worth 20,000 while now it is 160,000. In addition to the salary or fraction of the salary, he receives each month about 30 lbs. of flour and 5 lbs. of salt herring. His staff has since January been reduced from 22 persons to 6. There is not a kopek appropriated for carrying on the work, neither in his department nor in many other departments. (I visited one of the museums where I was told by one of the officers that those in charge are selling museum things in order to keep

---

[20]Georgii Kniazev.

going.) This poor cripple bread winner has to have a pair of special boots for which the shoemaker asks 70 millions. In order to get money the wife has sold her shoes for 22 millions, some books, etc., and in this way they hope to raise the needed amount. He on the whole is better off than some of his colleagues for he has no rent to pay. One poor girl in his office received one month 1,300,000 rubles in wages and out of this amount the government took out 1,000,000 for the famine area, leaving her enough to buy two pounds of bread.

In this Government of the Workingmen many of these workingmen who work for the government (except army and navy and in some cases railway men) are shamefully exploited. I know a man in the Foreign Office who studied in an American university and is quite capable. He receives 38 millions a month, out of which the government takes 10 millions for his paiok of 36 lbs. of flour and 10 lbs. of salt herring; 9 millions go for room rent, one million for union dues, etc., leaving him 18 millions (the equivalent of 100 lbs. of bread) with which to clothe and nourish his family. He receives his pay regularly while thousands of others get mere advances. One of the most puzzling questions in Russia is, "How do people live?" Every one asks the question and no one can answer it. The usual reply is, "I do not know; we live somehow." I am collecting some material on that subject for our archives.

In one of my former letters I called your attention to the high price of books. The other day I had a talk with a publisher who explained the causes to me. Though Russia has private publishing houses it has no private printing houses. All the printing is in the hands of the so-called Trust in which the workmen take a leading part. Through the union the minimum wage is determined and consequently the costs of printing have gone up so high and the price of books has so risen that there are no buyers and publishers are closing their shops. Six months ago a number of publications were born but the new economic policy and the minimum wage have killed them off. More Russian books of importance are now published in Berlin than in Russia.

In this land of freedom many contradictions may be noticed. Last winter the Central in the Petrograd system burned out and for months Petrograd was without a telephone. Recently a new Central was put up and announcements were made that the users of the telephone would be required to pay 75 millions when their phone was connected up and 50 millions a month. Few people were able to do this and consequently their phone was not connected. When the telephone authorities realized this they (through the Soviet of Petrograd) issued a decree compelling certain institutions to put in telephones. One is never sure of anything; he never knows when new taxes will be levied, when old taxes will be increased. Last December friends of mine received notice that they must pay 15 millions in advance for the use of their phone until June. They paid it but a few weeks later they were asked to pay more, etc. Recently the Soviet authorities in Petrograd called the proprietors of a number of high class restaurants and notified them that their licenses for the year would cost many billions. The proprietors asked for a day to think it over and when they returned they said that they had decided to close their places because they could not afford to pay. "How much can you pay?" They named the sum and in this way they dickered until they agreed, but they are not sure that tomorrow they may not be compelled to pay more.

In order to raise the value of the ruble the Soviet government has decided to reduce the emission of money, especially bills of small denominations, such as 100,000 and 1,000,000 rubles. In place of them, bills of 50 and 100 millions have been put into circulation. As a result there is a scarcity of small money all over Russia, and in Petrograd I have seen people run around with big bills which they were unable to change. From Odessa our ARA men telegraph for small bills because they are obliged to pay six percent to get a big bill changed. This is one way of making the ruble go up, by creating a scarcity. Another way of creating a scarcity is by not paying salaries, but of this I have already spoken.

Among the thinking men, including many Communists, little is expected from the Hague. The Communists say that the present bread crop is going to influence to a considerable extent the policy of the government. If the crop is good the leaders may decide to make no more concessions for the present; if it is bad they may yield the few points of principle that separate them from America even before this winter. Some Communists think that if they could hold out for another year or two the Powers will give in on the question of debts and private property and save the face of the leaders. In spite of the signs to the contrary there is a steady movement to the right. America is in the best position to bring the Soviet to its point of view and the red leaders ask nothing better than an agreement with America. The German Communists who are friendly with the present regime as well as other Germans are pushing the Soviet along the line of agreement with America.

June 25, 1922

The courier is about to leave and I am drawing my letter to a close. Please excuse me for making my letters so long, but I feel that the events that take place here are worthy of record. It is not necessary that you should read all that I write. I am going to write my business letters separately and briefly.

In regard to the teachers' appeal which was given to me in Petrograd,[21] I thought it might be of interest to the Department of Education. It is a true picture. Should you care to make it public, leave out Petrograd or any other indication as to its origin. Of course, the same is true of any other material that I send. I do not care so much for myself as for the poor Russians.

I am beginning to collect manuscript material dealing with the economic and social condition of Russia during the war and revolution. I can not get much but every little helps.

It is not likely that I shall go to Siberia, the idea had to be abandoned because of the likelihood of early closing.[22] It is possible that I shall remain as an observer for a couple of months and make a more thorough study of some problems. Every day is full of interest and full of pain. I am glad I have had two months in Europe recently because I convinced myself that I can throw off the gloom when I leave here.

This morning I received Lutz's letter of May 31 informing me that the Russian collection has reached New York. By this time it is probably in the Library. I am glad of that.

I am not buying very much because of the high prices and because we already have a good collection. Had we an abundance of cash I should have recommended that we purchase more books. It is the last call.

With best wishes,

★ ★ ★

Moscow, July 6, 1922

Dear Professor Adams:

I am going to acknowledge, though hastily, your good letter of June 7.

The situation here has not cleared up since my last letter. If I remember correctly I told you that the men on the spot—that is, Haskell, Brown, Goodrich, Rickard, Herter, etc—had recommended that the relief work come to an end this fall. This recommendation was cabled to Hoover. Day before yesterday a cable came from him for Haskell, Brown, Rickard, and

---

[21]A copy of the Petrograd teachers' appeal to the public protesting the economic situation of educators can be found in the Golder collection, box 32.

[22]At the time Golder was writing it was assumed that the ARA would close down its Russian mission with the autumn harvest of 1922. In July, however, the ARA decided to continue its child-feeding and food package operations in Soviet Russia into the spring of 1923 under a reduced U.S. staff.

Herter to meet him in New York, where Goodrich will also be, no doubt to settle the question of feeding in Russia.

Now as to my own plans. As I told you before, I am of some help to the ARA but I am not essential to run the show. Herter—and I assume that he represents the views of Hoover—is rather eager for me to stay on as long as I can and keep a look out and report to Hoover what is going on in a political and economic way.[23] Brown urged that also. At the same time I can get away whenever it should seem best. It seems to me that Hoover and you can better plan that. It seems to me that it would be wise for me to return to Stanford not later than the Winter Quarter. If Hoover is in office there will be other calls for me to go to Russia and it would help me if I should get away from here and look at Russia from the distance and get a little of the American point of view. I am quite out of touch and I am even hesitating on the use of English words. The Russian problem will not be solved in a day or two. . . .

With kindest regards,
Cordially,

★ ★ ★

Conversation with Professor X[24]

The other day I called on my good friend Professor X to talk over the Russian situation. Professor X is a scholar of international reputation and like many Russian scholars is now deeply and actively[25] interested in political questions. During the old regime he was a member of the Imperial Council in which body he had much influence as a liberal and an independent, for he was never a party man. When the Revolution broke out he was one of the few who understood its meaning and possible consequences and instead of joining political intriguers as some of his colleagues did he devoted all his time and energy to saving as much of Russian culture and as many of

---

[23]In fact, Herter first suggested to Hoover that Golder remain in Moscow as a political observer. On June 1, 1922, Herter wrote to Hoover that Goodrich was on his way to Moscow and was bringing along Golder. "I think the Governor's views are quite largely moulded by Golder, who appears to be a very able citizen and ought, I think, to be retained by us in Moscow as political advisor if nothing else." American Relief Administration, Russian Mission, Hoover Institution Archives, box 262, folder: "Herter, Christian A."

[24]Professor Oldenburg.

[25]Golder subsequently edited this to read "passively and formerly actively."

the Russian scholars as he could. He has the respect and the good will of the Whites and the Reds and his appeals from time to time to the Communists in behalf of education are not always in vain. Since 1917, Professor X has lost some of his dearest friends and relatives; he and his family have suffered from hunger, cold, and diseases, and yet all these sorrows have not embittered him for he regards them as purifications of his country and sees in the distant future a greater and better Russia.

When I put to him the question whether America should recognize the existing Russian government he said most emphatically: "No. I ask you not to do so not because this government is Communist but because it is not for the best interests of Russia, the Russia of the future I am thinking of. Our present government is not a real government but a number of not very well coordinated commissariats, sometimes working together, sometimes intriguing against one another. It is not a government on the promises of which you can rely, for the orders of the central authorities in Moscow may or may not be obeyed in Petrograd or Kazan. Before you recognize this government it should of its own accord and whole heartedly offer to pay its debts, admit the rights of private property, select honest, learned, and impartial judges who will judge each case on its merits and not according to instructions from party headquarters, and frame a stable code of laws. At the present time we have decrees, hundreds of them, made and unmade by a group of five or six Communists to meet the political needs of the movement. Many of these decrees are contradictory and no one knows whether he is acting legally or criminally."

"Suppose," I asked, "America recognized Russia and American capital came into the country to develop its commerce and industry, would that not shorten the period of suffering and bring nearer the period of stability which you have so much at heart?" "No, it will not," he replied. "Our salvation can not come from without but must come from within, and we, as a government and to some extent as a nation, have not yet confessed and repented; we have not yet the contrite heart, and until we have reached that state of mind nobody can save us.

"Suppose you came now into this demoralized country, full as it is of propaganda and passion, suppose you opened shops and insisted on an honest day's work and directly or indirectly brought pressure on an unwilling government to modify its institutions so as to make it possible for you to carry on its work. What would happen? The cry would be raised at once that you are exploiting the proletariat and the country would be thrown back into the hands of the extremists and we would have to go through once more a period of suffering. Wait another year or two until the Russian people of themselves bring about the changes which you think you can make by coming in now. Time is working for Russia and I wish you could see, as I do, the great transformation that is taking place in the character of the people.

"The most important of all is, of course, that they are learning how to work. When the Revolution broke out the masses were taught that they had a right to live on the capitalists, that the state would take care of them, that if wealth were properly distributed no one would be obliged to work more than two or three hours a day. What has been the result? The wealth of the country has been wasted and consumed, the population has become demoralized, and the country has been brought to the verge of starvation. It is now becoming clear to most people that these teachings were false and that in order to live one must work, but this lesson has not yet been driven in deep enough and it will yet take a little time. For the sake of Russia, the great Russia of the future, give us a little more time. I and many of my friends may not survive the next year or two, we may die of hunger and cold, but that is a small price to pay for the good of our country. Russia is like a patient recovering from typhoid fever and to whom much food, though he craves it, must be denied. Let us recover slowly, let us suffer some more the cruel pangs of hunger because it is the only way to get well and strong.

"Not only will Russia recover quickly materially but, I believe, also intellectually and culturally. All the suffering, all the misery we have endured and are enduring is teaching us Russians to think clearly and that is a great step in the line of progress."

★ ★ ★

Moscow, July 9, 1992

Dear Professor Adams:

. . . Herter has asked me to write directly to Hoover through him and therefore I am writing two kinds of letters, one about the general situation and the other about matters relating to the Hoover Collection and my connection with Stanford. I am, of course, sending you everything I write on any subject so that Dr. Wilbur and you may know what is going on and also to keep up our files.

I am now at work on several special studies which I trust to have ready to send soon. The secret police is becoming more and more interested in our welfare and I am not forgotten. They have nothing on me and I am not giving them the opportunity, but feel their watchfulness in a subconscious way and often catch myself looking behind me or about me.

Col. Haskell leaves tomorrow and Quinn remains in charge. It is doubtful whether the Colonel will return. Let me repeat again my hope that the ARA will get out of here soon and that Hoover will drop out of relief work altogether.

                                        With good wishes,

★ ★ ★

                                                Moscow, July 9, 1922

My dear Professor Adams:

There was something doing in Moscow and Petrograd this last week. I have already written you about the trial of the clergy. About a month ago eleven priests of Moscow were condemned to be shot and five of them were shot. After that the scene of excitement shifted to Petrograd where several dozen of them were on trial for resisting the laws of the Soviet, inciting revolt, and the general charge of counter-revolution, which covers a multitude of sins and may be determined and interpreted as one likes.

I told you also of the case of the woman who went to the trial and was arrested and locked up for two weeks or rather ten days. The trial is playing havoc with the nerves of some people and last week when I was in Petrograd I found the same poor woman going to the trial and denying herself food in order that she may buy something to eat for the prisoners. I saw that she was hungry and I insisted that she should have lunch with me. She refused at first but I finally coaxed her into it, but when we were through eating she told me that the reason she hesitated was the knowledge that if she did not reach the court house by noon she would have to stand up until five o'clock and she did not have the strength to do that. I wondered after all whether I had done her more harm than good. The trial came to an end May 5 with the condemnation of the Metropolitan of Petrograd, a prominent bishop, two or three professors, and a number of priests—altogether eleven men were sentenced to be shot. This sentence has stirred the thinking people very much.

The trial of the Social Revolutionists is still going on and another is being prepared. About a week or ten days ago over one hundred Social Democrats, many of whom were holding prominent positions in the government, were arrested and some sent out of the city. No one knows exactly why and for what purpose. It is assumed that the Communists have determined to crush any possibility of a future uprising by discrediting the leaders and the parties. With the arrest of the Social Democrats there has come to be a feeling that the left wing of the party is taking the upper hand. Trotsky, Bukharin, and one other less well known Communist are the three men who are behind the arrests and trials. A number of doctors have also been locked up this week because they dared to criticise publicly the

Department of Public Health. Fear of search and arrests is spreading and in some homes where I have been every bit of paper, such as for example the London Times and other foreign sheets, are being hidden or destroyed for fear they might bring suspicion and arrest.

I have been reading the papers with some care in order to see just what kind of a public opinion the leaders are trying to create. The general tone is no more retreats, no more compromise with the bourgeoisie, let the bourgeoisie understand that this is a dictature of the proletariat and that the proletariat only through the Communist Party will govern, and that the laws are revolutionary laws and will be interpreted from the proletarian point of view. This tone has had a very depressing effect on the non-Communists, some of whom had made up their minds that the best thing to do was to make their peace with the Bolsheviks, work with them to build up the country so that in the end a sane and sound Russia may evolve. They now see themselves condemned forever to be hewers of wood and drawers of water, with the sword ever hanging over their heads.

About a year ago a group of Russian émigrés, generals, and publicists who had served in the White armies and governments, wrote a book called Smena vekh,[26] published in Prague, in which they tried to show that the period of resistance to the Soviet government was over and that from now on all the Russian émigrés should make their peace with the de facto government and help to build up Russia. The Bolo press hailed this announcement with delight and even tried to get a certain amount of diplomatic success out of it. The generals who came back were received with honor and later assigned to some obscure post where they will never again be heard of and where they will ever be watched. Of the publicists, men like Professor Kliuchnikov[27] were invited to go to the Genoa Conference as experts, and from there brought back here to testify against the Social Revolutionists and to show how they plotted against the Soviet government with Kolchak at the same time when he, Kliuchnikov, was Kolchak's Minister of Foreign Affairs. This testimony led one of the prisoners to exclaim, "Kliuchnikov, you worked against us with Kolchak because we were too radical and now you denounce us because we are too conservative." Now that the Reds have gotten out of Kliuchnikov all that they wanted they opened their guns on him and during this last week there were some bitter attacks and the papers have given him to understand that

---

[26]*Change of signposts* (Prague, 1921).

[27]Iurii Veniaminovich Kliuchnikov (1886–1938) was a specialist in international law and privatdocent at Moscow University before the revolution. After Kolchak's defeat he emigrated to Paris; on his return to Soviet Russia in 1922 he worked in the Communist Academy.

he is after all a d—n bourgeois and that he had made a mighty mistake in thinking that in returning to Russia he would be permitted to bring back the country to bourgeoism. His wings are now properly clipped.

German affairs have taken up a great deal of space in the press. On July 6, Karl Radek had a very able editorial on the German situation in which he tried to develop the idea that it is impossible to bring about a government of the proletariat through democracy and that the course which the German Socialists are pursuing, in trying to compromise with the capitalists and landowners and militarists and working with them, leads them back to monarchism, and that the only way to save the situation is revolution and force and to establish now a real proletarian government and not wait for evolution to do that. The non-Communists interpret the events in Germany in an entirely different way. "Look," they say, "how the German people are rising up in their might to defend themselves against monarchist terror and what they are doing to establish a real democratic government." Some of the Communists would not at all be averse to see a monarchy reestablished in Germany on the theory that it would convince the masses that neither socialism nor monarchism is fit to be entrusted with power and therefore it should be handed over to the proletariat.

The economic situation seems to be improving. Food is becoming cheaper and there is more of it. The crop promises to be good and an editorial in the Izvestiia of July 7 makes the statement that "in all likelihood Russia will not only have enough food for herself but some grain even for export," and then goes on to say that the government should do all that it can to keep individuals from engaging in the export trade. The ruble is holding its own, about 3,800,000 to the dollar. Aside from food, which is cheaper than it was, but not as cheap as in America or Germany (I am talking about Moscow and Petrograd), everything else is high. Transportation is improving and now a through train Moscow-Chita is running close to schedule.

July 10

In yesterday's Pravda the Communists issued a long appeal to the Germans not to form a coalition government with bourgeois parties and to work for a proletarian government.

In the Izvestiia there was a report of the meeting of the All-Russian Committee on Hunger, of which Kalinin[28] is president and at which

---

[28]Mikhail Ivanovich Kalinin (1875–1946) was president of the RSFSR and chairman of the Central Commission for Aid to the Hungry attached to the All-Union Central Executive Committee (VTsIK), established July 18, 1921.

meeting he presided. It was voted to ask the foreign organizations to continue feeding until after the gathering of the crop and after that to devote most of their resources, not in buying food, but in building up the agricultural life, that is purchasing plows, etc.

Two matters were brought to my attention yesterday that are worthy of notice. Last night I met the director of one of the museums which has many treasures. He told me that his museum is without resources and that the government itself has commenced taking out things to sell. He showed me some things which were given him to sell to meet current expenses, one of these things I bought. From other museums I hear the same story and I have no doubt but the stories are true. Russia is consuming its capital.

The other matter is this. There is a government department that occupies itself with supplying wood for the locomotives of a certain railway line. Until some months back the government supported this department but more recently it notified it that it would have to be self supporting. In order to do this the department has handed over the forests to contractors, who, in return for the supply of wood which they furnish the department, help themselves to the rest.

★ ★ ★

Moscow, July 17, 1922

My dear Professor Coolidge:

Your letter of June 27 gave me much pleasure. I was glad to know that the books have reached you in good condition and that you are pleased. As I have already written you the book market is almost dead owing to the high prices. Dela i dni[29] has gone the way of all flesh after making three appearances. Other publications which have given promise in the past have already stopped appearing. New ones are cropping up. The other day I learned that Annaly, a new historical journal, has made its debut in Petrograd. I am going to that famous city tonight and I shall ask for an introduction. The long delayed and much looked for Krasnyi arkhiv,[30] Part I, is out, also another volume of Franco-Russian relations, 1910–1914, is out. I am sending both to you. No doubt you will find much to interest you but not as much as you expect in view of the publications of other countries.

---

[29]*Works and days* (1920–1922) was a scholarly journal that published the work of "bourgeois" historians.

[30]*Red archive* (1922–1941), sponsored by the new establishment, published many important documents on the background and cause of the revolution.

I gave your kindest regards to the ARA men, and last night I was at the Bakhrushins' and remembered you to the Professor crowd over there. I must confess I am bored by the scholars, very much bored, and I am very sorry for them. They are so humiliated, so oppressed that there is no life left in them and when they meet they talk poor shop talk and abuse of the government, especially our mutual friend Pokrovsky. I can forgive them that. I went to see him the other day and found him worn out. In addition to his numerous other duties he is now busy as accuser of the Social Revolutionists and his days are pretty well filled. On top of that Trotsky has taken a fall out of him [sic] and for a couple of weeks I tried to read the exchange of letters that have appeared in the Pravda. It is all about materialistic interpretation, of which I know so little because you never offered a course in that field. Trotsky hit with a club, but my poor friend Mikhail Nikolaevich struck back with a wand. I am afraid M. N. is slated for a back seat, in fact he has already told me that he must save himself for his scholarly work and therefore is obliged to give up some of his administrative duties.

I see Muravev and Sokolov often. The former was counsel for the SRs and finally withdrew from the case when he realized that the judges were determined to judge according to party policy and not according to law. Because he withdrew he has been disqualified from practicing at all. What the poor man will do I do not know. He was also engaged as counsel for the Patriarch and by disqualifying him a direct blow was given to the Patriarch. There will not be many brave lawyers to argue cases against the government. Sokolov has become a bit pessimistic about the political situation. It is bitter for him to acknowledge it.

I am not running around as much as before and therefore have more time for closer observation. I am beginning to understand a few things and making a few notes. It looks now as if I will remain here until fall and then return to take up my work at Stanford. On my way across I will see you and tell you what little I know.

Haskell left for New York last Monday. He will be joined by the other gods of the ARA where an important conference will be held. From them and from Herter who has recently been here you will learn much news if you run across them.

I have not yet heard from Stanford in regard to the books from Russia, whether they have reached destination or not. When I go to Petrograd tonight I will see to it that the remaining boxes of books are sent out. I am almost certain that you have two or three boxes there. I do not think it wise to buy any more books unless it is something special.

There is much to tell you and little to write. Please remember me to

Lord, Blake, Haskins, Kerner,[31] and any others who sometimes think of me.

Most sincerely yours,

★ ★ ★

Moscow, July 17, 1922

Mr. Christian Herter
Washington, D.C.

My dear Herter:

This last week was on the whole a quiet one. For some reason or other the leading editorial writers on the two official papers, Radek and Steklov,[32] kept very quiet. There was not a single signed paper by them until last Saturday. By that time it became quite clear that the Hague Conference was a failure and the two men named above burst into lamentations. They blame the failure of the conference on the Powers, and console themselves with the fact that they did not have much to give any way. Both emphasized the fact that the Soviet would make no more retreats unless it received compensation in the way of credit. Now that the Conference has failed the thing for the Soviet to do is to make separate agreements.

I was invited last Saturday to meet Citizen Frumkin, assistant Minister of Commerce.[33] Frumkin is an important Communist with considerable influence in the party. He was at one time quite red but office holding has changed his color a bit. We discussed the Hague Conference. He told me what most of us knew, that the Soviet did not expect any definite results. Nevertheless he felt that the two conferences, Genoa and Hague, were distinct victories, political and moral, for the Soviet government. Europe has to take notice of Russia and Russia is now a moral and a political factor in world affairs. On this point there is no argument. As to the near future, he admitted that the Russian financial situation is not particularly bright, but it is much better than it was.

In the first place he said that there is an improvement in transportation

---

[31]Robert H. Lord, Robert Blake, Charles H. Haskins, and Robert J. Kerner were Harvard historians.

[32]Iurii Mikhailovich Steklov (1873–1941) was a party and government official and editor of *Izvestiia*.

[33]Moisei Il'ich Frumkin (1878–1939) from 1918 to 1922 was a member of the collegium of the People's Commissariat of Food Supply (Narkomprod) and from 1922 to 1924 deputy people's commissar of foreign trade.

and mining and that meant a great deal. He undoubtedly exaggerates the improvement but I did not think it worth while to argue with him. In the second place the crop situation is very encouraging. Russia expects to have a surplus of grain amounting to 200 to 300 million puds. This may be sold, or what is more likely it may be kept as a reserve. If sold it will bring in money with which to buy foreign goods. Any way, Russia will not have to spend money purchasing food abroad. In this connection I asked him to explain to me what the Russian Minister of Finance, Sokol'nikov,[34] meant (see London Times, July 7) when he said that Russia had now large reserves of grain which could not be exported because of lack of transportation facilities. To this he replied that the only reserves he knew were those the peasants have unloaded recently in view of the approaching good harvest.

We next tackled Russo-American relations. He asked why we were not more friendly to his government. I explained that we are friendly enough and would open relations whenever our points of view agreed. Russia could hardly expect our bankers to lend her more money so long as the old debts were repudiated. I made it clear to him that I did not think our government would lend any government a single cent. He replied that Russia would be very glad to pay us the debts if she had the wherewith [sic] to pay. If she had credit to develop her industries she would have the money to pay. I pointed out to him that the two questions, debts and credits, must be kept distinct. The question of paying government debts and debts to our nationals is a political matter which our government handles, and that credit is a matter to be dealt with by the Russian government and our bankers. He came back by saying that, after all, the debtors and creditors are the same people, the bankers, and that the government is merely a go-between and that therefore debts and credits are bound together. I endeavored to explain to him that our large banks get their money from the small banks and the small banks from the people and that just now and as long as Russia repudiates her debts the American public would not lend a kopek, but whenever Russia acknowledges her debts and promises to pay them and thereby reestablishes her moral credit, the American people would be glad to come to the help of Russia.

He then said that French public opinion is guided largely by the fact that so many Frenchmen held Russian bonds and he wondered whether the same is true in America. I told him that I did not think so because on the whole comparatively few Americans held Russian bonds, but that with us it was a question of principle and honesty. He seemed to hint that our attitude towards Russia was greatly influenced by the French. When I took

---

[34]Grigorii Iakovlevich Sokol'nikov (1888–1939) was people's commissar of finance.

issue with that he remarked that "it is rather a peculiar coincidence that the American and French points of view are so nearly alike." He ended up by assuring me that if representatives of America and Russia could get together a number of misunderstandings could be straightened out.

In this connection I should like to say something about Krassin's visit to America next fall. A friend of Krassin's told me some weeks ago that Krassin had been invited to deliver a course of lectures in some educational institution in America next fall. I tried to find out the name of the institution but have not yet succeeded. In talking to Mr. Frumkin I referred to these lectures but he had a kind of blank [look] on his face, but knew something about the proposed trip. Krassin himself will be back in a couple of weeks and I will then learn more. If he is really going I am going to put him at the Cosmos Club and try and give him letters to people in the States. Shall I give him a letter to Hoover? The State Department may know something of this visit. Is there anything that Hoover would like me to do or would he rather that I keep my hands off? In putting him up at the Cosmos Club that is purely a personal matter. The people with whom I come in contact know quite well that I have no official standing whatever and there can be no misunderstanding on that subject.

There are a few other matters that may interest you. During the last week it became known here that Gorky had given out interviews in which he attacked the Bolsheviks. These attacks have been keenly felt by the leaders here judging from the fact that they protest so much. In yesterday's Izvestiia, Radek had a leading editorial where he took the tone that poor Gorky was never much of a statesman, that now he is under the thumb of the reactionary elements in Berlin and his vision is quite distorted, and that when the poor chap comes back he will see things differently.

Another bit of news that is stirring up the more thinking people is the rumor, pretty well confirmed, that on January 1 or sooner vodka will be openly sold. It is feared that the already demoralized Russian masses will go to pieces under it, now that all moral restraints, external and internal, have broken down. The purpose of the sale is to increase the revenue. The financial situation is very bad and many departments have not been paid for months and other departments have had their personnel greatly cut down. This is especially true of educational institutions. For next year the small schools will be left to sink or swim. It is quite clear that the Soviet government, like the people, is living on what it can sell and it may reach the condition of the people when it will have nothing to sell.

The trial of the Social Revolutionists still drags on. The Russian lawyers who for a time defended them and then withdrew from the case have been disqualified from practicing law. Under the circumstances it is dangerous for a man to take up a case against the government.

There has been called a meeting of the Soviet for August 3 and this has called forth some grumbling on the part of the provincial Communists who go on the theory that the fewer meetings the better. On this occasion the international situation will be discussed. . . .

> With kindest regards,
> Sincerely yours,

★ ★ ★

Petrograd, July 20, 1922

My dear Herter:

I reached here Tuesday morning, July 18, and at once made my calls on my friends, Red and White. That same evening one of my Reds telephoned me that Ioffe[35] would like to see me next day at one o'clock. At the appointed time I called on him and had an hour's conversation with him. Of all the Bolos that I have met he is the most polished and the most suave and the only one who really talks German well, for we talked in German.

After discussing the ARA for a few minutes, the work of which he praised, we launched out on the Hague Conference. He said that he never had any illusions about the possible outcome of these gatherings for it did not seem possible to get an agreement that would suit everybody. Nevertheless he considered the achievement of the two conferences satisfactory in that it swept away many prejudices; it taught Europe and America that the Soviet was not as terrible as some people said and that it is possible to do business with the Russians.

Now that these conferences are almost over the Communists are a bit divided as to what next. Some argue that Russia must tie herself closely to Germany, others argued for an alliance with England, but he, Ioffe, with a considerable following, is for an understanding with America. The two peoples must work together not only for economic reasons but also for political, especially in regards to the Far Eastern Question. If forced to it Russia can do much harm to the U.S. in the Pacific, if we have any doubts about it we might think what has been done in India. However, much as he desired it he did not see any possibility of working with America because American journalists had told him that the U.S. because of the Monroe Doctrine refuses to mix in European affairs and therefore it is not likely that anything would be done for Russia.

I, of course, pointed out the falsity of his assumption, and said that we

---

[35]Adol'f Abramovich Ioffe (1873–1927) was a Soviet diplomat.

have always had the doctrine but that did not prevent us from being on good relations with Russia and the other powers, etc. This seemed to satisfy him and we went on. He said that at Genoa many people had said to him, "How can we be sure that after you get the European capitalists into your power you will not again confiscate their property and repudiate your debts?" "In order to answer this question," he said, "one must look facts in the face. The present revolution is not a success and it is not likely that the Russians will try it again. The Communists still count on a world revolution but the next move will have to come from some other country than Russia. Until then Russia is not going in for socialization and nationalization to any great extent, unless other governments do. Russia is not going to try anything new alone and if other countries have revolution then it does not matter much to the capitalists where money is invested. For the time being Russia is as safe as any other part of the world so far as investments are concerned."

At the Genoa Conference many people said to him, "You are almost a capitalistic government, why don't you go all the way?" In reply he said to them, "Russia, that is, the Soviet government, must be different from other governments in order to have any support. We must retain our communistic principles even if we give up some of the practices, for without principles there are no communists. We have our principles and believe in them. Many of us have fought, suffered, and died for the revolutionary cause for many years, some of us have escaped the bullets of tsarism and if we can prevent it, we are not going to be assassinated by capitalism. We have given up all that is possible and we must not be asked to give up the principles in which we believe."

I recalled him from this flight to talk of more practical things, the payment of American debts. He repeated what so many other Reds have told me and will continue to tell me, that Russia is willing to pay debts if credit is given her to reestablish her economic life. When I pointed out to him that the American government would not extend any credit and that foreign capitalists would not be likely to make any loans until that question was settled, he took issue with me: "Why, we are constantly getting offers from American capitalists." "Capitalists of importance?" I inquired. "Yes, Vanderlip—not Frank Vanderlip—and others." I smiled and so did he.[36] "To

---

[36]This refers to the curious episode involving Washington B. Vanderlip, Jr., a U.S. businessman who arrived in Moscow in the autumn of 1920 and presented himself to the Bolsheviks as an entrepreneur with millions of dollars to invest and great influence in Washington. The Soviet leaders mistook him for the well-known U.S. banker Frank A. Vanderlip and consequently made a big fuss over him. He was

recognize and pay the debts to the U.S. would be a simple matter if it did not open the door to France and we are afraid of you because you are supporting France," he added. When I asked him what evidence he had that we are backing France, he acknowledged that he had nothing more than circumstantial evidence. I spent a few minutes' time trying to show him wherein our Russian policy differed from the French, and how much easier it is to come to an understanding with us than with France, that the conditions laid down by Hughes as regards debt and private property are not impossible.

I concluded by asking him whether he or any other of his colleagues had made a special study of the American question. He said no, that the American question had been lumped together with the European, that he and his comrades had assumed many things on general hearsay. We both agreed that it might not be a bad idea to form a special commission for that purpose and he promised to suggest that matter to the Moscow authorities next week. In parting he said, "Maybe you will mix in our affairs, even if you do not in European, because we are only half European." At this we both smiled and parted. It was a pleasant interview. He told me that he leaves shortly for China to be the Russian representative. Is he going there to do us good or harm? Please answer. I hear that he is to make a treaty with China and open negotiations with Japan.

On my return to the office of the ARA I found a message that Tsyperovich,[37] a very important and influential Communist, wished to see me today, Thursday, at eleven o'clock. On the way to him I ran into another Communist whom I have known for some little time and whom I regard as an honest and trustworthy man. He is of the opinion that Russia can be saved by America and in his way is doing all that he can. We had a long talk and among other subjects we discussed Dubrovsky of New York.

He told me many interesting things. For example, he said that after the ARA decided to come to Russia, Gregory's stories became known and that greatly frightened the Communists and they decided to be on guard. They put some of their reddest tovarishchs to watch us and to prevent us from repeating the Hungarian performances. That was not enough. It was also

---

received by Lenin, with whom he discussed various investment schemes, including his plan to "rent" Kamchatka. It was several months before the Bolsheviks realized their error. See E. H. Carr, *The Bolshevik Revolution,* vol. 3, pp. 282–85, and Adam Ulam, *The Bolsheviks* (New York, 1965), pp. 484–85. An eyewitness to Lenin's misplaced enthusiasm about Vanderlip was H. G. Wells, *Russia in the Shadows* (New York, 1921), pp. 78, 150–52, 164–68.

[37]G. V. Tsyperovich (1871–1932) was a Bolshevik economist and publicist.

necessary to put some one to watch over us in America and create a public sentiment for the Soviet and against us should we attempt revolutionary stunts. The man selected for this work was Dubrovsky. D. studied in the University of Kiev from which place he was expelled for revolutionary activities. He went to the U.S. and after a time entered Fordham College in New York and graduated from the dental department. He kept up his interest in Russian politics. When Martens was made Soviet representative he took in Dubrovsky, and he, because he had an American passport, was made the messenger between the U.S. and foreign ports, where Bolshevik information and money could be had. When Martens left, Dubrovsky remained. When it became necessary to select some one to watch over the ARA and create a public opinion Dubrovsky was chosen and given the post of Red Cross representative.

Dubrovsky's ability is not highly rated by the Communists, but he has proved himself not only useful but also profitable. He has accepted thousands of dollars for transmission to Russia, promising dollar for dollar, but paid in Soviet rubles according to the rate of exchange when the money was accepted. My informant told me that his father had 25 dollars sent to him and after many months he received enough rubles with which to buy six pounds of bread. I can readily believe that. Dubrovsky has also been useful as a propagandist for in each place where he tries to form a Red Cross circle he also attempts to organize a Communist group. Many Communists are agitating for his removal and the reason that it has not been done is that there is no one quite so well qualified (American citizenship) to take his place. However, it is likely that he will be called off this autumn, but that is not certain. How does this correspond with the information you have?

It was about 11:30 when I had my interview with Tsyperovich. He started out by praising the work of the ARA and made some comments on the crop situation, but nothing of importance. In a few minutes we were talking Hague Conference. "If the Conference ends in failure, as it is likely to," he said, "it will be a disgrace." What is Russia's next move? I inquired. "We will go along without help. Look outside," he pointed to the window, "and you will see we are working. We are moving slowly, to be sure, but we are going ahead nevertheless. The crop is fair this year, and what is more important our people understand that the Soviet government is doing its very best in its dealings with the Western Powers and if we fail it is not our fault."

After he had discussed the question in general for a time he led up to America. Why does America stand aloof and why does it support France? I explained to him as best I could our position and pointed out to him how much easier it is to come to an understanding with us, but emphasized the fact that our government, in my opinion, would never consent to treat the problems of "debts" and "credits" as one question, that Russia must first acknowledge and promise to pay her debts and then deal with the bankers about credits. He came back as many others do, that Russia is going to make no promises until she could see her way clear to pay, or in other words until she had credit. I replied that it seemed to me that he and his colleagues were fighting windmills and that the question is much simpler. "Suppose," I said, "they accept the American terms, promise to pay debts both to the government and to our nationals, ask that a mixed commission be appointed to study the debts question to determine its amount and the terms of payment, what would happen? It is likely that if your acceptance is acceptable to our government, a commission would be appointed, some form of recognition might possibly follow, and you would then have the opportunity to discuss with our bankers the question of credits." "That sounds so simple," he replied, "but I am afraid of a trap. The moment we obligate to pay our debts to you, which are insignificant, France and the others will demand the same terms. We are willing to pay them our debts if they will promise to pay ours, but on this they refuse to commit themselves. What assurances have we that after we have promised to pay our debts to your government your bankers will give us credit? If we had some assurances, official or non-official, on that point we might not hesitate. If a group of American bankers made us a proposition to give us credit and demanded as a sine quo that we acknowledge debts we would give it very serious consideration. It is a serious matter and we must go carefully. We must do what Ioffe and you talked about yesterday, appoint a special commission to study the American question, as we must study separately every European question and deal with each on its merits."

He asked me also to go and see men in the Foreign Office in Moscow and talk to them, but I thanked him and told him that I could not do that for I had nothing to propose, that I had no official standing, that I was a teacher of Russian history and interested in Russian problems and eager to see commercial relations established between Russia and America, but that I would be glad to talk to them should they desire it.

We talked for about an hour in Russian. He was not so easy to talk to as Ioffe, but he was much more in earnest, at least he seemed so. He talked less about theoretical subjects, though neither of the two men waved the red flag to any extent, and he took the stand that he knew America pretty well and that if our government desired to find a way out it could.

After talking with these men and others, I think that there is a strong desire to go after America now, but our friends the Bolos do not know how to tackle the subject. They are afraid of us and they still think that we are the deadliest enemies they have.

Friday, July 21

Last night Dr. Walker and I went to the Splendid Palace, the Monte Carlo of Petrograd. For some months Petrograd has been wide open and a number of gambling houses did good business but within the last week all but Splendid Palace have been closed. Why they were closed no one knows (rumor has it because too many officials lost government money), but one night the rumor spread that the Cheka was coming and all present made a rush for the door, leaving their winnings behind them. Splendid Palace is under special protection of the Cheka, but it is occasionally spoken of as the "ARA Palace." A certain percentage of the winnings go to the Soviet representative with the ARA with which he pays that part of the ARA expenses which the Soviet has obligated itself. Lately the average nightly share of the Soviet amounted to about 10 billions of rubles, or about 2500 dollars a night. All the ARA employees are paid up to date and there is enough left for the other foreign organizations.

Splendid Palace was full of people. At first the director was unwilling to admit us because we said that we did not intend to play but only to look on. When, however, he learned (by looking at us) that we were not Russians and when one of his assistants said that he had seen Walker in the ARA, the director gave us passes. It costs 3 million rubles to enter. All the tables were crowded, at many of them baccarat was played, Macao also had its partisans, but roulette had the largest audiences. I was told that the bank has four numbers but I could not identify them, aside from 0. Betting was heavy and the officials in charge had long, broad wooden blades and it kept them busy pushing the paper millions from number to number. There were also large round paper circles which could be bought from the bank, representing tens of millions. Gold was also in evidence. On the whole there were fewer old and young people than at Monte Carlo, most of those present were between the ages of 30 and 60. Where these millions come from, whether they are honestly secured, is a question.

Town Talk

The question of the sale of vodka which is to commence soon is causing considerable talk. The Soviet vodka will contain, so it is reported, 38% alcohol as against 40% of the tsar's vodka. Someone is supposed to have drawn a cartoon representing Nicholas Romanov sitting at a table in a dirty vodka shop drinking vodka with Lenin. The former has a glass with 40% and the latter with 38% and the tsar says to the leader of the proletariat: "Lenin, do you really think it was worth turning Russia upside down for 2%?"

Lenin's conscience is not at rest and he is all the time trying to break away from his sick room in order to go and apologize to the Russian people for the misery he has brought on them.

Krassin is going to America to negotiate with New York and Chicago business men.

"Expert" and "Export." In 1918 when the confiscation and nationalization of the property of the rich began, Gorky used his influence to organize an "Expert Commission" to appraise the works of art and to take care of them. In Petrograd the various things that were not smashed or stolen on the way were deposited in the Saltykov Palace which adjoins the British Embassy. The better artists of Petrograd refused to go on this commission because they were opposed to this wholesale confiscation and therefore various antiquarians were put on it. At first the museums were allowed to pick out some of the works of art and put them in their museums, but since the New Economic Policy has come the museums have been asked to pay for anything they ask and as they have no money they have not been able to take anything. The Expert Commission has no money and consequently it has been permitted to sell its things. Some of the most valuable objects are exported, others are sold by members of the Commission to themselves for their shops and in the end the "Expert Commission" has become an "Export Commission."

During the last week (July 10–20) few ships have come into Petrograd and this incident coupled with the break up of the Hague Conference has let loose many rumors. One is that the Allies are again blockading Russia and no ships can come in, that the Russian delegation has been sent out of England, that the ARA is closing up—all these rumors have affected the food market and prices have gone up with a jump. At the same time it was whispered about that there were serious uprisings in Pskov, Novgorod, Crimea, and other places.

The arrest on a large scale of people for political or church reasons continues.

Newspaper Items

Now that the Hague Conference is over and the capitalistic countries have presented a united front it is up to the proletariat of the world to do likewise. The Moscow Pravda of July 23 contained an appeal of the Russian Communist International to the Workmen (male and female) of the World in which the treachery of the capitalists, and also of the 2nd and 2nd 1/2 Internationals, is shown up and the duty of the proletariat of the world pointed out: that it must help economically (like the American Union of

Tailors, which has come to Russia and has invested millions of dollars in Russia, in partnership with the Soviet) in re-establishing Russia and politically by bringing pressure to bear on their capitalistic governments to help Russia and not to destroy it (for the Social Revolutionists will now again intrigue with France against the Soviet), and ends with "Long Live the Soviet" and "Down with the Capitalist Robbers."

Pravda of July 19 announces that all paper moneys printed between 1918–1921 inclusive will go out of circulation after October 1 (with the exception of 50,000 and 100,000 ruble notes); 1, 5, and 10 million notes of 1921 will retain their value until January 1, 1923. After that date only the paper money of 1922 will be recognized as legal. People having 1918–21 money may exchange it for 1922. Note: Outside of Moscow and Petrograd there is very little 1922 money to be found.

The Izvestiia of July 18 prints the railway tariffs, which is enclosed.

In order to help the peasants and win them over, the Soviet government has decided not to collect from them the seed advanced in 1920 until some future time and the seed advanced in 1921–22 until sometime in 1923–24. This applies only to the famine area. Izvestiia, July 23.

★ ★ ★

Moscow, July 24, 1922

My dear Herter:

I returned to Moscow yesterday and am again busy. I am afraid you will be shocked at my letter for it might seem to you as if I were taking too much part in political affairs. Perhaps I am, but it is with the big guns. Not only do I do nothing to which the Soviet can object, but I am really trying to help them. I am doing nothing to which they can object. However, should it seem best for me to come out, I can do that at any time.

It is quite likely that a special commission to study the American question will be appointed as a result of my interviews last week. At least I have heard indirectly that both Ioffe and Tsyperovich are going to urge it. Zinoviev and Nevskii[38] have indicated that they wished to talk to me but I have to leave Petrograd and could not remain over for the interviews. If this commission is appointed it will probably call on me for information. If you think it wise to send me an unofficial statement of the present position of our government on the Russian question it would help. I should like to have

---

[38]Vladimir Ivanovich Nevskii (1876–1937) was a Petrograd historian and party official.

it very clear, point by point, so that there may not be misinformation. Will you please write me at length on the whole subject. Do not use official paper and do not sign it.

★ ★ ★

Moscow, August 1, 1922

My dear Herter:

I went with Messrs. Flesh and Sherman[39] to Petrograd on Saturday and have just returned and this accounts for the delay in this letter. No great events have taken place here since last week but the river of life is not stagnant and there are one or two currents moving. The trial of the Social Revolutionists is drawing to an end and before this reaches you the fate of the prisoners will be known to you. During the last week the papers have urged that the accused be given the full benefit of the law, which means execution, but just the same they have not used that word. I should not be surprised if a large number of the accused were sentenced to be shot and out of that number the Soviet would show mercy to more than half. However, one Communist who talks as one having authority assures me that not one of the accused will suffer capital punishment. There are some interesting side lights on the trial. Bukharin, editor of the Pravda, the red organ that cries for the blood of the Social Revolutionists, is one of the prosecuting attorneys against the SRs, the right wing of the accused, and legal counselor for the left wing of the SRs, that part which turned state's evidence.

The echoes of the Hague Conference are still heard. Sokol'nikov, one of the delegates, came back and reported that the reason the conference failed was because the Western Powers had nothing to give. On the whole there is rather keen disappointment over the failure of the meeting, not on account of the money (because little was expected on that score), but because of the failure in propaganda and the failure of creating dissension between England and France. The cry is now: "We can get along without the help of the capitalists, our harvest is good, our hands are free to make separate agreements," etc.

As you know there is a conference this week of the leaders of the Communist party and the international question will be taken up.[40] I was

---

[39]Edwin M. Flesh was comptroller and Edwin Sherman was executive assistant of the ARA.

[40]Twelfth All-Russian Party Conference, August 4–7.

told in Petrograd that from that city letters have been written to Trotsky, Stalin, and other leaders calling upon them to take up negotiations with the United States.

A Persian delegation has been in Moscow for some time trying to make a commercial treaty but the negotiations do not lead to results because the Persians insist on the right of private property and freedom of trade. Since my last letter the papers have published the note from the Japanese government in regard to treaty negotiations and I note that Ioffe has been appointed to carry on the negotiations. This leads me again to ask the question whether it is for our good or harm. I should not be at all surprised to learn that throughout the Far East the Communists will know that almost the whole of the Russian Fleet in Kronstadt has been sold to Germany for scrap metal and the ships are now being broken up. The proceeds of the sale, I am told, are to pay for coal for Petrograd.

The political reaction of which I told you before is still going on. About two months ago the Russian Medical Association met and something was said at the meetings which displeased the government and which was published abroad. Since then many of the leading physicians have been arrested and some exiled and still others have been deprived of their positions. There will be no more meetings of the Medical Association for years to come. In Petrograd there were organized three or four years ago a Dom uchenykh, Dom literaterov, and Dom iskusstva (Houses of Scholars, Literary Men, and Art). Gorky was principally responsible for these centers through which it was possible to come to the aid of the intellectuals in question. But these were organized centers not wholly in sympathy with the government. Lately the papers in Petrograd, where these Homes are located, have started a violent campaign against them which may lead to the closing of these places. It seems to be the policy of the Red leaders to allow no organization over which they have no direct control to exist.

When Lenin started his famous retreat he made it clear that it was an economic retreat and not a political one. This was a compromise with the Left wing, in which are Bukharin and others, into whose hands were handed over the Church trials, the Social Revolutionist trial, and the numerous arrests that are now taking place. These men have tasted power and blood, and now that Lenin is ill, they have opened fire on the famous New Economic Policy, otherwise NEP. There have been rumblings for some time that NEP is unsatisfactory and now the fight comes out into the open. On July 29 there was a long article in Pravda against NEP in which the author pointed out that this policy is developing a new bourgeoisie, a new capitalistic ideology, which will in time lead to the overthrow of the proletariat and the establishment of the old forms of government. No one challenges this statement and not only the radicals are worried over the course of NEP, but even such men as Kamenev, usually regarded as a conservative, are uneasy.

In the first place, many of the Communists themselves or their friends, profiting by the laws of NEP, have gone into business and they are pushing the government more and more to the right and the danger is that the push may soon become so strong that the Lefts will be pushed out altogether. To do away with NEP is regarded by many as impossible and therefore some suggest that it be controlled better, that is to say that private initiative and freedom of trade should be limited as much as possible. No definite program has yet been proposed and it may be that this question will be taken up at the conference this week.

The government is now occupied with the question of collecting the prodnalog, the food tax. The overhead expenses are very large and there has been a proposal by the more sound of the leaders that the food tax should be changed into a money tax, but this proposal has met with opposition from many quarters, especially from the local authorities who always manage to have a part of the tax remain in their hands. One of the reasons given why the prodnalog should be taken is that with a large reserve of grain on its hands the government could always influence the market and reduce the prices. The general tone of the Communists is that everything must be done to develop agriculture and keep the good will of the peasants.

A new order has recently been issued but has not yet been put into execution that all army and navy officers 45 years of age or over must retire. One of the reasons for this is to get rid of a lot of the old time officers who have been made use of but not wholly trusted. Schools for Red Officers are being developed to supply the vacancies.

We are anxiously awaiting the result of the conference of the ARA in Washington which will decide the length of time we are to remain here. I am still of the opinion that we ought to withdraw as soon as we can. I am becoming more and more of the opinion that for the time being our government should continue its policy of leaving the Soviet government to stew in its own juice. I am sorry for the Russian people, but I do not see what can be done now with the Soviet. The reactionary (left) wave is on and we must let it spend itself.

With kindest regards,
Sincerely yours,

Town Talk

On a cold wintry day Lenin and Trotsky were driving in a sleigh and a snow storm came up. The izvozchik lost the way and the two passengers became quite excited. Lenin shouted, "Keep to the right," while Trotsky ordered that he "pull to the left." They kept this up, confusing the driver until he quite lost his head and knew not what to do. Fortunately the two passengers fell asleep giving the driver the opportunity to find the way. When they woke up they found themselves on a straight and well marked road. "Where are we?" they both exclaimed. "On the Nikolaevskaia road" (the road of Nicholas), answered the driver.

At the beginning of the Revolution, the government established universities everywhere promising to keep them on its own resources. Most of these have had to close because the government can not keep its promise. In some places those in charge of the institutions have tried to persuade the local authorities to take the support of the institution. The Smolensk government took the matter under serious consideration and has appropriated all the money that came from the fines collected from people who picked mushrooms without permission. At Iaroslavl, one of the cooperatives has contributed several sacks of onions towards the upkeep of the University.

★ ★ ★

Moscow, August 6, 1922

My dear Herter:

The most important event in Moscow at the present time is the Conference (XII) of the Russian Communist Party, which opened for business on the 4th. The first topic for discussion was the international situation and neither of the two speakers, Sokol'nikov and Radek, represented the Commissariat of Foreign Affairs. Enclosed you will please find a summary and free translation of those parts of their speeches which are of interest to us. Let me call your attention especially to Radek's words. It seems to me that he has summarized in a masterly manner the position of the Russian Communists and has cleared the air. For the time being the Bolsheviks have decided to construct Russia from within—by developing industry, by encouraging foreign commerce, and by increasing the agricultural production. I do not believe they can develop industry and all the information that I have leads me to believe that they are losing ground. Aside from purely economic reasons they will be unable to succeed along this line for political causes. They are afraid to allow industry to develop unless they can control it. They are going to make an effort and will subsidize it at the expense of the agricultural population.

As to foreign trade, they have great hopes, for they plan to sell large quantities of grain. Every bit of grain that can be taken from the peasant will be squeezed out of him and put on the market. I do not believe that the crop situation is as rosy as it is painted by them and I am sure that all this is done for effect. But anyway they will take much and by the middle of the year the famine will be felt again.

The government expects many unpleasantnesses in the collecting of the grain tax and that is seen from the numerous decrees and threats it issues on that subject. It is well known that the peasants are in opposition to the government. Recently, the Pravda stated it openly and proposed that in each village the Communists should have a small group of men made up of the bednota (poorest men) to look after the interest of the Party. In other words to have spies from the riff raff to denounce the more honest and the more industrious elements. The papers are full of promises to the farmers and reminders of what the Soviet has done for them, but all this falls on dead ground. In yesterday's meeting of the Party the question of the cooperatives came up and the opinion was strongly expressed that the Soviet must control them, otherwise the peasants will get away from the government.

This last week I spent a day in a village not far from Moscow in company with a Russian friend. We happened to be there on a Church holiday, and though there was little church there was much holiday, much singing and dancing. The peasants are little concerned with Communism and for them it does not exist. It has made no impression on them. In talking with one old peasant he told me that it mattered little to him whether at the head of the government there was a tsar, a king, or a president, but he did want order and system. "Now," he says "when I want something I am sent from bureau to bureau, from table to table until I am worn out and in the end I get nowhere."

The peasants are pretty well demoralized and there is stealing, shooting, and general lawlessness, much more than in the old regime. All the former restraints have been removed, moral and physical, and the instincts are getting the upper hand. The Soviet government pays little attention to the villages except in time of tax collecting. While I was in the village the harvest was being gathered and the reaping was done altogether with sickles and in most cases by women. The ears of grain are not well filled out and the yield will not be as high as was hoped. The question of the grain tax is on the minds of the peasants and they complain that the burden is quite heavy. With an old peasant I raised the question of the Church and asked whether in his village they held by the old or the new Church. "They tried to get us to accept the New Church," said he, "but we told them that if the Jews wanted a new Church we would not raise any objections, but as for us we did not want a new Church and did not want a new God, and they have left us alone."

In different parts of Russia the trial of clergy is going on. Of the ten priests (not all as stated before) condemned to death in Petrograd six have had their sentences remitted to long imprisonment and the case of four is held under advisement. In the meantime the organization of the Living Church is proceeding. At the head of the new organization has appeared a new figure, V. N. L'vov.[41] This man was Oberprocurator of the Synod in Kerensky's cabinet and he is the same man who did so much to muddle up the Kerensky-Kornilov affair in 1917. He is not very brilliant and a bit reactionary, but he is being used. At the present time there is an assembly in Moscow of delegates of the Living Church. Only progressive churchmen are admitted and it was the original plan not to allow laymen to participate, but in view of the fact that only 80 clergymen appeared the rules were changed and laymen who in many cases are more progressive than priests are being admitted.

This assembly has for its object to "purge" the Church of reactionaries and counterrevolutionists and put in their places progressive leaders who will recognize the Social Revolution and the International. Archbishop Antonin has been preaching sermons to prove that Christ was a revolutionist. When the Church shall have been purged then the Sobor (Convocation) will take place. At this Sobor the following questions will be taken up: the patriarchate, monasticism, church service, Old Believers, trial of the Patriarch and members of the former synod, marriage of bishops, etc. L'vov made the statement that there will be little change in the dogma, but marriage of the clergy will be decided in favor of it. Little by little there will be built up an official organization but its possible influence is rather doubtful. In connection with the church treasures, it may interest you to know that there is now going on the trial of a number of men for selling church treasures.

The trial of the Social Revolutionists is still absorbing public attention. The evidence is all in and in the course of the next day or two the verdict will be rendered. Within a week some one has published and scattered in a secret manner circulars threatening the Bolos in case they execute the SRs. In the circular it is stated that vengeance will be taken on the small fry of

---

[41]Vladimir Nikolaevich L'vov (1872–?) was a deputy to the Third and Fourth dumas, procurator of the Holy Synod in the first and second cabinets of the Provisional Government, and the middleman in the confused negotiations between Kerensky and Kornilov in August 1917. L'vov emigrated after the October Revolution but returned to Russia in 1922 as part of the Change of Signposts movement. When Golder wrote this letter, L'vov was attending the All-Russian Congress of the Living church in Moscow, but although he addressed the congress he was not, as Golder writes, the head of this church.

Communists since the big ones can not be reached. These circulars have led to the arrests of dozens of people, to the search of the homes of dozens more, and every person who has at one time or another taken part in public life is frightened, not knowing when he will be hit. It is getting on the nerves of people and many are probably needlessly scared. Among the scared are the Communists themselves and they are not at all of one mind as to what should be done with the prisoners. Some of the reds, especially the older men, insist that no death sentence should be passed because of public opinion abroad, etc., but the younger elements demand blood. Long before this reaches you, sentence will have been passed and then, of course, it will be appealed and the matter will drag on.

At the present time there are a number of Americans, oil concession hunters and others, in this city. You probably know more about them than I. Personally I do not see what they are up to unless it is a ballon d'essay. During the last three weeks all kinds of rumors about the plans of the ARA have been afloat, mostly to the purpose that we are drawing out. On the top of this come other rumors, that the Russian Baltic ports are blockaded, that a number of grain ships have pulled up anchor without discharging and more like that. As a result of these noises the price of bread has jumped. When I came here in June the pud of white flour was worth 9 or 10 millions and it is now 30 and 32 millions. The value of the dollar has remained about the same during that period, though wages have gone up about 10% (but have not been paid in many cases). As you probably know already, there is a surplus of textiles in Russia and of Russian production due in large part to the high cost of production. Since the new harvest has come in, many of these factories have sent their men out with textiles to trade for grain and there is throat cutting among them, so that the price of material is cheaper at a distance from the factory than at the place of production. From various sources I get information that the Germans find it impossible to do any business here and that the Swedes are also giving up in despair.

There are rumors of war and stories are afloat but they are not reliable. Though the army is reduced in number its quality is improved by better discipline and a general overhauling at the top.

In summing up, I should like to say that the situation is at the present a bit discouraging. The left wing is in the saddle and it is likely to remain there for some months until hunger pinches again or the industrial life or the transportation system or any one of a dozen important events come to pass. There is bound to be a swing back to the right. In the meantime the Bolos will spare no effort to spread their propaganda and they will do their best to bring about a revolution somewhere. It might not be a bad idea for us to watch our friend the Bolo emissary in Peking and in his relations with Japan.

With all good wishes,

★ ★ ★

Moscow, August 10, 1922

My dear Herter:

Since my last letter a few days ago the condemnation of the Social Revolutionists has taken place, as you know. The last day of the trial was exceedingly interesting. The judge turned to the prisoners and asked what would they do if they were freed, would they continue to fight the Soviet power? The prisoners replied that in the past they had fought the Communists as an evil influence for Russia and that they would continue to fight them in the future. What to do with them was a great problem and the whole Party deliberated. The Soviet diplomatic representative in Berlin came and used his influence and in the end they sentenced them [to death] but decided to keep them as hostages. It is not exactly the thing brave men would do.

In its editorials the papers call the attention of all their opponents to the sentence and warn them that something as bad will happen to them if they don't look out. At the same time, however, I question seriously whether there are going to be any more trials. Sometime ago I called your attention to the arrests of many Social Democrats and I have just learned that the Party has decided not to try them but to exile them to different parts of the empire.

The conference of the Communist Party has come to an end. What has been decided in regard to international affairs I have not learned. It is clear from their numerous references to the Hague Conference that the disappointment is rather keen over its failure. In regard to internal affairs the conference has taken one or two positive stands. The question that received most serious attention was NEP, or the New Economic Policy. In a former letter I pointed out how bitterly it was being attacked and it came under fire in this conference.

The objection to NEP is that it develops a bourgeois ideology which penetrates the masses and undermines the Communists. Its exponents are the cooperatives, the professors and students, and intellectuals in general, and the new literature. Zinoviev was the spokesman for the opponents of NEP and he was quite eloquent. He called his hearers' attention to the conference of doctors, of which I have already written to you. He pointed out how the friends of NEP through the legal press (that is, books published privately) are spreading the idea of school autonomy, cheaper credit (there is only one bank, the State Bank), six months' military service, and a minimum wage in gold rubles. These ideas are not in harmony with the Communist policy.

He next took up the NEP press, that is, the press that has developed since the New Economic Policy has come in and which is not run by the government, though it is severely controlled by the censorship. He stated that in Moscow alone 337 such publications have appeared and in Petrograd 83 and that through them the bourgeois ideology is being spread. One man approved the stand taken by France and Belgium at the Genoa Conference, another said that he disapproved of the assassination of Uritskii[42] as much as he did of Alexander II. The professors, of whom Zinoviev says there are 5000, are also a bad lot and so are the students, "most of whom are against us." In concluding his long speech, Zinoviev made it clear that though the Party has made some concessions in economic matters it will make no retreats in political affairs; on the other hand, it is going to take the offensive and there will be no freedom of the press for the bourgeoisie and woe to them who spread teachings opposed to the gospel of communism.

Since that speech was made and approved by the Party I have had occasion to talk to the professors and other intellectuals under fire and they said: "We are not afraid. We are hardened to suffering. We can not be worse off than we are today. They can not kill us all because they can not get along without us. Let them do their worst."

In regard to the cooperatives the Party has resolved to get control of them by having representatives in them. Zinoviev called attention that in a recent conference of an All-Russian Agricultural Cooperative there were 84 delegates of whom only 2 were Communists. The forcing of Communists into the administration of the cooperatives will undoubtedly work for evil and destruction, for the time being at least.

From all this you will see that the Lefts are still in control and that there are some hard times ahead. But notwithstanding all their efforts to stop the tide of normal life they can not do it for any length of time. The peasant will have nothing to do with them and they are looking more and more with favor on the old bourgeois. There was a time, two or three years ago, when the name "bourgeois" was a red flag to the workmen, but it is no longer so. Many Communists trust more and prefer to have former bourgeois business men in their offices than the new breed of Communists.

---

[42]M. S. Uritskii, chairman of the Petrograd Cheka, was assassinated by a Socialist Revolutionary in August 1918.

The agricultural situation is gradually improving and big industry is gradually deteriorating and that means that the conservative elements are bound to influence the Party policy and the leaders will be forced, sooner or later, to make retreats or be overwhelmed. I think they will make the retreats and save what they can.

Krassin is back and has been interviewed. He states that the Rapallo treaty[43] is a disappointment and that Russia will surely export some grain this year.

Last night I had a long talk with a representative of the Far Eastern Republic, a former professor of Moscow, who is now here to negotiate a commercial treaty with the Soviet government. He complained of the slowness of American capital to take advantage of the business opportunities in his country. We are, he said, behind the Japanese, the English, and even the Germans, who are beginning to pay attention. The Japanese are grabbing everything that is capable of giving a good immediate return, but are leaving untouched, for the time being, the big industries.

We are patiently waiting more definite instructions from New York and Washington as to the future activities of the ARA in Russia. The few words that have come through stating that the organization would probably carry on has been a great disappointment to the men here and in the field. But the men are loyal to the Chief[44] and to the organization and you can be sure that in so far as it lies in them and in so far as other duties and obligations will permit, every worker will remain at his post until the whistle blows. As for me, in view of the fact that I have no special duty here and am needed at the University, I think I ought to return to the States unless Hoover and the Stanford authorities think that it is more important for me to remain here.

> With kindest regards and best wishes,
> Sincerely yours,

Moscow, August 14, 1922

My dear Herter:

All is quiet along the Moscow River. There seems to be a kind of peaceful reaction after the two stormy months. There is no change in the

---

[43]The Treaty of Rapallo, by which Germany renounced all claims against Soviet Russia and cleared the way for the establishment of diplomatic and commercial relations between the two countries, was signed on April 16, 1922, six days after the start of the Genoa Conference. News of the treaty stunned the Allied powers.

[44]Hoover was known as the "Chief" among those who worked for him.

internal policy except decrees keep raining as much as before. I think that
the wise heads are planning something in the line of foreign policy, just
what I do not know. It is rather noteworthy that in the resolution of the
Communist Party last week little was said on that subject, probably
purposely so as not to bind the hands of the leaders. At the meeting of the
Party Chicherin's case was discussed but no definite action taken. It would
seem that at Genoa Krassin and Chicherin proposed different plans of
procedure and as Chicherin was the head his scheme was followed and
proved a failure. The Executive Committee is considering seriously the
advisability of removing Chicherin and replacing him with Krassin and
giving Krassin's job to Dzerzhinsky. No decision has yet been taken.
Krassin is leaving for England shortly. His trip to America is postponed or
given up altogether.

In connection with the trial of the Social Revolutionists there is one
episode that is worthy of your attention. The sentence was ready to be
announced a day before it was actually done and it was held back for fear.
When it did appear it was tied with the decision of the Executive Committee
that the condemned would not be shot but would be kept as hostages.

The Persian Trade Agreement has come to a stand still because the two
parties represented two opposing views. Progress is, however, made in the
postal and telegraph agreements.

The representative of the Far Eastern Republic has called on me a few
evenings ago to invite me to visit the Republic and to secure information
about the country, its laws, possibilities of commerce and industry, etc.,
and submit it to our government. I thanked him, promised to call it to
Hoover's attention, which I now do, and left it there. Should such a trip
seem desirable it would be wise to have a mining engineer along and a
trained business man. I do not suppose Hoover will care to take any action
but if he thinks the trip ought to be made I should like to know it at once.

It is more than likely that the four priests, including the Metropolitan
of Petrograd, have been executed.[45] The Living Church is having its
conference and is throwing out of the Church everyone who is not with
them and are building up an organization, on paper at least, after their own
desires.

The crop question attracts the most attention and the government is
issuing decree after decree threatening every one who does not hand over
its tax. In the meantime the price of grain has fallen, not to the consumer,
but to the seller. Reports have appeared in the paper that in certain parts of

---

[45]Of the ten Petrograd priests sentenced to death, four, including Metropolitan
Veniamin, were executed.

Russia—Tsaritsyn, the Volga—the poor peasants were so much in need of money and other things that some, during the winter, mortgaged the crops, others are selling their grain as low as 600,000 rubles the pud (or about 15 cents) and some for 1 or 2 millions. Yesterday Fox[46] from Simbirsk came in and I put the question to him and he said that in his part of the world rye is selling as low as 1,600,000 the pud. The speculators are buying it up and the government is alarmed and the State Bank is sending in its agents to buy. I do not see that this will help the peasants much. Some say that the peasants are selling their grain because they need money to pay local taxes, that they do it in order to have little left for the government to take. The government is displeased and keeps telling the peasants that they should be more grateful since the government has given them the land, the forests, the meadows, etc. The peasants in reply have made up a little song which is becoming popular and runs something like this. I am sorry that the translation does not bring out the rhyme of the song.

> The land is ours but the crop is yours
> The forests are ours but the wood is yours
> The meadows are ours but the hay is yours.

It goes on in this way to enumerate the so-called blessings of communism to the peasants.

With good wishes,
Sincerely yours,

★ ★ ★

Moscow, August 18, 1922

My dear Herter:

There is not a great deal of news and what there is will not give you a great deal of pleasure. The political movement to the left is gaining in speed. During the last two days many professors and literary men have been arrested and no one knows the reason why. It is in line with the speech made by Zinoviev that the Communist Party would take the offensive. Today there is a decree which makes it possible for the Soviet to send out the men arrested either into exile into some part of Russia or abroad. In Petrograd arrests are going on and I suppose elsewhere. There will be no trials, they made too much noise and do not reflect glory.

Yesterday a woman from Petrograd came to see me to ask me to help

---

[46]Edward Fox of the ARA.

her find out whether her husband is shot. Her husband is one of the four churchmen from Petrograd who has not been pardoned. With this woman came the old mother of one of the other four. These two women have been going from one functionary to another to learn the truth and nothing more. One bishop of the New Church tells them one thing and another bishop another. One of the women had to borrow a pair of shoes to come and some one paid her car fare. It was not a pleasant half hour I had.

The papers are full of the question of the grain tax. It is the only resource of the government and it is making every effort to get it, but the peasants do not feel kindly and will resist. Speculators are buying up much grain and they do it in a very clever way. They do not have offices or permanent places of business so that no tax can be levied on them. Next week I plan to go into the provinces to look around.

With good wishes,
Sincerely yours,

★ ★ ★

Moscow, August 22, 1922

My dear Herter:

I have just returned from a two days' trip to Petrograd. There as here I found much depression and excitement about the numerous arrests of the professors, literary men, old army officers, and others. Among those arrested in Moscow are the Russian lawyers who for a time defended the Social Revolutionists and later withdrew from the case. No one knows on what charge any of these men are arrested and no one is likely to know. There are going to be no more public trials. The other day a new decree was published which gave to understand that in the future there are going to be a number of "administrative exiles." This means that many of the arrested will be sent away to little frequented corners of Russia or abroad. To what extent these measures of repression will help the Communistic cause remains to be seen. In my opinion very little.

In Petrograd as in Moscow the tide is all towards the right, especially economically and that necessarily carries with it a political orientation. Improvements are going on everywhere, small business is coming up and going down. People are drifting farther and farther away from Communistic "ideology," to use their own terms. There is no doubt that our red friends will do all that they can to stop it, and they may succeed for a time, but before long they will have to get on the band wagon or be run over.

The American question is on the carpet but I am deeply disappointed at the men they have working on the problem. I am informed that Ohsol,

Mikhailovsky,[47] and one or two others who in New York are connected with Dubrovsky are the experts on the subject. The papers and books of the National City Bank are being looked up. I was approached confidentially and asked to help secure a list of such papers and books so as to help their location. I have confidence in the man who spoke to me about it. If you think it is wise to approach the National City Bank people on the subject you will, of course, do so and let me know. I have heard indirectly that Ioffe was asked to approach our Minister in China. Unless I am greatly mistaken there are other approaches to our government about which you know and I do not. Time is on our side and we need not hurry.

There are a number of Americans here, as you know already. Many of them represent themselves to be spokesmen for the Administration but the government here is not fooled and regards some of these Americans as crooks. Cold weather is coming on and most of these birds will be flying south before long.

I expect to be about these parts until the end of September unless there is a good reason why I should remain longer. If there is anything you wish me to do before I leave please let me know.

Sincerely yours,

August 22, 11 P.M.

Late this afternoon one of my Professor friends, a teacher of history, came to see me. He told me that he had been summoned before the G.P.U. (the new Cheka) and charged with having worked against the Soviet for the last five years, especially during the different periods of civil war, and that therefore he is a dangerous person and should be locked up at once, but the Soviet being kind hearted gives him the choice of either being locked up at once or leaving the country within a week. The Soviet takes upon itself to provide him with a visa to whichever country he wishes to go but the Soviet assumes that he will go to Germany. The Professor will have to pay his own traveling expenses. About 70 or 80 people have this choice. I have just been to call on the wife of the lawyer of the Social Revolutionists[48] and he is exiled to Archangel, but an effort is now being made to have him sent to Germany. She told me also that the Soviet is planning to send all these prisoners by special train to Petrograd and there load them all on a steamer to Germany, but the passengers pay all their expenses.

These poor people have no money and they are running around like

---

[47] J. G. Ohsol (Oesel) and M. Mikhailovsky of the Russian Red Cross.
[48] Muravev.

mad trying to raise some. It is very pitiful indeed. I know some of these men personally and they assure me that they have kept out of politics and they have no idea why they are being sent out. One professor argued with the G.P.U. and asked to produce one single act against him. He was asked, "Are you for us or against us?" "I am not for you," he replied. "Then you had better leave the country." Some of the best minds in Russia are driven out, among them are the philosophers, the literary men, the professors, the engineers, the lawyers. I do not know how Russia can get along without them.

Krassin is discouraged and says he does not know what it is all about. Kamenev says that he was not consulted (I do not believe him) and it is only today that he learned a few details and is trying to get one or two cases changed. He says that 70 are arrested in Moscow. Smidovich,[49] the vice chairman of the TsIK (and Kalinin's successor), said he knew nothing about it and when his attention was called to it by the wife of the lawyer, he sent for the man in his department who is in touch with the G.P.U. and asked him to submit a report on the case of the lawyer by noon the next day. At noon the next day he appeared and reported that the G.P.U. refuses to make a statement. He [Smidovich] has demanded it in the name of the TsIK and it remains to be seen whether he will get it.

The right wing of the Communists are quite discouraged and they fear that sooner or later their turn will come or a fight to the finish. It is the price, say the right, for NEP, but there is nothing to indicate that NEP will not be seriously attacked. Krassin's position is not an enviable one. He told a friend of mine who went to see him to consult with him regarding remaining in Moscow to remain if he had patience and that it was all uphill work.

Lenin is able to sit up. He sent for Krassin yesterday and the two spent an hour discussing the Hague Conference. What the result was I do not know.

August 24

Do you remember the story of the expulsion of the Moors, of the Huguenots, and of their kind? I feel as if I were living in that period. Everywhere poor intellectuals are running around trying to save what they can, to sell what they must, weeping over leaving their native land and

---

[49]Petr Germogenovich Smidovich (1874–1935), as an Old Bolshevik and Soviet official, played a leading role in establishing Bolshevik power in Moscow in 1917. In 1922 he was named vice-chairman of the Central Executive Committee (TsIK).

becoming wanderers over the face of the earth without means, without equipment. It is a heart breaking scene. I wish we in the United States could take care of these people for they would do so much to enrich our national life. Instead of them we allow all poor trash to come in. All these poor people ask is a piece of bread, work, and a place to study. Some of the men are unusually able. There are among them chemists, engineers of national and international reputation. What Russia will do without them I can not imagine. From all reports this is just a beginning. There is an understanding between the Soviet and Germany on the subject, for although the G.P.U. offers to secure visas for any country the exiles wish to get, yet when it comes to a showdown it is Germany they send them to. One man came to see me this morning who is on an important commission in the Foreign Office and knows many things. He, too, has to go and the Foreign Office is in despair.

Just a word about the legal side of the case. On August 14 the decree on that subject was issued. It organizes a special commission in connection with the Commissariat of Interior of which Dzerzhinsky is the acting head and into this commission the Commissariat of Justice sends a representative. Period of exile is for not more than 3 years (after that the exile may be refused a permit to return).

Radek had in yesterday's Pravda a long article in which he pointed out that European affairs may lead to war and therefore Russia had better get ready, especially in view of the fact that the invitation of the Baltic States to disarmament has not been accepted whole heartedly. In today's Izvestiia there is a note from the Commissar of Foreign Affairs on the disarmament question. I do not know what to make out of all this.

Sincerely yours,

Moscow, August 26, 1922

Dear Professor Adams:

. . . The Expulsion of the Moors continues. I have been trying to account for it but I am not sure I know what is in the head of the government aside from the desire to remove any influence which is in opposition to it. They are afraid of "ideology." There is a rumor going the rounds that the Soviet intends soon to call a Constituent Assembly and is preparing the way by removing obnoxious candidates and opposition. Perhaps, but I am not taking it seriously. Kamenev told some people that in a year the exiles will be allowed to return. Even if this should be true they would come back poorer than when they left, for they are disposing of everything to acquire a little money for traveling.

Sincerely yours,

Town Talk

Bim and Boom are the Russian Mutt and Jeff

Bim: What does the word TREST (trust) stand for?

Boom: T stands for Trotsky, R stands for razreshil (permitted), E stands for evreiam (Jews), S stands for svobodnuiu (free), and T is for torgovliu (trade). Trotsky Permitted the Jews Free Trade.

Bim: Did you notice that the initials R.S.F.S.R. read the same from right to left and from left to right?

Boom: Yes. It was done purposely so that Trotsky the Jew could read it from right to left and Lenin the Russian from left to right.

Bim: What is the heaviest thing in Russia to lift?

Boom: The Russian ruble.

Bim comes on the stage holding in his hands a cow's tail.

Boom: Bim, what does that mean?

Bim: I came to town leading a cow and as I passed the Glavmias (Meat Department) they came out and took the meat from me and left me the hide. I kept dragging it after me until I came to the Glavkozh (Leather Department) and there the hide was taken from me.

Boom: How about the tail?

Bim: As to the tail ("prokhvost") Lenin has not passed a decree. ("Pro Khvost," when written separately, means "about the tail," when written as one word it means "braggard" or "fool." "Prokhvost Lenin" would mean "the fool Lenin.")

★ ★ ★

Moscow, August 26, 1922

Dear Professor Adams:

I wrote you this morning and I am now adding a few words. We have just learned that in Odessa, Kazan, and, I suppose, in other important cities, arrests of professors and their kind is going on and I suppose that they, too, will be sent out.

Yesterday Trotsky gave out an interview to foreign newspapermen on the subject of the exiles. He said that in view of the disturbed conditions in Europe and the likelihood of war between Germany and France which would drag Poland in against Germany, it is not likely that Russia could remain indifferent. In that case Russia should not have enemies in the rear. In view of the fact that the professors and their kind have not been able to make their peace with the Soviet during the last five years they must be regarded as enemies. In case of war they would have to be shot and rather than do that the Soviet is sending them out. He also gave out a few statements regarding the ARA which were favorable to the ARA. In regard to Russo-American relations he said that the Soviet is waiting for America to move. I understand that Krassin has been refused permission to go to the U.S. and that the Soviet has refused to permit an American commission to come to Russia unless a Russian commission were allowed to go to America. Perhaps you know more about these things than I do.

Yesterday the Russian Political Red Cross, an institution that existed even before the war, was closed and its members are subject to arrest. This institution looked after the health and comfort of political prisoners of all kinds in Russian jails and is not to be confused with Dubrovsky's Red Cross. With the closing of this organization comes to an end, so far as I am able to learn, the last non-official organization in Russia, the ARA excepted. Everything else is in the hands of the Soviet. It is the most thoroughly centralized government in the world.

All this is confidential and for your inside information.

Cordially yours,

Moscow, August 28, 1922

Dear Professor Coolidge:

Just a line of sad but exciting news for you. The Expulsion of the Moors, or rather the "Burzhui,"[50] has begun and among the number are some of your friends. Kizevetter has to go, and a long string of others less known to you, and last but not least, your friend Iziumov.[51] Why in the

---

[50]Derogatory Russian form of "bourgeois."

[51]Aleksandr Filaretovich Iziumov was a Moscow historian specializing in seventeenth-century Russia; in the 1930s he was director of the Prague Archives.

world they picked on him is more than I can tell. He came to see me yesterday crying bitterly for he has no money. He left me saying, "I must hurry on for I am to be married today. I do not know any foreign languages but the woman I marry knows German and French." I gave him my blessing and your address. There are some 70 expelled from Moscow, a large number from Petrograd and from other places. All these are to be driven to Petrograd next Monday and there loaded on a steamer and shipped to Stettin. It is rumored that this is the first shipment. I must not forget to tell you that our friend Muravev is among the number.

Really and truly some of the best minds are in that crowd, not only professors, but also engineers, electricians, men that Russia needs. The poor devils have been given just one week to get out and they are running around trying to dispose of the few things they have in order to secure money for traveling expenses. What they will do in Germany or wherever they go God knows. Speaking of God I must not forget to tell you that recently a writer in the Pravda attempted to prove that a certain writer is a counter-revolutionist because he spelled God with a capital G.

I was in Petrograd the other day and secured another set of the Tsarskaia okhota[52] and shipped it to Stanford. This will give you a chance to get one from Adams. It may be that I can pick up a few books from the libraries of the expelled burzhui which will be thrown on the market. The prices are high and that is against our buying. Mel'gunov[53] is coming to see me this morning. He, too, hopes to be sent or to be allowed to go and establish himself in some other land. I wish our country had the wisdom to draw to itself these intellectuals and absorb them into our society which they would

---

[52] Tsarskaia okhota na Rusi (The tsar's hunt in old Russia), 4 vols. (St. Petersburg, 1896–1911).

[53] Sergei Petrovich Mel'gunov (1879–1956) was a historian, journalist, and leader of the Popular Socialist party. For several months Mel'gunov had been purchasing books in Moscow for Harvard University and may have been the agent Golder hired to purchase for the Hoover Library while Golder was traveling for the ARA. In June 1922, Mel'gunov was imprisoned for two months for his past association with the Socialist Revolutionary party. Golder, who encountered him shortly after his release, wrote to Coolidge on August 13: "He [Mel'gunov] is as pale as a ghost and says that he has had enough. He was told by the prison authorities that 'It was a misunderstanding,' and that is all the satisfaction he got. He is now anxious to shake the dust and take to the high road. I think, too, that he is done with Socialism and he is selling out his socialist collection. Socialism, he says, is dead, at least the old socialism." Mel'gunov emigrated shortly thereafter. See Golder to Coolidge, March 17, June 10, and August 13, 1922, Coolidge papers, file: "Correspondence, A–Z 1922/23—A-Winship 1923/4."

greatly enrich. Instead we allow to come in the very elements that we can not absorb.

Tomorrow I leave for Kiev, Odessa, Crimea, and possibly Kharkov. While there I will try to secure for you the publications you so much desire. . . . We are awaiting the return of Col. Haskell from New York. He will bring with him the latest news from the front and that may help me to form my plans. I am anxious to get out; it is getting on my nerves and I am a bit unwell in other ways. Then again I should like to get another perspective from a different angle.

I do hope I can reach New England before the autumn glow is all gone and before the professor friends of mine are all worn out with the years of work.

With kindest regards,
Cordially yours,

Town Talk[54]

Bim: What does NEP (New Economic Policy) mean?

Boom: Ne pomazesh, ne poedesh. (Literally it means "If you do not oil, you will not ride," but colloquially it means "If you do not bribe, you will make no headway.")

Bim: No, it means Novaia Ekspluatatsiia Proletariata (New Exploitation of the Proletariat).

In front of a big government building hung a sign with the letters VSNKh (Vyshyi Sovet Narodnogo Khoziaistva—the Supreme Economic Council) and three men—a Communist, a Russian merchant, and a Jew—passed by and looked at it and asked each other what it meant.

The Communist: Vam skverno, nam khorosho. (It is bad for you, good for us.)

Russian Merchant: Vorui smelo net khoziaina. (Steal boldly, there is no boss.)

The Jew: (reading from right to left) Kholera na sovetskuiu vlast'. (May cholera get the Soviet government.)

---

[54]This was an unpublished addendum to Golder's letter to Cyril Quinn of September 2, 1922; the first part of the letter was published in Frank A. Golder and Lincoln Hutchinson, *On the Trail of the Russian Famine* (Stanford, 1927), pp. 214–15.

Moscow, September 10, 1922

My dear Herter:

Strange as it may sound, my trip to the Crimea was stopped by the Turko-Greek war. We had made plans and had received permission to go in one of the U.S. Destroyers that was in Odessa—we even went on board—when word came that the said Destroyer should not leave because the others had been ordered to Smyrna. Consequently, we turned back to Moscow. On the way back we had a look into Russian speculation. Soon after leaving the Black Sea city, watermelons were offered us at the price of 100,000 the piece and twenty four hours later and several hundred miles farther the same melons were selling at 2,000,000 rubles and passengers traded watermelons for bread.

We met some refugees and had interesting stories from them. One told me that he was from Voronezh and had started for the Ukraine last spring taking with him his wife and two children. In the course of the months that had passed he had lost his wife and one child, the other he left in a children's home. He himself had been working for local peasants and receiving from ten to fifteen pounds of grain a day. In other parts of Russia wages are also paid in grain.

We came through from Odessa to Moscow without change of cars and it took us about 64 hours, as against 35 before the war. Our car was an International and quite dirty. I can not say that it was very comfortable.

On reaching here yesterday I was made glad by finding your two letters of August 8 and 21 and was pleased to learn that the Chief and Mr. Phillips[55] were interested in what I had to say. I note what you say about a possible government commission to Russia and the desirability that I remain here to

---

[55]William Phillips was under secretary of state. On August 8, Herter wrote to Golder, thanking him for his letter of July 17, which he called "just the kind of news that we want very badly and the Chief has read it from beginning to end with avidity." In his letter to Golder of September 20, Herter wrote, "Your reports are much the best things that are coming in to this Government at the present time on Russia. The above is not [only] my opinion but is practically verbatim a statement of the Chief's. He is most anxious to have you stay on as both he and the State Department, to which copies of all your reports are relayed, feel that it would be a serious loss to have these reports discontinued."

In his letter of August 8, Herter informed Golder that there was "just a possibility" that the U.S. government would send an investigative commission to Soviet Russia, "in which event the Chief would by all means wish you to stay on as you would be absolutely indispensable to such a Commission." Golder collection, Box 33. The idea for an American commission of inquiry was first proposed to Hoover and Hughes by Governor Goodrich on his return to Washington from Moscow in July 1922.

help out. My experience with the Col. House Commission[56] has knocked out of me any wish to be on another unless I have an important and responsible part to play. I would rather return to Stanford and take up my work.

Aside from my connection with a commission may I say that I hope that we will not rush matters in Russia, for I do not think the time is quite ripe. It is not worth while to send a commission merely to show up the short comings of the present regime. What we need is a commission that will get results and I do not think that this can be done at present. The Persian Trade Agreement has come to a complete stop, the German Trade Agreement is making no headway, and it is not likely that we can do any better because the same causes are at work. The Left Wing of the Communist Party is still in power and is even making successful offensives in an economic way. Not long ago an English concern secured a timber concession and an agreement was reached and drawn up. Within a week some of the younger and hot headed members of the Communists changed a clause which puts the whole concession in peril. The matter is being fought over and it will probably be straightened out, but it gives you an idea what is going on.

The Right Wing of the Communist Party is quite unhappy and leaderless but it hopes to take up the fight in a few months. At the next meeting of the Soviet in December we may look for a change. The Right Wing made a mistake when it conceded the political offices to their opponents and took for themselves the economic positions of importance. It looks now as if they will be forced from these places. The reason I think so is that about Christmas time or thereabouts there will be a change in the economic situation of Russia. To me the situation looks very bad. Not only is industry not developing, but agriculture is going back notwithstanding the reports to the contrary. The crop is not as good as it has been represented; in parts of Russia there is still hunger and in two or three months there will be famine on a large scale. This, of course, will not prevent the government from exporting some grain and from collecting to the full the grain tax. As long as the present policy continues I can not see any betterment. Please do not take my opinion too seriously; you no doubt have better sources of information.

In a week I expect to leave for a month and go to different parts of Russia, chiefly the Volga, to make a social, economic, and political study of the Russian village, the only producing unit in the country. I am eager to get a definite idea as to what is going on there, how the laws are applied,

---

[56]The Inquiry.

how the tax is collected, and how the peasant thinks. We in the ARA have not this information. I have it not, though I have had the subject on my mind for some time. As opportunities present themselves I will write to you. Yesterday I took up the subject with Col. Haskell and he seemed quite pleased over it.

This week I am running over to Petrograd where I am usually fortunate in picking up a bit of news. I shall probably see Zinoviev, who is just now playing a big part. I am also trying to get an interview this week with Radek who is an influential member of the Party and has much to do with shaping the International policy. I am not seeking too many opportunities to talk to the leaders because there are so many Americans here and because the American government is feeling its way through other means. Nothing of importance is going to come off during the next two or three months and I think I can spend my time to better advantage in the country.

When I have returned from the Volga and have attended to some affairs here I hope to start for the States. It seems to me important that I come back, even if for a little while, in order to talk over various matters, get a new point of view, discuss and help arrange the Hoover Collection. I should like, if I could, to give some lectures at Stanford during the Winter Quarter and then, if desirable, return to Russia for the remainder of the year.

I was in the opera house this evening and while there I ran into Mr. Sheinman, the president of the Russian Bank. You have heard of the gentleman before. He wishes very much to go to America for a week or two to discuss financial matters with American bankers and sounded me, for the second time, whether it would be possible for him to secure a visa. Being an official of the government he feels that it would be beneath his dignity to ask for one unless he were sure to receive it. He would like to come with his wife and in a private capacity, without a staff and without secretaries. Sheinman is not a great banker, not a man of the world, not a pleasing personality, but he has influence among the many reds who are like him. From this distance it seems to me that it might be wise to let him come. He would learn many things that would do him and his fellows good, and it would please the leaders here, which may be worth while in view of the fact that we are just now trying to get in touch with them. I am bringing this matter to your attention and you will do with it what you think best. It is a question of policy, of course. I made no promises to him. Should it be decided to grant him a visa you will, of course, let me know.[57]

---

[57]Sheinman was eventually granted a U.S. visa; in April 1929, while in New York City to drum up business for the USSR, he learned of his dismissal from all government posts, including the directorship of the State Bank. He had the good sense not to return to the Soviet Union.

The "administrative exiles" have not yet been sent out. I am told that the delay is due to the unwillingness of the German government to take so many of them at once. A few of the exiles have been begged off by the different commissariats, who insist that they must have them, and will remain for a time longer.[58]

★ ★ ★

Moscow, September 17, 1922

My dear Governor Goodrich:

Your letters of July 27 reached me this morning and some of the matters you touch upon are already ancient history. Our government has already made the suggestion of a "commission" and the result is known to you. I am given to understand that our man in Berlin muddled things a bit, but this may not be true.[59] The Russian government is keyed up to the American music and is ready to meet us more than half way. The papers of the National City Bank are being collected and other American matters are being looked into. The other evening I ran across our old friend the President of the State Bank, Sheinman. He asked again that I might interest myself in getting him a visa to go to America with his wife, without staff or secretaries, in a private capacity to talk with American bankers. He does not ask to be allowed to remain more than two weeks. I have written to Herter on the subject and have recommended that he be allowed to come. It would do him good to try to do business in America and he would learn much that would be useful to him and his Communist friends. I am not an admirer of Sheinman but we have to take the Communist officials as they are.

Had I known that you wished to have me write you regularly on the Russian situation I should have done so with pleasure. To Herter I have written at least once every week and if you are interested I am sure that he will let you read what I have written. I am sorry that I have no copies with me.

The swing to the Left which started about the time of the break down of Lenin is still going on. You know all about the trial of the Social Revolutionists, the execution of the churchmen, including the Metropolitan of Petrograd, the arrest and exile of the professors, doctors, engineers. Now

---

[58]The remainder of this letter is lost.

[59]Golder refers to the U.S. ambassador to Berlin, Alanson B. Houghton (1863–1941).

students in considerable numbers are being arrested; some are exiled to different parts of Russia, others to foreign lands and still others are deprived of all opportunity of finishing their education. I saw our friend S.[60] last night and he told me of a certain Social Revolutionist, who had been in prison for some time, who was brought to trial and accused on September 14 and on the following day, without being given an opportunity to defend himself, was condemned to execution. S. is trying to get the execution put off and he may not succeed. Muravev is still in prison and Sokolov does not know what is going to become of him.

This will give you some idea of the political situation. The Lefts are in control and the Rights are unhappy but are just now leaderless and helpless. They intend, however, to resume the fight. The fight is between economics and politics, and I who know little about economics am betting on economics. The economic situation is bad and growing worse. The government policy is ruining industry and everybody is realizing it. Factories are closing. I read the other day a confidential report of the metallurgical industry in southern Russia and it proved that unless the Government subsidized it it would have to close.

In the Izvestiia of Wednesday there is a bitter complaint by a member of the Rubber Trust against the government monopoly of foreign trade. He points out that this policy works against home industry and in favor of foreign. In April the Trust sold the War Department goods for which it was to receive payment in gold and with this gold buy raw material in London through, of course, the Department of Commerce.[61] For two months the Department of Commerce did nothing and in the meantime the price of raw material has gone up. In May the Rubber Trust desired to export overshoes to Poland and Latvia and it had to be done through the Department of Commerce. Until now no report has come from Poland and the agent of the Department in Latvia reports having sold 24,000 pairs at one dollar and ten cents the pair. At the same time the Rubber Trust had offers to sell 300,000 pairs at one dollar and seventeen cents the pair, the buyer taking all the expenses on himself, but the Department of Commerce disapproved. While in the north everything is done to prevent the Rubber Trust from exporting, in the south the agents of the Department are encouraging foreign manufacturers to bring in their rubber goods, because the Department receives a commission out of the transaction. In this way the Rubber Industry is daily losing ground. The writer concludes by saying that this monopolistic policy is also ruining other industries.

---

[60]Probably N. D. Sokolov.

[61]The People's Commissariat for Foreign Trade.

In the same issue of the Izvestiia another writer calls attention to the fact that almost all the crude oil in Baku is used up and before many months there will not be enough to supply the local need unless development work is undertaken in the meantime. Similar cries and complaints are heard on all sides.

The agricultural situation is not as encouraging as it was hoped. The Volga has done well. In Central Russia there was a great deal of rain and as a result much straw and little grain. In southern Russia, especially around the Black Sea, where I have been recently, the situation is most discouraging. There was little seeded last fall and spring, and that little was late, and it did not get a start before the hot days came on. There is hardly any seeding this fall. Famine will be in that part of the world within two months. Notwithstanding that, the government is making ready to export grain and will undoubtedly do it. The report is being spread that the crop is excellent so as to cover up the export. Please, do not misunderstand me— there is more than enough grain in Russia to feed all the people in Russia, but this is not going to be done. Those that have will eat and those that have not will die, but the government will sell in order to get money as well as to show the world that Russia, having a good crop, can stand alone. The collection of the grain tax is not going on as well as might be expected. Up to date only about 16% has been gathered in.

My dear Governor, I am telling you all this not in order to paint a gloomy picture, but to show you that before long the situation in Russia will become so bad that the politicians of the Left will be forced to the wall and the economists of the Right will be called in to save the country. The only way they can save it is by calling in foreign capital and on the terms of the capitalists. The Right will yield pretty much everything along economic lines but will save its face and the face of the Party by clinging to political power. I imagine foreign capitalists will have no quarrel with them on that score. It would not surprise me if the turn came about Christmas time, when the hunger became a bit acute.

The Turkish victories[62] have caused much excitement here and our theorists have been busy proving that Europe is about to topple and that the long expected world revolution will soon come. Strangely enough, among some of the Communists the desire of a World Revolution is less strong than it was. They say this: Russia suffered most during the years when she was cut off from the rest of the world, that is 1918–21, but since she has re-established contacts the situation has much improved. Should a revolution

---

[62]This refers to the Turkish army's success during the summer of 1922 in the war with Greece, which threatened Great Britain's dominance in the region and led to the convening of the Lausanne Conference in the winter.

break out in Europe it would be followed by destruction and no production, which would be disastrous for Russia. It would, therefore, be better to put off the World Revolution for a time.

Recently I have had a talk with a man who is closely in touch with the situation in Central Russia. He told me that in that part of the empire the reconstruction of Russia is going on. There the Civil War destroyed little, there the peasants never drank deep from the fountain of Communism, and now they are proceeding with their own affair regardless of the Tovarishchs. The land is being divided up among them on the basis of the Stolypin program, that is, private ownership. They have this motto: "We are for the Soviet government but against the Bolsheviks." They are not opposing the government but they work on the basis that the government will approve and the government is closing its eyes. The situation is worth looking into and I am going to visit that part of the world this week.

I had intended going into the Volga region, but I have been unexpectedly called to Switzerland in connection with the Hoover Collection and I shall have to give up that trip. I shall probably remain in Switzerland a month or so and then, I do not know. I may return to Stanford to resume my teachings. Perhaps by that time I may hear from Hoover or you. Please write me in care of our London office.

In closing this letter let me tell you an amusing story. One of the flunkies who went with the Russian delegation to Genoa related to his friends at home his experiences. He said that Lloyd George was particularly nice to him and often offered him cigarettes. "He had a beautiful cigarette case on which were engraved these words: 'To Lloyd George from England's grateful workmen.' Chicherin, too, was very friendly and we often smoked together. He also has a gem of a cigarette case on which is engraved: 'From his grateful workmen to Morozov.'" Morozov was a prominent Moscow manufacturer.

> With all good wishes,
> Sincerely yours,

★ ★ ★

Moscow, September 18, 1922

My dear Professor Adams:

. . . The situation, political and economical, is tense and is hard on the nerves. Just now entrance examination is going on and the subject most difficult to pass is the "political" examination, a catechism of Communism. The questions asked by the Communist examining board remind me of the examination by the Spanish inquisitors of which Lea speaks in his book.[63] I am not exaggerating. Boys and girls of 16 and 17 are put through a horrid examination which makes my blood boil when I hear of it. For example: "Do you justify the assassination of Alexander II?" The poor child does not know what to say. Should he say yes, he would be asked whether he would assassinate a Communist or some such person. The questions are oral. The report is now going the rounds that a similar examination is being prepared for the few professors who are left.

The housing problem in Moscow is most acute. Houses are being torn down or are tumbling down from lack of repairs and new ones are not being put up. Each day more and more people are crowding into the city on the theory that it is better here. There is an abundance of material for a book entitled "Government Confusion."

It is whispered about that in parts of Russia the peasants are refusing to pay the tax and that the most reliable of the Moscow red troops are being sent against them. I am not ready to believe all that.

When this reaches you the new school year will be in full swing. I wish I were with you. Here is hoping that you will finish your work.

With kindest regards,
Sincerely yours,

★ ★ ★

Moscow, September 20, 1922

My dear Herter:

I have just had a conference with Krassin. We discussed the proposed American commission. In this connection, I wish to call your attention to an unsigned article that appeared in yesterday's Izvestiia on the subject of the Russian-American commission. The writer refers to articles which have appeared in the New York Herald and the New York World criticizing the answer of the Soviet government to the American proposal. I told Krassin that other papers, like the New York Times, approved of it, and that from the information we had, no general conclusion could be drawn as to the attitude of the American press. He then went into a discussion of the commission. He said that he was present when the answer to the American proposal was drawn up and nobody had the least intention to offend in any way; on the contrary, it is the desire of the Russian government officials to

---

[63]Golder means the historian Henry C. Lea (1825–1910) and probably has in mind his *History of the Inquisition of Spain*, 4 vols. (New York, 1906–7).

draw nearer to the United States. They would rather tie up with the United States than with any other country and that was their feeling from the very beginning of the Bolshevist regime. At the time when all industries were nationalized the American factories were left free.

When the question of an American commission came up, the Soviet officials discussed three possible ways of meeting the situation which would be satisfactory to all concerned. (1) If America is ready to resume normal relations with the Soviet government, the Soviet government would be very happy either to receive or to send a commission to America to discuss the matter. (2) If an investigating commission were sent in, then out of self-respect Russia would like to send a commission to America. (3) A commission of business men to come to Russia to discuss purely business matters.

He then went back to the question of the attitude of the American press that the Soviet government offended the American government in its reply. He pointed out that the Soviet government had very little choice in the matter. The question was put to them in such a way that the Russians were obliged, in self-respect, to give the answer they did. It was pointed out to the Russians by our people in Berlin that about 30 persons would be sent in, who would request the right to go to every department of the government for information. When a slight objection was raised, the Americans pointed out that it was the Russians who were asking for money, not America.

Krassin pointed out that should a commission be sent to America, it would probably be composed of two or three persons of which he would in all likelihood be one, that the commission would attempt no propaganda and would do nothing which would offend the American government or the American public. However, if no such commission can be allowed to go to America then he would suggest that an unofficial commission of purely American business men should come to Russia to talk business.

Yours faithfully,

Moscow, October 2, 1922[64]

My dear Herter:

    This is probably my last letter to you from Moscow for some time for I leave tonight for London. . . .

---

[64]Golder's report to Herter of September 27, 1922, on his visit to Iaroslavl is published in Golder and Hutchinson, *On the Trail of the Russian Famine*, pp. 226–46.

I wish I had joyful news for you as regards the economic conditions in Russia. The reserve of raw material is being gradually consumed and the end is not far off. During the last week or two there have been alarmist reports as to the decrease in production of iron and coal, it has fallen below that of last year. I know from many reliable sources that former owners have been approached with a request that they take back their factories, but the conditions are such that they refuse. So far as I know, an American and an English company are trying to get a concession to work some land on terms acceptable to the Soviet government. The fall off in industry is alarming the Communists. In a recent speech to the labor unions, Rykov, one of the Commissars, pointed out how much more slowly industry is growing as compared with agriculture and if this continues the bourgeois peasants will get control and spoil the whole scheme of things, and he urged every effort be made to stop this. Though he did not say it, he intimated that the peasants should be made to bear heavier burdens. In yesterday's paper some other Communist came out openly advocating that the load should be made heavier for the peasant, that he should carry all the load. This may or may not be put into law, but it is adopted in practice for the peasant is almost the only producer in the state. Of course if the practice is carried too far the result will be the same for agriculture as it is for industry.

Perhaps the most important question under consideration by the Soviet just now is the Urquhart concession.[65] Lenin and some others are opposed to it and the matter is now in the hands of the Political Bureau of the Communist Party. You, of course, know that every important matter goes through and is settled by this body. Krassin is fighting for his political life for if that fails he will be in the same situation that Chicherin was when the Italian treaty was disapproved.[66] On the other hand should the Urquhart concession be accepted that opens the door to many other concessions of that kind. Qui vivra verra.

---

[65]Leslie Urquhart, the British entrepreneur and chairman of Russo-Asiatic Consolidated, sought to obtain a mining concession in the Urals, where his firm had operated before the revolution. Negotiations with the Soviet government for a long-term lease of the Russo-Asiatic's former mine at Kyshtim and other confiscated holdings were long and drawn out. The Bolsheviks were evidently divided over the idea of offering concessions as a form of compensation for expropriated property, and the Urquhart case became a political football within the party leadership. The Urquhart concession appeared to have finally been defeated in October 1922, only to be resurrected several months later. See Carr, *The Bolshevik Revolution,* vol. 3, pp. 354–55, 431–33, 477.
[66]It is unclear which treaty Golder has in mind here.

In Moscow the housing conditions are very bad. Old buildings are being destroyed and no new ones are going up, for under the present laws of property no one will build. About a year or so ago the government offered to return in ownership small houses and to hand over to organized societies larger houses on condition that they make the necessary repairs and pay rent. A number of the best houses were in the hands of the workmen and as they could not afford to repair them they offered one or more of the unoccupied apartments to people of means, provided they repaired the whole house. These terms were accepted in many cases and the necessary repairs made and in this way many of the nouveau riche secured roomy and comfortable places to live in, which put them outside of the law that limits each person to 16 square arshins (one arshin is 27 inches) of space. It seems now as if the Moscow local Soviet is going to formulate a special regulation extending this 16 square arshins everywhere, including the newly repaired apartments. Under these conditions it is not possible to go ahead. One never knows what is going to happen tomorrow. Let me relate another painful story. Of the intellectuals exiled, many had their apartments which they sold in order to get money to pay their traveling expenses. A few days after the transactions were made the Cheka appeared on the scene and announced that it falls heir to these apartments and that the sale was void.

Another comic or tragic thing happened a few days ago. Until about six weeks ago the State Bank had a monopoly of the foreign exchange business. Then a regular bourse was opened, making the transactions in foreign money legal, under the same conditions as prevail in other countries. This was announced as a great victory for sound business principles. As you know also the ruble has fallen during the month of September from 4 to 10 millions to the dollar. The other day the police surrounded the bourse and arrested and locked up all its members on the charge of conspiring to lower the value of the ruble. These kings of finance are now in prison and their pockets have been emptied of all foreign money.

The papers now devote much space to the question of the election of the Soviet. Yesterday Kalinin had a rather naive paper on the subject in which he called attention to the electoral system of Europe and America (he gave the Prussian system before the war as the present system in all democratic countries of the world), where power goes from one bourgeois party to another, but here, in Soviet Russia, it is different: the power is always in the hands of the Peasants and Workmen, but only individual Communists change.

I have no new light to throw on the proposed American commission. It seems to me that it would be wise if it could be brought about to have the Commission of Inquiry be sent in before long. Conditions here are bad and are now growing worse, but I feel it is merely the darkness before the dawn. Our friends the Communists will be forced to give up tinkering and undertake really constructive work on a private ownership basis or on such conditions as capital can accept. By the time our commission has fully informed itself the Soviet government will be ready to talk sense and then we can get down to business. It is not going to be smooth sailing but these difficulties have to be gone through sooner or later. I see but two ways open to the Communists here: either follow along the line they are on now and bring the country down still lower, which will help neither them nor anyone else, or yield to capital and save what they can and save their power as long as they can. I think they will take the second course. Of course there is still one more, and that is to involve the world in a war and have all go down in a heap. From the present threatening conditions in the Far East they get some comfort.[67]

> With good wishes, as ever,
> Sincerely yours,

★ ★ ★

Riga, Latvia, October 4, 1922

My dear Herter:

Just after writing you and before leaving Moscow for Riga, I had a conversation with Commissar Rykov. We discussed the American commission matter. He said that the question was seriously debated by the Commissars before a conclusion was reached. The Commissars could not see what other information such a commission could desire which the ARA did not already have. In his opinion the American Relief Administration is the best informed organization in the world on all questions relating to Russia. The fact that we desire to send in an extra commission seemed to the Commissars an attempt to kill time. Another factor which influenced the Commissars in their decision was that of establishing a precedent. Should they have allowed an American commission to come in, the French and other governments might have asked the same privileges.

The Commissars are extremely anxious to bring about relations with the United States. Rykov is particularly eager that American capital should undertake the development of Siberia and the Caucasus. Siberia because of the Japanese and the Caucasus because of the English. He attempted to scare

---

[67]Golder is referring to the tensions in Soviet-Japanese relations over the terms of Japan's withdrawal from Siberia.

me by telling me that the Soviet government is negotiating with different nations, especially with China and Japan, but I refused to excited over it and made very little of the negotiations. He then dropped that attitude. He told me that he had heard from one of the Soviet diplomats in Europe that the American government had accepted the counter proposal of the Soviet government as final and that he regarded the matter as ended.

I then took up with him the possibility of a way out and told him that I personally was very anxious to bring about relations between the two countries. He then added that if Hoover or Governor Goodrich would express a desire to send an unofficial commission to Russia, it would receive the same facilities and be given the same help as the official commission proposed by our Department of State. He also added that anyway the American commission would not be satisfied with merely official information and it would certainly try to secure unofficial information as well.

Incidentally he told me that the Argentine Republic had proposed to the Soviet government a loan of about £10,000,000 with which to purchase products in Argentina. The matter has not yet been acted upon.

He also brought up the question of the Urquhart concession. He said that it was the most serious matter that the Commissars have had to deal with for some time. Should they decide to accept the concession as it stands it would be a turning point in Soviet policy. The matter is seriously debated and will not be decided till some time next week.

With kindest regards,
Sincerely yours,

★ ★ ★

London, October 9, 1922

My dear Herter:

I arrived here Saturday, the 7th. Since my enclosed note to you written in Riga on October 4th, I have noticed two or three things in the papers to which I should like to call your attention.

One is a statement in the London Post of October 7th to the effect that Rykov has been dismissed from his post for inefficiency in his work and disreputable conduct in signing several decrees in a drunken state. If this is true, and I am not quite ready to believe it, then I dare say the reason he was dismissed was not so much because of drunkenness as because he leaned too much towards the Right. He had the reputation of being an honest and painstaking Communist, who was quite dissatisfied with the new political policy adopted by his colleagues on the Left. All that means that the Left group is still in power and control for the time being.

In this morning's paper I notice also that Urquhart's concession has been turned down as I had feared. I think the turn down of the concession was due rather to the influence of the left wing than to international politics, the last used merely as an excuse, but I may be mistaken.

Sincerely yours,

★ ★ ★

Paris, October 16, 1922

My dear Herter:

I do not mind offering suggestions because I do not expect you to act on them. During the last two weeks I have had an opportunity to view the Russian question from some distance and I have come to the following conclusions: It would be best for Russia and the world for the United States government to tie up with the Soviet authorities. It is not the Communists I am thinking of but Russia and the world. It is true that recognition of the Bolsheviks would strengthen them for a time, but it would be a dearly bought victory. By coming in official contact with the rest of the world, the Bolsheviks will ipso facto become respectable and respectability will kill them. If official representatives of other States were in Moscow and the Soviet diplomats in the capitals of the world, there would come into existence a moral force which would influence their actions. The presence of European diplomats would give support to the Right Wing of the Communists, which is in itself very important.

The Bolsheviks are very human and very parvenu and very eager to stand well in the eyes of their neighbors. If the United States should give them some form of recognition and should send to Moscow one of our big headed Americans, a man with plenty of good sense, a true democrat, who would invite the Bolos to his table and treat them as human beings he could wield much influence for good. I know all the objections that will be raised but we have got to do it for the sake of bleeding, suffering Russia. We can bury our pride and eat our words, if necessary, but we must save Russia and she is worth saving. I do not know any other way except the policy of waiting. If we wait the Bolos will kneel to us, but in the meantime thousands of Russians will have died and millions of others will have approached the state of savagery. We can gain more by treating the Bolsheviks as human beings than by calling them names.

You know that I do not love the Bolos and my suggestions are made purely for the sake of Russia, for the sake of America and the world. I think it is the best thing to do.

Sincerely yours,[68]

★ ★ ★

London, England
November 5, 1922

Dear Lutz:

Thank you for the San Francisco letter, even if it did make me homesick. I am glad you had such a happy summer, and I keep hoping that some of these days soon we can try one together.

I am all alone in this big building. Tomorrow I start back to Russia, and I am about as enthusiastic about that as I would be about going to hell. "Chacun à son tour." It is going to be a hard winter for me. Coolidge and Hutchinson will not be there, and so many of the other men with whom I used to be in more or less close touch will also be away. Then again, the moral situation is so bad. I mean the suffering, and I came in closer contact with the worst suffering than the other men. But we will survive it some way.

The Russian problem is a difficult one, and a painful one, and the Russians themselves make me weep and laugh in turn. I have told you something of the poor people there, and their psychology, and this morning I am going to put on paper the peculiar mental workings of the émigrés. Since my first return from Russia last spring, I have kept away from the émigrés and for these reasons. Many of the old and honored nobility have

---

[68]Herter passed on a copy of this letter to Dewitt C. Poole, head of the State Department's division of Russian affairs and American consul in Moscow in 1917–1918. Poole thought it worthwhile to send a copy on to Secretary Hughes. In his cover letter to Hughes of October 26, Poole wrote of Golder's appeal for political recognition of Russia: "The arguments he advances have been heard ever since the Bolsheviki came into power, but he states them with so much conviction that it occurred to me that his presentation of the matter would interest you." Poole reiterated his belief that political recognition would fail to encourage Bolshevik moderation: "Foreigners will be able to exercise real influence in Russia only so far as they have money or capital to give. This brings us right back to your declaration of March, 1921. I understand from talking to Mr. Herter that this also is Mr. Hoover's view. He has not been in any way persuaded, but very much interested, by Professor Golder's letter." U.S. Department of State, General Records, Record Group 59, reel 71, 861.01/511.

been forced to sell themselves to the Bolos, and now act as their spies. That scares me a little for I keep my mouth shut as a rule. My experience in Russia has made me suspicious of everyone who talks Russian. The great difficulty with the émigrés is that they have learned nothing and have forgotten nothing. When they come across someone who has come out of Russia, they pounce on him with questions, not for the purpose of getting real information, but for confirmation of their preconceived ideas. If you do not agree, then it is proved ipso facto that "you do not understand the Russian people and the Russian peasant." The very fact that all this misery exists in Russia might convince these nobles that they do not understand, but it is a waste of words. The point of view of these émigrés almost makes me a Bolo when I am with them.

You may wish to know what kind of information they would like to have. Well, it is this: "The Russian people and the Russian peasants are down on their knees praying to the old tsar's God for a restoration of the monarchy and all the satellites of the court." Of course, there are a few who know better, but they are overruled and overwhelmed with abuse and called Bolsheviks, traitors, and so on.

At different times, I wrote to you about a poor noble woman who has suffered so much, who has been in prison, and so on. I helped her to get out of Russia to join her sister in London, and she has been here about three weeks. I hunted her up and took her to dinner last night in a decent restaurant (nothing lavish) where she could have a good meal and hear a little music. I thought it would cheer her up, but I never made such a mistake before. As soon as she came in, she became as glum as night. I tried to explain it to myself by reasoning that it reminded her of her former life and said something about it. She gave me a queer look and exclaimed, "You do not understand. I am thinking of all the misery and hunger in Russia, and it is such a shame to be here enjoying myself. There we all hungered together. I knew, of course, that there existed amusement places in Moscow and Petrograd where people spent piles of money, but I never saw them, never went near them. Here I run into them everywhere." Then, changing the subject, she said, "The English women are so ugly, aren't they? The Russian women are much prettier." When I looked at her and the English women in the hall, I heartily agreed with her.

She went on to tell me something of her problems since coming to England. Being a religious woman, she goes to church often. The English clergy have offered a church building to the colony of Greek Orthodox and the building is, of course, like any other Church of England building and that fact jars on my friend. But what hurts her here is the crowd that gathers there. "In Russia," she said, "to the church came all those who were cold and hungry and all those who loved God. Here we have the old crowd of grand duchesses, comtesses, and their circle, with their display of dresses and jewels and the same old silly talk."

"What do they talk about?" I asked.

"Oh, of the restoration of the monarchy. The other day I had a visit from a former officer of the Imperial Guard, the same regiment to which my husband belonged. He tried to assure me that a tsar would soon reign in Russia. He provoked me so that I asked him whether he was a Russian citizen, in view of the fact that he did not dare to go back to Russia, he had not a Russian passport and was supported by non-Russian money. He drew himself up and shouted back at me, 'Madame, I am a member of the Imperial Guard, have been and always will be, and am ever ready to die for the Emperor.' How do you like that? But that is not all—the monarchists are agreed on the principle of the monarchy, but they fight like cats and dogs as to who should be monarch.

"Morally," she continued, "the émigrés are becoming demoralized and reveal the silly and false life of the old regime. My brother-in-law has told my sister that she is old and he is tired of her and he must have some soul-mistress and he is now running after Princess W., leaving my poor sister all alone. That is a common occurrence.

"They are now aping the rest of the world. Some are becoming Catholic, others are urging a union of the Church of England with the Orthodox. There is nothing real in all that. They do not love Russia, they care nothing for her. I would die for Russia and I wish I had never come out.

"Now that I am here, what shall I do? I hate work with all my body and soul. I wish I were dead."

My dear Lutz, this gives you an idea of what I go through from time to time. It is intensely interesting, but exhausting.

As ever yours,

CHAPTER FIVE

BOLSHEVISM AT A CROSSROADS
(November 1922–May 1923)

Moscow, November 19, 1922

My dear Professor Adams:

. . . Life here is hard and discouraging and so hopeless. I do not speak for myself, though it reacts on me more strongly than I like. I was interested to watch the effect on myself as I approached Moscow. The nearer we came to Russia the more I felt the gloom settling on me. Misery, depression, oppression, demoralization everywhere, but there is so little to do. But it is all interesting from the point of view of social science. It is a kind of vivisection experiment. In my letters to Herter I will tell you something of what is going on. I am glad to have the opportunity to supplement them with an occasional letter to you, where I can put in a few personal touches. It is not that I like to talk about myself, but merely to record for the sake of history the influence of life here on a person of average education and average ability of observation. My letters to Herter are read by many people and sometimes I am afraid some clerk in the State Department will betray me as Col. Ryan of the American Red Cross was betrayed.[1] It is not that

---

[1]Lieutenant Colonel Edward W. Ryan (1884–1923) was the American Red Cross representative to Estonia in 1920. After he surreptitiously accompanied an Estonian peace commission to Moscow in March, a report on his mission was leaked to the press by U.S. military intelligence; the resulting publicity compromised the American Red Cross with the Soviet government.

there is anything in my correspondence that carries harm to any one, least of all the Bolos. . . .

Cordially yours,

★ ★ ★

Moscow, November 20, 1922

My dear Herter:

When I reached Moscow on the 15th I found the Communist International in full session and since my arrival I have been trying to find out what is going on.[2] I have read the speeches, followed the discussions, and have talked with people and now I should like to make a report, though superficial, of the situation as it appears to me. I am assuming that the American papers have given and are giving full accounts of what is transpiring and that leaves me only summaries to make.

One of the first things that struck me on my return is the apparent unity of the two wings of the red party, which is due no doubt to the efforts of Lenin. This unity has resulted in a distinct move towards the Right, not as yet in deeds, but at least in words. I have read with a great deal of interest the speeches of Lenin, Trotsky, Bukharin, and Radek and I am deeply impressed by the unity of thought, which sounds like a program worked out beforehand.

Leaving out, for the present, the theoretical parts of their speeches and examining only those portions that refer to Russia, I find two lines of argument. One is an apology for the past failures and the shifting of the blame on others. The Communists, it is hinted, had no desire to force the extreme ideas of the party on Russia, which was not ready for them, but were compelled to do it by the war, as a war measure. The small trader was used by the bourgeoisie as a war tool and therefore in self-defense he had to be pushed out of the way. Another reason for the small success of the experiment is the lack of loyal employees. During the past five years, and at the present time, nearly all of the state employees were and are enemies of the Soviet regime. This is now being remedied by sending some of them out of the country and especially by taking the schools out of their hands and the training of loyal employees.

The other argument is the defense of the New Economic Policy. If I am not mistaken, I pointed out to you some months back that in the course

---

[2]This was the Fourth Congress of the Communist International, November 5–December 5, 1922.

of the last summer a bitter campaign was carried on against the NEP by the left wing, who saw in it tremendous dangers for the Party and possibilities for capitalism. In his speech, Lenin pointed out that NEP must be judged by its results and showed how in the spring of 1921 the peasants as a mass were bitterly opposed and even rising up against the Soviet, and that the workmen in the cities were discontented; but now the agricultural population is, as a whole, pleased with the regime, and the workmen, especially in Petrograd and Moscow, are contented. Under NEP commerce and industry have also developed. All these gains are to the credit of the Soviet and have been made without any loss of power on its part.

Among his many arguments, Trotsky brings out this one: NEP would be really dangerous if there were any likelihood that capitalism had any chance of endurance, but its days are numbered. The fact that the industrial situation in Europe and America is improving and that the capitalists are making war on the eight-hour day and other labor gains made by the war and revolution go to show that the workmen will not much longer put up with such oppressions.

Bukharin takes the stand that under present conditions the proletariat can do certain things and is incapable of doing others and when it attempts to do the impossible it leads to a loss in production, heavy expense, creation of a bureaucracy, and such like evils. This is what has happened in Russia and this is why NEP was brought in and, consequently, therefore, NEP must be kept until the time when the proletariat shall have learned more and more from the capitalists. This, of course, is also the idea of Lenin.

So much for the past, and now for the present. This phase Lenin also discussed. He dwelt on the improvement in commerce as compared with a year and a half ago. He does not, of course, state that a year and a half ago there was no legal commerce and that, therefore, he compares everything with zero. He states that progress has been made in light industry, but emphasizes the poor condition of the heavy industry and concludes that unless heavy industry is put on its feet not only are the Communists lost but Russia disappears as a civilized country. The only way to save it is either by foreign loans or by home economy. Loans seem to be impossible, foreign capitalists will not come to the rescue and therefore, Russia itself must bend all her efforts, must cut down on everything else, even schools, to save money. Russia already has twenty millions of gold rubles for that purpose.

Radek in his speech developed the idea that for the present the working-men of Europe have lost confidence in the Socialists and hope of getting power into their hands in the immediate future. The policy of the Communists should be to agitate among the workmen, quite regardless of party, for purely social betterment, shorter hours, higher pay, etc., and incidentally do a bit of propaganda work to prepare them to assume power at some future date.

Future. No definite plan or policy was stated but the inference is that NEP will be continued and the idea of concessions will not be abandoned. Both Lenin and Trotsky pointed out that the Soviet had nothing to fear from either as long as it held the commanding positions—political control and power of taxation, land, important industries, and railroads. For the present, Russia will have State Socialism and out of it will come real Socialism.

I do not know whether my summary of their speeches conveys to you as it does to me the swing to the right. For the present, the idea of a world revolution is completely given up. (I doubt even whether this Congress will pass any resolutions or make any plans for the immediate future.) State Socialism and the weapons of the ordinary socialists are accepted (there is even talk of the wisdom of coalition with Socialists). As for Russia, NEP is not only defended and justified, but is recommended as policy for the future. The danger of concessions is minimized. If I am not mistaken all this is done to prepare the public mind for the granting of concessions in the near future and for the extension of the policy of the New Economic Policy.

I explain this change of front in regard to the world revolution to the coming in power of the Fascisti and the general reaction in Europe and the swing to the right in Russian affairs and to the economic conditions of the country. Lest I mislead you, let me make it clear that this swing to the right is for the present purely a matter of words, at least insofar as big affairs are concerned. But the fact that the public mind is trained along the line indicated has significance. NEP is encouraged in a quiet way. The prohibition of the export of grain is removed, the cotton monopoly is about to be taken off. It is whispered about, and it sounds probable, that the present German minister is arranging for German firms to take over a number of cotton and other mills. The other day my attention was called to an item in the paper which may have some bearing on the future. It is this: the Soviet government has presented a man with an estate for life.

I am not dwelling on the economic condition of the country, which is bad. Heavy industry is in a critical condition and growing worse, especially in the South. Many of the state employees in Moscow have been unpaid for months, and in the provinces they are seldom paid, with results which anyone can judge by the numerous trials for plundering the "trusts" and grafting on the railways. In the provinces, the failure to provide for the employees brings about other evils. A man in whom Gov. Goodrich and I have confidence told me the other day that the buildings of his former estate, which during the last two years were used for school purposes, are now being sold by the local Department of Agriculture for fifty puds of flour in order to pay the employees.

Political conditions are worse, or rather the policy of persecution of all those who do not agree with the Communists and are likely to be dangerous in the future continues. Searches, arrests, and exile go on. It is in line with the policy outlined above in the speeches, that is to say the Communists retain political power in order to protect themselves against NEP and concessions to foreigners.

Yours faithfully,

Proposed Budget for 1923
Do not Vouch for Its Accuracy.
Comes from good source.

Budget	1,500,000,000 gold rubles
Commissariat of War	43%
Education	4%
Interior	17%
Finance & Supply	23%
Agriculture	5%
Propaganda, Nationalities, etc.	6%

★ ★ ★

Moscow, November 22, 1922

Dear Herter:

Last evening I had a long conversation with Radek, who seemed to be very pleased to see me and urged me to stay and talk to him. I was greatly astonished at his grasp of the foreign situation and of his knowledge of what is going in Washington. He takes the New York Times, the New York Herald, the Wall Street Journal, The Nation, and The New Republic. He has also a number of books on America. He follows closely the activities and speeches of Hughes, Hoover, and keeps an eye on Goodrich. He told me a lot of things which were quite new to me: of the influence of Hoover on certain newspapers, of Hughes asking Goodrich to make a speech on Russia in a certain place, etc. The thing that will interest you especially is the conclusions which he and some of his colleagues have come to. One is that Hoover and Goodrich are friends of Russia, the other is that Hughes is something more than a mere capitalistic lawyer, but a high-minded statesman, who achieved a distinct American success at the Washington Conference.[3]

We discussed, of course, Russian affairs. That there was a fight on NEP he admitted, but claimed that it is about over. Many of the Communists feared that as NEP developed the workmen would fall away from them, but this has not proved to be the case. The workmen are now better off than a year ago and at the same time more loyal, as was shown by the enthusiastic demonstration of November 7th (which I did not see). From this it follows, according to the arguments of the Right, that as economic prosperity increases, the loyalty to the Soviet will increase in proportion. The workman has now bread for his needs but he is demanding meat as well and the progress of NEP will give it to him. Under the circumstances the Soviet has nothing to fear from NEP; on the other hand it has much to hope from it, and therefore it should be encouraged.

He gave me his views on the question of foreign capital. He started out by saying that the Genoa and Hague conferences have convinced him and his colleagues that nothing can be gained by talking and talking. It is a waste of time. The Soviet is interested in deeds and not words and is ready to talk business with whomsoever comes along. The Soviet is equally convinced that it no longer has anything to fear from foreign military intervention or from any other kind of direct intervention and therefore looks with favor on foreign capital and will drive a bargain with it.

We took up Russo-American relations. He assured me that now the leading Commissars are convinced that the offer of the American government to send a commission was a friendly act. From this I was led to infer that it was not always so understood. The fact that our government has several times in the course of this year refused a visa to Krassin and other leaders and at the same time asked permission to send an official commission to Russia with powers to go into any department of the Soviet government and ask for official documents, etc., puzzled them not a little, especially Lenin.[4] It seemed as if we tried to humiliate the Soviet and

---

[3]The Washington Conference on Naval Disarmament took place from November 12, 1921, to February 6, 1922.

[4]Poole at the State Department read this passage and wrote to Herter on December 16 stating that Golder was being misled by the Moscow Bolsheviks and that these supposed American conditions were a "pure Soviet fabrication. No such conditions were stated or implied. They have been invented subsequently to excuse the blunder which the Bolsheviks now realize they made in declining the American proposal.

consequently it took the stand it did. He assured me that the Soviet desired nothing better than to tie up with America. I tried to explain to him the American point of view, what our motives were in asking for permission to send a commission, pointed out how much more important it is to send an official commission than merely a number of business men, and why the counter-proposal of the Soviet made a bad impression in the United States. He then asked me to go and see Kamenev and Chicherin and explain to them the American point of view. I told him that I preferred not to do so for fear that it would give my words an official importance which they were not entitled to. He then inquired whether I had any objection to meeting some evening at his home, in an informal way, the two men above mentioned so that we could talk over quite freely the situation in order to see whether the stupid formalities which stand in the way of bringing about better relations between the two countries could not be removed. To this proposition I agreed and it is planned for next week because I am going to Petrograd tomorrow for a few days.

I wish to goodness I knew a little more the mind of Washington for I would then be in a position to suggest action along the line desired. Before taking leave of Radek I asked him to write me a personal letter on the whole subject giving the views of his government. He promised to do so as soon as he had talked it over with his friends.

In regard to European affairs, Radek attaches much importance to Fascism and its influence in Europe, especially in Germany. He has information that the reactionary elements in Germany will "start something" towards the end of January or February. He does not think it wise for the German Communists to try for power just now.

Very truly yours,

★ ★ ★

Moscow, December 2, 1922

My dear Herter:

On Thursday evening, I called on Radek and on greeting me, he remarked that "our Russian-American affairs are progressing better than I

You might let Golder know this if you have a convenient way of doing so." In this letter Poole called Golder's reports "one of the most valuable sources of information which we have concerning current events and especially the currents of Bolshevik opinion at Moscow." Golder collection, box 33.

Herter passed a copy of Poole's letter on to Golder, who replied to Herter with some irritation on January 11, 1923, that he would be better able to perform his role were he not kept "in the dark" regarding the thinking in Washington, about which his Bolshevik interlocutors always seemed to be better informed.

thought. A few days ago, we received inquiry from Gov. Goodrich in Washington whether we would allow an American commission to come to Russia on the understanding that a Russian commission would be permitted to go to America later, should it desire to do so. We replied in the affirmative. Chicherin has now gone to Lausanne where he will discuss the subject more fully with Childs."[5] This is very interesting and I am now all ears and eyes. If we really mean business we can have our commission, for the Soviet leaders do not mean to let another opportunity get away from them. Radek told me that he made a fight [against] the "prestige diplomacy" and had some success.

He told me also that the International, which means for all practical purposes the Russians, are issuing instructions to the American Communists to cease all propaganda in America, to stop secret meetings in the woods, to discontinue publishing illegal papers, and "all such nonsense" (words of Lenin). It is the opinion of the leaders—Radek, Lenin, et al.—that the handful of foreign Communists in America are accomplishing little and they had better save their energy and use it in labor circles in the ordinary way. This, apparently, is in line with the policy outlined by Radek in his speech a few days ago, a summary of which I sent you.

Our conversation led us to the subject of the disarmament conference, which meets now in Moscow. Radek pointed out that Russia had little to fear from military invasion and that 100,000 soldiers are quite enough for the internal order of the country, the largest number being, of course, needed in the Far East. This statement was followed by a side remark: "I think America is quite right in refusing to lend money to any country that uses it for a large army." This was an illuminating sidelight.

We wandered on to the ARA and he told me of some of the discussions between the Comrades on the question of whether to allow it to come in. Some held that the ARA would learn too much and others replied that this was inevitable, that no responsible government or capitalist would come until he had learned "too much" and the sooner they learned it the better. Experience has shown that from this point of view the ARA has done much for the Soviet government. During this last year, the tone of the American press is much more favorable to the Bolsheviks than before and there is no question but that the ARA is largely responsible for that. Hoover was also seriously debated. Some feared that his object was to discredit the Soviet, but Radek and a few others held that Hoover, being an organizer, was interested in construction and not destruction. Time has justified this view.

---

[5]Richard W. Childs (1881–1935) was the American ambassador to Italy from 1921 to 1924.

The question of an economic advisor was taken up. I pointed out that capitalists would be more ready to make a loan to Russia if some prominent world-wide known man were in charge of the spending of it. He agreed in theory, but said that the matter had been discussed and fear was expressed that the advisor would not work for the best interests of Russia, though he added the case of Shuster of Persia proves that this need not be so.[6] I did not push the matter further for I realize that it is not so much fear for Russia as fear for Bolshevism that is in his mind.

You may be interested in a number of other events and movements in Russia. Chicherin's return to Russia a couple of months ago was marked by a new orientation in foreign policy. The Commissar of Foreign Affairs now stands for a rapprochement with France. One of the first evidences of this in a practical way was an order to the Russian members of the Russian-Polish commission on the question of returning to Poland books, manuscripts, etc., to satisfy the Poles, on the ground that the higher interests of the state demanded it. I have no doubt that in Lausanne Chicherin will back France rather than England. As a matter of fact, England is not in favor just now and the future of England is not regarded as bright. I note that Herriot[7] in France is saying more or less nice things about the Soviet. It looks as if the whole programme had been pre-arranged.

Meyer Bloomfield[8] has been here again, this time as a special representative of Secretary Mellon,[9] and, therefore, talked as one having authority. He promises to come again in May with a commission, but I have not learned whom he will represent at that time. I do not see what is gained by such missions.

Friends of mine who are in touch with the provinces tell me that the local authorities pay less and less attention to the decrees of the center and do pretty much as they please. I can easily understand that. Until now, the most important tie that bound together the center and the provinces was money, and now that little money flows from Moscow, the local powers pay little attention. Foreign capitalists who invest here will, for many years to come, have a double fight on their hands, in the center and in the

---

[6]W. Morgan Shuster (1877–1960), an American lawyer, was treasurer general and financial adviser to the Persian government from May 1911 to January 1912.

[7]Edouard Herriot (1872–1957) was a French radical politician and public official who visited Soviet Russia in mid-1921 and published his impressions in *La Russie nouvelle* (Paris, 1922).

[8]Meyer Bloomfield (1878–1938) was a prominent American lawyer.

[9]Secretary of the Treasury Andrew W. Mellon (1855–1937).

provinces. Contact with the provinces is now greatly endangered by the serious threat of closing certain railway lines (a number of branch lines are already ceased) because of lack of funds. Should this be done, the lines so closed will run down completely, for they are now kept up by a bit of repair here and there. Needless to say, the peasants along the track would help themselves to everything in sight. The most serious danger of all is the breaking off of relations between Moscow and the interior.

In the Pravda of November 29th, there is a statement that the Khlebpro-dukt, the government organ in charge of the grain, plans to export now one million puds of wheat and two million puds of barley to Germany. Later it may export to other countries.

The result of my knocking about in Moscow and Petrograd since my return has convinced me that the food situation is much better than a year ago. The market is full of things to buy and though high, people manage some way to find the necessary paper.[10] I ask people how they do it and they say "NEP." Those who do not engage in business sell their things and lend the money to those who do. There are, of course, thousands who have nothing to sell, can not speculate, and have no other work. These suffer very much. One of these days, this speculation is bound to come to an end for the same coat has already been sold a dozen times and is wearing out. Nevertheless, life is pushing the country into normal channels and the fight against NEP is becoming weaker. Small industry, of the domestic industry type, is once more springing up in the neighborhood of Moscow, and should foreign help come not too soon, a person traveling in a stage coach from Moscow to Petrograd ten years from now may find small nail smithies and spinning wheels in each village.

Heavy industry is declining and neither Lenin nor all his men can raise it until capitalism puts it on its feet again. In the Izvestiia of December 1, there is an article on the condition of heavy industries in which the writer estimates the value of the production of 1922 (in gold rubles) as one-fifth of that in 1913. The metal industry is at the bottom on the list. Thursday night at the opera, I ran into two of my Bolo friends from Tver, one is director of the Tver Textile works and the other is director of all the textile mills of that district. They told me that in some of the mills they had enough raw material to run them until January, in others they may have enough to pull them along until May and then they are through. The trust is trying to buy cotton in the States, but so many different bureaus are handling it that they are in doubt whether anything will come out of it. The trust itself has no money and, therefore, it depends on the Timber and

---

[10]That is, money.

Flax trusts to buy for it in exchange for their products, and all this transaction has to go through the Ministry of Commerce and I do not know where else. There has recently been organized a Russian-American bank, with a capital of $100,000 (so I am informed) and this bank has offered to purchase the cotton and give the Textile Trust six months' credit, but for one reason or another no headway is made.

Yours faithfully,

★ ★ ★

Moscow, December 4, 1922

Dear Fisher:[11]

Radek and I have become quite chummy and he was over for dinner at the Pink House tonight and talked most interestingly to the boys. He is exceedingly intelligent. Lately I have visited him at his home and we have had some interesting conversations, as you may learn from my letters to Herter.

Radek has been reading Foreign Affairs and has noted a number of American books he would like to have. I offered to get them for him and I am writing to you for them. You will have to find some fund for the purchase. We will get Russian books in return, but that is not to be taken into consideration. We are going to keep him supplied with American books of political importance and if there is no other fund your servant will foot the bill. It is exceedingly important for us to keep in good relations. Brown and Hoover will OK my request I am sure.

He has left me his copy of Foreign Affairs which he and Lenin have read. It is pretty well underscored and that makes the document one of political importance. I wish you could see it. I am saving it.

Good bye, old man.

★ ★ ★

Moscow, December 10, 1922

My dear Herter:

I have not much news to write to you. I am quite certain that you are much better informed about Russian affairs than I. Here two tendencies are

---

[11]Harold H. Fisher (1890–1975) was the historian of the ARA and chairman of the Hoover Institution from 1943 to 1955.

at work. One is more moral and political oppression, the other is more economic freedom. The Bolsheviks are experts in phrase making (and some believe in them, though Radek told us the other evening that phrases are not meant to be taken seriously) and they say that they have broken through the "military front," the "hunger front," and they must now crush the "bourgeois ideology front." Priests are still tried and sentenced, professors are still hounded, and now a campaign has been started against students. Some are exiled, others are forced from the schools of learning by decree and still others by a high tuition fee. These are not the only stupid things. Even such innocent organizations like old established historical and literary societies where old men gather to quarrel about the ablative absolute and the influence of the Salic Law on Magna Charta are to be closed. There is now a campaign being waged to put an end to the Academy of Sciences, the institution founded by Peter [the Great] and which has done such excellent work since then, and which is now the only center of Russian culture. There is another movement to close the opera and ballet. Of course, you know that it has taken centuries, at least scores of years, to bring the Russian ballet, Russian music to its present position and all this progress will be lost in a year or two if the opera and the ballet and the training schools are closed.

Economic freedom is making headway in various ways. All kinds of projects are up for discussion, and some are pulled out from under the noses of the various commissars so that they might have a chance to grow. The country seems to be ready for economic development but nothing is done because there is no money. The railway system is running badly in debt because it has no freight to transport and only a few passengers. The attempt to raise the fare has cut down traffic so much that the administration has on the quiet reduced the cost of tickets. I am told on fairly good authority that there are any number of locomotives, in fairly good condition, standing idle. In this connection I should like to call your attention to the talk that is heard in certain circles in regard to the locomotives that were made in Germany and Sweden. The orders were placed not so much because the machines were needed but in payment for political service, especially in Germany.

Today I had a call from a director of a cotton mill, of whom I have written you before.[12] He told me that his mill had enough cotton for another month and then he does not know. The government committee that has charge of the buying and selling of cotton has offered to sell his

---

[12]See Frank A. Golder and Lincoln Hutchinson, *On the Trail of the Russian Famine* (Stanford, 1927), pp. 228–31.

mill cotton at the price of 130 arshins (pre-war price about ten kopeks the arshin) of calico for one pud of raw cotton. This calico is to be taken to Siberia and there traded off for bread and this bread is to be taken to Turkestan to give it to the natives there so as to encourage them to plant cotton in place of grain. Turkestan produces very little cotton because of the scarcity of food and because of the mortality during the last few years due to war and famine. The director complained of the red tape which prevented his mill from getting the cotton it needed. In his district there is plenty of flax which he could secure and exchange abroad for cotton, but the numerous government monopolies and bureaus stand in the way. He told me that he was assured in February that the government monopoly in cotton would be abolished.

He spoke of the healthier tone in labor circles. His workmen realize the seriousness of the situation and submit to the orders issued. You will remember that in one of my letters I told you that in his factory about 45% of the cost of labor was being added for social trimmings. This 45% is being reduced to 28½% and will be reduced still more.

If his mill has to close, which now seems likely, it will bring much suffering. The peasants in the neighborhood have not enough food for themselves and grain is now imported and bought with flax. The workers in the factory have no flax. But it is not only in the factories that people are being thrown out of work. In today's Izvestiia there is printed the proposal of the Commissar of Finance that all government institutions should cut down their forces by 25%. There is no other work. From that point of view the situation is rather serious.

. . . With kindest regards and Christmas greetings to the Chief and you.

Sincerely yours,

★ ★ ★

Moscow, December 10, 1922

Dear Professor Adams:

. . . I am busy doing this and that. My writings do not show it but I am busy. Something has recently come to my attention which will interest you. In Moscow I come in contact quite frequently with the historians and with the economists. The war and revolution have affected these two groups in different ways. Before the debacle both groups were bookmen but after it the economists were dragged into government service, put in charge of bureaus, sent out into the field, etc. The historians, on the other hand, have remained bookmen. The difference between them is most striking. I hardly get a spark from the historians, they have become fossilized, reactionary, and are always trying to explain everything by historical precedents. Not so the economists. Contact with the world has sharpened their wits and I learn something every time I am with them. Some of them are, of course, a bore and stick as close to their economic laws as the historians do their precedents. . . .

With all good Christmas wishes,
Cordially yours,

★ ★ ★

Moscow, December 21, 1922

My dear Herter:

Since my last writing nothing of any great importance has come to pass here. The tendencies noted before are still working. The All-Russian Soviet meeting opens on Sunday and in the meantime the autonomous republics are having their soviets and some reflection is thrown on what may take place in Moscow. The most striking thing is the movement for a closer union with the center and for more centralization. Kalinin, in an interview, made the statement that the autonomous republics were the initiators of the movement, but I question it. The resolutions passed by the autonomous republics are too much alike to be from different brains. A movement like this is to be welcomed. The purpose of it, from the point of view of Moscow, is to be able to present a stronger and more united front, political and economic, to the rest of the world.

Another interesting development is the agitation to make every government institution, every local organization to be self supporting. This includes the railways and post and telegraph service, and provincial governments. From the point of view of the ARA it is bad, for we will have to depend more and more on the local governments who, on the whole, are poor in money and poor in cooperation. On the other hand, from the point of view of Russia, it is a commendable step, for it will teach the people to depend on themselves and to cease expecting help from outside. For the time being it will cripple the railways, the telegraph service, the school, the social and economic institutions, which are already in bad shape. The papers are full of decrees and discussions of reforms and they all begin and end with "let us" and "we must and should" until one is weary for he knows nothing can come of this talk. The laws are perfect. For every so many inhabitants there must be a physician, nurse, hospital, children's home, school, etc., etc., and no attention is paid to these decrees for there is no money. Yet the laws pile on, I suppose more for foreign consumption than local.

Yesterday there was a decree that every one having old gold rubles must bring them to the bank and exchange them for a gold certificate. With us one brings a gold certificate and gets gold and here it is just the other way. The object of this decree is to encourage or force people to subscribe to the 100 million [ruble] gold loan which the bank is issuing and one of the results of it will probably be police searches of homes for gold and confiscation of it when found.

The fight against the "bourgeois ideology" goes on. Today or tomorrow will appear a new publication, "The Ungodly,"[13] which proposes to discredit religion. I may send you a copy of it should it have enough merit. This month the first batch of "red professors"[14] will graduate and this probably means that the "white professors" will have to make place for them. Preparations are already made for the reception of the shining lights. Until now only those professors and scholars who had attained a certain preeminence, such as publications, etc., were entitled to the akademicheskii ration, but now this qualification is to be removed so that others may also benefit. In the same way the pay of the professors, which until now depended on the number of hours of teaching, is to be done away with and the teachers are to be put on a flat rate.

Russian art is being greatly threatened. Recently a commission from Moscow was sent to Petrograd to move some of the best paintings from the Hermitage and the Alexander III Museum[15] to Moscow, on the plea that Moscow is the capital and should have them. Petrograd has had a hard fight and has had to yield something, but it does not know where it is going to stop. If pictures can be moved from Petrograd to Moscow, why not to Rostov or Berlin? There is as much reason for one as for the other. Florence does not move her pictures to Rome just because Rome is the capital.

The opera and the ballet also are in great danger. The charge against them is that they are bourgeois and inculcate bourgeois ideology. Writers on the subject insist that Russia must have proletariat art, but none of the Communists have been able to produce any such art. Futurism is worked to death but futurism is no more proletarian than it is bourgeois. Lenin does not care for art in any form and the question will probably come up to him for settlement and it is more likely that he will kill it.

---

[13]*Bezbozhnik*, usually rendered in English as "the godless."

[14]Golder is referring to the graduates of the Institute of Red Professors, which was established in 1921 to train "red professors" to replace nonparty academicians.

[15]Now the Russian Museum.

Literature no longer flourishes. Private publishing houses are either closed or are absorbed by the government. Only Communistic publications flourish.

The other night I went to a symphony concert played by an orchestra without a leader, a Bolshevik innovation here. On inquiry I was told that the orchestra has a soviet of five persons that meets and decides just how the composition should be played. After the soviet has argued and decided its decision is laid before the orchestra as a whole and each player gives his opinion. When finally some agreement is reached, every player has to memorize or keep in memory just what force he is to give to each note. But the comic side of it is that when the orchestra is in action the chairman of the soviet, who is one of the players and sits where all the others may see him, makes all kinds of contortions and signs. The playing of the orchestra lacked life and I was disappointed with the leaderless orchestra. I have heard that the players, especially the older men, did not like it.

This is rather a stupid and newsless letter, but it is the best I have. You, at the other end, have lots of news, but we never get any here. I have to go to Radek and the other Communists to find out what is going on. It is not fair.

Sincerely yours,

★ ★ ★

Moscow, Christmas Day 1922

My dear Herter:

Merry Christmas to you. Please do not think me altogether a heathen just because I am writing to you today. There are two reasons for that. One is that the courier goes today and the other is that writing to folks in "God's country" is the most agreeable thing one can do today. I am not spoiling the Christmas atmosphere, nor peace and good will, for there is little of it here.

The most important thing that has happened here (and that is not very important) is the All-Russian Congress of Soviets[16] which opened on last Saturday night. No doubt the papers have reported more or less in full on the speeches and I will confine myself to a summary. I should like to say at the beginning that no great change will be announced, aside from the change in the form of federation. It has been planned to have a whole session devoted to international matters, but at the last minute the plan was

---

[16]Tenth All-Russian Congress of Soviets, December 23–27, 1922.

given up. Our friends are becoming cautious and do not commit themselves as readily as they did a few years ago.

On Saturday evening, 6 P.M., Quinn, Matthews,[17] and I went to the Bolshoi Theatre, where the Congress is held, and found it closely guarded from all sides. After some little difficulty we found our way to the diplomatic box which looked over the hall and the stage. The hall was brilliantly lighted so that we could see the delegates who filled every seat. In comparison with last year, the delegates seemed to be a much cleaner, less rough and more intelligent looking, and better dressed. Only a small part of their number were "intellectuals." I dare say that 90% or more of them were real proletarians, whose faces indicated strength, determination, and emotion. It was not the kind of material that was capable of always deciding for itself the right or wrong of a difficult question but it could be led through fire and water in the cause of righteousness. Our friends on the Left appeal to them in memory of ancient wrongs and future brotherhood of mankind and in this way gain their good will. If the reds can make good some of their promises, these proletarians will stand behind them; if they can not these very people will turn with bitter hatred against them.

The Congress opened with Kalinin the president in the chair. Lenin, who is very ill, could not be there, and the Congress sent him greetings and stood while some one in the audience started singing the International. It was sung with a will and was very impressive.

Kamenev took Lenin's place and in a three hours' speech gave a resumé of the internal and external condition to follow him. He said nothing new about foreign relations, but, of course, interpreted them differently. He spent a few minutes on America and related in a rather unfair manner the attempts of our government to send a commission. But it was not a point of any importance. From foreign affairs he went on to discuss the economic position of the country. In general one may say that he offered nothing new, nothing which is not already known to you. I was greatly impressed by one of the characteristics of the Communists, that is the love of polemics. He took for his key note an article written by Martov[18] in Berlin to the effect that the Soviet is not capable of carrying on in Russia on a socialistic basis and that the return of capitalism is inevitable. Kamenev's thesis was to prove that the Soviet will and can carry out the socialistic program. It is going to keep in its hands the "commanding heights," that is, a monopoly of foreign commerce, the heavy industries, the railways, etc. It is also going to keep political control. In these two ways it will be able to dictate the

---

[17]Philip Matthews, executive assistant of the ARA Russian mission.
[18]Julius Martov (1873–1923), Menshevik party leader,

future. Kamenev then went on to show that during the last two years great progress had been made in all lines of industry, which goes to prove that the Soviet is as successful on the "economic front" as on the military. By comparing production in 1919 with that of 1922 he is able to show great improvement. It is hardly worth while quoting these figures, most of which you already have.

Kamenev was rather honest in facing many questions. He stated that industry was run at a loss, especially a loss in raw material. He pointed out the limited market. In 1914 the internal commerce of Russia was about 4½ billion gold rubles (industry about 2½ and agriculture 2) and in 1922 less than 1 billion (industry 510 millions and agriculture, not including the food tax, 375 millions). When closely examined, he said, the figures of 1922 are really not as favorable as they look for most of the trade was by exchange of goods. Government organs did 65% of the 1922 trade and sad to say they sell twice as much, 23%, to private commerce than to government cooperatives.

He dwelt for some time on the evil effects of the fall in the value of the ruble as a result of too much emission.[19] In January 1922, 90% of the government expenses was covered by emission, 8% by income from the sale of forests, railway fares, post office, etc., and only 2% by taxation. Since then there has been great improvement. In September of this same year emissions covered 53%, government undertakings 30%, and taxation 17%. He emphasized the need of more taxation and made it clear what has been quite obvious to some of us, that the government is making an honest effort to organize the country on a sound basis. Whether with the limited human and money resources it can succeed in its attempts is another question.

Soviet Russia has the expenditure of a 20th century state and the income of a 19th century state. Industry and commerce of Russia of 1923 can not bear much more taxation unless it is more highly developed. To do this, foreign capital must give a helping hand. In his speech, Kamenev indicated that Soviet Russia is kindly disposed towards foreign capital and was ready to go a long ways to meet it. Foreign capital need not become frightened at the emphasis he laid on the government monopoly of foreign commerce. That question has been seriously debated among the Communists during the last few months and put to a vote a couple of weeks ago and barely carried. It is altogether possible that circumstances may force the party to

---

[19]That is, the circulation of more rubles.

reverse itself in the near future. In any case, the Soviet is always ready to make special arrangements.

In conclusion Kamenev touched on the question of NEP. He was positive that from the political point of view the Soviet had nothing to fear from NEP, but from the economic there was much danger. Without the peasant the city proletariat could not get along and whether Russia of the future is to be a bourgeois state or a proletarian depends on the peasant. He will favor the side that offers him the "best goods for the cheapest price." It seems to me that Kamenev has well put the question and there is nothing to add to it.

Last night, Sunday, Quinn and I went again. The most interesting part of the Congress is the discussion that follows each report. Delegates have a right to air their opinion and some of them do it with a freedom that is astonishing. Their points of view have little influence for every move is settled before hand, but the discussion gives the delegates an opportunity to blow off steam and the government an idea which way the wind blows. One peasant to whom we listened said this: "I have heard a good deal about heavy industry and light industry, about which I know nothing, but I know this, that if we do not have more education there will not be enough industry to talk about." He then went on to criticize the government.

If a delegate talks more than his allotted time he is brought to order by clapping of hands. If the chairman wishes to put an end to discussion he reads off a list of those who desire to speak and then puts the question, "Shall we have more discussion or not?" and gets the expected, "No, no." Motions are made, put, and decided by the chair. The delegates are not deeply concerned in these matters because most of them are Communists and know that the question is already decided by the party and he is to vote in the affirmative.

Aside from the Congress, I have little to report. I learn from good sources that some of the bread tax, that is, the grain which has been collected, is beginning to spoil in the poor warehouses. Russia is not prepared to house so much grain and to hold it as it does now. Some provinces have few facilities for that purpose and as a result the grain is heaped up in places little suitable for the purpose. The question of selling or not selling is still debated but not settled. All the arrangements for selling are already made, but as far as we know, grain has not yet been shipped out, though the papers are full of reports that this is being done or is about to be done.

There is going to be a new rounding up of church treasures, those that were left for carrying on the service. It is not likely that there will be any resistance.

We are having plenty of ARA troubles, but Quinn is handling them very ably.

> With best wishes for the year,
> Sincerely yours,

★ ★ ★

Moscow, December 26, 1922

My dear Herter:

I do not know how you feel about it, but I am quite discouraged with the results of my present efforts in Russia. Either there is nothing to report or I fail to find out what it is. The fact that I am kept in the dark as to what is going on at your end of the line makes my work stupid. I do not even know whether my letters reach my destination. . . .

> With kindest regards,
> Sincerely yours,

★ ★ ★

Moscow, January 2, 1923

My dear Herter:

The Tenth All-Russian Congress of Soviets came to an end on Wednesday. Aside from the formation of a closer union between the RSFSR, the Ukraine, White Russia, and the Caucasus states (which is in itself a very commendable deed), nothing constructive was done, or was anything destructive proposed. As I have had occasion to point out before, the Soviet is becoming cautious, it no longer waves the red flag. It now has principles and phrases but no policy, and its next move depends on the move of Europe and under the circumstances it does not bind itself at these meetings. Kamenev in his speech said something about the monopoly of foreign commerce but it was not taken seriously. On the question of concessions and relations to foreign governments and foreign capital, no commitments were made.

Most of the time was spent on money questions. Every commissar who reported made it clear that his department is badly crippled and is likely to be more so unless the government gives it credit. In his speech the Commissar of Finance, Sokol'nikov, pointed out that the government had no money and that from now on all institutions must live off their own. The only way to put the country on its feet is to decrease the issues of paper money and to increase taxation. In theory, everybody agreed with this statement and it was not challenged but he was attacked (almost came to blows with one important critic on the actual management of his department). He was asked, for instance, why the State Bank gives credit to private enterprise and refuses it to state undertakings, why he employs bourgeois trained bankers and not red experts. The answers were obvious but no one quite dared give them.

When it came to the question of taxation there was considerable hair pulling. Where is the tax to come from, agriculture or industry? Sokol'-nikov and some of the faithful said "agriculture" but pointed out that the whole taxation machinery must be reorganized. As it stands today one commissariat (Narkomprod)[20] collects the grain tax and another (Narkom-fin)[21] the trade and industry tax. Last summer this peculiar situation developed. The head of the state bank was made the head of Khlebprodukt (the organization to buy up grain) with authority to use state funds, and he had to compete against the State Bank which was engaged in exactly the same kind of transaction. He played the role of coachman and cook in Molière's "L'Avare."

Sokol'nikov favors the payment of all tax in money and not products for in this way it will create a demand for money on the part of the peasants and consequently the value of the ruble will go up (and incidentally the whole machinery of taxation will fall into his hands). Everybody of course knew that under the present conditions the giving up of the grain tax was out of the question because the paper rubles have little value. Some questioned whether the peasants could bear a heavier load, his condition is pitiful enough as it is, and if pushed too hard, he will reduce still more his arable area. Some of the Communists put the problem this way: The Soviet can not exist without industry, industry can not exist without agriculture and a market; in order to develop agriculture and a market it is necessary to put the peasant on his feet by establishing rural credits, etc., and in order to do this we must have money from heavier taxation, and this taxation must come from agriculture.

Agriculture is not in a very prosperous condition just now. Compared with farm products, the price of manufactured goods has gone up two and three times. The closing down of some of the branch railway lines and the possibility of putting out of commission several main lines will put the peasant in a bad way. In the paper of December 31, I find that in Tsaritsyn a pud of white flour costs somewhere about 30 cents in our money while in Moscow it runs as high as a dollar; in Rostov it is quoted as 22 cents and in

---

[20]People's Commissariat of Food Supply.
[21]People's Commissariat of Finance.

Minsk as 75 cents. I dare say that the farther from the railway, the cheaper the flour and the dearer the manufactured goods and consequently no market. The fall seeding is on the whole not more than a year ago, in some districts considerably less, and the prospects of a crop sufficient to sustain the whole population depends on climatic conditions, and in a country as large as Russia one can not count on that regularly. Should 1923 be an off-year, which God forbid, there will be another great famine.

Much time was spent by the Congress in discussing the industrial situation. One delegate took the government seriously to task for placing large orders (for political reasons) in Germany, Sweden, Czecho-Slovakia, while Russian shops have to close for lack of orders. Some of the important metallurgical works and machine shops, like Briansk, Mystishchensk, etc., are practically closed. Owing to the cutting down in the railway service, the coal mines have to reduce their output. It looks now as if more and more mills will have to shut down in the course of the next few months.

Internal trade and foreign commerce were taken up. Private trade is gaining fast on government institutions, that is, the cooperatives, etc. In January 1922, government trusts, etc., did 22.6% of business with government cooperatives and 20.8% with private stores and in September it was 8.2% with cooperatives and 30% with private. The monopoly of foreign trade as a "commanding height" was under fire and some one asked on the quiet whether it might not be a good idea to bring the force down from the height to watch the frontier so that less goods would be smuggled across. That much trade and contraband is carried on in an illegal way is beyond denial.

One of the striking things of this Congress was its open criticism of the government. It is no secret that the Communists have fights among themselves but they usually do not allow their differences to be known to the world. But this time some unkindly things were said about one another. Kamenev and Sokol'nikov were called down publicly and others were condemned by implication. It can not be denied that the absence of Lenin, the financial difficulties, the failure of so many of the schemes, the uncertainty of the future are causing some of the faithful to doubt themselves and to question their principles. There is a good deal of rumbling and such thoughts as "let's stop talking about commanding heights and New Economic Policy and let's look at everything from the point of view of industry and commerce" are being heard and even find their way into print. During the next few months these ideas will be heard and seen more often than today.

As to the immediate future in matters of commerce and trade there is no general plan. It is proposed to reduce industry to the limit of the market, for small as industrial production now is (about 20% of prewar) it is still more than the market can absorb. The industries that survive will have to be put on a paying basis, that means all the social trimmings will have to come off and in other ways the ground will be better prepared for real industrial development later on. In the meantime there is going to be much suffering because of much unemployment.

The immediate future looks very dark indeed, but there is light ahead. The government is making a hard effort to organize the economic state on the right lines but it has not the means. Without the aid of foreign capital little can be done and every day that the government puts off making its peace with the foreign bourgeois the problem of reconstruction becomes more difficult. The government is waiting for something to happen, for a war, for a quarrel between the Powers, for a bidding between big groups of capitalists which will turn to its advantage. It is a gambler's chance and the reds are taking it. But it seems to me that it is a losing game in the long run for them, for the forces of life are pushing Russia back into the old capitalistic channels and pretty soon the Communist leaders will of themselves put into practice ideas which they now regard as concessions to capitalism.

Lenin's health gives much cause for uneasiness and should he drop out the chances are that there will be a split in the Party. Trotsky is, next to Lenin, probably the ablest, but for some reason or other he is kept in the background, even by Lenin. Radek is one of the cleverest but I do not think that he has much influence on internal policies. Rykov, Tsiurupa, and Kamenev, the three men who have been designated as Lenin's deputies, are not men of his class. There are all kinds of possibilities and I hope that they will all turn out along the lines of peace and good will.

Sincerely yours,

★ ★ ★

Moscow, January 8, 1923

My dear friends:[22]

Your letter and one other were the only companions I had to watch with me Christmas Eve and, without saying more, you will realize how much I appreciated it. I tried not to think of Moscow but let my thought wander to the Oregon coast and to you. It was much more pleasant to live over last summer with your crowd than to dwell on the events of this winter by myself. I wish I could see your children and see in their faces the image

---

[22]Tom and Sigrid Eliot.

of the one who has gone and whom I loved. There are so few small children in Russia and of those few not all can be played with.

I quite understand what you mean by saying that I am sacrificing myself in what seems a hopeless cause. You are partly right and you would be wholly so were I spending all my time in feeding the hungry and nothing more. But I am trying to do something in addition. I am trying to bring the Russian and American governments together. Believe me that if they are not already on speaking terms Hughes and Hoover are not the only people to blame, as you seem to imply. You do not know that some of the [Soviet] leaders belong to a "hard neck" race and insist on saving and being saved in a special way. In the course of this last year, the American government has made two honorable essays to bring about better relations with Russia and both failed because of the Soviet authorities and for very petty reasons.

I am talking confidentially and therefore I feel free to say that some of the Red gods are a disappointment and do not come up to the estimate that I had made of their ability. Though they cry down the methods of the capitalist diplomats and statesmen, yet they resort to the same tools, and are as proud of a petty diplomatic prestige as any second grade ambassador in Europe. I have urged on some of them to give up "prestige diplomacy" and work for moral victory but I have failed. The Bolos are clever, they are tricky, but they are not big, and at times they are so stupid. Take the performances of the last day or two, the season of Russian Christmas, when the Communists (that is, the same as the government) paraded the streets, dragging trucks with representations of the divinities, pagan and Christian, making coarse remarks and vulgar gestures, which shocked not only the religious minded, but also the clean minded. Why do this? Why hurt people's feelings? Not very long ago the Vatican donated a large sum of money to feed the hungry and the sick in Russia. If the money was not honest money, the Bolos need not have taken it, but once they accepted the gift, it is only decent that the Church should not be insulted. It is neither here nor there that the Americans are hypocrites, narrow-minded, and all that. The fact remains that the Reds are eager to get our good will and more eager still to get our bourgeois capital, and yet they do the very things that will turn public opinion against them. You see why it is so hard to do anything for them and why it is not quite fair to put all the blame on Hughes and Hoover and their kind.

I am deeply pained to read what such publications as the Nation say on the relations of our government towards the Soviet. Why are the whites always wrong and the reds always in the right? Why is it wrong to murder Jews in Poland, lynch negroes in the South, massacre Armenians in Turkey, and not wrong to shoot dozens of priests, kill and exile scores of professors, and cause the death of hundreds of non-Communists, like you and me, by depriving them of their livelihood and their homes? Why is it wrong to jail Communists in America because they try to overthrow our government and not wrong to shoot counter-revolutionists in Russia because they try to change the government? Of course, you will say they are both wrong, with which I thoroughly agree, but why does not the Nation and the parlor-bolshevik condemn both in the same loud voice? When some time ago a New York legislative committee passed a measure aiming to keep certain teachers from teaching, the parlor-bolsheviks raised a howl that was heard from coast to coast, but in Russia hundreds of scientists have been deprived of their places and been hounded out of the country. The only comfort they got was the idea that they were not shot. Did the parlor-bolsheviks protest? Do you know that each teacher is spied upon, that each non-Communist student is watched, that in some schools none but Communists are admitted (the University of Moscow has 97% Jews and 3% non-Jews or Russians),[23] and in others bourgeois can get in only by means of lying, bribing. Knowing as I know all that, you can imagine what a mockery it is to read what the American radical papers have to say, to note the speech of Paxton Hibben[24] in New York that the Soviet government was the only honest government in the world.

I have no wish to make your heart ache as mine does to witness all the misery and suffering. The war is much to blame, so is the Revolution, Kolchak, Denikin, Wrangel, the blockade, etcetera, but they are not the only factors. Much of the sorrow of today is due to the intolerant policy of the Soviet government. I know a family, the head of which defended revolutionists in the tsar's court.[25] He held a high position in the Kerensky government; he has never opposed the present government, but because he could not whole-heartedly approve it, he was arrested and, without being given a trial, was ordered into exile. His wife has worried herself into consumption, one daughter is ill, and the whole family is about to become a wreck. I can enumerate case after case who are hounded for no other reason than they are bourgeois. The tsar's government never did that. At least it gave one a trial.

To live here is like sitting at the bed of a dying person. Day by day the number of cultured and educated people is being reduced. Last year there

---

[23]Golder is here passing along as fact an unfounded report he has heard in Moscow.

[24]Paxton Hibben (1880–1928) was a director of the American Committee for Relief of Russian Children, one of several small American relief committees sympathetic to bolshevism and a vocal critic of Hoover and the ARA.

[25]This is Muravev.

were three small (non-Bolshevik) groups where the questions of the day were discussed. This year there are remnants of two, and the next year there will be none. The peasants are not dying so fast, but are degenerating under the influence of the new ideas and the new teachings. In the end, Russia will come out, history teaches that, but the process is very painful.

"To starve further a scorbutic patient who had a morbid passion for salt salmon, until he acquires a taste for my particular brand of religion seems to describe the policy of our government at present. I can see nothing constructive or educative in Hughes's or Hoover's (overt) attitude."[26] I leave it to you, my dear Tom, to decide whether it is Hughes and Hoover or Lenin and Trotsky who are pursuing the policy noted above. You wonder why America does not enter into closer relations. Before going further, let me say that I have urged recognition. But I must say that political recognition will help nobody, it is a formal gesture and not more. What is needed is economic relations, industrial and agricultural restoration, and that kind of a thing. This is not a government matter. But let us look at that for a moment.

The American Relief Administration came here over a year ago on a special agreement to do a certain work. Believe me, we have tried to do it honestly; we have not mixed in politics; when we discovered men who were meddling in things that did not concern them, they were immediately dismissed. On the other hand, the Soviet officials were not always honest with us. From the very beginning, they blocked us, they discredited us and they are doing that today, and all that is done for political reasons. Last fall, the American Relief Administration was asked to stay for a time longer and on the same terms, but now the Soviet government is doing everything in its power to get out of keeping the terms and is making it hard for us to carry on our work. If the government is not willing to keep faith with us, who have come in here to help in caring for the needy, how can you expect capitalists to risk their money? You are economists enough, New Englanders enough, to realize that sentiment has nothing to do with such affairs. Believe me, my dear Tom, the fault is not wholly with the American Relief Administration, with Hughes and Hoover.

My dear Sigrid and Tom, please pardon the tone of this letter, its contents, and its length. When I use the term "you" I do not mean you personally. Needless to say, I have meant nothing in the spirit of bitterness. It is painful to watch gentle, cultured, innocent people suffer and hear gentle, cultured, innocent people in America applaud. The Bolshevik question is far from being simple and there is much in bolshevism that is

---

[26]Golder is evidently quoting from a letter he had received from Tom Eliot.

admirable. Some of its leaders are noble men, but large numbers of them are rascals who are crushing the spirituality of the movement. Some day when we walk along the beach, far from the pain and suffering, we can talk it over calmly.

This is not the kind of letter I meant to write you. It is an ungracious return for your cheery word, but you have always been kind and forgiving and I know you will bear with me now. In essentials, we do agree and if we seem to differ on certain questions, it is because we see them from different angles.

May this year bring peace and contentment. If I had my wish, I would have you on the Pacific coast, not too far from Stanford, where we could meet from time to time with our friends. Two days ago I prayed God that this request might be granted, but I can not do that today for yesterday the Bolsheviks burned God, Christ, the Virgin, the gods of the Orient, and left only the Communist gods, Karl Marx, Lenin, et al. I can not as yet pray to them; perhaps in time. Such things have happened.

Most cordially yours,

★ ★ ★

Moscow, January 11, 1923

My dear Herter:

The event of last week which shook the world was the "burning of the gods," and if our correspondents sent out all they had planned you have no doubt read a good deal on the subject. I should like to make one or two comments. In asking intelligent people on the Right and Left why such a stupid thing was done I was told that the only reason they knew was the desire to keep the "communist fire of enthusiasm burning" and that it was always necessary to have some stunt. There is one phase of this celebration that is necessary to point out. Orders were sent to the various provincial towns to carry out anti-religious acts. In these small towns the Jews are the most important Communists and the hatred of the Church elements will be turned against them not as Communists but as Jews and in this way the fires of hatred are kept glowing and some day they may burst out.

Industrially the situation is, to put it lightly, not improving. During the last few days several important factories closed because they had consumed all their capital. Others are reducing the output because there is an oversupply. At the same time, orders for goods are placed abroad. I am not speaking of locomotives, but of such simple things as sacks and, somewhat more important, pipes for oil. It is proposed to spend a number of millions of gold rubles in the purchase of pipes abroad, notwithstanding the fact that the pipe mills of Russia, which formerly supplied this article, are idle. The reasons are simple. The Russian mills can not produce as cheaply as foreign mills, they can not deliver as quickly and as surely, and they can not commence an order unless they receive an advance. They have no capital.

Those who are eager to see a real and healthy improvement in Russia need not, however, be discouraged. During this last week I have noted some things that are very encouraging. The more intelligent Bolos realize that things can not go on this way in the industrial world and they now agitate that the cost of production should be reduced to the point of meeting competition and that most of the country's industries should be put on the basis of "sink or swim." This agitation has been put into an order by one of the highest government organs (STO)[27] to some of the coal mines to reduce by ½ kopek (gold) the cost of producing a pud of coal within the next three months. The same question was taken up by the textile mills a day or two ago. To reduce wages is almost impossible and it would be a pity to see it done. The textile directors voted to pay during January from 3.5 to 7 rubles gold (for the month), which is little enough but more than they can afford.

The reduction of the cost of production will have to come from two other sources. First, reduction in the cost of social insurances, etc., which in some industries are more than 40%; that is to say that in addition to his wages each employee has set aside for him or for his social benefit a sum equivalent to 40% of his pay. In the last few days there has appeared a summary of a report of a commission studying the social insurance question. This commission found that the rate is very high, that none of the syndicates and trusts pay it all, that some have paid in only about 4.6% of their dues and that none have paid more than 26%, that no one has as yet received any benefit from this fund, and that it is not very clear where the money goes to. It is quite evident that reductions will be made here and in a very short time, not only in practice but in theory. It will clear the field for business undertakings.

The cost of production may be reduced in still another way: that is, more efficiency. Something is being done here, too. I noticed in yesterday's paper that in a certain region (with 179 districts) having Labor Bureaus, all but 28 were abolished and departments of government as well as private employers were left free to get their labor where they pleased. This is important, for until now labor could not be had except through these

---

[27]Russian initials for the Council of Labor and Defense.

bureaucratic and Communistic organizations. Of course, this is only a beginning in that direction, but other changes will follow.

The cost of production will be reduced by more efficiency. One hears a good deal of talk of the Taylor system,[28] and I am told that it has been put into operation in certain shops. But it is not likely that anything is coming out of it. The efficiency needed here is freedom in selecting directors, managers, etc. There is a beginning that way, too.

Of course, you know that the 8-hour day is for all practical purposes non-existent as a sine qua non. The law has been gotten around by permitting overtime work for extra pay.

Please do not misunderstand me. All I am trying to show is that life is forcing the leaders to normality. Under the present conditions Russian industry can not compete with foreign and all the improvements suggested above will help but little, but they are preparing the ground for healthy industry.

The hopes some of the Bolos held that agriculture will be able to put industry on its feet is not bringing results. Agriculture is not improving and the prospects for next year are not bright. There is a big shortage in work animals, seed, implements. One hears a good deal of talk here about tractors, but they will have as great a success as electrification. One of the first simple problems tractors have to face is the lack of strong bridges for taking the tractor to the farm; also there is the lack of spare parts, the lack of fuel, and, more than that, the conservatism of the average peasant.

Money, money is the cry everywhere. The Commissar of Food (who is in charge of the grain tax) complains that he can not transport his grain because he has not the money to pay the Commissar of Railways for freight and the Commissar of Finance refuses to advance the money. As a result the grain is spoiling in the warehouses. In order to get money it has been decided to increase taxation and this has become so heavy that many of the business houses say they will have to close. By the way, it may interest you to know that the State Bank in making up its yearly balance has discovered that it has fewer gold rubles now than a year ago.

One more thing and I am done. The rebuff received by Russia at Lausanne is making itself felt in her prestige in the Near East.[29] Persia has assumed a rather haughty attitude in her relations.

---

[28]This refers to the scientific management theories of U.S. engineer Frederick W. Taylor (1856–1915); these theories found adherents among the leading Bolsheviks, notably Lenin.

[29]The Lausanne Conference convened in November 1922 to discuss the Turkish

Moscow, January 18, 1923

My dear Herter:

At times I wonder whether my letters clear up the situation in Russia or muddle them up. Today I am going to try to clear up three apparently contradictory statements which you may have come across in my letters. In some of them I tell you that conditions are worse, in others that they are better, and in still others that they are hopeful.

Are conditions worse than a year ago? From the point of view of the Soviet government I say they are worse. Industry is going down and various attempts of the government to set it right put it farther back. Let us take the textile business. You know that in spite of its supply of prewar cheap raw cotton it has been working at a loss, except last October when it made a little more than expenses. Since then the government has put in a commission to regulate prices and as a result during the month of December the textiles were once more sold at a loss. If there is a loss at the old cheap prices of cotton how can the textile industry expect to support itself by buying high priced American cotton?

Notwithstanding the cheapness of bread in the Ukraine, it now costs three times as much to mine a pud of coal in the Don basin than before the war; a large part of this high cost is due to overhead, to the complicated organization of trusts, syndicates, and their fellows. On the other hand the production of wood fuel is much less syndicated and there the cost of production is less than prewar.

The greatest confusion is in the transportation department. It is no secret that the railroads are run at a heavy loss, in part due to the high cost of coal and in part to various other reasons. One big factor is the lack of freight. At each principal station one sees long lines of empty freight cars. But here is the tragic part: these empties are so poorly distributed that there are parts of Russia that need them and can not get them. This is a fact. In order to be self supporting, the railways raise the rates, but the wording and the instructions are so loosely stated that few know what is meant. The result of these high rates is a reduction in traffic. Except for third class and wagon-lit (for commissars, speculators, and foreigners), the passenger trains are empty. But it is the high freight rates that cause the harm. I am told on good authority that a pud of barley costs at the present time 3 millions (7 cents) in Simbirsk and the freight charges on it to Moscow are 7

---

question. The Soviet delegation, led by Chicherin, argued unsuccessfully to restrict international navigation through the straits of the Dardanelles and the Bosphorus. See Timothy Edward O'Connor, *Diplomacy and Revolution: G. V. Chicherin and Soviet Foreign Affairs, 1918–1930* (Ames, Iowa, 1988), pp. 121–26.

millions. There is now a proposal that freight rates should be paid in gold values at the point of unloading. The shipper will not know what it will cost him until the stuff arrives at destination.

The country is in bad condition commercially. The transportation system is in small part responsible. Just now the heavy taxation is crushing commerce. Dozens of stores are closing. The reason for this heavy taxation is the need for money. Some say it is to kill NEP, but I think that is secondary. In view of the fact that the supply of gold on hand is very small and foreign purchases have to be paid in gold, a decree has been passed or is about to be passed limiting the amount of imports. It is a self-imposed blockade. Everywhere one hears, "We are face to face with a catastrophe. In a few months there will be a crash—the factories will close, the stores will shut their doors, the peasants will stop sowing because they get nothing for their crop." In a country so primitive as Russia now is it is difficult for me to picture a catastrophe. If the factories close, the workmen will return to the soil from which they are removed by a generation. Trade will be driven underground, as it is already, or it will break out in some new form. Of course, conditions will grow worse but there will be no catastrophe in the sense that the term is used elsewhere.

To turn from this scene to a happier picture. Is anybody better off today than a year ago? Yes, thousands of people who have work, who have a little money for speculation, are better off materially. Bread is so cheap that even those who have a small salary can keep the wolf from the door. On the other hand those who have no work—and there are tens of thousands of them—are worse off, because last year they had some work and a ration, but now they have nothing. There is frightful suffering.

Though materially a large part of the population is better off, morally the thinking population is worse off. Last year every one expected great things from NEP. It was assumed that NEP would lead to the land of normal, or prewar life, but this has not come to pass. NEP is neither fish nor fowl. One man has defined NEP as a system of exploitation of the peasant and the squeezing of the merchant class for the benefits of the factory proletariat. Another made this statement regarding it: Before the Revolution, business in Russia walked on its feet; after the Revolution it walked on its hands; and now under NEP it walks on one hand and one foot.

Leaving the rich speculator out of consideration, the people who manage to keep body and soul together do so by hard work, by running from place to place, by selling the few things they still have. They barely get along. Now the government is going to tax them heavily—tax the furniture, the rooms, the pictures, etc., and they are wondering what is going to become of them. In this connection, let me tell you a story which is rather characteristic. It was told to me by a man whom I know well and whom you met. A few weeks ago, an artist was called to pass an opinion on a picture sold by an individual as a Rembrandt. The artist said that it was not. Next day he was summoned before the Cheka to give evidence because the seller was under arrest for misrepresenting the picture. The artist once more said that it was not a Rembrandt and gave his reason. The judge, a simple workman, in talking to the artist, while looking on the picture, said: "Now if you would only say that it is a Rembrandt we would let the man out of jail, but if it were a Rembrandt, I suppose we would have to confiscate it." This is the dilemma the tax payers find themselves in. If they say it is a Rembrandt it will be confiscated; if they do not say it they will be put in prison. If people had Rembrandts to sell they would not worry, but the difficulty is that there is nothing more to sell and the tax will have to be paid. But how? The feeling of a catastrophe of which I spoke before is noticed among ordinary people as well as among industrialists and merchants.

All that I have said above gives you the blues, no doubt. There is a ray of light nevertheless. I will go further and say that from the point of view of Russia of the future, the situation is very encouraging, much more so than a year ago. Our friends the Reds are learning and the lessons are not wholly lost on them. They have learned during the last year that the Soviet government is a poor business and industrial manager, that some things can be done better by private initiative than by the state. An interesting illustration of that appeared in the papers last week. The Cotton Trust, in order to encourage the natives of Turkestan to plant more cotton and less grain, has decided to send in a lot of grain to distribute among the planters. It called for bids. The government agencies asked 8 arshins of calico for a pud of grain and an advance; private dealers asked 5½ arshins and no advance. The helplessness of government departments is so striking that it is tragic. One government agency buys from another similar agency through a private contractor, and another private contractor takes the job of delivering the order. This system not only increases the overhead, but it also lends itself to graft.

Talking about contractors, let me tell you a story that goes the rounds. The Commissariat of Railways owes not only the government, but also private contractors. Each day these contractors gather at the Commissariat to demand their money and when they become too noisy a squad of Chekists are called out (Dzerzhinskii is head of the railways and the Cheka) and the place is cleared out. One old Jew was persistent, came day after day, and finally just before Christmas he was given 10% of the total money due him, for educational purposes.

The government can no longer carry all this burden and it is forced to drop one industry after another, one undertaking after another, or it will have to modify its system. Under the present legal and economic conditions in Russia private capital can not and will not touch industry and commerce. I know that a number of former Russian industrialists have been approached and asked to take back their factories but they refused because the terms were not satisfactory. If the factories are allowed to close up, the Soviet will lose its city proletariat, its mainstay. It is a difficult situation the leaders are in: it is either close the factories or hand them over to capitalists on a capitalistic basis. What will they do? I can not say, but I know this: they are giving the subject serious thought and the next congress of the Party in March is going to be one of the most important in the history of the Soviet government. They have got to face the issue and they have got to take into account the rumblings outside and inside the Party. It would be easy if they had only one point of view to consider, but they have three. Is a certain policy for the best economic interest of the country? Is it for the best interest of the Soviet government? Is it for the best interest of the Communist Party? It is not simple. Poor Lenin (with the aid of Stalin, I am told) is working on this problem. I wish him success.

I should like to say a word or two about certain political phases of the situation. I am told that Ioffe has recently written from China to his colleagues here to give up the idea of getting help from Europe and to pin their hope on America.

It is rumored here that England is encouraging Turkey to work for a federation which should include Georgia, Azerbaidzhan, and other regions now belonging to Russia. This may or may not be true, but I know this, that the little governments in that part of the world are making demands on the Soviet and the Soviet is doing all it can to satisfy them.

I spent the week end in Petrograd and saw a great deal of my artist friends, some of whom you met. I went with them to the ballet and Russian opera and I was quite carried off my feet by the harmonious setting, the poetic interpretation, and the artistic execution. It was a wonderful revelation to me, more so than ever before. All glory and praise to these Russian artists who have been able to carry on these hard years. My friends told me that they might possibly be able to hold out the remainder of the year but that is all. There is talk of a tour of Europe and America next year, but that is in the nature of a wind up. The ballet schools and the opera studios will have to close. It is such a pity that all these years of work, study, suffering, and spiritual and artistic enthusiasm should be allowed to go to waste. It is a loss not only for Russia but the world as a whole. I am so glad that so many of our young [ARA] men have had and are having opportunities to be present at these performances for it will influence their lives and they will carry this influence to America. We are giving Russia bread, but it is giving us something more precious in return. It is not only opera and ballet but in other lines of art.

As I have told you before, the government refuses to support the theatre and ballet because it is teaching bourgeois ideology. Last Monday night the opera was for the benefit of a Communistic organization and strangely enough the opera was a religious one. It had to do with people giving their lives for their faith, with crosses, priests, and bishops. In this morning's paper I noticed that a Communist was appointed director of one of the classic theatres of Moscow and that he recommends that the classic plays be thrown on the waste pile. We might as well put up a cross to the dramatic art. Du courage! Du courage! It is always darker before it is lighter. Qui vivra verra.

> Je vous serre cordialement la main.

A Little Journey into the Land of the Monks
(January 21 & 22, 1923)

Sunday being Christian prazdnik and Monday a Bolshevik holiday (Gapon Day, for Father Gapon of revolutionary fame),[30] I accepted the invitation of a Russian friend to leave ungodly Moscow for these two days to breathe the saintly atmosphere of Troitse-Sergieva Monastery, some forty miles distant. Though it is better than a year ago, train service in Russia is still primitive. One has to wait in line half an hour or more for a ticket, he has to stand or sit in unheated third class cars (on most lines there is only this class) with boarded windows (except at the very top where there are bits of ice-covered glass through which daylight penetrates with difficulty and at night there is almost total darkness) and inhale poisonous air. These passenger wagons are filled with bags and baskets and crowded with coughing, nose-blowing, and vile-tobacco-smoking passengers. The smoke, combined with the hot breath of the human mass, forms a thick foggy cloud which mounts to the frozen ceiling and causes a precipitation of icy water. In any country other than Russia there would be a loud outcry against this inhuman treatment of humans, but here the people are good natured and think how much better off they are today than two years ago when they had to travel in open box cars at the rate of speed of a snail. But good nature can not keep the feet warm and first one and then another of

---

[30]Georgii Apollonovich Gapon (1870–1906) was an orthodox priest who led a procession of Petrograd workers who were fired on by tsarist soldiers on January 9, 1905; the incident later became known as Bloody Sunday.

travelers begins thumping his feet on the floor in the effort to keep them warm until it sounds, especially to one dozing, like a company of new recruits on the march. When the train comes to a stand still, which is every few minutes, there is a hasty rush outside to run up and down the platform and as hasty a rush back because the air outside is beastly cold.

At last, after three hours of train bumping and feet thumping, some passenger shouted "Troitse" and we stepped out into a better world than the one we came from. The clean snow and green forests of this religious community are a refreshing change from the dirty and noisy streets of the red capital. We were fortunate enough to secure a clean room in the house of a Russian workman who made us quite comfortable. Before the war the monks had a guest house where they made visitors welcome, but this is now gone.

When I had had a bite to eat I went to call on Madame X, whom I have known off and on for some time. She and her husband are teaching school and doing with a right good will what they can to keep the lamp of science and religion burning. I had heard from various Russians, especially the émigrés, that in Russia there was a great religious movement, with Troitse as its center, which promises important political consequences in the immediate future. When I questioned my friends about this movement they replied that in an hermitage, off the main beaten path, dwelt an old monk, Starets Alexei, greatly beloved and venerated by all those who come in contact with him. He listens to the troubles of all those who come to see him, gives them sound advice, takes a personal interest in them, and sends them home with peace in their hearts. If this purely personal influence over a small circle may be called a movement then he is the leader of it. The other clergyman who attracts some attention is Father Florenskii, a scholarly priest, deeply interested in metaphysical questions too deep for the average educated man. At one time when he was professor of the theological academy he had a large audience, but now he touches only the few with whom he comes in daily contact. He has an even smaller following than Starets Alexei. When it is all sifted down it is evident that the Troitse movement offers neither encouragement to the Whites nor discouragement to the Reds.

While it is true that there is nothing to be hoped or feared, in a political way, from these movements, they have some significance when taken together with the deep spiritual awakening which, my friends claim, is now taking place, especially among the young intelligentsia, the very class that before the war fought for revolution and against faith and tradition. These young men and women are disillusioned by the results of the revolution and its teachings and are now turning to religion in search for the ideal. These statements were not new to me for I had heard them from some of my student friends who a very few years back were ardent disciples of Voltaire and Marx and wrote philosophic essays to prove the non-existence of God. Since then many doubts and questions have arisen which they are not able to answer.

Why has the Church, which they were told was built on lies, withstood the shock of the war better than socialism, which its adherents claimed was founded on truth? Why do the families of the nobles and the cultured, both trained in social tradition, support their trials and tribulations more manfully than the masses? Whatever the philosophic answer may be it is for the philosophers to say but the emotional answer among many is to turn to the Church. At least that is what my Troitse and student friends say and if they are right, Russia need not despair; for these young disciples will carry the gospel of the new spirit into every factory and village with the same fervent zeal that their fathers carried the revolutionary ideals. In view of the hounding of the non-Communist intelligentsia which is now going on I shake my head at this optimism, but my friends say that I am a man of little faith. They claim that the worst is over and they are now facing the sun. A year ago they and their friends were wholly occupied with the question of wood and food and now they are concerned with the higher things.

Interestingly enough they give the American Relief Administration much more credit for this renaissance than it seems to me it deserves. They insist that the ARA food packages, which some received from their friends abroad and others as general relief,[31] were just enough to pull them across from the material into the spiritual world. But that is not all. The ARA, they say, opened for them the window to the outside world, it put them once more in touch with their friends, it put new hope and new courage into their souls. It was the first sign of spring and of a better day.

When I returned to the room that night I found the master of the house and my friend around the samovar and I joined them. Our host is a tailor and works in his own home to avoid the heavy tax laid on shopkeepers. He talked very quietly of the early days of the revolution, of the idle hours spent as a mobilized tailor in the government work shops, and the busy hours after that in trying to earn enough to make the ends meet. When one of us said something about the present miserable condition of the peasants he flared up in an astonishing manner: "Let the rascals be miserable! It is their turn now!" he shouted. "They deserve to suffer as they made us

---

[31]By "general relief" Golder means ARA food packages distributed to groups and individuals at the discretion of the American relief workers.

suffer. Two and three years ago they rode into town with a pud of flour or a can of milk and acted as if they owned the world. In exchange for their bit of food they picked out the finest furniture, the costliest jewels, the best clothing. They got my warm overcoat. I used to wander from village to village in search of work and in payment for several days of hard work to fit them into their finery they gave me a few pounds of flour. Don't you waste any pity on them. Go to the bazaar and note who buys sugar and expensive cloth and you will see it is the peasants. Let them suffer, the scoundrels. They got my overcoat."

Early Monday morning I struck across the open country in the direction of the steeples of the monastic churches in the distance. After a brisk walk I entered a beautiful forest of evergreen trees, the same kind of forest in which, the legends say, St. Sergius wandered and prayed and made friends with the wild beasts. It was still and peaceful and as I followed the snow path and passed the deserted monasteries I thought of ancient stories, of castles, knights, and witches. After a time I came out into the open road and saw before me an old, long-haired, long-robed monk at work. He returned my greeting in a friendly manner and we entered into conversation. At first he was a bit suspicious but when I told him I was from America he burst out into a laugh and became somewhat more confidential. He laughed, he said, because he had a friend who went to America where he earned good money but when he heard of the Bolshevik Utopia he returned and now he is cursing the day that he left New York. After this he became more friendly and offered to lead me to the hermitage where he and his brothers were living. On the way we met several of them with axes and other tools on their way to the deep forest to work. We came to a high wall and as we entered we saw a number of churches and other monastic buildings. The churches were closed and sealed except for one old wooden chapel of quite primitive architecture, the original building of the hermitage. My guide took me there and handed me over to the good care of a middle-aged, peasant-looking monk who guided me about. We chatted as we moved along and when we came to a bench we sat down to have a good talk. The good man, when he realized that he had nothing to fear from me, was only too glad to open his heart and pour out his woes. ·

He and the other monks, he said, were organized according to the Soviet decrees into a workmen's artel for the purpose of cultivating the bit of land in connection with their hermitage. They raised enough food for their own needs and last year they had a car load to send to the famine area. They paid their tax, they conformed to all the laws and regulations, they kept out of politics, but all this did not save them from the hands of the local soviet, which had it in for them just because they were monks. Now the local authorities demand that the artel should pay a high rent for the use of the land and a heavy insurance, both of which amount to billions of rubles and is beyond their ability to pay. This demand is a pretext to force them out and break up the band. "Formerly," continued my companion, "we were accused of idleness and now we are not given a chance to work. All we ask is to be let alone. In the days before the revolution, when we read the lives of our saints and their loneliness in the deep forest, we used to pity them, but now there is not one of us who would not gladly retire into the wilderness in order to get away from this everlasting hounding. The persecution by the so-called Red Churchmen is worse than that of the Bolsheviks, for the latter touch mostly the body while the former torture the soul. Why can't they see that the Communists are using them as tools to destroy the Church and when they no longer have need of them will cast them out?"

"Father," I asked, "how do you explain this persecution of God's servants?"

"My son," he replied, "we have put to ourselves the same question. Most of our old men (startsy) see in these persecutions signs that the world is coming to an end and therefore it is in the order of things. But when will the end come, tomorrow or after tomorrow, who can say for to God a thousand years are as one day. Some of us do not think it is the coming of the anti-Christ for if that were so the Church would be persecuted everywhere in the world and not only in Russia. If it is not the end of the world then this present persecution is one of the many in history and after each of them the Church comes out regenerated. Whatever the explanation may be, we know it is God's will, it is in expiation for our sins, and for our good."

After this the conversation turned on the Soviet government. "If the Bolsheviks did not oppress the Church and rob the peasant," said the monk, "they might continue in power indefinitely. But their present actions cause discontent everywhere and if there is no revolt it is because the people are crushed and the Bolsheviks have the bayonets on their side. This fall I visited my native village in Tula and saw my three brothers and their families, ten persons in all. Last year they had a crop of thirty puds of grain and twenty of them were taken away as tax. Now they have little to live on, no seed for the spring and no animals for plowing.

"There is suffering everywhere, but it is not as intense as two and three years ago or even four. It was no uncommon sight to see men and women, formerly in high standing, dressed in rags trudging through mud and snow from the outlying villages and carrying sacks of frozen and rotten potatoes from which the black water ran. My son, there is nothing like religion to help a man in time of trouble. I have watched them, saint and sinner, as they passed by me during those hard times. The believer knew that he was doing penance for his sins and for those of Russia and that Heaven held a reward for him and a better future for Russia; the unbeliever suffered and rebelled like a dumb beast. The one became softened and the other hardened. You have no idea how many of the intelligentsia who formerly reviled God are now turning to Him with the prayer, 'Have mercy on me, a sinner.' "

Our conversation, or rather his conversation, was interrupted by the ringing of a church bell summoning him to service. He excused himself and I wandered out of the enclosure, passing the different brothers, one of them totally blind, engaged in various tasks.

In the afternoon we called on the monks of the Troitse-Sergieva Lavra, the mother of all the other monasteries in this part of the world, and found the brothers in great trouble. Several of their members were lying in the cold prison and no one knew what would be done to them. Their sin? From time immemorial the monks of this monastery were in the habit of taking their holy image of the Mother of God to the different villages for service. The villagers in return contributed to their larder and store houses such things as they could spare. A few months ago the monks decided to make another religious procession and asked the local powers for permission, which was granted. Before holding service in the different villages the assent of the soviet was obtained. When the brothers had made their circuit and had returned with a cart load of food the Cheka pounced on them, took the rewards of their labor, and even emptied their store houses and threw them in prison on the charge of carrying on counter revolutionary propaganda. They were put in the same cell with thieves who took from these old men their warm coats and left them to freeze. "They put them with even worse company," added one of the brothers, and I can merely guess who that might be. There is no redress, no trial, and the poor men will lie there until the Lett, the head of the local Cheka, sees fit to let them out.

Two or three of the monks received ARA food parcels and use them sparingly, the white flour for church days only. "It is not so much the food as the moral support which these parcels bring us that makes them so precious to us," said one of the monks.

In token of their gratitude they showed me their valuable collection of manuscripts and presented one of their books to the Hoover Collection.

★ ★ ★

Moscow, January 25, 1923

My dear Herter:

I have been thinking a good deal and asking many questions on the subject whether at the present time it would be profitable for foreigners to invest their capital in Russia. I have come to the conclusion that it would not be and attached to this letter I give my reasons. Please regard them as very confidential and I should prefer if your neighbors across the street[32] did not get a copy. But I leave it to your good judgment.

This stand does not contradict my recommendation that some form of recognition be given to the Soviet government provided it can be done with honor and self respect. I urge recognition because it will hasten the process of evolution and not because any immediate material profit will come out of it. As I have written to you more than once, changes for the better are constantly going on and it may be that some business concern might undertake something even now, but it would be dangerous for any one to recommend it.

As ever yours,

Individual and Property Rights

In Russia at the present time there are no fundamental laws, no basic principles of justice as in England, no constitutional guarantees as in the United States for the individual and his property. A person may be arrested at any time without warrant, he may be kept in prison indefinitely without trial, he may be dispossessed of his property without explanation, and he may be put out of his room without due notice. Each day new decrees are made, often contradicting those made the day before, and most of them are so poorly worded that only a Bolshevik lawyer and a Communist judge understand what is meant and they know because they get their instructions and orders from the prosecuting attorney and he receives his from the Communist Party. In some cases the decision is determined before the trial and in others it is changed after the sentence has been declared. It is Party advantage and not justice that the judges have in mind.

Then again, decrees have little to do with actual life. There are decrees which say that no man may be under arrest more than two weeks without being told the reason thereof, he may not be held in jail more than a certain time without trial, and yet every one knows that they are not observed. I know personally several such cases. On the other hand, many of the regulations of the Labor Code are not observed and the workman does not get by far all that is promised him. The much lauded Civil Code does not protect the individual against the government and its numerous institutions; the Labor Code has much to say about the rights of the employees, little

---

[32]That is, the State Department.

about his obligations, and nothing at all about the rights of the employer. This fluid legislation is very convenient for the Soviet for it can use it or not as it sees fit, but it is dangerous for the individual who has no such choice.

Interference with the Individual

In Russia at the present time the employer is interfered with in the carrying on of his work. His employees are selected for him by the Labor Exchange from the Labor Unions which in turn determine the rate of wages, the hours of work, the condition of labor, and to a certain extent the policy. A workman may not be dismissed without the consent of the Union and the shop may not close without the assent of the same organization. There is on record the case of a dismissed scrub woman who appealed her case and dragged the employer before twelve different government and Communist organizations and succeeded in the end in getting herself reinstated. A director of one of the trusts told me the other day that one of their factories was losing money and should be closed but the Union would not agree to it. The employer is also interfered with by the local soviets, the heads of which have their own axes to grind and must be satisfied; he is interfered with by the Rabkrin[33] (theoretically workmen and peasant inspectors but in reality a government controlling organ), which assumes the power of an administrative court; he is interfered with by the Cheka (GPU, as it is now called), which places no limit on its jurisdiction; and last but not least, he is interfered with by the unseen power of the Communist Party, which has a small organization (komiacheika)[34] in each factory.

Economic Reasons

In Russia at the present time the financial conditions are so disturbed that it is impossible to do big business. Decrees on financial matters follow each other so fast that they confuse. Last April it was decreed that all gold coins should be deposited in the State Bank; a few days later it was admitted in theory and in practice that dealing in coin was permissible; now it is proposed to pass decrees making the holding of gold coins a criminal offense. I could go on and enumerate other such cases, but that is hardly necessary.

The same uncertainty reigns in the taxation world. In place of develop-

---

[33]Acronym of *Raboche-krest'ianskaia inspektsiia*, Workers' and Peasants' Inspectorate.

[34]Acronym of *kommunisticheskaia iacheika*, Communist cell.

ing new sources of revenue the government is destroying the old ones by laying on them heavier and heavier loads. One never knows how much regular and how much special tax he will have to pay in the course of the year and how many times the assessment will be changed on him. Through the arbitrary power of taxation the government can confiscate not only the profit but the capital as well. Not very long ago Trotsky made a speech in which he pointed out that the Soviet had nothing to fear from capitalism so long as it had the power of taxation. Capital has no redress, no rights of which the court need take cognizance.

Labor is demoralized physically and morally. It is less productive, less honest, more costly than before the war. During the revolutionary years just passed the workman fell into the habit of loafing, because his pay was assured him, and stealing, because his pay was insufficient for his needs, and these bad habits have not left him entirely. In addition to this his mind has been poisoned by propaganda and he has been led to believe that the capitalist is a robber and a thief.

Another evil of the present regime is the government regulation of prices through its comparatively recently organized Komvnutorg (Committee of Internal Commerce). The textile industry, which last October sold its goods at a profit, was forced by the Komvnutorg to dispose of them in December at a price that was below cost. The government is an unfair competitor because it does not count the cost. It has collected millions of tons of grain from the peasants and now throws it on the market and ruins the peasant.

Of the evils of the monopoly of foreign trade, it is hardly worth while to speak. The two cases cited above (textile and grain) show what would happen to any undertaking were its market limited to internal commerce alone.

Modern industry and commerce can not make much progress without an efficient and business like transportation system, which is absent from present day Russia. No one quite knows what the policy of the railway administration is; no one is quite certain what the rates are today or will be tomorrow. On January 18, the administration announced that on the 20th a higher rate would go into effect. As I have had occasion to point out to you before, it is now proposed to determine the tariff not at the time the goods are shipped but when they arrive. This juggling with rates is ruining the peasants and the merchants and not helping the government. It does encourage illegitimate business and bribery and the recent convictions of men accused of underhanded dealings has not decreased the practice but it has increased the size of the bribe.

Moral Reasons

Every investor who plans to come to Russia must bear in mind that these years of destruction and demoralization have lowered the moral standard of the community, that sharp practices are winked at, that officials high and low are more corrupt than before the war. No one, office holder or business manager, is quite certain as to what will happen to him tomorrow and consequently he makes the most of today.

P.S. After writing the above I picked up the Ekonomicheskaia zhizn' [*Economic life*] of January 21 and found there an article by a well-known Communist economist on the special and illegal taxes laid by the local authorities on the people. Among the list are the following:

Tax on all those who profited by the revolution, i.e., merchants

Tax on the wages of workmen

Tax on rarities, such as sugar, kerosene, wine, etc.

Tax on stoves for the support of the fire department

Tax for the purpose of clothing the militia

Tax on chimneys, windows

Tax in grain on the peasants for doing this or failing to do that

In ten districts the writer found 38 different special and illegal taxes levied by the local authorities and used by them.

Moscow, January 29, 1923

My dear Herter:

This week I have neither good news nor great news to give you. The situation is not changing fast for the better. Silent forces are working for good and evil forces for evil, and it is a question of time.

The great difficulty is that we have here a lot of small men at the head of things who either do not understand or have not the courage of their convictions. There are only two really capable Bolsheviks, Lenin and Trotsky, and the one is quite ill and the other is side tracked. Most of the others are intent on preserving their jobs and all the privileges that go with them. We now have the sacred right of the office holder. These men do not want a change not so much because it is capitalistic but because it is opposed to their selfish interests. This explains the exorbitant tariff rates, the heavy taxes on private industries and the exemption of semi-governmental, the wasting of millions of rubles on factories that work at a loss and for the products for which there is no demand, and the impossible terms asked of concession seekers in the hope that they will not take them. The barrage of words does not deceive. The actual government is slipping out of the hands of the capable and honest men and is falling into the hands of the hangers on and the careerists. There is snarling among the commissars and fistfights among their followers and as a result of that there is chaos. This will go on, I suppose, until the capital is all consumed and then the fight will break out in the open among the adventurers and idealists.

What should be done is clear, but few have the courage and the spirit of self-sacrifice to do it. There was a time in the history of the Russian Communist Party when it was different. The position of the honest Communist is tragic beyond words. Formerly the ardent leaders kept up the enthusiastic spirit of the followers by appealing to high ideals, but this is no longer possible. No matter how hard they try, it is difficult to convince the average Communist that the New Economic Policy leads to Utopia and not to Capitalism. Every intelligent person realizes that the whole trend of things leads back to private property, individualism, and all the joys and sorrows that go with them. Not long ago I spent an evening in a Communist home and talked to two young Communist women. They told me how they worked and suffered for the cause in 1918 and 1919. "But we gloried in it then," they added, "because we were full of enthusiasm; now we have no enthusiasm." What a tragedy. They admitted what I had heard, that many of the younger members of the Party are resigning because they see in it nothing more than a political machine.

It is hardly worth while illustrating my statements by details. . . .[35] One bit of news may interest you. The commission which had been at work on a Russo-German trade agreement has been dissolved because of a disagreement among the Communists on a matter of no great importance. It does not really matter much in a practical way.

As ever yours,

★ ★ ★

Moscow, February 1, 1923

My dear Herter:

I leave tomorrow for Daghestan to be gone two or three weeks and hope to have, on my return, an interesting report to make.

---

[35] A two-page addendum of statistical material has been omitted here.

In this part of the world there is nothing very new to report. The same tendencies and movements indicated in my previous letters continue. Industry is on its downward course and no half measures can save it. In some of the mills and the factories the machinery is giving out and there is no money to replace it. There are all kinds of talks, conferences, and schemes but nothing comes out of them for they are all evading the main issues.

I had a call yesterday from a Professor of a Siberian university who told me that industry, especially iron mining, has come to a stand still. Live stock is greatly reduced because the government demanded last fall the payment of live stock as tax. In many villages the cows are left, but no bulls. The native population in Siberia suffers in particular. The situation in the cities is better than in the country.

P.S. Sunday Evening.

Radek, who has been away two months, has just returned and today I had a long talk with him. He told me a good deal about the European situation, which I need not repeat to you, and its possible influence on Russia, which may interest you. Of course, the fear here is that France may win out in the fight and then through Poland bring pressure on Russia. He has not had time to talk over the situation with his colleagues.

He has not been in touch with American relations and he could tell me little. We discussed the Goodrich cables[36] and wondered why nothing came of them. He told me that no conditions had been attached to them, but I called his attention to a statement made by Kamenev which contradicted his. But as I was not sure of my ground I did not follow it up.

In this connection I wish to call to your attention a conversation I had the other evening with a Communist who rather astonished me by his knowledge of Russo-American relations. We took up the question of an American commission and he was very anxious that we should not call it a "Commission of Inquiry." The commission could make all the inquiries it desired, but it must not call itself by that name. I pushed him for a reason and after a time he said that the mass of the small Communists would put a wrong interpretation on the name. It is already becoming more and more difficult to answer their questions. If a "Commission of Inquiry" should come the leaders would be accused of selling out, etc. "We've got to save appearances," he said. The poor reds have done their propaganda so well, they have made their ignorant followers believe many phrases and they now find it difficult to undo their own work.

---

[36]The "Goodrich cables" allegedly were communications sent from the United States by Goodrich to the Bolshevik leadership at Moscow about sending an American commission to Soviet Russia.

Returning to Radek. I ventured to suggest to him that if relations between our two countries were not progressing, it might be due in part to the bad impression of the recent Russian dealings with the ARA. I pointed out to him that our ARA workers had a much higher opinion of Soviet methods and officials a year ago than now and that it was in part due to bad tactics of the Soviet in entrusting important work to unimportant people. I called his attention to the fact that Nansen's recent visit was made an occasion for indirectly insulting the ARA by pointing out invidious comparisons which did not exist in fact, that Col. Haskell's coming has been passed off in silence, that up to date not a single official had called upon him. He pleaded ignorance to the facts but agreed with me that too many little people and tactless ones were handling delicate problems. He said that he would see Kamenev and call his attention to the stupidity of the system.

We touched on the question of foreign debts and their payments. He was of the opinion that this problem must be faced before long in a real and serious manner, but he added that this is less important than convincing the foreign capitalist that he can put his money at a profit. After all, he continued, it is useless to expect a government loan, and a loan from a foreign corporation will come, payment of debts or no, only when conditions for investment are favorable. This will come soon.

He has come back convinced that Russia must draw close to America and he is going to devote the next six months to the study of America. He has brought with him many books on American subjects. I have added a few which Fisher sent at my request. He asked for Hoover's recent book,[37] which I offered to secure for him. Please send me any recent American books on political and social subjects that you think may interest him.

He invited me to let him know of my return from Daghestan and accepted with enthusiasm my invitation to dine and spend the evening with me and our men and asked if he might bring some of his friends with him. I agreed to, of course.

A bientôt.

★ ★ ★

Moscow, February 8, 1923

My dear Herter:

I have been preparing for over a week to go to Daghestan to look into the famine situation for the ARA and had not intended writing you at all

---

[37]Herbert Hoover, *American Individualism* (New York, 1923).

this week, but in view of the fact that the Honorable President of the Daghestan Republic, with whom I am to go, puts off the voyage from today to tomorrow, I am here still and take advantage of the opportunity to drop you a note.

All is quiet along the Kremlin. Outside of it there is much talk about the high taxes and it is interesting to note some of the crooked ways that are followed to avoid paying them. In view of the fact that the amount of the taxes increases with the size of the establishment, many shops and stores are breaking up into smaller units. Something similar is going on among the salaried people; a man divides his salary, or has his office do it for him, among the several members of his family. Business is being driven underground.

In the Kremlin the much discussed question is how to reestablish industry and make it self-supporting. Trotsky and some other prominent Communists have been making a tour of a number of factories with a view of learning what can be done, where the cutting is to commence. The general opinion is that it has to be in wages, for low as the wages are they are still out of proportion to the production. Trotsky is working on this problem and it is likely that he will make a report on that subject to the Communist Party when it meets in March. It is even talked about that he is to be put in charge of heavy industry after that date. I hope that it comes true, for the situation demands a man with determination. It is a difficult job to reform the Russian industry and an unpopular one. Many Communists hold to the theory that the peasant and the bourgeois should pay all the losses in order to support the factory proletariat. But the point is being reached where the means are almost exhausted and an end must be put to this wasteful system. Trotsky will do it. He will close many of the mills, cut down expenses, and though he can not save the situation he can prepare the way for more business like methods.

The Urquhart concession is again being discussed and it is again coming up for action. You, of course, remember that the Soviet government never wholly turned him down and it has tried to impress on the public at home and abroad that the question of his concession is still an open one. Krassin is due back in a few days and it is generally admitted that he comes back on condition that some of his measures be put through. The Urquhart matter is his own pet scheme. In this connection I should like to call your attention to a conversation I had recently with a man who was present at an important meeting in which a number of commissars took part. The question of the monopoly of foreign trade came up and it was attacked by Sokol'nikov, the Commissar of Finance. Krassin defended it and gave as his reason for supporting it that it was a bait to those seeking concessions. If a man seeking a concession in Russia is sure that he will have a monopoly of the home market, he is more likely to go after it than if he had competition with outside competitors. The concessioners can, of course, by special stipulation secure the right to export abroad. The question of foreign trade is just now occupying the attention of many Communists and this subject as well as concessions will be discussed by the Party in March.

The situation in Germany is attracting much attention here.[38] The Whites are praying for war in the hope that it will bring about the downfall of the Reds. The peasants are also praying for it and for a similar reason, but they are outspoken against joining the army. The Reds themselves are quiet and the newspaper talk of fighting Poland in case the latter should attack Germany has been put an end to. The whole subject of war has been carefully gone into by the Communist leaders and it has been decided to make no hostile move unless attacked. Many of the smaller Communists are not satisfied with this decision. They are also displeased with the opinion of some of the Kremlin stars that this is not the time for a revolution in Germany and that it should be discouraged. The fire eaters take the stand that there is no time like the present for revolutions.

I do not expect many important developments here very soon and I plan to move about quite a bit in the near future. In view of the fact that Col. Haskell is in Greece and stands in well in Turkey I may go down there in the near future and do some work for the Hoover Collection which needs doing and which has not been done. It is an opportunity that must not be neglected. Col. Haskell will of course help me in every possible way. Our Russian collection is in good condition.

Sincerely yours,

★ ★ ★

Moscow, February 12, 1923

My dear Professor Adams:

Your letter of just a month ago was handed to me last night and since then I have been very busy. Sunday morning I had calls and writing to do. In the afternoon I went to a symphony concert given by a German director, later had a conference with Radek. After dinner I was invited by the President and Mrs. President of the Daghestan Republic to go with them to an opérette. I invited them to the opera or something of that kind, but they told me that they were bored by such serious things and preferred

---

[38]On January 11, 1923, in response to Germany's failure to meet her war reparations obligations, French and Belgian troops occupied the Ruhr region.

light comic opera. I went and was bored. Moscow audiences differ with the kind of performance that is given. The ballet crowd is in large part made up of tovarishchi, the opera audience is in large part composed of poor bourgeoisie, and today at the symphony I saw some real old time aristocracy or people of old refined families.

Just as I have pointed out to you before that Russian society is divided between "we" and "they," so is time differentiated between "then" and "now." Yesterday I was going in a sleigh when there passed us a man on a very fine saddle horse and the izvozchik turned to me and said, "That horse is a left over from then." Today when I saw two refined looking ladies, mother and daughter, in the audience, I thought of "left over from then." This gives you an idea what havoc the revolution has played with society. But the tide of life runs so strong that neither Lenin nor all his men can turn it out of its course and though the old society is gone for good the new comers are being pushed into the same direction as the old. . . .

With kindest regards and best wishes,

★ ★ ★

Moscow, March 15, 1923

My dear Herter:

On the 13th I returned from Daghestan where I had a most interesting experience among those wild mountaineers and bandits. Today I shall begin working on my long report and send it to you as soon as it is finished.[39]

Thank you for the letter of January 23. I am a bit discouraged with the attitude of our government on the Russian question. The situation is this. There is terrific pressure on the Soviet government from France and England for concessions, etc., especially from France. The leading Communists are afraid of both England and France because of their imperialistic designs, the one in the East and the other in the West. The Communists are most eager to come to an understanding with us because they know we have no political and imperialistic designs. To Americans they are ready to give their best concessions and on the best terms, any reasonable capitalistic terms, but they (the Communists) can not make general sweeping reforms such as we demand. They are ready to give to each concessioner individually what they can not admit as a principle. As one important Communist told me, "We can not go back on ourselves and our theories to that extent; it would be suicide for us as leaders and as a party. You have got to help us

---

[39]See Golder and Hutchinson, *On the Trail of the Russian Famine*, pp. 273–319.

to save our face and our standing. If you do not cooperate with us, then we will have to work with England and France." I think he stated the case fairly.

Yesterday I had a talk with Radek and we discussed the illness of Lenin. He is of the opinion that should Lenin die, Stalin would become the leader of the party. He has a very high opinion of the Georgian. It is possible, too, that Trotsky may in the future (in case of Lenin's death), play a more prominent part in foreign affairs. There may also be some other changes. In some circles, there is complaint against Trotsky that his is not a mind that balances all the pros and cons. He is very energetic and if given a certain piece of work to do, he does it with all his might, but he never does a finished piece of work.

Just now, the Communist theorists are in the midst of a hot discussion as to whether in the near future America will compete with Russia on the grain market. Somehow these theorists can not talk calmly about competition; to them it means a terrible conflict, a struggle between capitalistic powers or between the bourgeoisie and the proletariat, et cetera. . . .

I find a lot of odds and ends that may keep me here for a few weeks yet, and then when I leave it will be for good. As you know, it is my plan to spend several months in Western Europe in the interests of the Collection.

With kindest regards and best wishes,
Sincerely yours,

★ ★ ★

Moscow, March 29, 1923

My dear Herter:

As you may guess, American news has occupied the front page of the Moscow papers, especially the report of Hughes's speech to some ladies organization,[40] and the alleged interviews by Hoover where he has been made to come out against Hughes, or very near it. The editorials on Hughes's speech have been critical but not bitter, and there was nothing in them in the way of an ultimatum, as to what the Soviet would or would not do.

There is a restlessness and a pessimism everywhere, even among the

---

[40]This refers to Hughes's public reply of March 21, 1923, to the plea of the Committee for Recognition of Russia of the Women's International League for Peace and Freedom to reconsider U.S. policy toward Soviet Russia. Hughes reiterated the U.S. position.

Communists, and those in authority are in the mood of not resisting the pressure of life to the Right. Two months ago there was serious discussion of saving big industry by putting Trotsky at the head and other such measures, but now the situation in that field is so hopeless that there is a strong movement to hand over these undertakings into private hands, with the government as a partner, I suppose. I should like to add here that I think under the present state of affairs it would pay to have the government as a partner. The government partner could protect the other partner from many worries and would stand between him and the labor agitators and grafters.

The concession situation is this. Recently, two or three small concessions have been granted to former foreign owners of plants. A year ago the Soviet officials took the stand that there would be no compensation for damages, but this year this compensation is taken as a matter of course at the very beginning of the discussion. The only argument is about the ways and means. In principle the government is not yet willing to admit the whole 100% damages, but is ready to make it possible for the former owners to get their 100%. I am not sure whether I have made myself clear. What I mean to say is this: the government will assume a certain portion of the compensation and to make up the rest will give special privileges or some such arrangement.

In the concession agreements now drawn up the amount of the tax to pay is definitely limited. Collective bargaining is demanded but I do not see much to object to in that. The employer and employee come to an understanding elsewhere and they can do it in Russia.

Urquhart's concession is still causing discussion in the papers. Many of the critics are Russian engineers who apparently fear that they will be left out. If Americans should come in it is very important that they should put themselves in touch with the Russian engineers and not ignore them.

I will not trouble you with a longer letter today. Our mail is held up in the Customs as usual of late.

Ever yours,

★ ★ ★

Moscow, April 5, 1923

My dear Herter:

We have had an exciting week. The trial of the Catholic clergy, the condemnation, and the execution have all created excitement abroad as well as here.[41] I am not sure that you know all the nasty things that were said, for the newspaper men have been handled rather roughly of late and they are a bit scared. But I will not stop to discuss that now.

Last week there appeared small posters on the streets of Moscow (I am enclosing a copy which was saved for me and which you must send on to the Hoover Collection) against the Communist Party in the name of the Social Democrats. They were of course quickly torn down and this act was followed by numerous arrests right and left. The interesting thing for us and the painful thing for the Party is that these posters appeared in different parts of Russia at the same time, which goes to show that there is some kind of a secret organization at work which I did not suspect. Moreover, I am told that there is an underground press at work in Moscow and I have been promised specimens of its work. It would seem that the methods of attack and defense of the old regime are repeated.

The trial of the Patriarch is soon to take place and his friends have had much difficulty in getting lawyers. The Church has been so hounded that there is not an important lawyer left who is affiliated with the Church. A few lawyers of socialist leanings have been left and those who have been scared off, some directly and others indirectly, so that up to date no lawyers have been found. Then again there is no money for the trial—but more of this anon.

The Living Church, supported by the government, is very active and sometime this month it will call the sobor (convocation) which will condemn the Patriarch and legislate for the new Red Church. In order that there may not be opposition many arrests are going on among the lower and higher clergy.

The condition in the Communist Party is the most serious situation. It is cracking and some of the cracks are almost so big that it is difficult to step over them. Right in the Party there is a movement to do away with the dictature of the Party and run the government by the Soviet elected by the people as a whole. This movement is attracting attention and it has a small paper of its own. Bukharin and others have come out against it with the result that it has been driven underground.[42]

---

[41]A sensational trial of Catholic clergy in Moscow from March 21 to 25, 1923, was followed by the execution of Monsignor Constantine Butkevich (Budkiewicz) on March 31, despite (or perhaps in part because of) the protests of foreign governments, notably Poland and Great Britain.

[42]On the eve of the Twelfth Party Congress (April 17–25, 1923), two party factions, the Workers' Truth and the Workers' Group, stepped up their criticism of the lack of democracy within the party. See E. H. Carr. *The Interregnum, 1923–1924* (New York, 1954), pp. 79–82, 268–70.

As you know, the important Party Congress takes place the 15th of this month, unless it is again postponed. Last week and the first part of this week the Moscow Communist Party had its meeting to prepare for the Congress. In view of the fact that Kamenev and other leaders are members of it and made speeches, this meeting is pretty much of a guide as to what is going to take place at the big gathering. Kamenev in his address pointed out (1) that the Soviet started out as a Peasant and Labor Party. Since then a third partner, a silent one, to be sure, but a powerful one, the nepman or burzhui, has had to be taken in. As it stands today it is a combination of three parties having more or less different interests, but it is possible to combine and harmonize the interests of two against one. In the beginning the peasants and labor combined against the burzhui; now there is danger of a combination of the peasants with the burzhui against labor, unless labor changes its attitude towards the peasants. Labor is now living on the earnings of the peasants because industry is going down and it has to be kept going on the taxes collected from the land. These taxes are becoming too heavy. Two things must be done: the peasant must be furnished with a foreign market for his grain (which the Americans have now seized) and there must be a reform in the taxes so that they will not fall so heavily on the land.

(2) The next point taken up by Kamenev is the administrative machinery of the government. He states that 95% of the administrative machinery is in the hands of non-Communists. He proposes that the high bars to the entrance into the Party should be let down so that peasants, intelligentsia, and workmen may be able to jump over, and once in should be treated as equals. This, it seems to me, is a big step towards the right.

(3) Nationality Question. I may have had occasion to point out that there is much restlessness among the small nationalities, especially in the Near East. The Soviet has had to pacify them at a considerable cost, but it has not settled anything. The trouble is that the Georgians, Daghestanians, and others feel that Moscow is interfering too much, that, as my Daghestan friends said, "it is grabbing everything in sight." At the meeting of the party this month this nationality question will be seriously discussed.

In connection with this question there is another which seems to have been settled this morning, at least in the morning paper. Many of the so-called autonomous republics have been opposed to land nationalization and the matter was allowed to rest. In Daghestan, where I was recently, there is still private ownership of land as before, the only difference is that the government has grabbed some of the large estates and is keeping them in its hands. According to the morning paper the land question in the autonomous republics is left to be settled by these republics, which practically means that private ownership of land is legalized in Turkestan, Bashkiria, Daghestan, and other autonomous republics. This does not include Georgia, Armenia, Ukraine, etc. I assume that after the party meeting and the results of its action these republics will act as they please. I should like to add also that these autonomous republics are not going to be satisfied with having private land ownership alone. They will also insist on the right to dispose of their minerals on such terms as they see fit. Pandora's box is being opened.

I should like to add in conclusion that the political situation in Russia is more serious today than it has been ever since the ARA first came in. The leaders are on the run and they do not know what to do and the little fellows do as they please. What will happen after Lenin takes his eternal departure is a guess.

As ever yours,

★ ★ ★

Moscow, April 12, 1923

My dear Herter:

In my last letter I outlined Kamenev's speech and indicated the possible lines the Party Congress would take. Since then there has been much discussion pro and con for such a programme. Without going too far into the theoretical side of the discussion I will summarize the points at issue. There are three important questions and on their answer depends the immediate future of Russia. These questions are (1) economic, (2) political, and (3) nationality.

Economic.

What shall be the relation of the peasant to the proletariat and shall the peasant be exploited for the sake of the factory worker? The left wing (I do not think it is very strong) says "yes"; the right wing, which counts in its wing such men as Kamenev, Trotsky, Krassin, and Preobrazhenskii,[43] says "no." In yesterday's Pravda appeared Trotsky's report to the Party, his program, and its official approval by the Central Committee of the Party. Next week the Party meets and will either accept it or reject it, the chances being in favor of its acceptance. Behind the barrage of words the question is what shall be done with the Russian industry. Here are Trotsky's proposals.

---

[43]Evgenii Alekseevich Preobrazhenskii (1886–1937) was a Bolshevik economist.

(1) Labor should receive what it earns and no more

(2) Discharge all unnecessary employees

(3) Close down all factories that work at a loss

(4) Working hours to be adjusted to present conditions

(5) Let each factory live within its means

(6) Tax industry no more than it can stand

(7) Reduce buying abroad to a minimum and encourage home industry

(8) Invite and encourage foreign capital to go into industry

(9) Reduce restrictions on labor hire and union interference

(10) Impress upon the Communist directors in factories that their principal duty is to see to it that much is produced at a small cost and not to try to placate and to play up to labor

If this programme is accepted, and as I indicated, the chances are that it will be, the Communist Party has gone to the Right as much as any capitalistic political party. This programme, in other words, means "put industry on a paying basis."

In his speech before the Party Congress in the Ukraine, which took place last week, Trotsky touched on the question of the relation of the peasant to the proletariat. He pointed out the dangers of exploiting one class against the other and demanded that the peasant should not be taxed more than he can bear and that he should have enough left to enable him to develop his land so that he may grow richer and the country with him. Trotsky also pointed out that one way to help the peasant is by creating a foreign market for his surplus grain. I had hoped that he would touch the question of the monopoly of foreign commerce, but he dodged it, probably purposely. The doing away with the monopoly is a point in the programme of the Right, but I dare say that this time the question will be compromised.

Political.

What shall be the relation between the Party and the Soviet? A certain number of the Party are for a separation of the two and judging from the way this position is attacked I should say that it has a considerable following. Trotsky touched on it but walked around it. The question will come up next week and in all likelihood there will be a compromise and a trade. The "politicals," that is to say, the men who believe that the Party should run the Soviet, will vote with the "economists" (Trotsky, Kamenev, et al.) in return for their support. Personally I favor for the time being the control of the Soviet by the Party, for with all its faults it is an organization and has a certain amount of power. Without it there would be much anarchy and wasteful decentralization.

Nationality.

In the federation entered into sometime ago the Caucasus Republics (Georgia, Armenia, Azerbaidzhan) were treated as one and this has caused much ill feeling, especially in Georgia, where one clique intrigues against another. Georgia is a trouble maker and only about a month ago Kamenev and Kalinin had to go down there to pacify the insurgents. I think I called your attention to the fact that Georgia has demanded that all the valuable Georgian manuscripts which the Russian Academy of Sciences has in its possession should be given back to the Georgians and the point was granted. What the small nationality states demand is that the Soviet should establish a second chamber, similar to our Senate, in which all the states should be represented by an equal number of persons, as in our Senate. This is most interesting from the political science point of view. Then again the federated states demand more control over their resources and industries. In his speech which he made in Kharkov the other day Rakovskii[44] came out openly for that. These are a few of the nationality questions. The leaders in Moscow fear decentralization and rightly so, but I question whether they can resist the pressure.

As I have indicated in another letter, and you can judge for yourself from the number of burning questions that are coming up, all is not well within the Party and many of the leaders are frightened. There are numerous arrests in the army, and the air is poisoned with wild rumors. The foreign situation created by the trial, condemnation, and execution of a Catholic priest has alienated foreign opinion.

Trial of the Patriarch.

We had known for some time that the trial of the Patriarch was to come off in the near future. Last Friday it was suddenly announced that the case would come up this Wednesday, yesterday. Five volumes of charges were against his holiness and these volumes were in possession of the prosecuting attorney and he would allow no one to see them. "What's the use?" he said. "The evidence is clear. There is even no need of witnesses. In two days all will be over." Before the 11th came, the day was postponed to the 17th, but in yesterday's paper there was a notice that no definite date had yet

---

[44]Khristian Georgievich Rakovskii (1873–1941) was chairman of the Council of People's Commissars of the Ukrainian Socialist Soviet Republic.

been fixed. It may be that the trial will be held over until after the Party Congress. There has been some change in attitude. Until now the prosecuting attorney in the other trials tried to show that the Patriarch is the cause of all the trouble and in a summary of the charges which appeared last week this same attitude was maintained. But now the evidence will try to show that he was a tool in the hands of a certain Bishop Nikandr.[45] This is the attitude taken by the court in the Catholic trial and it may be that Nikandr will be sentenced to be shot and the Patriarch spared. There is, however, no reason to suppose that the Party may not decide on something else by the time the trial comes off.

Let me conclude this long letter by saying that I think that the steps taken by the Party at this next meeting are worthy of praise. The leaders are facing the issues bravely. They are going to appeal to the Russian masses, the peasants, for support and they are going to do everything to win their confidence. The proletariat will fall into second place and it is left to sink or swim as is industry. In the same way the leaders will play up to win the good will of the nationalities. I suppose the extremists and office holders will fight and for a time being there may be trouble, but I hope that it does not become serious. If Russia can work out its salvation through evolution it ought to be encouraged.

This afternoon I am going to have a talk with Radek and will tell you his opinion. Tonight I am going to Petrograd and may pick up bits of information worth knowing. Next week is the time of the Congress and I expect to be present for a part of it and then I leave Russia. It is going to be interesting from now on, but I will have to leave the excitement to someone else.

With kindest regards and best wishes,

P.S.   You may be interested to know that the attitude of the government towards the Social Revolutionists has changed for the better and they are treated much better now.

★ ★ ★

Moscow, April 19, 1923

My dear Herter:

The Party Congress opened Monday with Zinoviev making the leading speech. Trotsky's important report on industry is to come off Friday, giving

---

[45]The case against Metropolitan Fenomenov Nikandr, as with that against Tikhon, was dismissed.

statistics which he did not give the other day. Yesterday there was a set-to between the so-called "Left" [and the "Right,"] which believes in the new idea, let us call it the Trotsky idea, though he is only the spokesman. When the debate was over and the ground cleared the Lefts were beaten because when the question was put to them how they would reconstruct industry under their scheme they had nothing but words to offer. Before this reaches you the results of the Congress will be known to you so there is no use predicting.

In his speech Zinoviev came out whole heartedly for the monopoly of foreign trade. By this time you are well aware that the Bolsheviks, like other politicians, have in mind the public in their speeches. As a matter of fact, the wall of foreign trade monopoly is beginning to tremble. The other day there came out a decree that Russian industrial and other such organizations may sell their products abroad and may purchase the things they need including supplies for their workmen. Organizations which have nothing of their own to sell but need to buy abroad may sell the products of other organizations. The monopoly of foreign trade is used for bargaining purposes and the government is always ready to grant special privileges.

It is hardly necessary for me to point out that the proposed reforms in industry are not going to save it. It is too far gone and in bad hands. Only foreign capital on a large scale can do something. I still believe that it would be best to take the government as a partner otherwise there will be no end of trouble from little fellows and it will save the face of the government.

There are great changes going on which our newspaper men do not always see and therefore do not report. The little information that was sent out by members of the ARA will also be cut off as the organization leaves.[46] I hope our friends in Washington will not be dogmatic in their statements as to what the law is in Russia or what the situation is here, for most likely as not, they will miss it. If the time comes, and I think it is not far off, when it should be necessary to send in a commission it would be wise to give it definite instructions and a list of definite questions otherwise it will be lost in the mire of Soviet legislation.

Since writing you last time I have had two conversations with Radek. We touched on the execution of the Catholic priest and he assured me that had not Poland interfered in the role of protector of the Catholics in Russia, Butkevich would not have been executed. I took it for what it was worth. In the case of Tikhon, whose trial comes off next week, Radek said that if the Patriarch will express regret for his past deeds and promise to work

---

[46]At this time, with its famine relief mission accomplished, the ARA was preparing to withdraw from Soviet Russia; the last group of American relief workers departed in July.

with the government in the future he will get off easy. What Tikhon will do or say no one knows, for no one, not even his lawyer, has been allowed to come near him, while members of the prosecuting attorney's office have been to see him often. The Patriarch is no longer young and his friends fear that his troubles and confinement may have affected him both mentally and physically. Before this reaches you the result of the trial will be known.

Radek and I took up also the question of the American debt and I made the statement that recognition would probably not come before Russia acknowledged the debt. He replied the usual thing, that Russia could make no promises until she saw her way clear to pay. "But," I put in, "in forty or fifty years Russia ought to be able to pay." "In twenty-five years," he answered, "we will either be able to pay or we will be out of it." I then went on to say that if Russia would promise to pay I had no doubt that the American government would give her very easy terms, so easy that Russia could if she desired use those terms in dealing with France. "If that could be done I think we would agree," said Radek. I said nothing that he did not know before and I do not know how much importance to attach to the fact that he jumped at it this time. It was agreed between us to let the matter rest until he had a chance to talk the matter over with his colleagues. I saw him again yesterday and he reported that owing to the Congress, he had had the opportunity to see only two men and they were of the opinion that if something practical could come out of the plan it would be worth following it up. I expect to have another meeting next week but I do not intend to touch on the question unless he does. I am telling you this merely to point out that the time is not far off when they will be ready to talk business.

The result of the Foster trial[47] was hailed here as a great victory and I am not at all surprised to see in the wake of the acquittal the organization of the Communist Party of America. The Workers Party was a Communist organization in disguise and in one of my letters I called your attention to the decision of the last International not to do underground propaganda in America but to work as a labor organization. Soon after that the Workers Party was organized and now it has come out in the open.

The nationality question threatened to make trouble but the leaders have decided to yield all along the line on the theory of giving the nationality leaders all the rope they want. "If," said one of the Moscow leading Communists to me, "we tell the small nationalities that they must study Russian, they will refuse to do so. If we tell them to study their own

---

[47]The trial of U.S. socialist William Z. Foster (1881–1961) in March–April 1923 on charges of violating Michigan's law against criminal syndicalism ended in a hung jury.

language and help them they will insist on having Russian schools. That is your experience in America, I believe." He is right and it is the right theory.

There is going to be considerable decentralization in smaller matters. "The things the local governments pay for the local governments ought to control" is the cry. Students of Political Science and lovers of American government institutions ought to feel gratified the way these institutions are being taken up here, not because of any love for them but because life is forcing them on these people. I have already spoken of the Second Chamber or whatever its name will be, where all the nationalities and autonomous states in Russia will have equal representation.

Theoretically, the Party will control the Soviet, that is the last ditch, but at the same time the doors of the Party will be opened to admit those who may wish to come in. The other day a large group of former Social Revolutionists asked admission and they will be initiated.

There are numerous political arrests and imprisonments without trials as well as exilations [sic]. The other day a letter came from a prison camp along the White Sea telling of the harsh treatment received by a number of administrative prisoners, so harsh that eleven of the exiles locked themselves in their house and set it on fire. The central authorities in Moscow promised to improve conditions.

★ ★ ★

Moscow, April 23, 1923

My dear Herter:

I am taking advantage of Quinn's going to the States to drop you a line.

The Party Congress is still on and I suppose it will come to an end in a day or two. It is a great disappointment to me for I had hoped something good might come of it. We have words and nothing but words. The most striking thing is the part that Krassin took. Never before has he appeared so prominently and never before has he been so outspoken in favor of making concessions to foreign capital. But I fear it is his swan's song. I hear that he is to be removed from his present post.

The great noise made about lightening the burden of the peasant is a great joke, as you will see from the speeches. The facts are these: The government expects to collect 500 millions in gold from agriculture while last year it collected 400 millions. The money to be levied will be in rye units at the rate of 70 kopeks for a pud of rye. The local powers will not have the right to levy but will receive a percentage of the total collected. I have never seen such a farce as the speeches made, summaries of which I enclose. Some of our two-faced politicians should study them as models for platform writing. I have no time to discuss them in full. You can do that for yourself.

Let me sum up the situation. The Congress was a fight between the "politicals" and the "economists," the Zinoviev group and the Krassin group. In the beginning, Kamenev, Trotsky, and others were with Krassin, but something happened and they deserted him. If it is not that, then there is something underneath all that I do not understand. I am informed that the leaders as a whole decided to continue the old policy and to stand out as leaders of the world revolution. The European situation gives them some encouragement. Had they yielded to the Krassin cry they would have lost out morally in the eyes of the world proletariat.

For this coming year I see the same continued pressure on the peasants. Trotsky will in all likelihood be put at the head of industry and he will close many plants, and throw many people out of work, but I do not see that this is going to put industry on its feet. There will be more experiments and more planning and more propaganda and more pressure on the few intelligentsia left over. I am quite discouraged with the turn of affairs but there is nothing to do but wait. The Party is divided, but for the time the breach has been mended, but I do not know when a new crack will appear. Lenin's health or illness is a big factor. Everyone who had an idea to forward quoted some verse of the Lenin Bible.

Please excuse this poorly and hurriedly written letter.

With good wishes,

P.S. The trial of the Patriarch, which was to come off today, is again postponed. About two weeks ago the lawyers in the defense were allowed a peep into the ten volumes of evidence against the accused. A few days ago the charges against him were made public and now the lawyers can not get a look at the evidence. The lawyers for the defense have asked for fifty tickets to the trial and they were given six, and these six are in prominent places so that those who use them will be marked.

★ ★ ★

Moscow, April 26, 1923

My dear Herter:

The Party Congress came to an end yesterday and the resolutions adopted were along the lines indicated in the speeches and in my letter. How these will be carried out remains to be seen. Zinoviev made the concluding speech and he repeated again and again how united the Party is which is very strong proof that it is not. He ended by asking the boys to stand together and all that kind of stuff.

The Party is not united but instead of being a "right" and a "left" wing is broken in pieces and no one knows just what he wants, except that he does not want what the other fellow recommends. Lenin's death may "start" something but it is not safe to prophesy. I can not see anything hopeful ahead in the immediate future.

With kindest regards,

★ ★ ★

Athens, May 8, 1923

My dear Herter:

I had intended writing you my last Russian letter in Russia but during the last few days I was busy with odds and ends and did not get around to it. Col. Haskell and I left Moscow last Wednesday afternoon at four o'clock and arrived at Odessa Friday afternoon at two o'clock. We went on board a U.S. destroyer and sailed at five, reaching Constantinople the following morning, the 5th, at ten o'clock. For some reason or other, the destroyers would not take us farther and therefore we took passage on an Italian boat and sailed for Athens that evening and landed here yesterday morning. Since then I have been busy with matters relating to the Hoover Collection.

To return to Russia. I should like this morning to sum up the situation in that sick country. From the material point of view Russia is in some respects better off than two years ago. Food is cheap, the famine is pretty well under control, and the prospects for a good harvest are bright. From another point of view, Russia is not so well off as two years ago. At that time it had large reserves of raw materials, factories and shops fairly well equipped, railway tracks and bridges in more or less good condition, public and private buildings fit for occupation. Now all this is changed for the worst and this is so well known that I need not dwell upon that.

In regard to food conditions Russia is returning to the period of 1918 and 1919, when there was a shortage of food in the cities and plenty in the country districts. With the exception of Petrograd and Moscow all the Russian cities are decreasing in population, some of the inhabitants are moving into the country, others have died, and then there is a general decrease in the birth rate due to fewer marriages, the practice of abortion, and the lower level of morality. Industry and trade are going down and there will be much more unemployment than now. The proposed reforms by Trotsky, though sound and necessary, will bring about great hardships. Trade is taxed out of existence. This we see right before our eyes. The

Arbat street, which leads to the Pink House where some of us live, was a year ago full of open shops. But now about half of them are closed. The other day Telford[48] and I took a walk and in an area of two blocks counted twenty-five closed stores and fourteen open ones. This is more or less the situation in other parts of the city and in other cities. The few shops that are left are largely under government control and most likely running at a loss.

The health of the Russian population is not so good as it was because their vitality is greatly diminished. In the country certain diseases have spread and there is neither the moral force nor the medical science to check them. In the cities tuberculosis is making rapid headway, especially among the more educated group. There is hardly a home where this unwelcome guest has not settled himself comfortably and is destroying the lives of the young people. This is the most heartbreaking scene we have to look upon in Russia of today. One feels so helpless because he can do nothing because he is powerless to change the moral conditions. This disease as well as others are brought on in large part by worry. I may have called to your attention the case of Mr. Muravev, a very able lawyer, who defended Kamenev and his colleagues in the tsar's court and saved them from prison. Muravev tried to do the same for the Social Revolutionists last year and for his pains has been exiled. His wife has worried and when I took leave of her she was in bed and there is little likelihood that she will rise again. There are two young girls in the family and I do not like to think of the tragic fate that awaits them.

Of all the gloomy pictures of the Russia of the immediate future that of the young women is the darkest. There seems nothing but tears, rags, and disease ahead of them. I am talking of the girls of the better families. So many of the young men from twenty to thirty-five have been killed off during the wars, some have fled the country, and a large number of those who have remained have become demoralized. There are few marriageable men for decent girls and even if there were there is nothing of home life to look forward to. With the best of intentions and good will two young people working together can not make a decent honest living. They will be crowded into one room and will be obliged to live an abnormal life. This is the fate of most young women of the old regime. Even prostitution does not pay, for as one of our ARA men (who has gone and left us) said, "You can get any girl for a square meal."

In other respects there is a lowering in the moral tone both in the city and the country. The law of self preservation has forced people to justify all

---

[48]Charles Telford of the ARA.

means to attain their end. It is the air that children breathe in the streets, and mothers have complained to me that their children talk of things that shock their parents. In the country the lower price of grain has encouraged moonshine and there is much drinking. The moral force of the Church and the fear of the civil law is gone and as a result the sexual life of the community is lower than it was in the old days. The training which the peasants have had during the last five years in seizing the property of the landholders has encouraged them to help themselves to the good of their neighbors.

Of political conditions I have little to say that is new. The Communist Party is in power and intends to hold the "heights." It will probably open the doors a bit and let others come into the field. The Party has no hold on the mass of the population and is not very strong. I think we will have to drop the terms "right" and "left" and speak more of cliques, for the Party is pretty much made up of small groups, each having some special hobby. As time goes on and hard times come, the number of cliques will increase and the hatred of one towards the other will grow. Notwithstanding all the cruelty the Party has not succeeded in crushing all opposition but it has driven it under ground.

In another letter I sent you a circular which had been posted on the walls of Moscow by the Social Democrats and promised to send you other underground literature. Unfortunately the man who gave me the circular fell into the hands of the police and is now in prison. I have learned on good authority that there are several secret organizations in Moscow with branches in the provinces. There is little to be expected from them because in the first place they are divided, there are too many of them, and in the second place they have no ideal to work for. They are ready to throw a bomb, ready to risk their lives to stick a poster on the wall, but beyond that they are lost. The Bolos fear them and suspect them of working together with the counterrevolutionists outside and with foreign governments. This explains the numerous arrests of the Russian intelligentsia in Russia and the efforts to exterminate them. The lot of the Russian intelligentsia, the few that are left, is now much harder than three years ago. He is hounded from pillar to post and the Bolos take the stand that the non-Communist intelligentsia is either for the Party or against it. All those who are not for will be crushed during the next two or three years if the present policy is maintained.

I should like to say a word on the trial of the Patriarch. When I left, the trial had been postponed, for what reason I do not know. One of the Patriarch's lawyers succeeded in seeing his client and found the old man very ignorant and misinformed as to what had been going on. He did not know that the Metropolitan of Petrograd and the other clergy had been shot, he did not know that Butkevich had been executed, and he had been led to believe that if he would take a certain stand all would be well. Before the charge against the Patriarch had been made public the lawyers for the defense were allowed to look over the ten volumes of evidence against him but they could not use their opportunity to advantage because they did not know what to look for. Since the charges have been made they have not been allowed to examine the evidence.

This letter concludes my Russian series. I do not say this with any pleasure, no more than I took leave of that country with pleasure. As I stood on the destroyer looking over Odessa, tears almost came into my eyes at the thought of the misery and suffering endured by those big hearted and fine people and I felt so sorry for them. That, no doubt, is the feeling of every ARA man when he leaves Russia. Yet there is nothing more that we can do. We are leaving and that is right. We have done a monumental piece of work, for in addition to feeding the hungry we have started forces at work that are bound to have results. I do not feel like a deserter, but more like one who fights and runs away and will live to fight another day.

I am glad that this letter writing has given me an opportunity to know you a little better. I hope my letters have not tired you and have not misinformed you too much. I expect to spend the remainder of the summer in different parts of Europe in the interest of the Hoover Collection and should I come across any information that may be of interest to you I will send it on. I shall, however, keep off Russia for I have little confidence in the newspaper reports and the rumors that come out of Russia.

Sincerely yours,

JOURNEY IV
1925

CHAPTER SIX

REDS
AND WHITES

Golder returned to Soviet Russia in September 1925 to attend the two hundredth anniversary celebration of the Russian Academy of Sciences and to discuss with Soviet officials and scholars his idea of establishing a Russian-American institute to study the Russian Revolution. The visit gave him an opportunity to observe the changes in Soviet politics and society that had taken place since Lenin's death in January 1924.

Golder, accompanied by Governor Goodrich, was joined in Leningrad by Colonel William Haskell, the only other American to have received an invitation. On the eve of their departure from the United States, the American press speculated that the visit of these three former ARA representatives might be politically significant, which moved Secretary of Commerce Hoover to issue a statement reaffirming the Calvin Coolidge administration's policy of nonrecognition.

★ ★ ★

Diary

September 1

Arrived at Russo-Finnish frontier at 10:40 A.M. Remained at Finnish side until 12:30 and then started for the Russian. As soon as the Russians found out that we were delegates to the Jubilee of the Academy of Sciences they extended to us every courtesy. They would not examine our baggage, gave us free transportation, and put our baggage in the best coupé. We left Beloostrov at 2 P.M. and arrived at Petrograd a little after three. There we were met by a committee from the Academy of Sciences who took us with our baggage to the Hotel Europe and gave us royal suites. During the evening we spoke with reporters from the leading Leningrad and Moscow papers. They were very courteous and frank in their expressions. They remained until about 9 P.M.[1]

Leningrad shows more prosperity than two years ago. More stores are open and filled with goods, mostly of cheap German manufacture. Clothing and shoes are priced higher than in the U.S., that is to say, goods of the same quality. Hotel Europe is changed—a new type inhabits it—men and women who would not have been tolerated here before.

It would seem that the Jubilee of the Academy of Sciences is a great event and much is expected.

September 2

Governor Goodrich and I went to the Academy and saw everyone busy. The Jubilee is a national affair and everyone is excited. Went to the Museum of the Revolution and found the girls grateful. The old director has been sent into exile. The girls said that they were better off materially than before and they looked better fed. Went to the Hermitage and there learned that a similar situation existed.

In the afternoon went to see one of the merchants. He insisted that from the private business man's point of view conditions are no better than before. For the time being, he insisted, taxes were not so heavy, but they might grow heavier any time. There is no law. Educational conditions are bad. Children of former bourgeois are not allowed into higher educational institutions.

After dinner I called on Professor P.[2] He said that for those teachers

---

[1] On his exit from Soviet Russia in late September, Golder wrote to Lutz: "When I reached Russia I learned that for two months before my coming, the papers had much to say about my visit and its political importance. Notwithstanding Hoover's denial of having anything to do with my trip, the Moscow papers carried special Washington dispatches stating that Hoover had come out with a statement that my trip had political importance. You can not beat them. They published interviews by me and put in signed articles by me which I never wrote." Golder to Lutz, September 29, 1925, Hoover Institution Internal Records, series D-04, box 148b. The articles Golder refers to are in Krasnaia gazeta, September 10 and 12, and Izvestiia, September 11.

[2] Probably Ivan Pavlov. Goodrich's diary for September 2 documents a meeting of Golder and the governor with Pavlov. James P. Goodrich papers, Herbert Hoover Presidential Library, West Branch, Iowa, box 18, file "Russia: Diary, 1925."

who had work and pay there was enough food, but those who had no work suffered sadly. He would not admit for a moment that the "moral" conditions had improved. Affairs of state are conducted from the point of view of the Communists. In educational institutions students who are qualified but who are of the bourgeoisie are not allowed to enter, but others of the proletariat, who are not qualified, are forced in. As a result, science makes no headway and Russia's future looks dark indeed. As a result of today's talks it would seem as if the material situation of those who work and have money is better. Outwardly the situation looks much better. Streets are cleaner, building is going on, street cars painted, cafés full.

September 3

This morning Governor Goodrich and I went to the Academy of Sciences and secured tickets. Thence to the Hermitage. The Hermitage is richer than before because a number of paintings and objects of art which formerly belonged to members of the royal family are now in the Museum. It was a great pleasure to visit the place.

On the way back to the hotel we saw a large number of soldiers in front of the Winter Palace preparing for review. Colonel Haskell says they lacked discipline and were not much of an army.

Late in the afternoon I called on N. M. B. Her family is pretty well broken up. Her husband left her and her daughter Kira is a widow with a two-year-old baby boy; the older son is just out of the army and is married and father of a baby boy. The youngest son prepared himself for technical school, and he got in but was kicked out because he is a burzhui. The poor boy is up against it and does not know which way to turn. The mother works in the Department of Education but gets little. On the whole they are better off because they have enough to eat, but otherwise the situation is no better.

From there I went to see the old dowager who danced with Cassius Clay, and her two nieces. They were greatly depressed with the situation. They named numerous people who had been recently shot and imprisoned. They spoke of Prince Golitsyn.[3] His wife died and the father and son are imprisoned. My friends found the circle of their friends gradually decreasing in number and they feel as if their turn would soon come.

After dinner I went with the Governor to visit some of his friend's friends. It was a Jewish family which lived packed in two rooms for which

---

[3]Prince Vasilii Dmitrievich Golitsyn (d. 1927?) was director of the Rumiantsev Museum until his arrest in March 1921.

they paid 30 rubles a month. The head of the house is a watchmaker and since he does not work for wages he is regarded in a category higher or lower than the workmen and therefore pays higher rent. Formerly he had a stove, 4 rooms and paid 75 rubles rent.

Tonight Col. Haskell left for Moscow.

September 4

Spent the morning in the bookshops. Books have gone up in price since 1922, but good books and beautiful binding are still cheaper than in 1914. There are a number of good buys. I should like to buy and buy.

Late in the afternoon we had a call from S. F. O[ldenburg]. He commented on the improvement in Russia since my last visit. He pointed out the change of attitude of the government towards the Academy. For the coming year the Academy will have an income of 2 million rubles as against 300,000 three years back. When I raised the question whether the Academy should have help from outside, he came out sharply against it. He believes that Russia should stand on her own feet.[4] He thinks that the time for recognition is ripe and that recognition would greatly help Russia. Every intelligent foreigner who comes to Russia helps. He admitted that the lot of the old intelligentsia is still difficult. He claimed that the better elements in the Party are against harsh measures. He had a good word to say for Rykov and stated that Trotsky is, on the whole, the ablest of the leaders, but not very influential just now. He does not agree with the other leaders and was removed from the army.[5] The fear of a Napoleon is ever before the Communists.

After dinner I went to call on one of my book dealers. He has good quarters for which he pays 20 rubles a month. Being employed in a store he is classed as a "workman" and gets all the privileges of a workman. He has a beautiful collection of antiquités and fine bindings.

Saturday, September 5

In the evening there was a gathering at the Academy of Sciences, the first formal opening of the Jubilee. Big autobuses brought for the purpose

---

[4] According to the entry in Goodrich's diary for September 5, Golder specifically offered the financial assistance of the Laura Spelman Rockefeller Memorial Fund to maintain the academy. Oldenburg turned it down, just as he had in 1921 when the same fund offered the academy $500,000. According to Goodrich, Oldenburg "said it was much better to starve for the present in order to bring the government to the necessity of supporting the Academy."

[5] Trotsky was forced to resign as people's commissar of war in January 1925.

from Moscow were lined up to take the guests to the Academy, which was brilliantly lighted up. The crowd outside watched the guests and government officials come in. At the head of the stairway were the President, Vice-President, and other officials of the Academy who met and greeted the guests. The hall was full of people in all kinds of dresses—the Mongols, Chinese, Japanese, and others in national costumes were most conspicuous. Refreshments were served. Sometime during the evening President Karpinsky[6] made an address of welcome which nobody heard and all applauded.

Sunday, September 6

Noon. Since 11 o'clock there has been a parade of the Young Communists and workmen. It reminds me of the days of 1917. There is however a great deal of difference. The parading is just as ragged but it has more pep. Each group of Young Communists has a band of its own, made up of its own members. A great deal has been done for the young workmen. Lenin's name figures prominently, but not the names of any of the other leaders. There were numerous flags with the usual mottoes. Little by little the Soviet succeeds in getting its ideas into the heads and hearts of the proletariat.

Have received several letters from my Moscow friends, all extending me invitations to visit them. One woman wrote on old stationery with the crest of her noble family. The old bourgeoisie is hard to keep down.

Duranty is here getting about on a pegleg. It is rather pitiful.[7]

Governor Goodrich told me the history of the note in which the American government indicated a desire to send a Commission to Russia in 1922. Goodrich and Borah[8] had persuaded Harding to do that, knowing full well that Hughes would oppose it. It was also understood that Goodrich would be a member of the Commission. When that had been done they tried to get Skvirsky,[9] the representative of the Soviet government in

---

[6]Aleksandr Petrovich Karpinsky (1847–1936) was president of the Academy of Sciences.

[7]Walter Duranty (1884–1957), a *New York Times* correspondent, had been in Moscow most of the time since 1921. His foot had been amputated as a result of injuries he suffered in a train wreck on the Paris-Havre line in November 1924.

[8]William E. Borah (1865–1940) was the Republican senator from Idaho.

[9]Boris E. Skvirsky was the unofficial representative of the USSR in Washington. He arrived in 1921 as a representative of the Far Eastern republic and stayed on after the republic's demise, setting up a Russian information bureau and publishing a monthly called *Russian Review*. See E. H. Carr, *Socialism in One Country*, vol. 3, pt. 1 (New York, 1964), p. 464, where he calls him "Shvirsky."

America, to cable to his government to accept without conditions the invitation. Before doing so he wished to know whether Goodrich would be on the Commission. Goodrich could not give him official assurance and Skvirsky refused to telegraph, though he at first promised to do so. When the Soviet government received the word through Ambassador Houghton in Berlin, it feared that an unfriendly commission would be sent and therefore it began to play down conditions which killed the whole thing.

7 P.M. The opening of the exercises of the Academy was rather interesting. The Academicians sat on the platform. When Kalinin came in there was considerable cheering but when the President of the Academy came there was more. There was still more when Glazunov[10] appeared to conduct his own composition. When Lenin's name was mentioned there was some cheering but not a great deal. The International was well sung by the children's choir. Lunacharsky made a long but interesting speech after which Oldenburg read an address on the history of the Academy. A recess was taken for a few minutes and then came Beethoven's 9th Symphony. The interesting part of the symphony was the chorus of orphan and poorly clad children. They did very well indeed. It is probably the only children's chorus in the world to sing such a composition. Like all singing by Russians, it sounded like church music.

Later in the day I called on N. M. B. She says that conditions are much better now than before, but it is still difficult to find work. She is connected with the Education Department. She complains that students are so busy with self-government, with meetings of pioneers, with delegations and inspections that they have little time for study. Lower schools are crowded and there is not enough room for all who wish to attend.

At 8 P.M. Governor Goodrich and I went to the banquet in the Museum of Alexander III. As we entered, we saw hundreds of people, men and women, some in full dress. Tables covered with the choicest zakuski[11] were to the right and to the left of us. There were all kinds of cured fish, caviar, salads, meat dishes, and any amount of liquor—brandy, vodka.

About 8:30 the word to "fall to" was given and everybody crowded around the tables. After a time the crowd moved into the large hall where the dinner table was set. Scholars of the same specialty had tables set aside for them. The historians had a table for themselves. Each table was loaded with wine, mineral waters, fruit, and sweets. The dinner was long and in numerous courses. When about half through, the President of the Academy

---

[10]Aleksandr Konstantinovich Glazunov (1865–1936) was a composer, conductor, and director of the Leningrad Conservatory. He left Soviet Russia in 1928.
[11]Hors d'oeuvres.

made another speech of welcome which few heard. He was followed by Kalinin, the German Ambassador, Lunacharsky (who spoke in four languages—Russian, French, German, Italian), and other Bolos. The Bolos tried a bit of propaganda as they always do. When they were through, different representatives were called upon and they expressed the greetings of their country or university. While they were talking, others were eating and it was difficult to hear what was said. As the night advanced it became more and more noisy and the efforts of the officials of the Academy to bring quiet failed. We went home about 1 P.M. singing "for he is a jolly good fellow."

The banquet was the first occasion for the Russians to dress up to eat as before the war. This banquet was quite like old times. There was food and drink in great abundance and much gaiety. It was interesting to watch the efforts of the French and German scholars to impress themselves upon the audience.

Monday, September 7

As we were at dinner today a messenger came post haste and asked us to go to the Academy to see the demonstration. We did not finish our meal and hurried down stairs, but it was almost a half-hour before we got away in the bus. The demonstration consisted of the workers of the Gosizdat.[12] They had a band with a red flag and after marching in front of the building they turned around and stopped to make and hear speeches. We got away before the speechmaking was over. Went to the opera to hear "Ruslan and Ludmilla" by Glinka. It was beautifully done. Art is not lost in Russia and the chances are that it will continue to develop.

Tuesday, September 8

This morning I visited the museums of the Academy and the Library. In the course of the day I had a talk with members of the former intelligentsia. It is quite clear that systematically and surely the Soviet government is getting rid of them. With an exception here and there they have been removed from the archives and Communists—most of them who have little knowledge of archive affairs—have been put in their places. From that point of view conditions are worse than three years ago. Those who hold their places fear that sooner or later they will go too. They are being watched and their movements reported. Those who have no work suffer

---

[12]Russian acronym for the State Publishing House.

greatly. In many cases all opportunities for making a living through intellectual efforts are closed to them. Teaching positions are scarce and the censorship of the press is so rigid that publication of books is out of the question. Owing to limited means, many are forced to give up their living quarters. One man earns 60 rubles per month and has to pay 48 for rent. He now has to sell his books for he has to move into two or three rooms.

With two or three I discussed the relation of the peasant to the tsar and they agreed that the peasant was hard to understand. They agreed too, that the peasant is not against the Soviet but probably not for. Provided the peasant was not taxed heavily and had the government do things for him the peasant was agreeable. One or two who had been in the villages said that a few were electrified and that books were now found in places where they were never before seen, that a great deal was being done for the common man.

The Bolos are being divided into several classes. Some are earnest and self-sacrificing, but narrow and fanatical. They regard non-Communists as their enemies. One of my friends who had been excused from service and was replaced by a Communist went to his successor for a recommendation without which he could not get a position. The Communist replied that he could not recommend his "class enemy" and refused to do anything. There is another class of Communist that is wholly worthless and selfish. They have saved nothing of the old and they take nothing of the new—but live on their wits and appetites and find excuses for all they do.

Wednesday, September 9

This afternoon the Leningrad Soviet invited the honored guests. We all met in the palace of the Duma, now known as Uritskii's Palace.[13] A presidium was selected of local and foreign celebrities, of whom I was one. The meeting opened with a long speech by Zinoviev lasting nearly an hour. It was little more than an exposition of Marx, Lenin, and the Communists. It was well delivered and the tovarishchi gave him much support. He was followed by Oldenburg and others, among them I as representative of Stanford. I did not remain to see the end.

In the evening I went to see the ballet. There were parts of three ballets—Petrushka, Act 3 of Prince Igor, and tableau 5 of the Sleeping Beauty. It was all beautifully and artistically done and was a great delight. Most of the foreigners who had never before witnessed this spectacle were

---

[13]The Tauride Palace was for a time named after the assassinated Cheka chief M. S. Uritskii; it later reverted to the original name.

greatly delighted. Now that the Communists are again encouraging art there is reason to believe that the ballet will continue to prosper.

Thursday, September 10

One more banquet—almost as brilliant and abundant as the other. There were speeches but no one paid attention on account of the noise. The festivities commenced at 6:00 and lasted until 10:30 or thereabouts. At the train station there was a large crowd, a military band, and soldiers. A special train of ten Pullman cars was at the service of the guests. Altogether there were three trains. The trains were quite comfortable and clean. I caught a bad cold.

Friday, September 11

A reception committee and a band waited for us at the Moscow station. Each delegate was assigned to a hotel and put into a bus. Governor Goodrich was on hand at the Hotel Europa where I was put up. Moscow people try to outdo Leningrad in hospitality for nothing is charged for meals at the hotel.

In the evening we went to the Conservatory where we heard more speeches in praise of Communism and greetings in honor of the Academy.

Saturday, September 12

This morning it poured but we went to the Kremlin and got wet. At 2:00 a luncheon was given at the Bol'shaia Moskovskaia hotel which lasted until 4:00. After that I went to visit M. L. The situation is pitiful indeed. Two members of the family are in exile in Perm and barely able to earn enough to support themselves. Natasha, the daughter, plays the violin and her earnings support her and her father. A third member, the husband of one of the daughters and father of two small children, is in prison. Food has to be taken to him for the rations in the prison are not enough to keep him alive. At home there are six children and six adults, one of whom is working. He does not earn enough to keep the family in the bare necessities of life. It is pitiful and heartbreaking. No one knows why the two were exiled and the third put in prison, nor does anyone know when they will be let out, nor when other members of the family will be locked up.

Dined with C. & P. They admit that the process of evolution was not what they foresaw, and were ready to admit that certain plans of the Bolos may work out. Production has increased, agriculture has developed. Quality of production has not come up to pre-war. Cost of production has been kept down by bookkeeping because depreciation and overhead are not taken into consideration. Operating expenses is the only item that is counted. They said that a number of very able men have been developed in recent years among the workmen and Communists. As soon as one of these gets into a position of responsibility he thinks less of theories and more of production. Dzerzhinskii is one of these men, Piatakov[14] is another, Sokol'-nikov is a third, et al.

As to the crop, there will probably be about 350 million puds for export. The crop has been good but the rains are preventing threshing and much grain will be lost.

Much credit is needed for machinery.

Sunday, September 13

In the afternoon I went to call on S[ergei] B[akhrushin] and found the situation from every point of view worse than it was in 1923. S[ergei] looks old and worn and the family has been crowded into three small rooms, one of which is a bath. Their friends are disappearing one by one and their positions are being taken from them. The future looks gloomy and gloomier.

In the evening I went to the concert and ballet. It was good. Gel'tser[15] gave her famous military march and did it well.

Monday, September 14

Spent part of the morning with Gov. Goodrich interviewing in the Department of Agriculture. There will be about 350 million puds to export—this includes all kinds of grain.

In the afternoon (5 P.M.) there was a meeting of the Moscow Soviet. Kamenev made the principal speech and it was full of propaganda—worse than anything so far. This was followed by speeches by the representatives of the Academy and visitors. When it came to my turn Kamenev asked me to speak in Russian, which I did. The meeting dragged on until almost 8 o'clock.

The banquet was supposed to take place in the Hall of the Nobles[16] at

---

[14]In 1925 Dzerzhinskii was chairman and Piatakov deputy chairman of the Supreme Economic Council.

[15]Ekaterina Vasil'evna Gel'tser (1876–1962), legendary dancer of the Bol'shoi ballet.

[16]Golder refers to the Hall of Columns in the House of Unions, the former Nobles Club of which the hall was the ballroom.

8:30, but it was postponed until 9:00. It was after 10:00 when it started. The hall was beautiful, with its marble columns and its lustre. It is the same hall in which the SRs were tried. There must have been more than 1000 people in the hall. There was an abundance of rich food and choice wines. About half way through, the Commissars began to speak—Kamenev, Litvinov, Lunacharsky. I left after midnight and the speaking was still going on.

Tuesday, September 15

Had a busy day with Gov. Goodrich, visiting different ministries. In the afternoon I went to hear Keynes[17] lecture on the economic conditions of England. The meeting began late so I did not remain to the end. Madame Anna Alexandrovna[18] came to dinner. She has gone from white to pink and is fast growing red. With her I went to visit a Russian family where a number of people were gathered. What struck me most of all is the general acknowledgment that the Soviet government has done much for the common man. There is a desire to make peace with the reds and work with them. There is not even talk of the return of the old.

We discussed the economic situation. Russia can not supply the demand for certain goods and at the same time there is much unemployment. Thousands of people are on the land where they are not needed. This unemployment is explained by the fact that there are not enough factories to employ all—not enough machinery to create all the goods that are demanded. As soon as industries develop, the surplus labor will be taken up.

Futurism is passing and realism is returning. The new and young writers are beginning to talk about style and are trying to acquire it.

A[nna] L[ouise] S[trong][19] is one of the "uplifters" of Russia and a great propagandist of the Soviet government. She told Gov. Goodrich that she is investing her money in short-term loans (90 days) at 1¾% a month. This she calls "benevolent capitalism." She is also ready to offer her services to Americans who are seeking concessions and thinks that because of her friendship with Trotsky she can get inside information. She is very keen to earn much money. She has a room in one of the houses which cost 20 rubles a month. There she has hidden away an electric heater which she

---

[17]John Maynard Keynes (1883–1946), the British economist, according to Goodrich, annoyed his hosts by attacking Lenin and Leninism. Diary entry of September 14.

[18]Golder probably means Ol'ga Aleksandrova, a former aristocrat and previous employee of the ARA in Petrograd.

[19]Anna Louise Strong (1885–1970) was a radical American journalist and activist.

uses when no one is looking. In this way she uses up lots of current for which the others pay.[20]

Last year history, literature, and humanitarian sciences were abandoned, but this year there is a return to them.

Monday, September 21

On Friday I had a long talk with Radek and Mrs. Radek. Judging from their tone they were badly hit by the last Communist storm.[21] It would seem as if he were sidetracked from West European affairs, for he is now giving more of his time to Chinese. He is now Rector of the new Chinese University and plans to make, with the help of Chinese scholars, a thorough study of Chinese questions. He is eager to come to America and I am going to see what can be done. He is not wholly pleased or sympathetic with some of the Soviet policies and talks almost of "we" and "they."

On Saturday I saw Pokrovsky and Mrs. Kameneva[22] with whom I left in written form more details as to the Russian-American Association for the study of the Russian Revolution. They were of the opinion that favorable action would be taken.[23]

In the course of the day I saw some of the old professors. They complained of the difficulties and almost impossibilities of publishing anything. Some of them are writing for the archives.

Saturday night I left for Leningrad and reached my destination on time on Sunday morning. Gantt[24] was at the station to meet me and I went to Hotel Europe. Later I went to Gantt's home. He is doing excellent work.

---

[20]Goodrich wrote in his diary for September 16 that Strong "has developed into a usurious bourgeois."

[21]Radek's political fortunes were on the downswing owing to the defeat of the Bolshevik-inspired revolution in Germany in October 1923 and his association with Trotsky. Radek was removed from the European section of the Comintern and, in May 1925, made the head of Sun Yat-sen University in Moscow, an institution dedicated to training young propagandists and agitators for the Chinese Communist movement. See Isaac Deutscher, *The Prophet Unarmed* (Oxford, New York, Toronto, 1970), pp. 203–5.

[22]Ol'ga Davidovna Kameneva (1883–1941), the wife of Lev Kamenev and the sister of Trotsky, was president of the All-Union Society for Cultural Relations (known by its Russian initials, VOKS), attached to the People's Commissariat of Foreign Affairs.

[23]In November, Golder received word in Paris through the Soviet Embassy that VOKS had accepted his proposal.

[24]W. Horsley Gantt (1892–1980) was a physician who served with the ARA in

After dinner I called on some more professors and had a long talk about Russia and Russian affairs. Among other things they brought out the point that Russia has always been experimented upon. First one ruler gets an idea and brings up a whole generation on that idea, then comes another ruler with another idea and upsets everything and all the experience is lost and wasted.

In regard to the present political situation they pointed out that anti-semitism is growing in Russia, especially in the army. In part this is due to the old feeling and in part to the tactlessness of the Jews. They are crowding the Russians from their places. In the universities, as the old Russian professors are pushed out, Jews are put in their places. Eight out of ten of the new Red Instructors are Jews.[25] That this anti-semitism is growing is in line with what A—— told me and he gave that as a reason that the strong hand of suppression is necessary.

★ ★ ★

Helsingfors, September 29, 1925

Dear Professor Coolidge:

. . . I have had an interesting time in Russia but I am ill physically and in every other way. The strain on one's heart and mind is still great. All our friends are a bit worse off than when we left them in 1922–23. Last year, history and other humanitarian studies were wiped off the slate and hardly one of our friends has a place left. Gautier[26] is out, Bakhrushin is out, et al. They all look older. But it is not only the Whites who have suffered. I went to see Radek and he, too, had a bad jolt. He has been taken off the European work and made rector of a Chinese University in Moscow. In other respects, materially, the country has made much progress. Russia is interesting but it leaves me exhausted. . . .

★ ★ ★

Petrograd in 1922–1923, at which time he began his long association with the physicist Ivan Pavlov. Gantt returned to Petrograd in 1925 to study at Pavlov's Institute of Experimental Medicine.

[25]This statement cannot be verified, but in any case Golder is merely repeating something he had been told, probably by one or more of the displaced professors.

[26]Iurii Vladimirovich Got'e (Gautier) (1873–1943) had been a professor of Russian history at Moscow University; in 1925 he was associate director and head librarian of the Rumiantsev Museum.

Helsingfors, Finland
2 October 1925

Hon. Herbert Hoover
Washington, D. C.

Dear Chief:

I entered Russia on September 1 and came out on the 29th. The four weeks that I spent there were passed in the two cities of Leningrad and Moscow. It was a little over two years since I had been there and I was struck first of all by the outward material prosperity. Streets are being repaired and cleaned, houses are painted and constructed, stores are open and filled with goods. There is hustle and bustle in the streets, not unlike the years 1914 and 1917. There is, however, one well marked difference and that is the lack of color, the absence of well-dressed people, especially women. It is a drab and rather monotonous looking crowd that one notes running here and there in search of a job or bent on other material pursuits.

Russian material progress is especially noticeable in industry. Little by little production is climbing up to the prewar level. This year it is about 80%, next year it may be 90%, and in another year or two it may reach 100%. Some of the Communists are jubilant over this success but the more thoughtful shake their heads. They are a bit discouraged with the quality of the output and they realize also that to reach in 1927 or 1928 the 1914 level is no great cause for rejoicing. The factories are still running with the old and worn out machinery and no capital is laid by for the purchase of new equipment and there is danger that the time may soon come when factories may close for lack of machines. This is true to a certain extent even today. There are thousands of idle people, there is greater demand for textile goods than can be supplied and yet no more is manufactured because there is no more machinery. England and France have been appealed to for credit but as yet with little success. It is understood, however, that as soon as France settles her debt question with the United States she will regulate her debt with Russia and encourage her bankers to offer credit to Soviet industries.

The textile mills are running full time but other industries are not so prosperous. There is considerable unemployment, much more than seems on the surface. In addition to the idle proletariat in the cities there are thousands of former factory workers who have fled, during 1917–1922, to the country where they are not employed to the best advantage. Some are returning to the cities and this accounts in large part for the growth of the population of Leningrad and Moscow.

As reported the crop this year is unusually good, but unfortunately the early rains have caused much damage to some of the grain. As a consequence the amount of export will be less than anticipated. It is not likely that the total amount of food exports will exceed 300 or 325 million puds.

Internal commerce is practically in the hands of the government organizations (cooperatives, trusts, etc.). Private trade is legal but is burdened with so many taxes that it is having a hard time holding its own. If this keeps up it is likely that this kind of commerce will be confined to certain lines that can best compete with the government. Most of the goods displayed in the windows are of home manufacture and not of a very high grade. Clothing, shoes, and such things are much more expensive than in the United States. Food is cheaper than at home. When I say "cheap" or "dear" I mean from the point of view of the dollar; from the point of view of Russian wages everything is dear and some things beyond the reach of the great mass of people.

I think it may be said with safety that the population as a whole is as well off today as it ever was in its history. The peasants are probably more prosperous now than in the time of the tsar. They are out of debt, they practically own their land, and are not heavily burdened with taxation. It is proposed to reduce the tax next year and exempt entirely the poorer farmers. The object of this move is more political than economic but the fact remains that the peasants will benefit and they are not greatly concerned with motives. Workmen who are employed are at least as well off and there are many who insist that they are better off than before the war. Their pay is fairly good, their hours of labor short, they are not crushed with taxes, they pay low rents, and they enjoy privileges that no other class of the population enjoys.

The only class in Russia that is not as well off as before the war, that in some respects is worse off, is what is left of the old bourgeoisie and intellectuals. No "white" is allowed to occupy a position that a "red" can fill and as positions are becoming scarcer and competent "reds" more numerous the "whites" are forced to the wall. They present a very pitiful picture. They do not know what to do and to whom to turn. This is especially true of artists, writers, and teachers. Engineers, economists, and other technical experts, whose services are still needed, are treated better; but even they are never sure what the next day may bring forth.

It is not only the food question which worries the "whites" but also the constant fear of arrest and exile. Since the death of Lenin and the movement and talk of restoring the monarchy in Russia, the Cheka has been busy in getting out of the way all those who might possibly be implicated in a possible plot. It is the émigrés abroad with their silly talk that are largely responsible for the suffering of those at home. Though terror still exists it should be made clear that it affects only a very, very small class of the population, that is to say the handful of old bourgeoisie and former intelligentsia. The great mass of the people are not touched, they are freer now than they ever were in their lives. They pay little attention to the Communists and their decrees and do pretty much as they please.

It is admitted by all, even those who hate the Bolsheviks, that the Soviet is stronger today than three years ago, and that there is little likelihood that it will fall or be overthrown. The workmen, as a whole, are for the Soviet and will fight to maintain it. They regard it as their government and they believe that they are governing and they take a deep and personal interest in its welfare. The peasants do not desire the return of the old regime but are not very enthusiastic over the new. They accept whatever favors the Bolsheviks offer them without feeling any gratitude. It is hard for the toilers of the soil to forget what they had suffered in the hard years. The Communists admit that they have as yet failed to win the peasant and now every effort is being made to get closer to him. To the peasant the Soviet is still "they." It will be difficult to overcome this feeling because so many of the Soviet leaders are Jews. Anti-semitism is gaining, particularly in the army, among the old and new intelligentsia who are being crowded for positions by the sons of Israel. Among the methods adopted to get the good will of the peasant are the reduction of the tax, the letting up on the religious persecutions, the building of schools and places of entertainment, the introduction of machinery, and the electrification of the villages. Certain villages are already electrified.

The old bourgeoisie is completely crushed. Three years ago there were not a few who predicted an early fall of the Soviet and boasted of the fact that they had never worked for the government. There were even a few who belonged to secret organizations. If I recall correctly I sent you a circular that was being passed around in an underground way. There is no more of that. The fear of the Cheka has put an end to it. There is no resistance left. There is also another reason. Many of the more thoughtful whites have come to the realization that there is more to the Soviet than they had thought, that it is really doing good work for the people as a whole, and that the best thing for them to do is to fall in line and help. The Communists, however, do not trust them and not only keep them at a distance but continually dangle the sword over their heads. I doubt, however, whether the sword will come down.

Since my last visit there has developed a strong feeling in the Party itself. The last fight has left some sore scars and they are not healing very fast. In talking to some of the men hurt they referred to their opponents as "they" and openly criticized their internal and external policies. There is no reason to think that this is the last fight. The Communists are sailing uncharted seas and every time that it is necessary to change a course they get into a wrangle. While Lenin lived he gave the orders and now there is no big boss.

The question of propaganda in foreign countries is seriously debated. Many are of the opinion that it should be brought to an end, at least for the time being, and that an attempt should be made to live in harmony with the rest of the world. This faction is slowly gaining ground but it is difficult for the opposition to give in without a fight. For the time being there is a kind of compromise and a change of tactics. Fewer propagandists are being sent to foreign countries and more foreign delegations are invited in and shown the blessings of the Soviet regime. While I was in Russia there were several delegations present and others were expected. The Jubilee of the Academy of Sciences was made use of for propaganda purposes. Whether this new propaganda system is going to be more successful than the other remains to be seen. Foreign governments can not object to it. The people at home who see the cost of entertaining foreign delegations do a bit of grumbling. It seems to me that the peak of the propaganda movement has long since passed and that it will gradually die down to insignificant proportions.

Although there has been marked material improvement during the last three years yet there is no noticeable intellectual and spiritual progress. The old scholars and the old learning are looked upon with disfavor and the new has not yet qualified. The physical and exact sciences are encouraged but the humanitarian and theoretical studies are frowned upon and last year wholly abolished in the universities. There is no freedom of speech and the press is wholly in the hands of the government. The censorship is here more rigid and more stupid than in other states. Universities are practically closed to the children of the former bourgeoisie and even the lower schools are not always open to them.

Leaving out this small and rapidly disappearing circle of the former bourgeoisie the Soviet does all that it can to spread education and physical culture among the masses and gives them opportunities which they had never before enjoyed. It has to a very great extent succeeded in putting finer ideas of manliness into them and confidence in themselves. They now feel like free and independent citizens which they had never before felt. As far as the budget will permit much is being done for the children. They are organized into clubs, they are given musical instruments and taught to play them, they are conducted on excursions and through museums. The only draw back to education, especially in the two large cities, is that the children are being constantly called out to "demonstrate" before delegations, to march on holidays, to meet to discuss programs of study and other such things. The poor children have but little time to study their lessons. Out of this mass of children the new leaders are to come forth. They have different environments than those possessed by their teachers and there is every reason to believe that during the next ten years there will arise many differences of opinion between the two generations and that the younger will fight for the leadership.

Now that the war, famine, and the bitterness of the revolution are over one begins to notice a return to normal life. This return to normality manifests itself in different ways. Five years ago the young revolutionary writers prided themselves on the roughness of their expressions but now they are beginning to be concerned with matters of style. Extreme impressionism is on the wane and in its place is a return to realism. One is no longer proud of dirty clothes, and starched collars and well tailored suits are coming back into fashion. There is more respect for law and order than three years ago. Life is gradually falling into normal lines. Another manifestation of this normality is the craving for wholesome literature, for sports, and for funny movies. The influence of America in Russia is stronger than ever.

Jack London and Sinclair Lewis are well known writers, Douglas Fairbanks and his company are famous the empire over, our efficiency is talked of and admired everywhere, and to go to America, to be American, to be as efficient as an American comes nearer the ideal of the average Russian than to be a commissar. This American influence is bound to restore normal attitudes and lead people to concern themselves with practical and wholesome questions rather than with abstract theories and discussions of abnormal questions. I wish that we could speed this process of development by establishing closer relations. I do not see what is to be gained by waiting. We could exert much influence in that country and help restore Russia and mould her along our lines. We could at the same time learn something from Russia. We are going to be obliged to change our whole attitude on the Russian experiment. The Bolsheviks have not accomplished what they set out to do but they have come a bit nearer to it than we thought possible. It will not do to be dogmatic on the question.

So far as I have been able to learn there is little change in the attitude of the Soviet towards foreign powers. There is always the deep desire, which is shared by reds and whites, to establish closer relations with the United States. Aside from the United States the country that is now attracting attention is China. Some of the Communists feel that the Far East is going to play a great part in the world affairs and that it needs careful study. A special Chinese University has recently been created and Karl Radek has been made its rector. Its object is to study China; not so much the diplomatic history of China as the soul and thought of the people. Chinese scholars are going to be invited and intense research will be pursued.

I should like to summarize this letter by saying that during the last three years Russia has made great material progress, that the Soviet has strengthened its position, that the lot of the masses has been made better and that of the small intelligentsia worse, that there is a return to normal life, and that contact with the outside world, especially America, would greatly speed this movement towards the normal.

The Jubilee of the USSR Academy of Sciences
September 5–15, 1925[27]

Two ideas brought about the celebration of the two hundredth anniversary of the USSR Academy of Sciences. Members of that institution had in mind to glorify science, to honor their predecessors, and inspire their successors. Political leaders saw an opportunity to show to the foreigner that the Soviet is the friend of learning and to the native that the foreigner is the friend of the Soviet. To carry out this ambitious program the Jubilee was planned on a grander scale than is usually customary. It would, however, be a mistake to assume that propaganda was the only thought back of the undertaking. Russia had been living a drab-colored existence for so long a time that there was everywhere a yearning for a bit of change, for a bit of color, for something to take the attention away from the black night just passed and concentrate it on the bright day ahead. Taking advantage of this state of mind and in order to create a new point of view the leaders made the Jubilee a national holiday, a kind of Thanksgiving Day. For the first time since 1914 the country had neither war nor famine and could satisfy its strong feelings of hospitality and welcome the stranger as a guest and not as an interventionist, child-feeder, or concession-hunter. For the first time since the formation of the revolutionary government the highest institutions of learning in the world recognized it by assembling in its capital and under its flag. For the first time in more than a decade Russian scholars had the possibility of meeting their colleagues from abroad and to talk of other things than food and raiment. All elements of the population welcomed the event and few begrudged the cost in time, labor, and money.

To give an idea how carefully the celebration was planned and how thoughtfully each guest was looked after I will relate my own experiences.

---

[27]Published in the *A.R.A. Association Review* I, no. 3 (October 1925). The ARA's Sidney Brooks wrote to Goodrich on October 28, 1925, that Golder's Jubilee article "ought to amuse everyone when the Review comes out. Doctor Golder let himself go and did himself proud." Goodrich papers, box 15, file "Russia: Articles, Statements, Correspondence, 1925–42."

As soon as it become definitely known that Governor Goodrich and I were going we began to receive letters and telegrams from representatives of Soviet institutions offering us free visas and assurances that while in the territories of the USSR we would have special low rates on all transportation lines and in all hotels. At the Russo-Finnish frontier, where we crossed, all custom regulations were waved aside and we were notified of new instructions giving us free rides on all steamships, trains, including sleepers. At the Leningrad station we were welcomed by a large reception committee and taken to Hotel Europe where we were lodged in magnificent style. There was always some one near at hand to advise, guide, and help. At the headquarters the bank cashed our checks without discount, the post and telegraph transmitted our messages without cost, and on the street the police let us break ordinances without arrest.

The festivities commenced on the evening of September 5 with a reception at the Academy of Sciences. Busses were brought especially from Moscow to carry the delegates to and from places of meeting. Around the hotel and along the way, the crowd, hungry for excitement, stared at us good-naturedly and occasionally cheered. As we marched up the broad stairway leading up to the receiving line we were caught by the cross-lightnings of the cinema-man. From the point of view of the guest the movie-man nearly wrecked the show. He was a privileged character, went everywhere and at any time, got between the stage and the floor, and when least expected turned his flash on the orator or the auditor and there was nothing else to do but swear. After shaking hands with the dignitaries we were marched into the grande salle, which was filled with somberly-clad people. This black monotony was somewhat relieved by the picturesque costumes of the representatives of Asia, including Thibet, and of the different nationalities of the empire. From the point of view of color the Europeans were a disappointment for none wore his cap and gown though some scholars brought them along. There were a few persons with massive gold chains about their necks which we took to be head-ushers until we were informed that they were "Gelehrte aus Deutschland." The guests took their tone in dress from the hosts. Most of the Russian professors had on their historic prince alberts and the commissars wore up-to-date tailor-made business suits.

Sunday morning we had a great surprise. Towards eleven o'clock the Nevsky became filled with men and women, boys and girls, with brass bands and red banners announcing to the world the "Union of Science and Labor," the "Brotherhood of the Proletariat and the Scholar." Lenin's name, Lenin's face, and Lenin's words were conspicuously displayed but strangely enough there was not a reference to any other leader. The only differences that I could see between this procession and those that I had seen in 1917 were that the young proletariat of today marched with firmer step and head erect, due to gymnastic training, and had a band made up of its own members. Score that for the Bolos.

In the afternoon there was the solemn opening of the exercises in the Philharmonic Hall. The Academicians and some of the commissars occupied the stage and were the target of numerous cameras and were almost blinded by the strong lights turned on them by the movie operators. It was not a "tovarishchi" audience. Kalinin was cheered, Karpinskii, the President of the Academy, was more warmly received, and Glazunov, who stepped up to conduct his own composition, was given an ovation. This invidious class distinction did not show itself again and after this when a representative of the dictatorship of the proletariat appeared he was given the honor due him. Beethoven's 9th Symphony was played and the chorus was beautifully rendered by a group of orphan children and their teachers. Put down another plus sign for the Bolsheviks. Most of the afternoon was, however, taken up with rather long speeches and Lunacharsky distinguished himself by repeating his Russian speech in German, French, and Italian. This stunt he performed several times in the course of the ten days.

Sunday night was the first of a series of never-to-be-forgotten banquets. Those at Leningrad took place in one of the large and very artistic rooms of the Russian Museum (formerly Alexander III). In the hallway were tables filled with "zakuski"—choicest caviar, delicious smoked fish, carefully cured meats, domestic and imported cheeses, pickled vegetables and fruits, spiced foods, hot and cold dishes, vodkas, cognacs, brandies, and other liquids that took away the breath but stimulated the appetite and the brain. When we had partaken of all these good things we went into the banquet hall and sat down to eat the innumerable courses. It was a gay and festive affair. The room was brilliantly lighted, the orchestra played enchanting music, the wine flowed on, the tongue loosened, the heart opened and we loved humanity, red and white, as never before. At first we toasted our neighbor at our side, then we drank to the health of our colleagues across the table, and towards midnight we went, champagne bottle in hand, in search of our numerous friends to drain a glass of kindness for auld lang syne. We fell on each others necks and with lips still moist with the bonnie liquid we kissed and consecrated ourselves to science. The toastmaster banged, the orators shouted but they could not drown the music of the clinking glasses nor stop the outgushings of long pent up expressions of friendship nor still the music of throats dry these many years. Governor Goodrich says that it was late when we went home, that he had to hold on to me, and that we sang "For he is a jolly good fellow" and other such songs. Being an absent-minded professor I can hardly be expected to remember such details.

The days that followed were filled with excursions and pleasure parties during the day, concerts, banquets, and speeches during the night. In looking back over the program as a whole one is struck by the fact that the Academicians spoke too little and the politicians too much, considering the occasion. We would not have minded it so much had there been a little more variety in the contents of their discourse but every time an official opened his mouth there flowed forth the blessings of Communism and the curses of Capitalism. Each charge against us as "burzhui" and our governments as oppressors of the masses was loudly applauded by the red-ties and red-kerchiefs in the audience. Some of us have a suspicion that years of this kind of oratory have made the dictators of the proletariat incapable of any other. Before the Jubilee was over they got a taste of their own medicine and did not like it. Keynes, the noted English economist, came over and was asked to make a few talks and give his opinion. He did so and in polite but no uncertain language said that he did not think much of the Bolshevik experiment. Later one of the Communists confided to me that he thought that Keynes forgot that he was only a guest and when I ventured to hint that some one forgot that he was only a host he replied, "Oh, that's different." Just the same, I think that the "tovarishchi" would have accomplished more had they talked less.

Late in the night of September 10, after another banquet, the Jubilee party left, in special de luxe trains, for Moscow. Here the organization machinery did not run so smoothly principally because the guests had to be quartered in many hotels. But what Moscow lacked in organization she more than made up in hospitality and during the five days of the celebration she would not take a cent from any of us for room and board. The banquet of the city of Moscow was held in the beautiful Hall of the Nobles with its pure white marble columns and thousands of lustrous lights. The china, glass, and silver were those of the nobles, the wines were from vineyards of the grand dukes, and the ceremony was that of the Moscow boyars. Sometime between the seventh and eighth courses and between the last red wine and the first white champagne, Kamenev, followed by his staff, in the manner of a Velikii Kniaz Moskovskii,[28] made the rounds of the tables, stopping to chat with this guest and drink to the health of that one. "Plus ça change plus c'est la même chose." Life has developed certain traditions, certain ways of doing things and under the same circumstances we usually act alike.

But why go on with this description? The ARA boys are not interested in speeches which they would not hear if they could and in banquets which

---

[28]Grand prince of Moscow.

they could not eat if they would. I must, however, say something about the ballets which were given in our honor. Most of the ARA favorites were there but as there were so many of them and to mention some and leave out others would arouse jealousies I will not name any. So far as I know no one bought silk stockings for grandmother Gel'tser and I am safe in making special mention of her. She danced the same "Marche Militaire" I saw her dance in 1914, soon after the outbreak of the war. The proletarians and democrats cheered her as lustily as did the capitalists and monarchists and for a moment I forgot that eleven cruel years have intervened between these two performances. At Leningrad Semenova[29] is developing into a star of real importance and Andreev[30] is still one of the great opera singers of the world. If it were not confessing to a weakness I would admit that the hours spent in the two opera houses were the most enjoyable of my stay in Russia. I should like to add for the encouragement of the friends of Russian art that the situation looks more encouraging now than three years ago.

The Jubilee came to an end on September 15, after which the party broke up. All of us were offered free trips to different parts of the empire and some accepted. I remained at Moscow and Leningrad to deliver the numerous messages of love which the married men of the ARA charged me with. The young women recalled with deep emotion their ARA sweethearts, married and unmarried; they laughed with joy at the memory of the Pink House suppers, the Hermitage soirées, and the Blue House get-togethers[31]; they wept bitter tears over the fact that thousands of miles separate them from their loved ones; and they asked me to say that they are ready to give up father and mother, even husbands, to join the "Ameri-kantsi."

★ ★ ★

The following are excerpts from Golder's Paris diary of November 6–13, which he sent to Harold Fisher at Stanford in the form of a personal letter.

November 6, 1925
Yesterday I had a talk with my friend the artist Benois, whom you have probably met at Leningrad. He is preparing the scenes from some big thing

---

[29]Marina Timofeevna Semenova (1908–?).

[30]Pavel Zakharovich Andreev (1874–1950).

[31]The Hermitage (a prerevolutionary restaurant) and the Blue House (a residential building nicknamed by the ARA) had been used as ARA facilities in Moscow.

at the opera. He is in a bad state of mind. He does not wish to break with Russia, he hates to become an émigré and at the same time he realizes that should he return, his life would be an endless pursuit of a piece of bread. Here he gains enough and a little over, but he suffers in other ways.[32]

Parisian society is divided into two classes: one wishes to hear nothing but good of Russia and the other nothing but bad. When Benois and his family arrived at Paris, Madame Krassin, an old friend of theirs, called. There was nothing to do but return the call. As soon as he did that, some of his other friends turned their backs on him. So it goes.

Madame Krassin invited me for tea en famille yesterday. She is a kindly woman and has three or four young daughters who talk good English. Her son is in Hollywood trying to become a movie star and in the meantime working in a store. I should judge that Mrs. Krassin does not have a very happy time socially. She asked me to call again, which I will probably do. Krassin, as you know, has been transferred to London and Rakovskii to Paris.[33] Rakovskii is more of a Parisian than Krassin, has more friends in Paris, and these have intrigued to get him here. Last night Mme. Krassin did not know whether her husband, who is now in Moscow, would accept the position. There is a feeling that he should not hold two important positions, Commissar of Foreign Trade and Ambassador. I have an idea that he will accept the ambassadorship, if for no other reason than his family. His children are European-trained, attractive looking girls, and I can imagine how out of place they would be at Moscow. One of the girls is very keen to enter an American university.

Entering American universities is not such an easy affair and thereby hangs a tale of woe. When in Moscow, six young instructors of the new type came to me and asked my help to secure visas to go to America to make studies in economic subjects.[34] They are working on their theses and in view of the fact that America is the most highly developed country economically they wished to go there. I made some inquiries about them and found them as represented. They were highly recommended to me by

---

[32]Benois arrived in France from the Soviet Union in 1924; he never returned to Russia.

[33]Krassin, since December 1924 the first Soviet ambassador to France, was made ambassador to London in November 1925, at which time Rakovskii, who had been Soviet plenipotentiary in London since 1923, replaced him in Paris.

[34]The six instructors were Pavel Aleksandrov, Semen Guberman, Boris Livshin, Israel Segalovich, Aleksandr Ugarov, and Maksim Shchukov. They eventually received their U.S. visas, apparently thanks to Golder's intercession.

Gorbunov, the secretary of the Sovnarkom,[35] Pokrovsky, of the Commissariat of Education, Steklov, the vice-president of the Academy of Sciences,[36] and Professor Kafenhaus, a teacher of economics.[37]

On the strength of this evidence I wrote to the State Department and the Chief asking for a visa. The young men said that while waiting they would proceed to Berlin and work in the libraries. When I arrived in that city they came to see me to report that they had no success at the consulate. I went there and was handed over to the mercies of a young clerk by the name of Burt, who read the law to me. My protégés, he said, could not go as students, because they had not been accepted as such by any accredited school in America. When I pointed out that they were not really students, but merely instructors, and that they were going to work in our libraries, etc., he replied: "They are either students or teachers. If students they must show credentials that they have been accepted, if teachers, they must show that they are going to teach." There is just one other possible way and that is as visitors. "But," said Burt, "they may carry on propaganda." When pointed out the unlikeliness of that he shut me up by saying that it is better to keep out 99 innocents than to admit one red.

From him I went to the Consul General who started out that he did not like the Bolsheviks, that they are a d——. However, he promised to look into their case but warned me that he would not give them the benefit of the doubt. I left it there, but in the meantime I asked Harvard to accept the men as students. I do not know what will come of it. I am so sorry that the Department of State under Kellogg[38] is becoming so hard-shelled.

While in Berlin I called on his excellency J. G. Schurman,[39] to whom I had a letter of introduction from Castle of the State Department.[40] His

---

[35]Nikolai Petrovich Gorbunov (1892–1944) was secretary of the Council of People's Commissars (Sovnarkom).

[36]Vladimir Andreevich Steklov (1863–1926) was a mathematician and had been vice president of the Academy of Sciences since 1919.

[37]Lev Borisovich Kafengauz (Kafenhaus), a former Menshevik, was professor of economics at Moscow University and chief statistician at the Supreme Economic Council. See Naum Jasny, *Soviet Economists of the Twenties: Names to Be Remembered* (Cambridge, 1972), pp. 143, 193.

[38]Frank B. Kellogg (1856–1937) was U.S. secretary of state, 1925–1929.

[39]Jacob G. Schurman (1854–1942) was a professor of philosophy and president (1892–1920) at Cornell University and American ambassador extraordinary to Germany, 1925–1930.

[40]William R. Castle (1878–1963) was a former student of Archibald Cary Coolidge at Harvard and served from 1921 to 1927 as chief of the Western European Division of the U.S. State Department.

adjutant came out and reported that Schurman was very busy, but that he would see me for a minute. This made me hot, and I said that I did not care to see His Excellency and waste his valuable time. His adjutant began to explain and I went in and stated my Hoover War Library problem. When he learned that I had been in Russia, he insisted that I should stay and tell him all about it. I replied that it was not worthwhile wasting his precious time since I knew that we did not agree. He asked that I should tell him. I made a short report and ended by saying that Russia, in order to make more headway, must have credit.

"Don't you think," said His Excellency, "that this lack of credit is due to her peculiar system of government?"

"How do you explain France and Germany's lack of credit?" I asked.

"Oh, they have been in the war," said the learned doctor.

Our diplomats as well as other diplomats, make me sad and gay. Be it said to the credit of the Chief that his commercial attachés are very much ahead of the diplomats. There is considerable feeling between the two branches of the service and the diplomats would like to keep the other fellows down.

Talking about diplomats, let me tell you of my interview yesterday with the first secretary and chargé d'affaires of the Bolo embassy. Both men are Armenians, the chargé a rather polished man.[41] The question was when would America recognize Russia. I replied that when Russia would pay her debts and stop interfering in the affairs of other people. They replied that Russia is ready to make peace with America if America would give her a chance. We did not get anywhere. We agreed, however, that unless Russia got money somewhere, she could not advance much further.

11 P.M. November 6

I had an exciting afternoon and evening with the Russians. Early in the afternoon I went to call on a Russian lady who was just come from Moscow and who plans to go back. She told me she has a hard time of it here. The émigrés greet her rather coldly. They start in by saying: "Have you just come out? All respectable Russians have been out some time." When they learn that she intends to go back, their contempt reaches beyond endurance. Under the circumstances the poor woman avoids the Russians, especially the Russian women. She longs to return, but when she thinks of the hardships that await her and her family she gets a chill. Her daughter was

---

[41]The chargé was Jacques (Iakov) Davtian, first counselor in Paris in 1925 and later Soviet ambassador to Poland.

almost turned out of the university because she could not answer this simple question: "What is the difference between the terror of the French Revolution and the Russian?" The girl answered she did not see any difference. At these words the Communists voted to put her out as a dangerous element. Fortunately one of the committee was a friend of her friend, an old revolutionist, and he quieted them down. She was called back and told that the difference is very great. "The Russian terror is for the good of the masses," and therein lies the difference. This lady's second daughter is now in the university and there is no telling what questions will be put to her.

Later in the day I called on General Golovin, an old acquaintance, and a very intelligent man. I discussed with him the proposed organization for the study of the Russian Revolution and asked his cooperation. He said he would do anything, provided that his name and that of the Bolsheviks do not appear together.

Tonight Miliukov dined with me and spent the evening. He has become more reconciled but still believes that recognition strengthens the hands of the Bolos and delays the happy day. I asked what he meant by the happy day, and so far as I could judge from his answer, he meant a return to capitalism and a democratic form of government. Should the United States recognize Russia he would not seriously object.

He told me an interesting story. While in America a few years ago Francis[42] invited him to St. Louis. A dinner party was given in his honor. While every one was happy Francis called on a friend to read from his (Francis's) book Miliukov's speech to see how eloquent it was. Miliukov listened but could not recognize it until it finally dawned on him that it was the speech which a certain novelist put into his mouth in a story and it was this speech that Francis had copied.[43] After the dinner the guests came to Miliukov and praised the "Russian Demosthenes."

I asked him whether Root had understood the situation in 1917. He was of the opinion that he did. "Anyway," said Miliukov, "I had a long talk with him and painted conditions in their true dark color." "Buchanan," added Miliukov, "knew the situation in Russia better than Paléologue,[44] but his book has many mistakes.[45] For example, he said that I visited the

---

[42]David Francis, former U.S. ambassador to Russia in 1917 and author of *Russia from the American Embassy: April, 1916–November, 1918* (New York, 1921).

[43]This is probably the speech Miliukov supposedly delivered before the duma, published in *Russia from the American Embassy*, pp. 35–39.

[44]Maurice Paléologue (1859–1944) was the French ambassador to Russia, 1914–1917.

[45]Sir George Buchanan, *My Mission to Russia and Other Diplomatic Memories*, 2 vols. (London, New York, and Toronto, 1923).

embassy before the Revolution. I was never inside of it and had little to do with the ambassador. Buchanan lied to me once. It was rumored that Buchanan went to the Emperor and painted conditions in gloomy colors. When I asked him about it he denied it, but later in his book he admitted it. When Milner[46] came over, my friends arranged that I should sit next to him in order to enlighten him. I was honest with him and gave him the true situation but later I learned that in his report he painted everything—the loyalty to the emperor and empress and the state of the army—in bright colors."

Then I put a rather unfair question to him: "Mr. Miliukov," I said, "could anybody have saved the situation in the summer of 1917?" He hesitated a bit, and finally said that he thought he could have. When I pushed him a little, he did not make it clear to me how; but he intimated that Kerensky was much to blame for the débâcle. Miliukov defended himself against the charge that he stood out for Constantinople.[47] "If Russia could have had peace with Constantinople, I should not have lifted a finger to secure it. When I came into power the Allies had already agreed that Russia was to have it, and there was nothing else for me to do than to stand by them and the agreement. They pushed me farther than I dared go. In my first note I did not overemphasize our relations with the Allies and at once Paléologue jumped on me. I knew the state of mind of the Russian public better than he, but he and the others insisted, and when I did not do as they said, they plotted against me. Albert Thomas[48] was one of the causes of my downfall. He joined forces with the Soviet."

I inquired about the talk of Palace Revolution.[49] He said: "There is no question whatever, but that it was planned. Unfortunately those who were implicated have failed to tell about it. Guchkov is quiet, Alekseev is dead, and L'vov left no papers behind, although he told me a great deal about it before he died."

Miliukov feels that he should devote the rest of his life to his country and countrymen. He is of the opinion that the monarchists' talk and

---

[46]Lord Alfred Milner (1854–1925) was British secretary of state for war, 1916–1918.

[47]As foreign minister in the Provisional Government, Miliukov's position was that in any peace accord Russia should be given Constantinople in accordance with the agreement between the Allies and the tsarist government. This issue was at the heart of the controversy over a "peace without annexations" that led to Miliukov's resignation on May 2.

[48]Albert Thomas (1878–1932), French Socialist minister of munitions, led a mission to Russia to urge the Provisional Government to launch a military offensive against Germany.

[49]A coup to oust Nicholas II on the eve of the February 1917 Revolution.

movement are pretty near at the end of the trail. He is urging his country-men to forget their ideas of Bolshevik Russia and study the real Russia as she is today. He does not look for revolution in Russia, but for evolution with the possibility of help from revolution. He thinks that salvation will come from the peasants. He would favor American help to the peasants, but not to industry, for fear the Bolos would use that to keep themselves in power. Monopoly of foreign commerce is the institution he would like to see destroyed.

Sunday, November 8, 5:00 P.M.

It has been a full day so far. Early in the morning I had a call from a Russian revolutionist, formerly a member of Kerensky's entourage, but now holding a position in the red government. He had a great plan to save humanity. The trouble is that scientists and scholars of all kinds are shamefully neglected. They live on the crumbs of the earth. It is a shame that the great organizers of the world do not give the question the attention it deserves. Albert Thomas is interested and if Hoover could be aroused all would be well. But before either Thomas or Hoover can do anything, the Russian peasants must learn to read and write and in order to bring that about they must have pencils and writing paper. From this you can see for yourself that the salvation of the world depends on pencils and writing paper. America, which is so deeply interested in such questions, will surely see it in the proper light and will furnish the necessary means. Now, Fish,[50] please take up a collection to buy pencils and paper to teach the peasant to read and write in order that Hoover may organize science, which will improve your position and the world will be saved.

. . . Later in the day I saw some of the Russian émigrés. How they quarrel and hate each other, but unite in cursing the Soviet and all the Russians who in any way cooperate or live under its flag. The poor Russians who are not red and who live there, but who come out occasionally for a breath of fresh air, are treated shamefully and are forced back. I do not know whom to pity more—the whites in Russia or those outside.

Tonight Mr. Jacques Davtian, Chargé d'Affaires de l'Union des Repub-liques Sovietistes Socialistes, dined with me. . . . Davtian wished to know on what terms Russia could have recognition. I made it clear to him that Russia would have to promise to pay her debt to us and promise not to interfere in our affairs through propaganda. He agreed that Russia must have credit and that she could not get it in Europe, and that America is the

---

[50]Fisher.

only country that could advance it. Moreover, Russia would rather grant concessions to America than to the European powers, because we have no political motives. He felt sure that the debt question could be arranged to our satisfaction, if we really meant business.

I took up with him the question of propaganda. He assured me that the Soviet government did not carry on propaganda, and I took no issue on that. As to the Communist International, he claimed that it was an international organization and that for its acts the Soviet was not responsible. The Soviet did not support it, its resources came from annual membership fees, and it had just as much right to do as it liked as did the Second International or any other private organization. I made it clear to him that this argument would not go down with us: if that was his attitude, and that of his government, it was a waste of time to discuss it. He laughed and said that he could not understand why a country that was so sound economically should fear the propaganda of a few agitators. I agreed with him that there was nothing to fear, but pointed out that in both questions—propaganda and debt—we must take into consideration public opinion and psychology. After thinking a moment he said, "We must find some way to satisfy public opinion." He claims that Zinoviev has very little influence on the government, that the men who run things are Rykov, Kamenev, and Stalin, and that Trotsky is again coming to the forefront.

Friday, November 13, 8 P.M.

. . . This evening I called on Peter Struve, former revolutionist, philosopher of socialism, professor of economics, and now editor of a monarchist paper, supported by a former oil magnate.[51] Struve quickly warmed up to his theme and jumped from his seat and poured hot shots into the left wing. He sees no possibility of evolution in Russia, for evolution means the ruin of the Bolos. The only salvation lies in political revolution. That, too, looks rather far away. Under the circumstances Russia is in for a long hard siege. The Bolos will not evolution and the country will not revolution, and there is your vicious and endless circle. He will not for a moment admit that there might possibly be a flaw in his argument.

When I ventured to hint that by his not having been in Russia for many years, there were some things that he did not see, he denied it and insisted that because he looked from a distance he saw the situation much better

---

[51]Peter Berngardovich Struve (1870–1944)—former liberal leader and Kadet, deputy to the Second Duma, and later foreign minister in the Wrangel government—in Paris was the editor of the journal *Vozrozhdenie* (*Renaissance*).

than those who were inside. After much talking it came out that by "political revolution," he did not mean a complete turnover, such as occurred in 1917, but what we would call an evolution towards the right. When that was made clear, I agreed with him, except that I think the evolution is going on, and he denies it. I then put the question to him whether the political evolution, or revolution, whatever we called it, would not be hastened by economic help from outside. A few minutes before, he had pointed out that only such help would bring about the "political revolution." When, however, I put my question to him, he replied, "As an economist, I can not imagine such a possibility. Bankers would not be so foolish as to let them have money." Here is another vicious circle: Only economic help will bring about the hoped for change, but economic help is unthinkable. Russian Bolshevism exists because its industry is parasitic and just as soon as industry should become self-supporting, it would throw over Bolshevism. This raises the question of why the Bolos try to get money to build up industry and make it self-supporting. It is too complicated for me.

The first few meetings with the whites, I told them about our plan to create an organization to write the history of the Russian Revolution. They smile good-naturedly, and assure me that only they can do so. The reds are sure that the whites can not; the whites insist that the reds have not the proper point of view, and both are agreed that an outsider has no business to touch it at all. They are very encouraging.

Friday, November 13, 8 P.M.

This afternoon I called on Kerensky, who was very glad to see me. I raised the question of recognition with him. He said that although as a politician he could not champion it, yet as a man and a Russian he would be glad to see it done. What is needed to upset the Bolos is contact with other people and a healthy development of the country. He has no objections to propaganda; that is for America to look out for. He, like other Russians and Europeans, is thinking of the great need Russia and America have to stick together against Japan. I told him that this question worried the Europeans a great deal more than the Americans. On the whole he comes nearer to the American liberal opinion about Russia than any of the others.

From him I went to Maklakov, former member of the Duma and, until recently, Russian diplomat.[52] He feels that Russia is changing fast and that

---

[52]Vasilii Alekseevich Maklakov (1869–1957), leading Kadet and deputy to the Second, Third, and Fourth dumas, was named ambassador to France by the Provisional Government, although the October Revolution occurred before he took up his post. He remained in Paris, coordinating the activities of the various Russian embassies until France recognized the Soviet Union in 1924.

the pressure is all from the peasants, and that sooner or later the Communists will have to give up their communism and get down to capitalism. As
he looks ahead, he sees the little Communists in office carrying out the
orders of the big capitalists. We got into quite a discussion as to recognition.
He said, at first, that he hoped that America would not step down from her
high position and recognize the reds. When I asked what that high position
was, he referred to a note of Colby which said that America would not
recognize the Soviet until the Soviet was recognized in Russia.[53] When I
inquired how that was going to be determined, he admitted the difficulties.
He then went on to say that if America recognized Russia, it would and
should insist on the payment of the debt; it should insist that not only
should its own citizens be paid for the property confiscated, but also the
Russians; that the Soviet should crush the International.

I took issue and pointed out that we have no more right to interfere in
Russian than we have in French affairs. All that we could do was to protect
our citizens and ourselves, and outside of that we could do nothing. We
wrangled on this point for a time and finally he said that he was thinking
of recognition de jure. If, however, it was only de facto recognition, it was
not necessary to emphasize these points. I finally put it up to him whether
he thought that recognition would do Russia good or harm. He admitted
that he was uncertain, and that he could imagine a time when recognition
would help to bring pressure on the Bolos to swing to the right. He was
not sure whether the time had yet come or not. He said that the moral
prestige that the Bolos would gain by American recognition is not worth
taking into consideration.

After summing up these conversations, I should say that the émigré
leaders are very much at sea as to the policy to be pursued. None of them
wishes to come out strongly against American recognition, for fear it
would at some time count against them. Kerensky is distinctly in favor.
Miliukov would approve of it, if the Bolos were made to accept our terms.
Maklakov thinks that the time may soon come when recognition will be of
great help in changing the course of the Communists. Struve is the only
one who preaches against it, but he was for intervention and blockade, was
the minister of Wrangel, and is now the agent of the monarchists.

---

[53]Bainbridge Colby (1869–1950) was U.S. secretary of state, 1920–1921. His diplomatic note of August 10, 1920, said essentially that the United States could not
recognize a government that was unrepresentative and "based upon the negation of
every principle of honor and good faith and every usage and convention underlying
the whole structure of international law." See Frederick Lewis Schuman, *American
Policy toward Russia since 1917* (New York, 1928), pp. 179–82.

JOURNEY V
1927

CHAPTER SEVEN

HOW THE MIGHTY HAVE FALLEN![1]

On September 10th, 1927, Lincoln Hutchinson and I sailed from New York on the Gripsholen. I should like to say a good word for the boat. I have been on larger ships but never on better. The food was delicious, the cabins comfortable, and the service excellent. There was no begging, no outstretched hands, no collection for musicians, sailors' widows, etc. The Swedish Company takes care of all these and does not pass this responsibility to the traveling public. Would that the other steamship companies used some of their dividends to pay the employees.

From Sweden we went to Finland where Freddy Lyons[2] and his beautiful wife did everything possible to make our stay in that country very pleasant. We left Helsingfors on the night of September 24th and at one o'clock on the following day we were at Leningrad. This city has not as yet a regular taxi-system, only a number of broken-down automobiles that compete with the droshkies. It is not a fair competition, however, for while the izvozchik has to watch his horse, the chauffeur goes on the train platform to snatch passengers. We took one of these autos to the hotel but after one experience we went back to our friendly izvozchiks and their more comfortable droshkies.

---

[1] Published as "A Trip to Russia," *A.R.A. Association Review* 3, no. 1 (January 1928).
[2] Served with the ARA in Soviet Russia, 1921–1923.

Hotel Europe, where we stopped for a day, is very comfortable and reasonable in price. For two large rooms and a bath we paid about eight dollars a day, including tax and service. Food was cheap, that is to say cheap for foreigners. A four-course dinner was seventy-five cents. Wines and liquors are very dear but vodka is cheap.

Since 1925, the time of my last visit, Leningrad has greatly improved. A number of new buildings were going up and some of the old ones were being repaired and painted. The Winter Palace has been given a coat of light green and white which I am told was its original color. Wherever one turned one could see preparations for the Tenth Anniversary Jubilee.

Notwithstanding these improvements Leningrad is becoming more and more a provincial city and is living on its past glory. It still has museums, theatres, opera, and ballet but they are not fully supported and some of the best artists are being attracted to Moscow.

We reached Moscow on September 27th and found the capital full of hustle and bustle. In addition to a very efficient bus system Moscow has a taxi-service run by the city. It is cheaper to go by one of the city taxis than by droshkies. Whether these taxis are self-supporting is doubtful. Besides the city taxis there are a lot of broken-down cars (no better than those in Leningrad) doing business on their own account. They are neither comfortable nor cheap. The two kind of taxis are parked side by side near the Bolshoi Theatre and we noticed that the chauffeurs of the city taxis discouraged passengers from making use of their service and pushed them on to their competitors.

In Moscow we stopped at the Savoy, a very comfortable hotel. Everything in Moscow is more expensive than in Leningrad. Two small rooms and a bath cost about twelve dollars a day, including tax and service. During our stay the price came down somewhat. Our good friend and former European director, Walter Lyman Brown, was at the hotel and told us that the same rooms cost considerably more a year ago. While the price of the rooms came down during the six weeks that I remained in Moscow, the cost of food went up from two rubles twenty-five kopeks to two rubles fifty kopeks for a four-course dinner. The hotels are run by the municipality and I was interested in the clever scheme to make the guests pay promptly and not allow the bills to run up. The city tax increases with the size of the bill. On small accounts you pay 10% and on large accounts as much as 40%. The waiters and officials of the hotel, having no personal interest in the hotel, have devised a counter-scheme to defeat the purpose of the municipality. Large bills are divided up into small bills so as to keep down the tax to the minimum.

While the food is abundant, manufactured goods are scarce, dear, and of poor quality. Some of the simplest things are unattainable. One sees long lines in front of government stores, which are usually empty of goods. Along side of them are a few private stores that sell at very high prices goods made in government factories. In other words the government factories do not begin to supply the demand and a considerable part of what these industries produce is bought up by private dealers while the government stores are empty.

During our stay in Russia there was a shortage of white flour and sugar. Coffee is not to be had at all. On the other hand, there was plenty of delicious fruit, as good as can be found anywhere. The Russians have not only learned to raise good fruit but also to pack it and to export it to the nearby states.

Drunkenness is on the increase. Vodka shops, intoxicated men, women, and children are in evidence everywhere. The revenue from the sale of alcoholic drinks is a very important item in the national budget but a dangerous method of state support. The Russian peasant and workman is too backward culturally to have much self-restraint and now that the village stores have little to offer in the way of goods, the peasant is apt to waste his substance on strong drink. If this state of affairs continues Russia is likely to fall behind more and more.

When we came to Moscow in September, we saw a great many of the homeless children. They were dirty, ragged, neglected and ran the streets in packs like wild beasts and they had the animal look in their faces. I saw them gnaw at raw bones just as dogs do. By November first they had been gathered up and sent out of the capital so as not to be in sight of the guests who came to the Jubilee.

Would that I could say something nice about the cafés. After a certain hour at night they are little better than rendezvous joints. One feels nothing but pity for the untidy painted women one sees in these places. They look more like poor mothers trying to make a living for the hungry babies at home than irresponsible flappers.

Where, and, oh where are the beautiful women that Russia once had! They are not in the cafés, not in the streets and not in the homes. The hard years of suffering are beginning to tell. The young generation is growing up without color in their faces and without joy in their countenances. People rush here and there with jaws set, eyes fixed, minds bent on one thing—the securing of the daily bread.

There is considerable unemployment and unless commerce and industry develop, the number of unemployed will grow. The annual increase of population is about 2% and primitive agriculture can not absorb the newcomers who rush to the few cities. One need not be a prophet or a pessimist to predict serious trouble if present conditions prevail.

Wages are low. The average office workers receive from fifty to one hundred twenty-five rubles per month. Rents are cheap but everything else, especially manufactured goods, is high. How to make ends meet is a problem, but the Russians have had considerable experience in solving it.

The church war is seemingly over and it is hard to say who is victor. Church organization has been broken up, church attendance has fallen off, but there is no reason for believing that the institutional Church may not rise again. The truth of the matter is that the Bolsheviks are pretty well worn out by the ten year effort to push one hundred fifty millions uphill. It is no longer a question of pushing them higher but of keeping them from sliding back. The passive resistance of the ignorant peasant is dead weight and bears down the strongest. Recently the Government, to avoid too many holidays, put the church feast days back on the old church calendar. Stories circulate of the way the peasant ignores the Government. It is said that when the peasant youth returns from the army they are taken to the church for a "purification" service, in which they renounce the Communists and their teachings. When the peasant girl (some of whom go to school in the cities and work in factories) returns to the village, her mother and father hand her the old dress and say, "Now daughter go to work and no city nonsense."

While at Moscow we took in some of the plays. At the Art and Malyi Theatres they put on two revolutionary plays. I doubt whether anywhere else in the world could one see such artistic performances as in these two play houses. In so far as dramatic art is concerned, Russia still leads.

I wish I could say as much for the opera and especially for the ballet. It seemed to me as if the ballet is not as good as it was. Perhaps I was too much influenced by the new revolutionary and propaganda ballet "The Red Poppy." The red was so much in evidence that it was nauseating. The scene is laid in China where the Chinese and English capitalists oppress the Chinese masses until the Russian reds come on the scene to save the proletariat and start the revolution. Gel'tser is the leading lady, and her reputation does not keep up with her years.

The men and women who used to be at the head of the cultural institutions when the ARA was in Russia are gradually being replaced by others. Whether that is to be counted as a step forward or backward depends entirely whether you have or have not the Marxian point of view. A Communist is now at the head of the Hermitage and there has been considerable tinkering with the Academy of Sciences. The old white professors are gradually being crowded out by the young red professors. What the old have done we know, what the young will do remains to be seen. The latter have not the background of the former, but they know their catechism.

Text books are published in large numbers, but few literary works because the censorship is rigid and buyers few.

I remained in Russia long enough to accept an invitation to attend the opening exercises of the celebration in honor of the tenth anniversary of the Revolution. . . .[3]

From the point of view of preparation, program, and execution, this celebration was not in the same class with that of the Academy of Sciences two years ago. Hurrah for the professors! If there was a detailed program for the November celebration I did not see it; if there was a banquet I was not asked to it. I was invited to visit factories and other "aspects of Soviet life" but I declined with thanks. On the evening of November 6th, an official of the Cultural Relations Society brought me a ticket to the military review on the day following and promised to call for me about ten o'clock. After he left I learned that the review would begin at nine o'clock and those that did not get into the Red Square by a quarter to nine would stay out altogether. After waiting for my guide until eight thirty I set out alone and reached the entrance to the square two minutes late. The police formed a chain and announced that no one would be admitted. This made no impression on the crowd which gently pushed by the policemen while they shouted "Nelzia, Nelzia."[4]

I found a place on one of the platforms, not far from Lenin's Mausoleum where those in authority were stationed. The exercises began with the playing of the International by numerous military bands. Voroshilov,[5] the Commander of the Army, walked up to where President Kalinin was standing, saluted, and invited him to inspect the troops. The two walked by the front line, then got into a car, and in a few minutes ended the inspection. After Kalinin returned to his place the troops filed by the stand where the commissars were gathered and saluted. The monotony of this performance was somewhat relieved by the picturesqueness of the Wild Division from the Caucasus.

While watching this review I could not help but recall similar occasions. In 1914 I saw Nicholas II, in 1917 Kerenskii, and in 1923 Trotsky review the troops. How the mighty have fallen and how much blood has been wasted in these thirteen years! How little there is to show for it!

---

[3] Here Golder reproduces the text of the invitation, which was sent out over the name of Ol'ga Kameneva as president of the U.S.S.R. Society for Cultural Relations with Foreign Countries.

[4] "It is prohibited."

[5] Kliment Efremovich Voroshilov (1881–1969) was the people's commissar for military and naval affairs.

On the stand behind me were two American radicals Margaret and Charlie. Margaret was keen to see women soldiers and whenever a company of small sized men passed, she exclaimed, "Here comes the Women's Battalion." Bringing up the rear of the infantry were a few Red Cross nurses dressed in skirts. This made Margaret quite furious. "Women should march with the men," she shouted.

"Would you quarter them with the men?" asked Charlie.

"Quarter them separately," retorted Margaret.

"You had better put a steel wall between them," added Charlie.

Margaret got over being sore when she saw the Cheka troops. "Three cheers for the gay pay yu,"[6] she screamed out. When a moment later she caught sight of the sailors of the paper fleet, dressed in smart uniforms, Margaret let herself go with "Zdravstvuit1,[7] sailors." This outburst quite disgusted Charlie who remarked: "The way the women fall for brass buttons is a sight!"

The military review which lasted for nearly three hours was followed by a civilian parade, which dragged on until evening. At nights the streets were illuminated. Celebrations, similar to that of Moscow but on a smaller scale, were carried on in various parts of the vast country. In this way is the revolution being deepened and engraved on the minds and hearts of the people.

I cannot conclude this paper without a word about the growth of pro-American feeling in Russia. As the years roll on, the work of Herbert Hoover and the ARA looms bigger and finer and legends are beginning to gather about the Americans. They are not only able and efficient but also big hearted, broadminded, unselfish, ready to help those in need without any ulterior motives. It is to America that all classes of Russia look for future economic guidance and help. America has the capital, America has the men, and the skill. America has the good will and America has demonstrated she has no political interests in Russia. America alone understands the needs of Russia because America is a continental country like Russia.

The Communists have stopped calling us names. They eventually realize that the ARA came to Russia to help and not to play politics. The policy of our Government has been consistent, quite unlike that of England, which is hot and cold in turn. Trotsky even went out of his way to pay us a left-handed compliment when he said that there was more liberty in the United States than in Soviet Russia.

---

[6]The GPU.

[7]"Hello."

I think this pro-American feeling will grow. Whenever the time comes when diplomatic relations between the two countries are resumed Americans, especially ARA men, will receive a warm welcome and hearty cooperation. I am also certain that Americans, especially former ARA men, will do their best to justify the confidence and admiration of the Russian people.

APPENDIX

Conference Between Governor Goodrich and Representatives of the Soviet Government consisting of Messrs. Kamenev, Krassin, Sokol'nikov, Litvinov, and Rykov, in Mr. Kamenev's office on Monday, June 19, 1922, at 3:00 P.M.

It was agreed at the very beginning that none of the conversations which would take place should appear in print. Gov. Goodrich said that before leaving America President Harding and Secretary of State Hughes asked him to talk over with those representing the Soviet government the situation with a view to removing the obstacles that stand in the way of an understanding, but he wished it to be understood that he was here not in any official capacity, but as a private individual.

Rykov welcomed the Governor and said that he was glad to know that the Governor has been working with a view to bringing about a better understanding.

Gov. Goodrich then took the points in Secretary of State Hughes's note,[1] touching on (a) Safety of Life, (b) Private Property, (c) Sanctity of Contract, (d) Freedom of Labor.

In regard to the question of Russian courts, Litvinov said that all citizens who had not complotted against the government are as safe here as anywhere. To this the Governor replied that in America every person arrested has the right to know on what charge. Kamenev replied that during the period of the Revolution and Civil War, the Cheka was in control, but

---

[1] A reference to Hughes's diplomatic note of March 25, 1921. See above, p. 151, n. 56.

after the break-up of the Civil War a new organization took place. At the present time, only the civil courts are empowered to try cases. Each person arrested has a right to know within two weeks on what charge and within two months he must have a trial. The courts are elected by the soviets, regardless of party. At the present time there are 57 such courts in Moscow. According to the new law, the highest form of punishment is five years' imprisonment, except for persons accused on the charge of spying, banditism, and betrayal of government trust, but even in these cases the prisoner has the right to be tried by the highest civil courts.

The Governor next took up the question of the demonstration which is to take place tomorrow, June 20th, and asked whether it was done with a view to demanding the death penalty on the accused Social Revolutionists. Kamenev said that the Russian citizens have a right to demonstrate and that the government cannot interfere and the government does not know what kind of flags and cries will be made, but no matter what kind of a demonstration it is, it will not affect the judges of the merits of the case. So far as he knew no extreme measures or any unlawful acts would take place, and he was sure there would be no lynching. The purpose of the demonstration is to express loyalty to the Soviet government, the existence of which loyalty the Social Revolutionists deny. Not only that, but the Soviet government has allowed the prisoners rights that no other government would permit, as, for example, the right to bring in legal counsel from the outside, among whom is one man who was minister in a Royal Cabinet which signed the Treaty of Versailles, which is now generally condemned.

Gov. Goodrich next took up the question of the arrest of the A.R.A. men in Odessa and pointed out the evil effect such a news item would have on American public opinion.[2] He said that if American employees are found guilty of serious charges, the matter should be brought to Colonel Haskell, who would take care of it. Kamenev said that he had already taken up the matter with Col. Haskell and he quite sympathized with the American point of view, however, the war and the revolution have so disorganized the telegraphic communication and the material welfare of Russia that it was very difficult to communicate with officials in Russia in a short delay of time.

Gov. Goodrich next took up the question about Radek and the Berlin agreement which assured the prisoners freedom from the death penalty. To the Governor it seemed strange that a private individual should have the right to bind the government and the courts in such a trial. Kamenev replied

---

[2] In fact the two Americans had been only briefly detained, and the incident was not publicized.

that the agreement was made between political parties which, though it had a moral value, did not bind the Soviet government and did not bind the court. Rykov broke in by saying that the Soviet government has had no time to pass judgment on the Berlin agreement, except on the clause which gave the prisoners the right to bring in counsel from outside. Gov. Goodrich raised another question as to the condemnation and execution of the five priests and wished to know on what charge they were executed. Kamenev explained that because of the hunger, the government needed all the financial support it could get and, therefore, undertook to collect the church treasures, which treasures belong to the government by right of the decree which separated the Church from the State. The priests opposed the government in this. They incited revolt and resistance to legal authority which led to bloodshed and murder and on these charges they were tried, found guilty, and executed.

Gov. Goodrich next took up the question of private property and asked to know to what extent does private property exist in Russia, and coupled with this another question whether a contract made between two individuals to the advantage of one could be annulled by the courts at the request of one of the parties and whether the government could annul a contract because it was disadvantageous to the government. Kamenev replied that the workingmen's government has nationalized property, first in land and second in industry, and from this stand the government cannot and will not recede. He added that the tendency in other governments is along the same lines. But this nationalization has come to an end, and at the present time the Government is doing all it can to encourage people and capital to go on and profit. For example, the old law of requisitioning from the peasants has been done away with and a regular tax system has been established. Furthermore, according to the present law, the peasants are not required to divide their land oftener than once in nine years, which gives them time to profit by their holdings. As to the question of whether contracts could be annulled by one or the other of the parties, Kamenev and the others present agreed that could not be done unless the contract was illegally drawn up. For example, if, as it happened recently, a man having bread came to a hungerer with bread and demanded in return extortionate values, such a contract the court may dissolve. The object of the law was to prevent exploitation. Sokol'nikov, Commissar of Finance, said that at the present time individuals have no limit placed on them as to the amount of money they may have or as to the number of buildings they may have or in any way limits placed on their property except land. In the matter of inheritance, the limit is placed on 10,000 gold rubles.

The question was next put to Krassin: Suppose a man sold his wheat to another man at 50 cents a bushel, but the next day the price of wheat went up to two dollars, could the seller break the contract on that ground? Krassin and others agreed that it could not be done. Krassin pointed out that during the last two years, from the time that the Soviet government has made contracts with foreigners, not a single contract has been broken. Litvinov added that, even during the old Tsar's government, there existed a law which gave the government the right to break any contract which was disadvantageous to the government.

Gov. Goodrich took up the other question of whether labor had any control in industry under the present laws. To this Rykov replied that it had not. The employer was free to make a contract with its labor unions as elsewhere. Labor, however, had an indirect influence in industry in that it had representatives in the government organization known as "Gosplan," which has for its object the planning out of the economic reconstruction and development of Russia. The employer is free to have in his service union or non-union men as it seems best to him. Gov. Goodrich then raised the question of the nationalized industries and wished to know whether there would be any objection on the part of the Soviet government if an American should take a concession of a Russian industrial plant and should invite the former owners to participate. Krassin replied that the Soviet government had no objections, that the American who took the concession could have in his company anyone he pleased. However, he said the Soviet government would not recognize contracts made by former owners with foreigners.

The question of the establishment of foreign banks in Russia was next taken up. Sokol'nikov said that at the present time the State Bank has the monopoly of the banking business and foreign banks who wished to come here would have to discuss the question with the government through the Commissariat of Finance, and would have to come to a special agreement with it. At the present time there are two or three other Russian banks in Russia such as the Central Cooperative and the Southeastern Bank in southern Russia, but they have a charter from the State Bank.

The next question was the debt of the Russian government to the American government and to American nationals. It was agreed by all that the amount of the debt is very small, and it was pointed out by Krassin that the several American industrial plants were not nationalized and that the Singer factory had been nationalized under the Tsar's government under the suspicion that it was a German concern. Krassin went on to say that there was no great obstacle to regulating the debt between Russia and America, that the amount was small and all that was needed was a free discussion between the two parties, intimating that it would be necessary to recognize the Soviet government first and discuss afterward. Gov. Goodrich made it very clear that the recognition of the debts must come before political recognition, that the recognition of the debts on the part of Russia would give it a moral credit in the eyes of the American people. Unless the Russian government were willing to say that it is ready to pay the debts as soon as possible and is ready to give obligations to compensate American nationals for confiscated property, no good could come out of discussions. Without that no American capital would be invested in Russia. Kamenev said he understood the psychology of the American people and he wanted us also to understand the psychology of the Russian people. Ever since 1905, the different political parties, including the Kadets, have plainly stated that they would not recognize the debts of the Tsar. From this principle, the Soviet government could not recede. However, it would be possible to pay the debts by taking up the matter in a business-like way. If arrangements could be made to secure credit, the debts would be taken care of in that way, but debts and credits go together. Krassin broke in by saying that the question of debts brings with it the question of compensations and the question of compensations brings with it the question of counterclaims.

After the discussion had gone on in this way for a few minutes, Gov. Goodrich made it very clear that if an understanding is to be reached between the two governments some way must be found out of this difficulty. The United States government can not and will not give a loan to any government and if Russia secures money in America it will come from private sources and the bankers and the money lenders of America must be assured of Russia's willingness to pay the debts. Krassin said that his government can not accept the principle of recognition of debts, but is willing to negotiate on the question of payment of debts. Kamenev inquired to know what guarantee the Soviet government would have that if it recognized debts it would get a loan either from the government or from private sources. Rykov said that if the Soviet government were merely required to make the promise of payment, but not the payment, he was willing to commit himself. Gov. Goodrich replied that, of course, he could not give any guarantees, but he felt sure that American capital would be ready to come into Russia as soon as Russia's credit was once more established. Kamenev came back by saying that Russia is a rich country and is willing to pay the debts, but did not think it right to commit itself unless it saw a way of paying them. To this, the Governor replied:

"You have no faith in yourself to pay your debts. We, on the other hand, have faith that Russia will pay her debts," and added: "You are wasting your time with America unless you are ready to recognize the debts and issue obligations promising to pay in the future."

Kamenev said: "Why is it that since Russia owes less to America than does England, you are doing business with England yet you refuse to have anything to do with us?"

The Governor replied: "Because England has not repudiated her debts and you have," that the question of the amount of debt is not as important as the principle.

Rykov raised this question: Suppose Russia recognized its debt to America, the products and help of which it needs very much, would that not lead to recognition of the debts to France, the products and help of which Russia needs less? He concluded by saying that Russia would be very glad to discuss the matter with the United States if it did not involve her with the other powers.

Gov. Goodrich tried to make it very clear that the United States is not tied up with France or with any other power.

At this point, the conversation changed to other subjects. Krassin wished to know whether it would be possible to send to America objects made of gold and precious stones to be sold there or to be pawned there for money with which to buy seed. Gov. Goodrich replied that it would not be possible, but he was not sure.

Rykov asked whether the Russian government had the right to demand a refund of the money which Bakhmetev spent in Washington with the cognizance of the American government.[3] Gov. Goodrich asked to be excused from answering this question.

Rykov also wished to know whether arrangements could be made by which the citizens of each country would have civil rights in one another's countries. When asked to explain what he meant it came out that what he really had in mind was whether Russians would be allowed to go to America and whether the Russian government would have a right to sue in American courts. This question was left unanswered.

In conclusion, Kamenev said that he hoped that Gov. Goodrich was convinced that the Soviet government had a real desire to come to an understanding with the United States, that there was no great obstacle to the question of the recognition of the debts, but in order to fully discuss the matter it would be best for the two governments to appoint persons fully authorized to take up these questions.

The meeting broke up about 5:00 P.M.   F. A. GOLDER

---

[3]Boris Aleksandrovich Bakhmetev (1880–1951) was ambassador of the Provisional Government to the United States; after the October Revolution he remained in the United States, and the White House continued to recognize him for another five years. The money in question was funds of the Provisional Government that Bakhmetev had used to settle claims against Russia, mostly war contracts, by American manufacturers and businessmen.

Index

ABOUT THE EDITORS

TERENCE EMMONS is a professor of Russian history at Stanford University. He is the author and editor of numerous scholarly articles and books on Russian history, most recently *Time of Troubles: The Diary of Iurii Vladimirovich Got'e* (1988).

BERTRAND M. PATENAUDE is a lecturer and writer on Russian history. He received his Ph.D. from Stanford University in 1987. He is editor of several books, including *Soviet Scholarship under Gorbachev* (1988).

HOOVER ARCHIVAL DOCUMENTARIES
General editors: Milorad M. Drachkovitch (1976–83)
Robert Hessen (1983–)

The documents reproduced in this series (unless otherwise indicated) are deposited in the archives of the Hoover Institution on War, Revolution and Peace at Stanford University. The purpose of their publication is to shed new light on some important events concerning the United States or the general history of the twentieth century.